MW00327518

B SALSITZ:N SALSITZ
Salsitz, Norman, 1920-
Three homelands
gn
1138551780

Jefferson County Public Library
APR 2005
Lakewood, Colorado

JEFFERSON CO PUBLIC LIB, CO

Three
HOMELANDS

Religion, Theology, and the Holocaust
Alan L. Berger, *Series Editor*

Three
HOMELANDS

*Memories of a Jewish Life
in Poland, Israel, and America*

NORMAN SALSITZ
with STANLEY KAISH

Foreword by WALTER REICH

Syracuse University Press

Copyright © 2002 by Syracuse University Press
Syracuse, New York 13244-5160
All Rights Reserved

First Edition 2002

02 03 04 05 06 07   6 5 4 3 2 1

The paper used in this publication meets the minimum requirements
of American National Standard for Information Sciences—Permanence
of Paper for Printed Library Materials, ANSI Z39.48–1984.∞™

Library of Congress Cataloging-in-Publication Data

Salsitz, Norman, 1920–
    Three homelands : memories of a Jewish life in Poland, Israel,
      and America / Norman Salsitz with Stanley Kaish.—1st ed.
    p. cm.—(Religion, theology, and the Holocaust)
    ISBN 0–8156–0734–2 (alk. paper)
    1. Jews—Persecutions—Poland—Kolbuszowa. 2. Holocaust,
    Jewish (1939–1945)—Poland—Kolbuszowa—Personal narratives.
    3. Salsitz, Norman, 1920– —Childhood and youth. 4. Holo-
    caust survivors—United States—Biography. 5. Holocaust surviv-
    ors—Israel—Biography. 6. Kolbuszowa (Poland)—Biography.
    7. Kolbuszowa (Poland)—Ethnic relations. I. Kaish, Stanley,
    1931– . II. Title. III. Series.
DS135.P62K6637 2002
940.53'18'092—dc21
    [B]   2002010939

Manufactured in the United States of America

Jefferson County Public Library, CO
C1138551780

*To the memory of my parents, Isak and Esther
Saleschutz, which is constantly with me from the
past, and my beloved wife Amalie, children Esther
and Bruce Dezube, grandchildren Dustin, Aaron,
and Michael, and nephew Edwin Salsitz, who
bring so much joy to the present, and whose
futures seem so limitless.*

NORMAN SALSITZ

*As time has passed, the Kaish family has grown.
Now, in addition to children Harvey and Steven,
and their wives, Michele and Julie, Lois and I find
ourselves blessed with grandchildren Michael,
Jeremy, Alex, and Harrison. These efforts are
dedicated to all of them with love.*

STANLEY KAISH

Norman Salsitz and his wife, Amalie Petranker Salsitz, experienced the events described in these vignettes. They are the coauthors of *Against All Odds, A Tale of Two Survivors* and *In a World Gone Mad: A Heroic Story of Love, Faith and Survival*, with Amy Hill Hearth. In addition, Mr. Salsitz (as told to Richard Skolnik) is the author of *A Jewish Boyhood in Poland: Remembering Kolbuszowa* (Syracuse University Press) and was a major contributor to *Pinckas Kolbusov (Kolbuszower Memorial Book)*, edited by I. M. Biderman. This latter volume is a tribute to the two thousand Jews of Kolbuszowa who died in the Holocaust and contains nearly all of the five hundred photographs of shtetl life Mr. Salsitz saved from destruction so that we may remember.

Stanley Kaish recently retired from a thirty-five-year career as professor of economics and dean of the Undergraduate School of Management at Rutgers—The State University of New Jersey. He is the author of two books, *Microeconomics, Logic Tools and Analysis* and *Handbook of Behavioral Economics* (2 vols.) with Ben Gilad as well as numerous articles on economic and financial subjects.

This collaboration with Norman Salsitz grew out of conversations occurring during their long-standing friendship. It became evident that despite the publication of three previous books about Salsitz's remarkable life, there remained need for another, for he had many, still-unwritten tales that deserved to be recorded and preserved.

Contents

PART TWO   # The War—Tales of Life, Death, Hope, and Despair

PART THREE   **Surviving the Holocaust**

PART FOUR   **Getting a Foothold in the Golden Land**

Illustrations

Foreword

WALTER REICH *

Norman Salsitz, born in 1920 in Galicia, in southern Poland, is surely one of the wonders of the world. I've never met anyone with a memory as acute, precise, authentic, encompassing, or organized as his, or anyone more adept at conveying such memories through the compelling power of storytelling. That he has now done so in *Three Homelands*— and that he has done so in a way that brings to vivid life a world that was destroyed and the forces that destroyed it—is a gift to us all and to our time.

In a book that he wrote with his wife, Amalie Petranker Salsitz, about their survival as Jews during the Holocaust, *Against All Odds*, and in one that he wrote about his childhood in the southern Polish town of Kolbuszowa, *A Jewish Boyhood in Poland*, Salsitz provided the storyline of his life from birth through the end of the Second World War, and provided a sustained view of the world from which he came and which, together with its inhabitants, was exterminated.

In this new book, he provides more, much more. The hundred stories that fill this volume overflow with that world's details—its characters, its habits, its lessons, its wisdom, its foolishness, its courage, its conflicts, its pain, its exultation. Accumulated in this way, they burst the boundaries of the form that they take—personal vignettes—to become a rich, multicolored, layered, and exquisitely detailed tapestry that displays a life as if it still lives, and that invites us into its moments and its rhythms with an invitation we simply can't refuse.

The way in which Salsitz saved and then made available the images

---

* Walter Reich is the Yitzhak Rabin Memorial Professor of International Affairs, Ethics, and Human Behavior at George Washington University and a Senior Scholar at the Woodrow Wilson International Center for Scholars. He was the Director of the United States Holocaust Memorial Museum from 1995 to 1998.

he captured in the photos he took as a teenager in Kolbuszowa finely parallels the way in which he saved and has made available in this book the images he captured in his memory at that time and in the decades that followed it.

In one of the vignettes in this book, "The Photographs," Salsitz tells us of his life as a photographer in Kolbuszowa. Having owned one of the three cameras that existed in that town during the years before the Second World War, this boy with Hasidic earlocks and dress assembled the town's Jews for portraits that captured, singly and in groups, who they were and what they did. In 1942, as ever more Jews were being "deported" to their deaths, Salsitz retrieved those photos and others, totaling some five hundred images, as well as personal documents; bundled them in forty waxed-paper-wrapped packages; secreted each package in the attic or roof of the barn of a local Pole; attached to the last package a list of the barns in which he had secreted all of the previous packages; and retrieved them all two years later, after the Germans were in retreat, by which time, posing as a Catholic Pole, he had reached the status of a high-ranking officer in the Polish army. After the war he showed those photos to survivors from his town and then to others—and he shows many of them, now, in this book.

It was this organizational penchant, combined with Salsitz's focus on capturing and preserving images of reality, that also characterized his collection of memories, his packaging of them into stories that convey those memories with fidelity, and his distribution of those stories in books and the vignettes presented here.

And I have immense confidence that, in their rich detail, these vignettes are authentic and reliable.

My late mother grew up in his town, and my late father grew up in a neighboring larger town, Rzeszow, that Salsitz visited often both before the Second World War and during it. It was, in fact, in Rzeszow that the Germans established a ghetto into which they funneled many of the Jews of the region, including the Jews of Kolbuszowa. And it was, in fact, from that ghetto, conveniently situated on a railroad line, that the Germans "deported" by cattle car, to the gas chambers of Belzec, the nearby death camp, the ghetto's Jews—including Salsitz's mother (his father was murdered in Kolbuszowa), his five sisters, their husbands and their children. As it happens, it was also from the Rzeszow ghetto that relatives of mine were deported for gassing, some of them no doubt in the same gas chambers in which Salsitz's family members were murdered, together with at least six hundred thousand other Jews.

During my childhood I heard, from surviving relatives, the names of many of my family members, both those who had been killed and those who survived, as well as vignettes about the towns in which they had lived.

When, less than a decade ago, I first met Salsitz, and he learned who my relatives had been and where they had lived, he told me, unerringly, not only their names but also, in each of their immediate families, many of them consisting of eight or nine siblings, the exact order of their births, whom they had married, the names of their children, the towns to which they had moved and the occupations they had taken up before the Germans had invaded. One day, opening my mail, I found a photo of a Zionist group in Kolbuszowa, taken by Salsitz when he was fourteen, accompanied by a note in which he identified, along with the precise date on which the photo had been taken, my mother ("the one in the hat"), her sister, and their cousin. The great majority of the people in that group would be murdered within eight years of the date Salsitz took that photo; but, in having taken it, and now in telling us stories in which they and many, many others in that town and elsewhere come alive, he memorialized forever who they were, what they were and the Jewish life in Poland of which they were a part.

One always wonders, in reading a memoir about events that took place half a century and more ago, and about the people who played a role in them, whether or not the memoirist is being accurate in citing names, dates, and events. Indeed, one inevitably wonders how such accuracy is even possible. As a psychiatrist I know that such accurate recall is extremely rare. But, based on the knowledge I have about a tiny part of the world that he describes, I can testify, with awed confidence, that Salsitz's memory is remarkably accurate indeed.

But accuracy, though necessary in telling a true story, isn't enough. The talent needed to tell that story, the insight required to find its essence, and the ability the storyteller must have to draw the reader into it, are what animate that story's actors and events, and what enable us to participate in it as if it's our own. Salsitz has that talent, insight, and ability to an extraordinary degree, and the stories that he produces—that gush out of him in a robust, brilliant, and endless stream—leave us enormously full of knowledge about a world that is no more, and enormously hungry for the next story, and the next, and the next one after that.

With the help of Stanley Kaish, who has enhanced the grace and concision of these stories, Salsitz escorts us through his boyhood, his family, his community, his struggle to survive the Germans, his life posing as a Polish officer, and his life in his new home, America; and through it all we want to know what happened next. We want to know more about the town, the labor camp, the German killers, the Jews who were killed, and those who managed to hide and to fight. Painful though it is, we want to know the reality of the life of Jews in a Poland where, hunted by Germans, they were also sometimes hunted by their former neighbors and friends, Catholic Poles, and killed by them—not through organized roundups, shootings, and gassings but with pitchforks and axes that pierced chests and split heads, and that ended the lives of Jews who had managed to hide in holes in the ground but who, alas, had not hid well enough to elude the neighbors who sought to kill them. Salsitz tells that story as well and in detail. That detail provides added insight into a phenomenon—the instances of killings of Jews by Catholic Poles during the Second World War—that only recently came to the public's attention with the appearance in 2001, in the *New Yorker* and then as a book, of Jan Gross's *Neighbors,* which is about the murder of the Jews of Jedwabne by their Catholic Polish neighbors.

And, with enormous illumination, Salsitz tells the story of Holocaust time—the story of what happened, day after day, and month after month, as the German vise was tightening and as Jews sought to escape the asphyxiating squeeze of its murderous grip. He tells of the randomness of life and the randomness of death, of cheating fate and, more often, of being victimized by it, and of the nobility and terror that marked the human spirit in that time.

Finally, and most strikingly, Salsitz brings us into the nearly unbelievable saga of his amazing life and, without embellishment or pretense, teaches us about a character the story of whose life illustrates the drama and the possibilities of our time.

Norman Salsitz is an extraordinary man and this is an extraordinary book. I know of nothing else like it.

Preface

STANLEY KAISH

Norman Salsitz and I have been working on this book, on and off, for ten years now. The project developed out of my reading and reviewing his two previous books, *Against All Odds* and *Jewish Boyhood in Poland*. The first is the narrative he and his wife Amalie wrote of the Holocaust, how it caught them in its web, destroyed their families and friends, brutalized them, and how they ultimately survived. If you haven't already read it, do so. You will agree that it is aptly titled. The second book is the story of prewar Kolbuszowa, the shtetl in which Norman grew up. It captures vividly the daily life and times of this Jewish community, poised, unknowingly, on the edge of the abyss. We meet Norman's parents, sisters, teachers, and neighbors, going about their business of working, praying, studying, matchmaking, living their lives in a prewar Poland that was very much in harm's way. The book is a gem.

In the course of discussing these books with Norman, I learned that he had many, many more stories from both periods and beyond that he hadn't included. Some elaborated nuances of the stories previously told. Others broke fresh ground, extending the story beyond the end of the war and into his experiences as a penniless immigrant to the United States. In particular, he had a number of stories about his father from whom, it turns out, Norman received his gift for storytelling. I agreed to help him to preserve these experiences.

Since those initial conversations, I have had the pleasure of spending countless fascinating hours with Norman, reliving events from his life and the lives of others, long departed, who lived in Kolbuszowa, in Rzeszow, in Cracow, in places I never imagined existed, often under unthinkable circumstances. There were stories, that left me lying awake with wet eyes afterwards and others that left me weak from laughter. The stories came from many worlds and were told in many voices. One week I would be listening to Norman telling tales of the shtetl, of the customs, characters, observances, and how he and his beloved family fit in to the setting. The next week more painful narratives are drawn from the Holocaust. I heard of the hardships endured, the hazards survived, the near-death experiences. Later the stories involve reliving the early years of Norman Salsitz in America: coming over on the boat, looking for help from the family, struggling to get started in America while still longing to go to Israel. Before we were finished we had written one hundred stories that we have organized into four parts: Vignettes of Jewish life; The War-Tales of Life, Death, Hope and Despair; Surviving the Holocaust; and Getting a Foothold in the Golden Land.

Naftali Saleschutz was the ninth and youngest child of a well-to-do ultra-Orthodox father and mother, Isak and Esther Saleschutz. He attended the public schools as well as *cheder* and yeshiva until he was seventeen, living in a land where the Jewish and Polish populations enjoyed an uneasy and largely separate coexistence. That world changed radically with the German invasion of Poland. Naftali soon found himself in a ghettoized world, walled off, where crowding and hunger and German brutality forced the family into a desperate state. Eventually the ghetto was emptied, his father shot before his eyes, and his mother and sisters taken to Belzec death camp and exterminated. Naftali was conscripted into a labor camp, only to escape and live with a fugitive band of Jews, deep in the surrounding forest, struggling to survive both the Germans and hostile Poles. Subsequently he became a freedom fighter, a partisan working with a Polish underground that wouldn't have accepted him if it had known he was a Jew. Next we find him, not in the black caftan and side curls of the Hasid, but in the snappy uniform of the Polish army officer, clean-shaven and ostensibly a Catholic. He had morphed into Tadeusz Zaleski, and in a position of military prominence, he found himself able to help the surviving Jews who found their way back to what they thought was home. But soon he had to flee Poland; and so he escaped to Germany, then came to America with his new bride, and found himself an immigrant living in a walk-up apartment in the Williamsburg section of Brooklyn, with no money, no training, and few prospects. He hoped for a helping hand from his uncles who had come to America decades before, but with one exception, the extended family left him pretty much to make it on his own. And make it he did. A remarkably short while later, his world had become that of the successful suburban businessman and real estate developer, the builder of more than a thousand homes in his newly adopted land. He went from one needing help to one who raised tens of thousands of dollars for Jewish charities.

One evening I asked Norman why it was that so many survivors of the Holocaust came to this country without any money and had become so successful. He thought for a moment and told me that it was because if you survive the Holocaust, you realize that "nothing is impossible." Norman Salsitz's life, while not impossible, is certainly improbable. It seems the stuff of fiction. But each time you begin to think, no, this couldn't be so, a document, a witness, a picture, an encounter, confirms that indeed, improbable as it seems, the memories harvested here are from a full and exciting Jewish life. I am delighted that Syracuse University Press is giving us the means of sharing these stories with a broad public. I hope you enjoy reading them as much as I did hearing them over the course of the last ten years.

Each of these stories is written so it may be read independently of the others. Recognizing that some readers may elect to skip around while others will read through from start to finish, we have repeated some background material where necessary.

PART ONE   Vignettes of Jewish Life

My Father, the Storyteller

My father, Isak Saleschutz, was a gifted storyteller. He would tell stories to illustrate a point, to drive home a lesson, or simply to entertain, and because he possessed unusual talent as a raconteur, people tended to be willing listeners, savoring the unfolding narrative in rapt anticipation of its outcome. He would draw from Jewish scripture, or traditions, or folktales, or simply the everyday lives of our people. Put a question to him, and his answer would begin with, "Let me tell you a story."

In the shtetl, everyone had a nickname. My father had several. He was known to many as Itche Naftalis: Itche because it is a familiar form of his given name, Isak, and Naftalis because his father's name was Naftali Saleschutz. People were often identified by both their own and their father's first names. They were also named in terms of the town they came from. My father's father, for example, was known as Naftali Dibiser because he lived in the village of Dubas, which was five kilometers from Kolbuszowa, and by extension, my father was sometimes called Itche Dibiser. Finally, because of his propensity to spin a tale to answer a question, my father was also affectionately known as "Itche with his stories."

Isak Saleschutz, the author's father, in 1934.

It is sixty years since his death, but the love of storytelling did not die with him. I have inherited this trait. I have also inherited several of

3

the names. While people now call me Norman, I was named Naftali after my grandfather. Since my father, as the son of my grandfather, was known as Itche Naftalis, I, by the same logic, am Naftali Itches. What is more, while he was called "Itche with his stories," my wife has, on more than one occasion, been heard commenting to a sympathetic listener, "There he goes again—Norman and his stories."

Since I share my father's name and I share his interests, and to some extent his talents, I, Naftali Itches, begin these narratives by repeating the favorite words of Itche Naftalis:

"Let me tell you a story . . ."

My Father, the Storyteller

The Tax Assessors

In Poland, taxes were levied differently than in the United States. In the United States, the government taxes everybody who falls into a given category in the same way and depends on its citizens to report the correct amount. The government trusts you until it catches you cheating. If it catches you cheating, then you're in trouble. But until you're caught, you're considered an honest person.

In Poland, each individual was taxed differently, depending upon who and what he was. The government would assess taxes annually, on a case-by-case basis. For instance, in our town there was a director of Internal Revenue and he appointed three assessors. These were prominent men, usually Poles, who would get together and discuss everyone's income. They would say, "This man, on the basis of his lifestyle and other personal factors, should pay so much." Jews were usually discriminated against and were assessed higher taxes than the Poles.

In 1936, a new director was appointed to the Internal Revenue and the new director decided to appoint a fourth assessor to assess income taxes in our town. The fourth assessor selected was a Jew. It so happened that this Jew and my father were dear friends. They were disciples of the same rabbi and used to go twice a year, on the holidays, to visit with the rabbi. Since his good friend was an assessor now, my father expected that his taxes, which usually increased from year to year, would finally decrease or at worst, increase only slightly.

So you can imagine my father's surprise, when he got his notice to pay taxes and they were three times higher than the year before. He ran immediately to the director of the Internal Revenue and he yelled and screamed about what they had done to him.

The director asked him, "Why are you yelling so much? Every year we raise your taxes a little and you never make a commotion. This year you come in screaming like a wild man. Why is this year different."

My father answered, "Let my tell you a story . . ."

In Heaven there exists a tribunal. Everyone who ascends to Heaven comes before God, the chief judge. One day, a goldsmith's hammer came before God and demanded that the blacksmith's hammer be punished by banishment.

The goldsmith's hammer says to God, 'I demand that you banish the blacksmith's hammer forever. He is a nuisance. Look at what he's doing. The racket he makes is terrible. When people go by the blacksmith's shop, they nearly go deaf. And the blacksmith's neighbors cannot sleep in peace at night. Please eliminate it.'

God asks, "And what of a goldsmith's hammer?"

The goldsmith's hammer answers, "Now if you go by a goldsmith's shop and listen when he uses his hammer, you can hardly hear a thing. The goldsmith's hammer doesn't disturb the peace; people in the neighborhood sleep at night."

God looks at the blacksmith's hammer and says, "Well he's making a very good argument. And he's right about the noise. What is your defense?"

The blacksmith's hammer says to God, "May I ask a few questions?"

"Yes."

And he asks the goldsmith's hammer, "What are you made of?"

"Of steel—iron."

"What do you work on—what do you strike?"

"Gold, silver."

"Ah, you see, you are made from iron and you strike gold, silver, and other precious metals. You hit strangers. But a blacksmith's hammer, what is it made of?"

"Steel."

"And what does it strike?"

"Steel."

"That's right. Brother hits brother. The blacksmith's hammer must make a racket. It must clamor for the whole world to know that a brother is beating a brother. But not you, you are like a stranger beating up strangers. You can afford to work quietly."

So my father said to the director of the Internal Revenue, "This is the

first year that you have a Jew as an assessor. A brother striking a brother
... Do I have to explain more?"

"No," said the director. "Your story says it all." And he lowered my
father's taxes.

In Poland we paid two taxes, a gross tax—based on the volume of
business we did—and an income tax—based on how much profit we
made. The income tax used to be 1 percent of the gross tax, so if you paid
100 zloty a year gross, you paid 1 zloty a year income tax. In the year following this incident, my father's income tax was inexplicably increased
almost ten-fold, to about 10 percent of the gross tax.

Again he ran to the same director of the Internal Revenue and asked,
"What did you do to me? The law says I have to pay 1 percent of the gross
tax for income tax and you're making me pay 10 percent!"

The director sat back in his big chair and said, "Mr. Saleschutz, last
year when you were unsatisfied with your taxes you told me a story. Do
you have another story to tell me?"

Not surprisingly, my father said, "Yes, let me tell you another story."

"Once there was a peasant who grew wheat in his fields. As you
know, when wheat is cut, it is bundled into sheaves to dry out in the field.
As the wheat dries out, no rain must touch it, or it will ferment and be
ruined.

"The peasant cut all the wheat and laid it in sheaves out on his fields.
Then he waited. The weather, which had looked fine, began to change.
Suddenly the peasant saw clouds coming. He gathered all of his children
together and instructed them to bring the family wagon into the fields.
He said, 'we must bring all of the wheat into the barn quickly, before the
rain comes.'

"The peasant was smart. He knew that he didn't have time to make
more than one trip to the field, so he had his family load the wagon as
high as they could with wheat. They piled so much wheat on the wagon
that when they got to the barn door, it couldn't fit through. Raindrops
started to fall.

"The peasant, was desperate. He turned to his wife and said, 'Go into
the kitchen and get the magnifying glass. Bring it quickly.' "

" 'What do you need a magnifying glass for?' "

" 'Don't ask questions, just get it.' "

"She brought the magnifying glass and he grabbed it from her hand.
The wagon was loaded with so much wheat that it was four times the size
of the barn door, but the peasant held up the magnifying glass and looked
through it at the barn door. Lo and behold, the glass enlarged the door so
that it looked ten times bigger, and he said to his wife, 'while I am look-

ing at the entrance to the barn, you go in fast with the horses and the wagon. It will fit and we will be saved.' "

My father looked at the director of the Internal Revenue and he said, "What did you do? You took my gross tax and you looked at it with a magnifying glass, and then you went in fast with the income tax."

"Perhaps you are right," the director said, and once again, he lowered my father's taxes.

The Logical Jews of Kolbuszowa

Science and technology were changing the world everywhere. Everywhere, that is, but in the old study hall (*Beth Hamidrash*) in Kolbuszowa. There the old Jews of the town spent most of every day, around the stove, happy to be out of the cold, studying Talmud. For the most part, they considered the same texts their ancestors had considered and wrestled with the same issues of Jewish law, morality, and procedure that had worried countless generations of Jews before. In the Kolbuszowa *Beth Hamidrash*, time stood still.

One reason time stood still here was that there was no railroad to Kolbuszowa. The nearest one was in Sedziszow, some twelve miles away. Hence its noise and its steam and the immensity of its power were never clearly perceived by the regulars of the study house. Nor was its ability to produce change by bringing new goods and new people with new ideas yet established in the community.

One evening, in the midst of a particularly arid discussion of dietary laws, Mendel, a pious Jew, mentioned to the others that he had seen the train in the next town. When he got a reply that was no more definitive than a distracted "nu?", he proceeded to describe what he had seen. He observed that the train appeared like a row of houses, set on a street. The lights would be on and the chimney would be smoking and all of a sudden, at a signal, the street would start to move. There was one special house in the front, he observed, and this special house pulled the rest. It was this special house that had the fire in the chimney and it was this house that pulled and led the others.

Having delivered himself of this description, Mendel sat back to await commentary, but for a long time none was offered. The old men of the Kolbuszowa study hall rocked and stroked their beards and contemplated these images.

At length, the member of the group who usually interpreted new experiences said, "Aha. I understand how it works. It is all a trick. There is nothing special here. There are horses hidden in the first house pulling the others."

"But I saw no horses," said Mendel. "You are mistaken."

And his companion replied, "You saw no horses because they were covered up. What you did see were clear signs that the horses were present. You said you saw steam coming out of the first wagon when the train started to run. The reason there is steam is that the horses are sweating while they are running and pulling the wagons. You can also see that when the train stops at the station, there is water that comes out from the first wagon. That proves that when the horses stop running, they must relieve themselves, and that water you see is the horses urinating."

The other Jews, accustomed to studying the familiar, not the novel, contemplated these two descriptions and decided that the more logical description must be the second one. All the things that are being told about the train are really nothing more than a story. They agreed that there are horses, and the horses are pulling the covered wagons.

It was at that point that a third old Jew suddenly stiffened, eyes alight with a new insight that was apparently developing in his mind. He slyly

An artist's interpretation of a discussion taking place among orthodox Jews.

made this observation. "I bet it's the same with this thing called a tele-graph. When the operator squeezes down on the key it gives out a noise. I bet there is really a dog there. If you take a dog and squeeze his tail, then it will hurt him and he will show his pain by barking. I bet the barking is a telegraph. This is something where you squeeze the tail on one side and the voice comes out on the other." .

The others stroked their beards, rocked back and forth, and gave this considerable thought. Technology was intruding new ideas into the Kol-buszowa study hall that evening.

My Grandmother's "Cholent"

Mmm, *Cholent.* How we loved the sabbath staple eaten in every Jewish home in Kolbuszowa, possibly in every Jewish home in Poland. A pun-gent brew, made from potatoes and beans and chunks of meat, and fla-vored with fat from the beef and chickens and geese consumed by the household that week, *cholent* would simmer from Friday afternoon until noontime on Saturday, in anticipation of the close of prayers and a return home from the synagogue. While the potatoes and beans were important ingredients, the most important was the fat, because the amount of fat was a reflection of the meat content of the meals eaten the week before. A rich family would have a fatty *cholent* with more meat in it. A family that ate relatively little meat during the week got by on a *cholent* that was mostly potatoes and beans. It is almost as if there were some divine social engineer compensating the poor and punishing the rich through the *cholent* recipe. Even then, before our awareness of the subtleties of cholesterol in the diet, *cholent* was called the miracle food. The Jews had enjoyed more than their share of miracles over the centuries, but the greatest miracle of all was said to be the fact that they could eat a hearty serving of *cholent,* lie down for a nap afterward, and live to get up again.

During the winter, buckwheat or barley was often used instead of the beans and potatoes. Since buckwheat was a considerably more expensive ingredient, there must have been an important reason for its substitution, and indeed there was. The week when the Torah portion describing the Jews crossing of the Red Sea was read was known as "Shabbat Shira," or Singing Sabbath. It bore this name in recognition of the role the sparrows had played, singing with the Jews during the crossing of the Red Sea. Just as the Jews traditionally put buckwheat or barley, left over from the *cholent*, out in the snow to feed the sparrows during the winter to thank the birds for singing with them at the their deliverance from Pharaoh, it was to mark the biblical recitation of that event in the Book of Exodus (14:30–15:18) that they put buckwheat or barley in the *cholent* in the first place. So the *cholent* was notable, not only for its sustenance of daily life, but also for its commemorative significance in the history of our people.

My grandmother, as was typical of the other Jewish women of the community, never missed serving *cholent* on the sabbath. However, her family was not one of those that was endowed with riches. My grandfather, Leibush Awrumalis (Berl) had been an extremely learned scholar, and he married the daughter of the wealthiest family in town. Unfortunately, the family businesses suffered financial reversals, and the couple had to rely on the meager income he could produce as a teacher. As brilliant as he was, and as outstanding as his students were, his earnings as a teacher were never more than modest. I remember hearing stories in which he was referred to by a nickname, *Zemike Greetz*, which meant "potato soup." He was called that because potato soup was all he could afford to eat most days during the week. On the weekend, though, he would look forward to enjoying the bolstering infusion of *cholent* following prayers.

As a practical matter, many of the shtetl women had the baker keep their *cholent* warm in his bread oven. He didn't charge them for this service, and since cooking on the Sabbath was forbidden anyway, there was no use in every one burning fuel to heat the *cholent*. There was, however, one major drawback to letting the baker maintain the *cholent* in his oven. Not all of the women were as fastidious in observing the dietary laws as my grandmother, and she worried that when her pot of *cholent* shared the oven with some less pure then her own, the fumes it absorbed would be enough to contaminate it. So she took to sealing the pot with a bead of dough all around the cover to make sure it was air tight and no nonkosher fumes could reach it. Each Friday, she would bring her tightly sealed *cholent* pot to the baker where it sat in the warmth of his great oven.

The women's pride in their *cholent* was evident to all who heard them talk of it. It was symbol of the role of the woman of the house as provider of sustenance, as well as an indicator of her skill at managing the food budget. A woman's ability to offer a rich *cholent* to the men after prayers was important and respected. Unfortunately, for my grandmother, however, her financial circumstances were very strained. There were weeks when very little meat graced their daily table and the traditionally nutritious *cholent* was not possible. She would scrimp on the fat, and occasionally, be forced to scrimp on the potatoes and beans as well.

My grandfather didn't seem to take notice. He was engrossed in his studies and his teaching. And since the pot was sealed when it was brought to and from the baker, no one but my grandmother knew exactly what was in it. She could have asked for help, of course, but pride prevented her from doing so, or admitting that there were financial problems. She carried her sealed pot with the same grace when it was brimming with fat as when the mixture was thin, consisting of mostly water and potatoes. No one would know how needy they had become.

At length, there came a day when there were neither potatoes, beans nor fat. There were no ingredients of substance. There was only water and she proceeded to boil it and seal it into the *cholent* pot. Off she went to the baker, with her pot, sealed with the dough, and containing nothing but water. Her head was still high, but she knew that in the household there would be disappointment after prayers when the pot would be recovered, opened and its meager contents revealed.

There is a Yiddish saying, *"men knapt di baken, zei zolen zain roit."* This means, sometimes you have to pinch your cheeks so people will think they are rosy. They were not rosy, but you pinched them so people would think they were. And so it was in my grandmother's kitchen that day. Returning with the *cholent* pot, she placed it on the table, stripped away the protective dough, and opened it to be served.

And my grandfather looked in, looked at my grandmother, ladled out a generous helping from the pot, put it in his bowl, smiled, and said as he always did at the postprayer meal, "Mmm. *cholent.*"

My Father, the Storyteller

The Boots

He would tell stories and we would listen. Sometimes we laughed. Sometimes we would cry. We always learned. For my father's stories weren't meant just to entertain, although they never failed to do that. They were also to make a point, to teach a lesson, to underscore a point of importance. Let me repeat a few more and you will see what I mean.

He told us about the time the Russians occupied our town Kolbuszowa in Galicia in 1915. They were extremely hostile to the local population. And it goes without saying that if they were hostile to the townspeople, they were doubly abusive to the Jewish population, because that's the way it was. They would rob and plunder the Jews in the town. Whatever they saw, they demanded, and if you were slow to hand it over, they would beat or even kill you. This happened to a watchmaker in the town. He was slow to respond to a demand that he turn over his stock of watches. He and his wife and their son were killed and the watches taken. After that, the Jews responded quickly. Property could be replaced, they realized. Loss of life was more permanent.

Boots were a favorite target of the Russians. If they saw a Jew in the street wearing a good pair of boots, they would throw him down and pull off the Jew's boots. All the Jews knew that if they wore their boots onto the street, the chances were they would be lost before nightfall. Jews were not fools. They stopped wearing boots. The only Jew who wore his boots on the street was—you guessed it—my father. He was no fool either, although the manner in which he wore his boots made everyone laugh and made the Russians think that surely he was.

My father had a very good pair of beautifully crafted boots. He also owned a pair of new shoes called *shtivoletten,* shoes like today's loafers with no laces, which also were a promising target for the Russians. My father wore them both in the street with impunity, but always one of each: a boot on one foot and a shoe on the other. When the Russian soldiers saw him with one boot and one shoe, they laughed, and called him a fool, and left him alone. He told them, when challenged, that he only had one shoe and one boot. He had lost the others and had to wear them this way. They had no use for one boot and one shoe and they never took them. Every day he changed. One day, the left boot and right shoe; the next the right boot and left shoe. He wore them constantly, and they were never stolen by the Russians, who didn't bother remembering that yesterday, the boot had been on the other foot.

I recalled this story from the First World War when the Germans came twenty-five years later. I, too, wore my boots and shoes in this same manner, one of each, switching back and forth. What worked for the father worked for the son: two "fools" who kept their boots about them while everyone else was losing theirs.

Two Brothers Meet

During the American Civil War brother fought brother. The politics of the time drew ideological as well as geographical lines across family landscapes. Sometimes by accident, sometimes by intent, blood kin stared at one another across hostile borders.

During World War I, my own family found itself in an analogous situation. Yankel Rothbard, (my first cousin) went to America in 1909. From the melting pot emerged Jack Rothbard, who found his place in his adopted country, worked hard, and took

Moishe Rothbard *(right)* was in the Austrian army during World War I while his brother, Jack Rothbard Yankel, served in the U.S. Navy.

hold. By the time the war started, Jack was an American citizen. He volunteered for the U.S. Navy and in a short time found himself in uniform, back across the sea, in Europe.

Meanwhile, Jack's brother Moishe had remained in what was now the enemy camp. He found himself called to active duty in the Austrian army and served in another sector. Jack knew his brother would be activated from the reserves to serve in the army and could have used this fact to be exempted from service. However, he kept this information to himself while applying for service because, like so many immigrants, he was grateful to his adopted country and wanted to serve.

Since the navy had sent him back to Europe, however, he thought it a shame to have come all this way and not have an opportunity to visit with his brother. Visit! As far as their respective governments were concerned, they were supposed to be killing one another, not visiting. Nevertheless, they corresponded to see if there were not some neutral ground where hostilities could be left at the door and brothers could embrace.

In due course they hit on Trieste, which was a neutral port at the time. Moishe was fighting on the Italian front and due for a leave. Jack, at the same time put in for a liberty from the navy; and so it came to pass that two brothers, one in the Austrian army and the other in the United States Navy, took a day off and came together in the port city of Trieste to embrace and reminisce, while all around them others continued to fight the war that was designed but, alas, not destined to end all wars.

The Pogrom

Terror paralyzed the Jewish community. Mobs of peasants roamed the streets beating any Jew they came upon. The windows of Jewish shops and homes were shattered and the stores stripped of their wares. Sacks of clothing, food, hardware, anything portable, useful or not, were hauled off by the looters. They pounded on the doors and dragged Jewish men and women from their homes and paraded them through the streets, taunting them, beating them, spitting on them, raping them, breaking them, and eventually, killing them. Pleas brought derision. Resistance brought retaliation. Surrender brought mortification. Flight was the only escape possible.

No, this wasn't *Kristallnacht* in 1938 Nazi Germany. Hitler hadn't come to power and authorized the official abuse of Jews. Quite the contrary. This was a celebration. The time was May 6, 1919, one year to the day before my birth. The place was Kolbuszowa, Poland, the town my parents and eight brothers and sisters called home and in which I would grow up. The event was the independence of Poland, won at the Versailles conference as a by-product of World War I, after 123 years of occupation by Russia, Germany, and Austria. The Polish people were euphoric, and what better way could be found to express their euphoria over their freedom than to stage a pogrom against their neighbors, the Jews.

After World War I, the Jews, like everyone else in Europe attempted to return to normalcy. Many younger men had fought in the Austrian, Russian and German armies. Others had run away from Kolbuszowa during the 1915–16 period that the Russians occupied the area. With the end of hostilities, these refugees returned, as did the veterans, to start life anew. Our family, which had been in business before the war, was beginning to resume its commercial activities.

The trouble began on Saturday, May 3, following the Polish Constitution Anniversary Day parade. A group of unruly Poles gathered on the outskirts of town. At the time, Kolbuszowa was fortunate in having a strict Austrian in charge of the local police, a sergeant named Herman, who confronted the mob and dispersed it. After church on Sunday, May 4, a few sporadic beatings of Jews took place. On Monday, which was market day in Majdan, fifteen kilometers from Kolbuszowa, large numbers of peasants came from the countryside to swell the local population. By the evening they began to riot against the Jews in Kolbuszowa. Once again the police, led by Sergeant Herman, were able to disperse the mob. When told by his superiors to shoot up in the air, he dismissed this advice scornfully. "I was taught that you shoot up in the air to shoot birds, not people." Relief was temporary. On Tuesday, May 6, market day in Kolbuszowa, the peasants returned in yet greater numbers and overwhelmed the police, disarming them and, in many instances, sending them running. Lawlessness and violence took over, and the beating and pillaging that were the Kolbuszowa pogrom rampaged all day long.

Having been in the community all his life, and done business with Poles during that time, my father and mother sought out a Polish family that would provide shelter for them and their children until the storm blew itself out. How ironic it is that such an activity became a rehearsal of a scenario Jews would act out again in a few years. They would rely on good will and old friendships to produce a helping hand. Most times they would be disappointed. Fear and greed would win out, and they would be turned away or worse, taken in and betrayed.

In this case the outcome was more favorable than my cynicism would anticipate. My parents and their eight children went to hide with a family named Ogonek. Mrs. Ogonek was a peddler who used to sell small items such as soap and chicory from town to town. She bought her merchandise from my father, usually on credit, and would go out to sell it. Next day, she would come in to get additional items and go to a different town. He had always been generous in extending her credit, and they had a good and friendly relationship. That was why it was so strange when at first her husband rejected them, but at last, in return for some consideration, the Ogoneks took the family in and let them hide in the attic.

My family hid in the Ogoneks' attic for three days, escaping the physical violence that surely would have befallen them if they had been out. For three days, they watched through the attic window and saw Mr. Ogonek and his daughter Wanda return with bag after bag of looted merchandise. A Jew in the attic was certainly not going to stand in the way of this opportunity for riches. At times my father was amazed to see our own family heirlooms carried in by the Ogoneks among their booty. Since they knew we were safely in their attic, it seems there was nothing to stop them from breaking into our house and carrying off some of its contents.

Altogether, nine Jews were killed during the pogrom. Hundreds were wounded, forty-five were raped, and many were maimed for life. One little twelve-year-old girl who had been raped repeatedly by Polish peasants lost her mind and remained largely mute until the Germans killed her twenty-three years later. A ninety-two-year-old man was killed, as were two women. Several Jews fled to the Jewish cemetery, hoping to be safe there. Instead, five of the nine killed during the pogrom were killed there.

When the Poles were later asked why the toll had been so high at the cemetery, they explained that it was because the Jews there had fought back. This had been a group of strong young Jews who were veterans of World War I. The Poles killed them with pitchforks, axes, and knives.

There were also a few bizarre acts of compassion by the Poles. In one house that they broke into they found Necha Schrek, wife of Avrum Schrek (called the *Lecht Zier* or the candlemaker) nine months pregnant and about to go into labor. Schrek was horrified when the Poles picked up the bed with his wife on it, and then watched in amazement as they carried her to the home of Rogala, a Pole who had been friendly to the Jews. Rogala took her in and she gave birth to her son, Nissin. Meanwhile, the Poles then turned on the husband Avrum and beat him nearly to death. They left him lying unconscious and bloody in the middle of the street. He probably would have died there had not another group of ten or twenty Poles come upon his motionless body and, thinking him dead, gathered around and urinated on him. Ironically, the flow of the urine revived him, and when they left, he was able to crawl back to Rogala's house. Rogala hid him in the stable, and after the pogrom he told this story of his survival. No one ever explained why the mob saved her and beat him.

The story became widely known, and for the rest of his days, the baby born that day, Nissin, was affectionately known as *Pogromchick*. Unfortunately the rest of his days were relatively few in number. The family emigrated to Germany, but were thrown out when Hitler came to power. They returned to Kolbuszowa, only to be killed with most of the Jewish population of our town.

Another Jew who told a remarkable story of deliverance was Hirsch Kleinman, whose hardware business had made him one of the richest men in Kolbuszowa. The mob caught and beat him as well, throwing him senseless into the overflow area surrounding the town well. He, too, was revived by the cold water and escaped to tell the tale.

The pogrom finally ended when (1) the Poles were exhausted from their rampaging, looting and killing, and (2) a small detachment of troops was sent from Rzeszow to quell the fighting. These soldiers doubtless saved many Jewish lives. To their credit, they arrested five Poles, although it seems a pitifully small number to hold responsible for three days of rioting that killed nine people. Two were identified by dozens of Jews as responsible for one of the killings. A military trial was held the same day and the two were immediately taken to a tree in the center of town and executed. Only one other man who had actively participated, a fellow named Sus, got a significant jail sentence of ten years. At the end of that time, however, he was back in Kolbuszowa, living with us as if nothing had happened. Pogroms in Poland, it seems, were as natural and periodic as the seasons.

One aftermath of the killings in the Kolbuszowa pogrom was a great deal of international notoriety. The *New York Times* and the *Jewish Forward* led the media in denouncing the pogrom in America. President Woodrow Wilson and Polish Prime Minister Jan Paderewski had a personal relationship stemming from the Paris Peace Conference. It had been Paderewski who persuaded Wilson to include independence of Poland as one of his Fourteen Points. Wilson appointed one of his early financial supporters, Henry Morgenthau, Sr., to head a delegation to Poland to investigate. While there had been pogroms all over Poland, and the delegation went from town to town to learn about the violence, they focused on Kolbuszowa, where the death total had been the highest. Their report led Paderewski to formally denounce the events that had taken place. Arthur Goddard, a member of the delegation, later wrote a book titled, *Poland and the Minority Races*, which explored the roots of Polish anti-Semitism and described the Kolbuszowa pogrom in detail. May 6 became synonymous with the violence, and as will happen when things are desperate enough, the date became the subject of some gallows humor. When someone was particularly mean or petty in the daily rigors of life, he would be told to cut it out. "This isn't May 6, after all." On the other side, the Poles made up lyrics to a popular national song, changing them from "Welcome May, golden May, for all Poles a glorious day" to "Third of May, sixth of May, kill the Jews for a glorious day." They celebrated the event and sang these words whenever they felt it appropriate to taunt their Jewish neighbors.

In a perverse way, the pogrom saved the lives of many of Kolbuszowa's Jews. An estimated 25 percent of the Jewish population of our town emigrated from Poland to America. That didn't include the Saleschutz family. Although my oldest brother Avrum had already left, my father was reluctant to give up the traditional Jewish existence we had. He was convinced his children would lose their observance of ritual and the dietary laws. My father's brother, Shulim, who had gone to America in 1890, read of the pogrom and bought and sent the family nine tickets for passage to America. This was a most generous act on his part since he had very little money. My parents and the seven children at home at the time could have used them any time during the following year. My father, weighing the pros and cons of leaving or staying, ultimately made the fatal decision to stay. It was during that year of decision that I was born.

Eventually we stopped talking about the Kolbuszowa pogrom. Some who were maimed bore the marks in their limps and their pains. Others, who had lost friends and relatives, were the beneficiaries of the healing power of time and its dulling effect on memory. Jewish lives returned to normal, but it would soon be apparent that the three days of the pogrom were just a rehearsal of what was to become normal for the Jews of Poland.

The Tale of the Yeast Box

One day in the spring of 1920 a number of children fell ill in the little town of Kolbuszowa. The symptoms—headache, weakness, fever—caused little alarm, for they were common to many childhood diseases. But by the next day some of the children were dead. In the ensuing days several more died before at last the ulcerous and unmistakable scarlet rash of smallpox appeared in others of the sick children.

The authorities took such measures as they knew, closing the schools, setting up what passed for a hospital, ordering the citizenry to report all known or suspected cases of sickness. But there the town's defense ended. For Kolbuszowa was an isolated and backward place, in a remote corner of minor Poland known as Galicia. An empty, sandy plain called "Sahara" encircled the town, the plain itself hemmed in by looming forests. The twentieth century had found it difficult to penetrate these barriers. No automobile stirred the dust of Kolbuszowa's narrow streets, and only the soft glow of candles and kerosene lamps lit its windows against the black country night. It was not that the people of Kolbuszowa were utterly ignorant; the existence of automobiles and electricity was well known. It was simply that such things belonged to another world, the world of outside, the great world of Cracow and Warsaw and beyond. So, too, with smallpox vaccination.

And so when the outbreak turned epidemic, there was neither panic nor even surprise, for who had expected otherwise? After all, most people were perfectly safe from the pox, having long since suffered through it, thereby gaining immunity. As for those who were not immune—mainly the very young—well, the disease would cripple a few, and there would be some who would never again choose to linger before a mirror, but most would live and be well. Unless it were very bad, no more than two or three in ten would die.

It was bad enough. The weeks crawled slowly by, each claiming more dead than the one before. Finally a kind of numbness settled over the town. Stories of suffering and bitter loss had become common. People discussed death in their neighbors' families as casually as if commenting on a spate of mildly unpleasant weather. It took some unusual or ironic twist to excite real interest: an improbable recovery just when the victim seemed lost; a sudden death days after apparent return to health; a beautiful girl ravaged by the disease while her plain sister escaped without a mark. There was no shortage of such stories—for the pox could be capricious. One of the strangest involved me and my father, Isak Saleschutz.

If Kolbuszowa had an expert on the progress of the epidemic, it was Isak Saleschutz. A devout Hasid and a leader among the town's Jews, he naturally knew its impact on his own people. But he also spoke fluent, unaccented Polish and in his business had many dealings with gentiles. From them he learned that the pox was no respecter of any religion. Confirmation of the fact was simple; he had only to look out across the square to the Catholic church. During the epidemic there were rarely fewer than half a dozen funerals held there, and one day he counted ten.

He also had another gauge of the epidemic's severity. In Kolbuszowa women baked their own bread, and my father sold yeast, which came packed in solid, well-planed wooden boxes. Almost every day some grim-faced man or woman would appear at the door asking for an empty one of these boxes. He gave the boxes without question, for he knew their intended use: Kolbuszowans were not given to useless frills, and an empty yeast box made a perfectly adequate coffin for a dead baby.

At such times, the storekeeper tugged at his full beard and thought anxiously of his own family. His wife Esther had just given birth to a son, their ninth child. The others ranged in age from toddlers to teenaged sons and daughter nearly ready for marriage. The older ones had survived earlier epidemics, and now Isak Saleschutz prayed that his younger children might likewise be spared.

For a time it seemed as though his prayers were being answered. The day of the ten funerals came and went, the epidemic began to wane, and none of the Saleschutz children had even caught the disease. But one evening when Isak came home from the house of worship (*Beth Hamidrash*), Esther met him at the door and drew him aside.

"Naftali is sick," she said.

The infant, barely six weeks old, lay in his cradle crying hoarsely. To Isak, the tiny forehead seemed to burn like the heated stones in the bathhouse.

"How long has he been like this?"

"It just started this afternoon."

Isak sighed. "It will be best if no one else learns of this."

Esther understood. If the authorities heard of the child's sickness, they might order him to the hospital. No one was certain what went on in that place. Some swore that the sick were poisoned, so that they could be quickly buried and so kept from spreading the disease. Whatever the truth, it seemed that very few who entered the hospital came out alive.

Esther sat with the child all night. Sometimes the fever left him, but it always returned, stronger than ever. She tried to nurse him, but his stomach could not keep the milk. It was the same during the next night, and on the following afternoon Isak received an urgent message to come in from the store. Even before he reached the room, he could hear the wails of Naftali's sisters and brothers.

The boy now lay quiet and perfectly still. Isak listened for a heartbeat and heard none. He held a mirror and then a feather to the infant's nostrils. The mirror showed no trace of fog, and the feather not the slightest movement. Esther was a strong woman who rarely had use for tears, but now she sobbed softly.

"Oh, Itche, the others are all living and well. This one was here already. Why couldn't he have stayed, too?"

The storekeeper was known as an authority on a great many subjects, but for his wife's question he had no answer at all.

In the morning, as always, Isak Saleschutz went to the prayer house. After his daily prayers, he sought out a stout, ruddy-faced man known as Meyer the Carrier (*Meyer Treiger*). Meyer the Carrier earned his way by doing odd jobs of almost every description. The epidemic had made him a busy man, for one of his functions was that of an unofficial undertaker.

The two men went first to Isak's store, where they sorrowfully fetched an empty yeast box. They went to the Saleschutz home. Esther had wrapped her son's body in a clean white shirt, and Meyer the Carrier placed the little bundle in the yeast box and closed the lid. Isak knew Meyer the Carrier well. "A glass of schnapps, Meyer?" he suggested.

"Well, I don't know. A little one, maybe." Meyer the Carrier set the box gently on the floor.

Isak poured two small glasses of the clear, strong drink. "*L'chayim.* May the epidemic end with this, and may we know no more sorrow."

"*L'chayim.*"

The men downed the schnapps, and Esther offered egg cake.

"I shouldn't," said Meyer the Carrier.

"Not even one piece?"

"Well . . . maybe just one."

Meyer the Carrier had nearly finished his egg cake and a second drink when he suddenly glanced sharply around the room.

"Reb Itche. In this fine house you have mice?"

"Mice? Impossible. We have an excellent cat."

"I'm certain I heard a mouse squeak. Listen!"

Now Isak and Esther heard the sound. The three adults scrambled around the room trying to flush out the mouse. Suddenly Isak pointed.

"The box!" he cried.

Meyer the Carrier tore open the lid and drew back the folds of the shirt. In his little coffin, Naftali Saleschutz blinked against the light, scowled, and irritated by the yeast dust in the box, squeaked out another tiny sneeze.

Superstition ran deep in Kolbuszowa. People still spoke darkly of the evil eye, and spat three times on waking from bad dreams, lest the dreams come true. Naturally, then, there were many who found a portent of the future in Naftali Saleschutz's miraculous escape. Surely he would enjoy long life, fine health, good fortune, or some similarly uncommon and happy destiny.

As it turned out, there was some omen or portent in my survival, for I was that infant. Grown to a man, I would cheat death more than once, and my destiny would be uncommon indeed. But if the interpreters of signs had glimpsed some shadow of the truth, they glimpsed only a shadow. They did not foresee—nor, foreseeing, could they have believed—the hideous irony with which time would twist their glad prophecies. The time would come when I would wonder bitterly why fate had withheld from me the simple peace, the gentle oblivion of a small grave under a large oak tree dug by Meyer the Carrier.

But that time was for the man. For the child there was only the bright spring of new life. As the epidemic faded to memory, the tale of the yeast box became merely another anecdote recalled at family gatherings, and the little universe of Kolbuszowa went on much as it had for the past half-dozen centuries.

Some Jewish Humor from the Shtetl

Many of America's comedians have been Jews: Jack Benny, Eddie Cantor, Woody Allen, George Burns—whose two sisters, Esther and Mamie, married two of my father's brothers, Sam and Max. With very little effort, one could cover a page with Jewish names and not-so-Jewish names that are nevertheless the names of Jewish comedians. Often they draw their material from the tribulations of daily life, choosing to make a joke of the tricks fate plays on all of us. It must be in the blood. Kolbuszowa humor doesn't sound very different. Let me give a few examples. You will see what I mean.

Weddings were big events in our town. Since there were no movies and no theater, and no money to attend with even if there were, people looked forward to events like weddings. The trouble was, just as there were no movies or theater, there were no buses or cabs either. If the wedding happened to be in the next town, and you wanted to attend, you had to arrange transportation. Usually a family would rent a carriage or wagon from one of the farmers and arrange to have him drive them there. And that is how it was that a certain Jewish father and mother found themselves, along with their sons and daughters, all dressed in their finest and sitting behind a peasant farmer in a wagon being pulled by a rather skinny but nevertheless willing horse. They were all chatting among themselves when the wagon came to a hill. The peasant stopped and told the family that the load was too much for the horse. They would have to get out and walk along beside the wagon until they got over the hill. They did, but in the rolling countryside, it was not long before they came to another hill and then another. Each time, the peasant had them get out while the horse pulled the empty wagon to the top. Finally, they were past the hills, but they hit a patch of sandy ground. There was no way the horse could pull the loaded wagon through the sand. Out they went to walk until they were past the difficult terrain. The same happened when they hit the muddy patch, only this time it was a little worse. The men had to help push the wagon through, while the horse pulled. At last, the group arrived at the wedding site, somewhat the worse for their efforts. The peasant turned to the father to be paid. The father looked at him and said, "I had to be here. I wanted to go to the wedding. My wife and my children had to be here as well. They wanted to go to the wedding. You had to be here because you wanted to make some money. But tell me. I want to ask you. Why did you drag along the horse?"

This tendency to use humor to make light of daily adversity carried through all aspects of life—even death. When disaster struck or calamity threatened, it was often faced with *galgen humor* or the humor of someone going to the gallows. For example, in one family there were three brothers who were 100, 98, and 95 years old. Alas, one winter day, the 95-year-old brother died. The oldest said to his 98-year-old sibling, "I always knew that our little one wouldn't last long."

Another 100-year-old man lay on his death bed. While he had been a good and virtuous Jew all of his life, he had never earned much money, and the room he lived in was tiny. Its small size was accentuated by the gathering of his many children, who packed the room at his death scene. The old man struggled up on one elbow and bade the children to leave the room. "My *neshuma* (soul) wants to get out of my body," he croaked, "and there's no room for it in this room."

Another, in much the same circumstance, also bade his children leave the room. His *neshuma*, he claimed, was too bashful to leave his body in the presence of so many people.

Finally, there was the old man who lay dying, and in a moment of final lucidity, made some final requests of his family regarding the preparation of his body by the burial society and the funeral procession that would take place. He said, "When you carry my body to the cemetery, don't go past the tavern. I went in there every day for the past eighty years, and I will want to go in again. Don't carry my casket too high. You know, I have always been afraid of heights and I will get dizzy. But most important, when you do the ritual washing of the body, don't wash me under the arms. I am very ticklish there, and I don't want to start laughing when I am dead."

Or what about the poignancy in this bittersweet tale of a major flood that hit a small Jewish town. As the waters washed over the lowland a desperate father grabbed his youngest child and put him on his shoulder to carry him to safety on the higher ground. When they had finally reached security and he could put the child down, he looked at him solemnly and said, "We have lost all of our material things, our house, our property. I could have rescued gold or jewelry or furniture, but instead I brought you to safety. I want you to remember how important family is, and when I am old, if the same situation occurs, you will take me on your shoulder and save me."

The little boy looked at his father and solemnly replied, "No, Papa, I can't do that."

"Why not?" asked the shocked father.

"Because," he replied, "when you are old, I will have a little boy of my own to save and I will have to save him."

This was a tale my father used to tell to remind us that a parent's responsibility to a child was not necessarily going to be matched by that of the child to his parent.

Then, as now, religion played a big role in some people's lives, and they would pray every day; and it played a very small role in the lives of others, who would make their annual visit to *shul* on Yom Kippur. We had a jeweler in our town named Shuniek Arzt who had developed a great skepticism for organized religion, and he particularly resented the strictures it put on activities on the Sabbath. Hasidic Jews could undertake no worklike activity from Friday sundown through Saturday. Everything they might normally do during that period had to be finished before. As a result, women were busy cooking, baking, cleaning the house, and washing the floor. Since you couldn't tear paper on Sabbath, the men had to prepare toilet paper the day before. We would use newspaper cut into little squares, and on Friday, the squares for the following day had to be prepared and set aside. Any finger or toe nails that were to be cut would be cut on the day before. Sabbath was a day of prayer and contemplation. It was against this background that Shuniek Arzt used to refer to religion as the rabbi's cow.

He told the tale of a Jew who came to the rabbi on Saturday in a state of alarm. "The cow fell into the well," he cried. "What can we do?"

The rabbi looked up from his studies and said, "There's nothing we can do. It is Saturday."

"But the cow will drown," the Jew pleaded, "and besides Rabbi, it is your cow."

"My cow?" said the Rabbi in alarm. "Then we must save it because *tsaar bal chaim*," which in Hebrew means, "you cannot torture an animal."

And so it was that life, death, marriage, religion all become grist for the mill of Jewish humor from the shtetl.

More Jewish Humor

Poverty was a common experiences among the shtetl Jews in Poland. While perhaps 10 percent were very well off, and another 40 percent were somewhere in the middle, a full 50 percent of the Jews in our town had to be considered poor. Only two things relieved their burden. One was the *mitzvot* of *tzedakah,* or charity. Jews were mandated to help those less fortunate than themselves, and they had established an elaborate network of societies and private charities within the communities that offered support. The other was humor. The Jews had an endless number of stories, laden with irony and self-deprecating wit, that circulated over and over again. Some involved retelling of events befalling people I knew. Others were tales from another time and place.

Both *tzedakah* and humor are combined in the tale of the poor, traveling Jew who found himself in our town, alone and among strangers one Friday afternoon. It was not an uncommon situation. No matter how poor, or how hungry a Jew might be, he knew that he could be certain of a good Shabbat meal. Many, who traveled from town to town begging for a living, made it a point to be at the door of the synagogue on Friday for the evening prayers. The tradition was for the more well-to-do among the regular congregants to take the poor Jews to their homes and to share their food. I know from my own childhood that it would be a rare Shabbat meal that didn't see at least one stranger having dinner with us. My mother always made it a point to prepare for the extra diners my father would inevitably bring home with him.

It happened that one Friday, an unusually large number of itinerant beggars were waiting at the synagogue door. As the worshipers filed out, the beggars asked each to take him home for dinner. Some congregants replied that they were unable to. Others readily agreed, and one by one, each of the beggars found himself matched up with a benefactor, until there was just a single one left waiting at the door. Inside, there was only one worshiper, a tinsmith by trade named Moishe Laibale, who had lingered a little longer than usual, and as he exited he found himself confronted by the beggar, asking to be taken home.

"I am sorry, but I can't take you home. I am no wealthier than you," the tinsmith told the beggar. "I barely have enough to feed my wife and children. If I show up with you for dinner my wife, who has one of the worst mouths in town, will curse at me for bringing you home. I don't need that aggravation."

"You must take me. I am all alone. It is Shabbat and I am hungry. You can't refuse me," countered the beggar.

The two dickered back and forth with the tinsmith trying to explain his inability to provide and the beggar just as insistently clinging to his arm, alternately pleading and demanding.

Finally, the beggar's persistence wore Moishe Laibale down. He said, "All right. I will bring you home. There isn't enough food for another at the table, but I will share my portion with you. Whatever, I have, you shall have half."

And with that, he led the beggar to his house. When he went in, his wife, Dobcia, greeted him with a smile and a "Gut Shabes," but over his shoulder she saw the stranger coming in as well.

Her mood changed immediately. "Who is this?" she demanded.

Her husband sheepishly replied, "This is a poor man who I have brought home for dinner with us. I have agreed to share my portion with him."

Dobcia was furious. "You know we don't have enough to feed ourselves and our children decently." And she let out a stream of curses, which are bad enough in English but far worse in Yiddish. As her hapless husband cringed under the barrage, she culminated with a wish that he get eighty-eight boils (*makes*) on his body and suffer eighty-eight black days (*schwarce yuhr*).

"Eighty-eight boils," repeated the husband in dismay. But then he brightened and turned to the beggar, who was standing behind him.

"Remember," he said, "You get half. Forty-four of the boils and black days are for you."

There were many other stories about these Shabbat dinners for the poor. They often revolved around the desperately hungry beggar wolfing down his one good meal of the week. For example, there is the story of the efforts of one family to make conversation with their guest. The dialogue went something like this.

"So tell me, do you have a wife?"

"A brother too.

"Do you have a sister?"

"A brother-in-law too."

"Do you have a daughter?"

"Sons too."

The exasperated host said, "Why do you always answer like this, with more information than I ask for."

The beggar replied, without putting down his fork for a moment, or stopping his chewing.

"I know what the next question will be. This way I save you the trouble of asking, and save myself the time in answering."

And so saying, he reached across the table, spearing another piece of chicken with his fork.

The tables got turned somewhat when the town organized the Shabbat feeding of the poor more systematically. They prearranged who would go with whom by assigning each poor man to a family. Cards were prepared, each with a family name on it, and these were distributed to the poor at the synagogue.

It was customary for all to bathe at the *mikva* (public bath) on Friday afternoon, before the Friday night service, and all the Jewish men, rich and poor, hosts and guests, would strip down and sit in the steam room together, sighing and soaking out the burdens of the week. Without their clothes, and with their beards, one Jew looked pretty much like another in this setting. So it was that one poor Jew who had received a card naming a family that would host him in a short while decided to inquire of the Jew sitting next to him on the bench if he knew the family in question, and what type of meal did they provide. These situations lend themselves to strange twists of fate, and it turned out that the naked Jew on the bench was the very one who had been assigned as a host. He thought for a moment and then replied.

"Yes, I know this family. You can have a good meal there, but you will find that they are very generous with the fish and challah, but stingy with the rest of the meal. My advice would be to eat as much of the fish and challah as you can because you won't get much else. They will be stingy with the meat, the cake, and the *tsimmis.*"

Everyone dressed then and went to the *shul,* and they were matched up and went home to eat. Naturally, the poor man didn't recognize his host in this setting as the man he had spoken to through the steam. After all, he now wore his black silk coat and his fur *streimel* (Hasidic sable hat) and looked very different. When they got home, the host told his wife about their conversation in the *mikva* and had her set before their guest an extra large portion of carp and challah, which was quickly devoured.

"Would you like a little more?"

"Yes, if you don't mind." And another portion of fish and challah was served him, and this, too, was eaten to the point of discomfort. The poor Jew was sighing with contentment over the bulk of fish and challah that his stomach now contained, when the wife served the soup. It was a huge bowl of chicken soup, heavy with fat and noodles, and lima beans, filling the room with its tasty aroma. So delicious was its flavor, that the poor Jew forced himself to squeeze in just a little bit of the soup and he sat back, stuffed as he hadn't been on many a Shabbat.

This was unfortunate for him, because the wife then proceeded to lay on the table a baked goose, and then generous portions of *tsimmis,* a mixture of dried fruit, honey, and baked carrots. And then came servings of cake and tea and cognac. Alas, the poor Jew could eat none of it, having gorged himself on fish and challah. All he could do was sit and quietly curse the unknown man in the *shvitz* (lit., to sweat; by extension, the steam bath) who had given him such bad advice.

My father often used this story to point out that you can ask too many questions, and try too hard to get the edge in your dealings with others.

One of the more interesting traditions that grew up within the Jewish family was the granting of *kest* to a new son-in-law. This was the practice of having a new son-in-law move in for a brief time with the family of the bride. During the period of *kest*, the bride's family would feed the couple and take the opportunity to teach them some of the practicalities of married and commercial life. My father used to teach my sisters' husbands about his business, and we all got to know them at the family meals.

It happened that one Shabbat at the synagogue, a poor Jew came up to my father and asked to be taken home for dinner. Being a good, and well-to-do Jew, he agreed and was leading his guest to the door. When he turned around to welcome him in, he suddenly found himself facing, not one, but two guests. The poor Jew had been joined by a younger man.

"Who is this?" my father asked. "I agreed to bring you home, not your friend."

"This isn't my friend," replied the poor Jew. This is my son-in-law. My daughter recently married him, and I promised him *kest*. He eats his meals with me. Since you are going to feed me, it is only right that you feed him too so he can eat his meal with me."

Jewish humor and storytelling of this sort that focused on the basics of food, charity, and worship probed the heart of our lives in the shtetl. Awrumale Nachims was another poor Jew who lived in the town. Like so many religious Jews, he was wise and respected for his knowledge, but was unable to establish a reliable source of livelihood. He lived a hand-to-mouth existence, borrowing and begging what he could. We gain some picture of his existence, as well as his native wit, from his observation, made while smoking a cigarette that he had rolled himself, that he was never happy when he was smoking. When asked why that was, he replied with a talmudic melody:

"The cigarette is never the right size to enjoy. When I am smoking a cigarette made from tobacco I begged from someone else, it is too thick to burn properly. When I make a cigarette from my own tobacco, it is too thin."

It was this same caustic sense of humor that led Awrumale Nachims to observe to his neighbors that two kinds of people caused wars: bicycle riders and Jews. Invariably, the neighbor would scratch his head and ask, "Why bicycle riders?" He would say, "Why don't you ask, 'Why Jews?' It is because everyone naturally thinks that Jews are the source of all trouble."

Awrumale Nachims had two very rich neighbors. One was named David Narzizenfeld, and was known as Schwarzer David for his black beard. The other was named Nachum Auchisiger. Both were extremely wealthy, but Awrumale hated one and loved the other. Once again, we asked him why this was so.

David Narzizenfeld owned a quarry that produced gravel that he sold to the municipalities for covering the roads. Every day he would walk the five kilometers to the quarry, carrying a simple lunch of bread and onions with him. He worked and sweated in the quarry all day with his laborers, interrupted only when he sat by the river to eat his simple lunch, washing his meal down with water drawn from the passing stream. He would walk back late in the day and rise to repeat the ritual the next morning. He earned a great deal of money but apparently derived little luxury from it. Awrumale Nachims loved Black David because he was rich and didn't enjoy it. "I have no money and don't enjoy it. He has plenty of money and doesn't enjoy it."

He had strong resentment of Nachum Auchisiger, however. He owned a dry goods store from which he earned a handsome living. Unlike David, however, he lived right up to the limit of his wealth, dressing well, eating and drinking abundantly, enjoying the finest of cigars and cognac, and belching loudly and comfortably after each enormous meal.

"I hate this rich man," he often said. "It is bad enough that he has money. It's worse that he enjoys it so much."

While we are recounting stories involving poor men, let me tell you of the poor Jew who had never seen a mirror before. One day at a flea market he sees a broken piece of mirror for sale, and when he looks into it, he is astonished. He sees his father in the mirror as he looked just before he died, and says, "Oy, Papa, what are you doing in the glass? I haven't seen you in such a long time." He is of course, looking at his own reflection, which he has never seen before. Fascinated by the miracle of being able to talk to his father, he buys the glass and takes it home to his basement. Every day, before going to the synagogue, the Jew goes down to the basement to talk to his father. He tells him of his life since he passed away, and what he does each day. As he comes to spend more and more time in the basement, his behavior provokes the curiosity of his wife. She has heard him talking to someone but has no idea who it is. So one day, while her husband is at synagogue, the wife goes down to see what is going on. There, she finds the mirror, which is totally foreign to her also. When she looks into it she is shocked to find it is occupied by one of the homeliest women she has ever seen. "I don't understand," she muses. Why does he spend so much time down here talking to such an ugly old witch?"

To round out this collection of Jewish-related humor, I have a story about Jews told to me by my Italian partner, Joe Rulo, when we were building houses together in Jersey City. He came to me one day with a question that had been posed to him by his new daughter-in-law, Kathy. She was curious about the *mezuzahs* she often saw Jewish girls wearing on chains around their necks. She had heard a story about what was in them and had asked him if he could confirm it with his Jewish partner. I told him I would oblige. What had she heard? What she had been told was that when Jewish boys were circumcised as infants, their mothers saved the clipped foreskins, which they would dry out and put into this golden box. When a Jewish boy became engaged, the first thing the mother gave the fiancé was this container with the foreskin in it. She had heard that it was very special because it was the symbol of being a Jew, and was to be worn day and night and never taken off.

At first I thought he was kidding me, but then I realized that even in the United States, where a Jew and an Italian were business partners, there was this much ignorance about who we were and what we believed.

I then told Joe the story of the Italian who often observed one of his Jewish friends kissing the *mezuzahs* fastened to their door posts when they went into and out of the house. When the Italian learned that the *mezuzahs* contained the Ten Commandments, he told the Jew that he thought that was a beautiful custom that he would like to imitate since the Italians also believed in the Ten Commandments. The Jew bought the Italian a beautiful *mezuzahs* as a gift, but the next time he came to visit he didn't see it mounted on the door. When he asked why it wasn't there, the Italian sheepishly told him he didn't know how to put it up. When he opened it, the instructions on how to mount it were in a foreign language written in funny letters that he couldn't understand.

Unfortunately, the story I told him was just that—a story. The one he told me, which sounded even more contrived, represented a true belief about the nature of Jews and their customs.

The "Streimel" and the "Chosen"

Moishe Bombach was missing. The entire Jewish population of Kolbuszowa was waiting for him on that bitter cold day in the winter of 1930 and he had simply disappeared from the sled that was bringing him from the train station of Sedziszow to Kolbuszowa, twelve miles away. His family swore he was on the sled when it left the train depot. He was not on it when it arrived.

Naturally, there was great concern over the disappearance, but nowhere was it greater than in the household of Chaim Shaya Berkowitz, the *dayan* (judge) of Kolbuszowa. Moishe Bombach was to marry the *dayan's* daughter that evening. Since the bride's father was *dayan* of Kolbuszowa and a respected member of the rabbinical court where the law was interpreted, everyone, whether invited or not, was present in anticipation of the wedding. They were there to share the *dayan's* joy, but also to share the food and drink, and they were there for the entertainment to be provided by the *Badchan*, a jester hired for the occasion. They were concerned for the bride and groom but they were concerned for themselves as well. The long-awaited day of celebration was in jeopardy.

While everyone knew Moishe Bombach was missing, no one in Kolbuszowa knew exactly what he looked like. As with most weddings among the Hasidim, neither bride nor groom had set eyes on one another before the day of the wedding. It was an arranged marriage that brought a scholar to the bride's household and gifts and security to the groom. The *dayan* was delighted with the match, for Moishe Bombach was reputed to be a scholar of great promise. Although he was missing, there was no reason to believe he had changed his mind. The bride had been reported to be of sweet disposition. The marriage would bring him *kest*, support and financial security as part of the *dayan's* household. And most significantly, it was known that he was immensely satisfied with the engagement presents he had received—presents young men in his circumstance hope for. There was a gold Shafhausen pocket watch with a long, golden chain that he wore, spanning his waist from pocket to pocket. He had loved to open it with a flourish when asked the time, and to feel its weight in his hand. Like most teenage Hasidic grooms, he was concerned with matters both spiritual and temporal—especially as measured by his gold Shafhausen watch.

But if the gold watch was a source of great joy, the sable hat he had received for the event had filled Moishe with near bliss. This, too, was part of the tradition. Every married Hasidic man had a sable hat, or *streimel*, which was worn only on Saturdays or holidays and on special occasions like weddings or engagements. The hat was a traditional remembrance of an order issued by the bishops in Germany during the Middle Ages that all Jews must wear hats made of cat skin and rat skin as a means of inflicting humiliation. So detested was this requirement that several hundred years after the order was lifted, the Jews of East Europa com-

Moishe Kornfeld, the author's brother-in-law, wearing his streimel.

memorated it by sparing no expense in importing the finest sable tails and fashioning them into a young man's most prized possession, his *streimel*. With his watch and his hat, Moishe Bombach was genuinely pleased with the prospect of marriage. The bride? That would just have to take care of itself.

When the sled arrived with only Moishe's parents and sisters aboard, but without the guest of honor, speculation ran amok. Perhaps a Polish peasant had kidnapped him for his gold watch. Maybe the furs in his hat were so attractive, foul play had befallen him as a result. No doubt had he been traveling alone such speculation would have prevailed, but as it was, the family knew that the *chosen* or groom had been seated right behind them on the sled. Could he have fallen off? Surely he would have held on with both hands.

And so amid the speculation and bewilderment, it was decided that the sled would retrace the road traveled in search of the missing bridegroom. And they had best hurry. It was extremely cold, and if he had fallen off the sled, his feet would freeze quickly.

The shadows were already long across the road, for night comes early in Poland in the winter. Back they went, along the road, with the wind rising and the snow drifts attesting to the severity of the recent storm. As they rode back they called over the wind the name of the *chosen,* "Moishe, Moishe." And then through the gloomy twilight as they rounded another bend in the road, there he was. Moishe Bombach, talmudic scholar, sat in a snow drift up to his chest. Facing him, one could see his head poking out of the snow that covered the rest of his body, and in front of him, he held the round box with his *streimel.*

The horses drew the sled forward to the spot where these two odd parts of Moishe's presence were exposed in the snowbank: his head, with its wispy, goatlike red beard, and the box with the sable hat. He sat in the snow as if in the stocks in a New England jail, unable to move, shivering in the cold, his head covered with a peasant winter hat—but he survived.

They freed Moishe Bombach from his snowy prison and bundled him into the sled for the trip back to Kolbuszowa. On the way, he related what had happened. He had been seated on the back of the sled with the round hatbox containing the prized *streimel* protectively situated in his lap for safekeeping. Moishe held onto the sled rail with one hand and the hatbox with the other. The sled had been flying over the snow, the wind howling, the runners of the sled making a loud hissing noise. As they thus traveled from the station, Moishe had taken his hand from the box for a moment and reached into his vest to check the time with his new gold Shafhausen watch. Once having established the time, he paused to test its weight. His gaze lingered a bit on this prized possession and he had let his thoughts wander. Suddenly a gust of wind had come up and threatened to blow his other prized possession, the *streimel* in the hat box, off his lap. Moishe let go of the railing to grab the hat box when just as suddenly, it was God's will that the strong wind blew the box with the *streimel* off the sled. Moishe, long on talmudic analysis but not too gifted with common sense, jumped from the sled to retrieve the box with the *streimel.* He landed in the six-foot snow drift, and as snow filtered into his collar and up his sleeves, the horses galloped away, pulling the sled to Kolbuszowa. Moishe had landed with his rump down, and his feet up and in front of him, sitting and unable to move. He yelled and called for them to stop, but to no avail. As the sled receded into the distance the usually distracted Moishe suddenly became very focused. The *streimel* in the round box in front of him was safe. However, he realized that he wasn't. Indeed, in the dire situation in which he found himself, his very survival was in jeopardy. Moishe normally prayed three times a day. He had been doing this since childhood. The blessings and importunings were uttered quickly and as a matter of rote. If God were to hear them, he would have to be paying close attention. Today was something very different in Moishe's life. Today the prayers were offered with a special intensity. They were very clear. A number of promises may even have been offered in return for deliverance.

It was to be four hours before he was rescued and returned to Kolbuszowa.

The next day the wedding took place. Most of those present had never seen Moishe before. Those who did know him had found him to be petty and self-concerned. But today he was different. The bride, who was in truth somewhat plain, was given special attention by Moishe. The boisterous crowd that he might normally have resented was welcomed. After the ceremony, he greeted everyone with warmth and animation. It was observed that Moishe, although short and skinny and not a handsome man, wore a constant smile on his face, which actually led some to call him quite attractive. He was dressed in his best Shabbas black silk clothes and across his waist, from pocket to pocket ran the golden chain on his Shafenhaus watch. On his head, crowning him on this day of his wedding and day after his deliverance, was his most precious possession, the sable *streimel*.

And it glowed with a luster that was extraordinary, even for the high standards of the furriers of the day.

My Father, the Businessman

Money mattered a great deal to the Jews of Kolbuszowa. Most of them were poor, and money, essential in the struggle for survival, was hard to come by. With no public welfare system the Jews built up their own form of social safety net. Those with a little more supported those in need. Sometimes they extended liberal credit. Sometimes they gave outright charity. Either way, it was important that both giver and recipient clearly understand and agree on the matter of which it was. Many a friendship foundered on misunderstanding—whether actual or merely convenient—of whether the money was expected to be returned.

As a successful businessman, my father usually found himself in the position to extend credit to customers who needed it. Occasionally, however, he found himself short of funds and in temporary need of someone else's consideration. Let me give you a few stories that point out how he dealt with each situation.

Somewhere between credit and charity falls the interest-free loan. You expect to get it back, but without gain to yourself. My father made many such loans. He had a fund that he used to finance people to help them make a living. Usually he would lend one hundred to two hundred zlotys at a time to Jews who were unable to accumulate the needed capital to finance their business ventures. With the money, they would go to a market in a different town and buy chickens, eggs, geese, or whatever was available there at a better price than it was at home. They would bring their purchases back to Kolbuszowa and sell them, usually at a small profit. Then they repeated the operation the next day, at a different market in a different town. Again a tiny profit would be added to the income of the family, and with it they would buy their own necessities of life: bread, kerosene, milk, sugar, and so on.

There was only one restriction on the capital my father provided.

Usually he would give it out on Sunday, and he insisted it be returned the following Friday. He had no hesitancy in lending the same amount to the same person the following Sunday. He just wanted to get it back over the Sabbath, hold it, and then lend it again.

This lending and returning and relending would go on for years. Usually, there was no misunderstanding about what was expected, and things went to everyone's satisfaction. One time, however, one man who we called Eliash did not return on Friday with the two hundred zlotys he had been lent. Nor did he come back the following week or the week after. One day, just when my father decided he was gone for good, he showed up. Better late than never, one might think. Not this time. Eliash didn't want to belatedly return the two hundred zlotys.

Instead he said, "I need to borrow a hundred zlotys for a half hour. I have an excellent opportunity to make a quick profit, but I need it now." No mention was made of the other money already owed.

My father said, "Come, Eliash let's talk about it. Let's sit down, have a cup of coffee and a piece of egg cookie, and discuss the project."

And he talked, and he talked dragging the discussion well beyond the half-hour Eliash said he needed the money for the deal. My father purposely dragged out the time, even though Eliash professed to be in a great hurry.

At length, he said, "Well, Eliash, it appears you do not need the money any more. You said you needed it for a half-hour, but we have been drinking coffee and eating egg cookies far longer than just a half-hour. I guess the opportunity has passed."

That was the way he expressed his disappointment and anger that the original money had not been returned. There was never an explanation offered. He just had no intention of giving Eliash any more.

Berish was another Jew who used to borrow from my father. One week he didn't return his hundred zlotys either, but he did come around and my father confronted him.

"Berish, you owe me a hundred zlotys."

Berish said, "No, I don't owe you the money. It is you who are guilty. You caused the situation by lending me the money and putting me in your debt."

He must have meant it, because he never returned the money.

One man who always returned his money was Kiwtche Leistner. He was a philanthropist at heart and liked to lend money to his friends, much as my father did. The only trouble was, he had no money to lend. So, every week he would borrow five hundred zlotys from my father and lend it as if it were his. He had the pleasure of doing the *mitzvot* of charity, and my father had the double pleasure of making his friend Kiwtche feel good about himself and seeing that needed capital was received by some of the poorer Jews in the town. He was a kind and generous man, but he had a sense that it was important that the terms of an agreement be honored. In times of need, he could be flexible, and he had little patience for those who sought to take advantage of him.

While I usually think of him in this role of capitalist benefactor, giving aid to people, I learned, quite by accident, how he reacted when the shoe was on the other foot; that is, when it was he who owed money and couldn't repay it. It came about when my wife and I were in Israel in 1949. She had a lot of family there: a grandmother, sister, three uncles and cousins. While we were on Allenby Street in Tel Aviv, a man hailed me and I recognized Kuba Alter, from Rzeszow. Seeing me triggered a memory in Kuba Alter, and he called over some friends, introduced me, and told them he wanted to tell them a story about my father. It seems that Kuba Alter was a major wholesaler in Rzeszow, and we were customers of his. In that relationship, it was he who sold merchandise to my father, and extended him credit when he didn't have the money to pay immediately. As Kuba told the story, one time my father came to buy some merchandise, and as he was loading it up, he didn't offer to pay right away.

Kuba Alter asked, " 'Reb Itche, what about the money?' "Your father didn't want to say he didn't have the money," Kuba told us. "Instead, he told me a story."

" 'Once upon a time a peasant wanted to buy a cow that would provide him with abundant milk and cheese. He went to a Jew he knew who sold cows and said to him, 'I am coming to you because I know you are honest. Please sell me a good cow.' The Jew picked one out from his small herd and assured the peasant he was getting a good cow. Two weeks later the peasant was back, both hurt and angry. 'The cow you sold me,' he complained, 'doesn't give milk. You said it was a good cow, but it isn't.'

The Jew took the cow and said, 'You are wrong. This is a good cow. It doesn't run away, it has a pleasant disposition, it is a good cow.'

'But it doesn't give milk,' the peasant complained.

The Jew said, 'you didn't ask for a cow that gave milk. You asked for a good cow. Believe me, if this cow had milk to give, it would give you her last drop. She would give it because she is a good cow, but she happens to have no milk right now.' "

Kuba Alter told us he understood from the story that my father had no money at the moment, and this was his way of saying so. He was also saying that being a good and honest man, he was assuring me he would pay as soon as he could.

He laughed, as he told the story, and added, "I gave him the merchandise and sure enough, two weeks later I had my money."

That's how my father was when it came to business.

The Words of My Father

Even today, nearly sixty years after the Germans killed him, I think of my father as one of the wisest persons I have known. I have been through a lot since then, done a great many things, and known intelligent people in every walk of life. Still, this community leader, this successful businessman, this learned scholar, this loving parent continues to shine in my estimation more brilliantly than ever. I particularly remember his words. He was a unique individual with a great talent for communicating and pressing his viewpoint by telling a gentle story that inevitably yielded a moral or a message that far transcended the events of the tale. Let me give you some examples of his words. You will see what I mean.

Tzedakah, or charity, plays a prominent position in the Jewish scheme of values. The Torah commands that men of means are obligated to provide for those in want. Nevertheless, it is not uncommon now, and it was not uncommon then, for a plea for *tzedakah* to go unheeded. My father used to describe it this way:

"Once upon a time, there was a Jewish man who had grown extremely wealthy. He owned vast tracts of land and the rich forests that grew on them. One time while out in one of his forests he lost his way. His path twisted and turned, and the more he tried to find his way, the more confused he became. By luck, he came upon a peasant who knew the forest like the back of his hand, and the rich man asked the peasant if he would lead him out.

"The peasant agreed, but while they were walking toward the edge of the woods, a great thunderstorm came up. While sheets of rain pelted down and lightning flashed, huge thunderclaps shook the ground. The noise was deafening, but in the middle of the din the peasant suddenly stopped and shouted, 'Listen, do you hear that?' "

"Hear what?" asked the Jew, his ears ringing from the thunder. "That cricket. I hear a cricket," the peasant said. The Jew strained, but amidst the roar of the elements, he could hear no cricket. The peasant bent down and picked up the small cricket from the leaves. They walked on through the storm a bit further, when the Jew stopped.

"Do you hear that?" he asked the peasant.

"Hear what?" the peasant replied.

"The clink of a gold coin," the Jew said, whereupon he bent down and pulled a gold coin from the leaves that carpeted the floor of the forest.

The moral, said my father, is that we all hear what we are preconditioned to hear. No matter how clear a plea for charity is to you, it will fall on deaf ears of someone for whom *tzedakah* is not recognized as a mitzvah.

As you might expect, my father was generous to his family, as well as to strangers. When my sisters married, he always made sure they had dowries that went beyond the norm. He gave them big houses and helped set his sons-in-law up in business. He was the same way with his relatives, and with many of the people he did business with. Credit was generously extended and debts likely to be forgiven if a borrower's fortunes turned against him. When people commented on his generosity, they were sometimes rewarded with this in reply:

"Which would you rather be," he would ask, "a pig or a cow?" The shrug that usually greeted the question was met with an elaboration. "A pig has value to people. They use its skin for leather and its flesh for meat. So does a cow have value. People get milk, butter, and cheese from a cow. The difference is, a pig is only of value after it is dead. You have to kill it to enjoy the benefits it offers. A cow, on the other hand, is valuable, and provides the means for well-being while it is alive." He would pause, and stroke his beard.

"I'd rather be a cow than a pig. I want to give and be valued for what I have to give, while I am alive. I want to give," he would emphasize, "with a warm hand. The alternative is to have it taken later when my hand is cold."

My father was not only generous with his money. He was also willing to give his time and talent to teach a lesson when it seemed appropriate. For instance, one day he was out and noticed a groschen, which was the equivalent of a penny nowadays, lying on the ground. A child who saw it there, passed it by, not bothering to pick it up. My father didn't hesitate to walk over and pick the groschen out of the dust himself. But he didn't put it in his pocket. Instead he brought it to the fruit stand and with it bought ten cherries. He then dropped one of the cherries where the child could see it, and the child hurried over to pick it up. My father dropped another, with the same result. The child picked it up, as he did, one at a time, with all ten cherries that my father dropped.

At that point he called the child aside and said, "Do you see, you didn't want to bother to bend down to pick up the groschen. You walked right past it. Yet you bent down ten times to pick up the cherries I bought with that coin. If you had picked up the coin yourself, you could have saved all of that effort." The child showed some understanding of his message that the worth of things isn't always what it appears to be. If you know what value lies within an object or a person you can prosper at perhaps one-tenth the cost and effort.

He had a somewhat more subtle variation on that allegory when he told the story of the Jewish merchant who used to travel among the Polish beekeeping peasants to buy the honey produced by their hives. He traveled with a barrel attached to four wheels which he used to store and transport the honey. The technique he used was to fill a gallon (*gasior*) jug with honey from the hive and then to pour the contents of the jug into the barrel. He would pay the peasant an agreed sum for each gallon emptied into the barrel. To keep count of how many gallons had been poured, his custom was to take off his yarmulke, put it on the ground, and put a groschen coin into the skullcap as a token to keep count. When the hive was empty, he would count the coins in the hat and multiply that number by the agreed price of a gallon of honey.

One day he came upon a beekeeper whom he hadn't dealt with before. The peasant, it turned out, was a thief. As the Jew was transferring the honey he would go from the hive to the barrel, and often had his back turned on the peasant. This was an opportunity not to be missed. Seeing all those coins in the yarmulke, the peasant waited until the Jew's back was turned and stole some of the coins. At the end of the day, when the Jew and the peasant were settling up, the Jew counted the coins in the hat and paid the price of a gallon of honey for each one present. The Jew knew the count was short and surmised what had happened. He shrugged, and smiled and paid the amount owed based on the coin count. The peasant, of course, couldn't acknowledge that he had stolen the coins, so he accepted the amount, but vowed not to do business with that particular Jew again.

My father used this story to point out that if you steal a penny from a business partner, in the long run it can cost you five hundred times as much. He was never quite clear, however, on the question of who was the bigger thief, the peasant who stole the coins or the Jew who got the honey for nothing. That was for his listener to decide.

And then there was the story he told when my mother began to get a little chubby from eating too much. In commenting on it, he would say, "She is getting fat from our sins." People would look at him. That was a strange thing to say, she is getting fat from sins. What did he mean by that? He explained that whenever he or the children left over any food, mother used to become quite upset.

"Eat!" she would say. "It is a sin to leave over food." Most times we would just push away from the table, saying we were full. Well, if we were going to sin, it didn't mean she had to also. She wasn't going to commit the sin of throwing out leftover food. Instead, she would eat the food herself.

"She got fat," he said, "because of our sins. Because it is a sin to thrown away food."

Be that as it may, he did have a strange habit when he drank his morning coffee from the large, half-liter cup he always used. Each morning, he would add exactly eight lumps of sugar to the coffee. That seemed a lot of sugar, but not excessive. What was strange was that he would never stir the coffee. The sugar would just sit at the bottom of the cup. People wondered about this strange, seemingly irrational behavior, and he explained it. "I don't like coffee that is too sweet," he said. "If while I am putting in my eight lumps of sugar, someone comes in and disturbs my count, I won't know where I am. I can ask them, how many I have put it, but they won't know because they aren't paying attention. I am liable to start over again at one, and end up with more than the eight lumps of sugar I want. Then, if I stir it, it will be too sweet. This way," he concluded, and I never knew if it was in jest or he was serious, "it doesn't matter. I don't stir it anyway because I don't like sweet coffee."

Thus, my father controlled events in his life, just as, he said, did his friend Moshe, who used to fight with his wife constantly. One day, during a particularly serious fight, she threatened to hit him with a broom. To avoid the blow, Moshe scurried under the bed, just about the time my father came into the room and inquired what was going on. When he heard Moshe was under the bed, he said, "Moshe, come out from there."

Moshe said, "I will not!"

"Why not? Why won't you come out?" he asked, and Moshe answered.

"She wants me to come out. I won't because I want to show her who is the boss around here."

My Father, the Storyteller

Sometimes Less Is More and Sometimes More Is Less

As a businessman my father was frequently exposed to customers and suppliers who would offer exaggerated claims and explanations. As a wise man, he knew that excess and exaggeration weren't necessarily the most persuasive tools. One could often be more effective with a more modest selection of rhetoric.

For example, he used to tell the story of five tailors who were opening shops along the same street in Warsaw. Finding themselves in a difficult competitive situation, they each wished to stress the superiority of their services. The first put a sign in his window advertising, "I am the best tailor in Warsaw."

Certainly, this was a strong claim that would have been more effective had not the second posted the notice in his window, "I am the best tailor in Poland."

Clearly this claim would have won a following were it not for the third tailor who claimed, "I am the best tailor in Europe."

Superiority throughout the continent should have won the day, and it would have, were it not for the fourth tailor, whose sign claimed, "I am the best tailor in the world."

The fifth tailor was stymied only for a moment. Of course, he might have claimed to be the best in the galaxy or the universe, but those dimensions were unknown to him. Instead, he posted a dignified sign reading,

"I am the best tailor on this street."

My father made a similar point when one of his suppliers who had failed to deliver on time, or one of his customers who was late with a payment would offer a wide assortment of elaborate excuses. He told the story of a triumphal Napoleon who had issued an order to the effect that when he entered a town, all of the bells in all of the churches should ring in acknowledgment of his victory. As a result, the air was filled for weeks on end with the ringing of church bells. On across Russia he swept, accompanied by what appeared to some to be the joyous pealing, and to others, the mournful tolling of the bells. Abruptly, one day, he approached a town where his army was met only with silence. No bells, pealing or tolling, welcomed the conqueror. Angered that his edict was being ignored, Napoleon demanded that the mayor of the offending town be brought before him.

"Didn't you know about the order I gave? Why aren't your church bells ringing as I commanded?"

The mayor said, "I have ten excuses I can give your lordship as to why the bells aren't ringing. The first is, when the Russian army left, they took all the church bells with them." The second is . . .

"Say no more," Napoleon commanded. "The first is reason enough."

My father used this story when people explained over and over again why something had or had not taken place. Only one explanation was needed—provided it is a good one.

My favorite of these allegories of his involves the poor Jew who dreamt of finding wealth somewhere in his lifetime. As he dwelled on the matter there came to his attention the existence of a far-off kingdom rich in many things, but which had never known or seen onions. The Jew decided to find his fortune by introducing the onion to this kingdom. So he put a bushel of onions into a bag, and with the bag on his shoulder, set out for the kingdom. Since the distance was great, he traveled, on foot, for three years and eventually arrived at its walls. He asked for an audience with the king and when this was granted, he told the king that he had something rare and wonderful for him, and to show it, he would cook a meal for the court. The Jew then gathered the ingredients for a stew, and from his bag, he took some onions to complete the recipe. When it was all cooked, served, and eaten by the people of the court, there was unanimous consent that the Jew had truly brought something marvelous to the kingdom. The onions would enrich their lives, and in return they wanted to enrich the Jew for his contribution. The king took the bag in which the onions had been carried and filled it with an equal weight of gold. The Jew was overwhelmed. This was riches beyond what he had hoped for. He bade farewell to the kingdom and with the bag of gold on his back began the long, three-year journey back home. When, at length he got there, he was by far the richest man in his town. His friends implored him to tell them how he gained such wealth and how they too might achieve so much. To one, he confided that he had introduced onions into the far-off kingdom. When he was there, he recalled, he did not see any garlic either. He was certain, he said, that the king would be grateful if the Jew were to bring garlic to his kingdom.

And so, the second Jew loaded up a bag with garlic and retraced the steps followed by his friend to the far-off kingdom. As anticipated, the kingdom had never experienced garlic, and when the Jew cooked a meal that contained its aroma and flavor and served it to the court, they proclaimed that this was a gift worth even more than the gift of onions received many years before.

"How shall I reward this Jew?" asked the king of his advisers.

"You gave the other Jew a bag of gold for the onions," one suggested. "Give this one the same."

The king thought about it, and said, "No, a bag of gold was suitable for the onions. But the garlic this man has brought is even more precious. We must reward this Jew with something even more valuable than gold."

He pondered the matter and with a flash of insight, the king declared. "I know what to give him that is more valuable than gold." And he gave the Jew a bag of onions.

It was through stories such as these that my father gently instilled in us an appreciation of life's ironies: that less can succeed over more, but that more can turn out to be less; and, that no matter how right you are, for all practical purposes, you can turn out to be very, very wrong.

In My Mother's Kitchen

Of the five senses, it is my sense of smell that is most effective in evoking memories of times past. One whiff of raspberries cooking can send me back seventy years to my mother's kitchen, where she has a big pot simmering on the stove. She had an annual ritual of preparing raspberry syrup for our family and for giving it away as presents to her friends. This syrup was highly prized for flavoring foods, particularly hot tea, and for its medicinal powers. Those favored to received a bottle considered themselves fortunate indeed.

Each year she made precisely 350 bottles of syrup. Its preparation required, of course, the wild raspberries, which she bought from the local peasants, and also enormous amounts of sugar, which in Poland was an extremely expensive commodity. The government monopolized sugar production and used the product largely for export, as a means of earning foreign currencies. The world price for sugar was very low, about five groschen per kilo. But since little found its way into the domestic market, prices in Poland were twenty times that and generally too high for most people's budgets. A kilo of sugar costing one zloty required a day's wage for the average worker. Our family was the exception. Because my father was a wholesaler of a wide variety of products, including sugar, we bought sugar, not by the kilo, but by the ton. Naturally, it was intended

Esther Saleschutz, the author's mother, in 1934.

for resale. To my mother, however, it was just available, and she would liberally help herself to the sugar inventory to make the syrup. She would fill the house with the sweet aroma of raspberries cooking down to make 350 bottles of a delicious syrup that no one else could afford to make in quantities of more than five or ten at a time.

I think my mother's instinct for giving away food came from the extent of poverty she had experienced as a child. Like so many shtetl Jews, her father had little money. And like so many consumed with study, he didn't seem to mind. While his name was Leibush Berl, he was called Leibush Awrumalis and was acknowledged to be one of the outstanding scholars in the region. He spent his time studying the Scriptures and earned a little money by teaching. One of the stories told to emphasize the extent of the family's impoverished state held that when celebrating Passover they passed around for the six of them, not six hard-boiled eggs, but two. One was divided into quarters to be shared by the four children. The other was halved with a portion eaten each by the mother and father.

Oddly, this material impoverishment enriched my mother intellectually in a unique manner. Her childhood house contained but one room, and this served as kitchen, living room, bedroom, and most importantly, classroom. Because there was no place else to go, she would be present in the room while her father tutored the young men seeking his enlightenment. She would listen as over and over again they recited the weekly portions of the Torah, and as a result, after many years, she found she could recite the Bible from memory. While most women of her time received no formal Jewish education, my mother could both read and understand Hebrew. The women in the town who didn't read Hebrew would sit around my mother in the synagogue and repeat the prayers she would recite. Because they prayed through repetition of the Hebrew my mother chanted, she was called the *zugerin* (talker). In our home, during the week, the women would gather to knit, and pluck feathers and gossip about local happenings. On Saturday, my mother would read the Tsenerene to the women after the meal. The Tsenerene was a Yiddish translation of the Bible, which of course was the language they all spoke, but once again, few could read. The result was that the women in our town not only learned to recite the prayers, they also grasped an understanding of the Bible stories as well.

The smell of bread baking is another sensory treat that transports me back to childhood. My mother didn't only give away the raspberry syrup. She also made it a practice to bake huge challahs and large loaves of bread for the holidays, and she would seek out the needy families in the community and be sure they had the bread and soup to eat. There were no social security or government welfare programs to support widows or the needy. Private charity was quietly given in many forms by those who could afford it to those less fortunate. She had a standard gift package consisting of twelve sabbath candles, a quarter of a liter of wine for the Kiddush, a roll of chicory, a packet of tea, and a kilo of lump sugar. These she prepared for distribution in large numbers whenever we celebrated a special event in the family such as a wedding or a birth.

We children—there were nine of us—sat around the kitchen while the bread baked. It was warm and comfortable, and my mother would be knitting one of the sweaters she seemed always to be working on, and singing to us in her beautiful voice, or telling us stories. She was a quiet, but by no means simple woman whose whole being was dedicated to her responsibility to my father and us children. Almost miraculously for those times, all nine of the children to whom she had given birth survived childhood. Infant mortality was common in Kolbuszowa, with one of her friends only seeing four of her eighteen births surviving. My mother often spoke of how grateful she felt for the blessing of not losing any of us. As the youngest of the nine, with five older sisters to look after me, I was, I will confess, a little spoiled from the attention I received from the ladies of the house.

The comforts of this idyllic childhood dominate my memory of my mother. Named Esther, as a result of being born on Purim, she was in every sense a queen: wise and gentle, generous and amusing. As her wool would be used up when she was knitting, she would only knit faster and faster. When the inevitable question came as to why she was going so fast, she would reply with a twinkle, "So I can finish the sweater before the wool runs out."

This kitchen, with its cooking, its singing, its storytelling, its reading of the Tsenerene, its telling and retelling of family stories, its love and its warmth—this kitchen and millions like it in Jewish homes all over Poland are what the Germans turned irretrievably to smoke and ash during those terrible days of the mid twentieth century.

My Father, the Storyteller

The Rabbi and the Miser

My sister Matil was going over my father's books one day and came upon a payment made for which she could find no corresponding bill. Since the family business in Kolbuszowa was an extensive one—we traded in a broad variety of goods with vendors from all walks of life—she searched, questioned my brothers, rechecked the records, and finally went to ask directly about the mysterious draft.

My father sighed, stroked his beard, looked off for a moment and at length told her the following tale:

Some years back, in Cracow, there was an extremely wealthy, but extremely miserly Jew. He had made a great deal of money as a trader and seemed intent on taking every zloty with him to the grave. When less fortunate Jews came to him to seek financial help he chased them away. Yeshivas (academies of talmudic studies) would constantly seek funds, and to all, his answer was a uniform rejection. Beggars asking for a few groschen to buy bread would meet a similar reply. This rich Jew was consistently stingy and lacking in charitable compassion. Not surprisingly, he earned the contempt of his community. The Jewish tradition is a charitable one, and this rich man so violated the spirit of that tradition that no one questioned that he deserved to be shunned.

As if to underscore the extreme stinginess of the rich miser, there lived in the same neighborhood another wealthy Jew who was completely opposite in attitude to charity and need. He was as generous as the first man was stingy. No one ever left his door without a supporting hand filling an empty purse. The yeshivas knew that they could rely on him for funds, and the synagogues praised him for his generosity. The contrast could not have been more marked if it had been designed intentionally.

Ultimately the miser took sick and died. No one grieved. No one felt that the community had suffered a great loss. In fact, the disrespect they felt for this man was so great that they did not even want to bury him among respected citizens. If he wouldn't be one among them during his lifetime, they didn't want him among them forever after. They took the issue to Rabbi Jehoshua Ben Josef, who was both wise and famous for his book *Maginey Shlomo, (Defendant of Shlomo)* and told him of their feelings; and the learned Rabbi said he would think over the matter. He was very familiar with the miserly behavior of the now deceased rich man and held him in no greater esteem than did the broader community. At length he held that the miser's behavior had been so bad that he indeed did not belong among the righteous Jews of Cracow. He would be buried along the fence of the cemetery, an area isolated for thieves, adulterers, and other nondeserving Jews. The funeral would not be a traditional one. No minyan would sit to pray for him. No Kaddish was said. The miser's death was marked by a bitterness among his neighbors that matched his own behavior during his lifetime.

At about the time the miser's health failed him, the business fortunes of the community benefactor also suffered a serious reversal. In this case, however, he wasn't the only one who was impacted. The entire community paid the price. Beggars still came to his door but occasionally, and then with growing frequency, they would be sent away empty-handed. The yeshivas continued to ask for support from him, but the money they formerly got without question was less forthcoming. The stream of charity slowed and then stopped completely. The generous rich man's financial condition had deteriorated so badly that he gave nothing to those in need.

The neighbors felt great compassion for him. They knew that he had always been available to them in their bad times, and they felt called on to reciprocate his acts of charity. A collection was started in his behalf, and when it grew to a significant sum, it was offered by a grateful community in the spirit of sharing to this generous man who had given so much and now had apparently lost everything.

A delegation of citizens was selected, and they brought the community's offering to the failed philanthropist. To their shock and dismay, their charity was rejected.

"No, I cannot take your money," he explained, "for in truth, I gave you nothing. All of the giving, all the support, all of the good deeds you give me credit for did not originate with me."

The neighbors were stunned with disbelief. "If not from you, then from whom?" they asked.

And the generous rich man, so venerated in the Jewish community looked away and said, "All the money I gave you came from the man you buried by the fence in the cemetery. He demanded that I promise under oath that I would never betray that he was the source of that charity." These were charitable deeds done anonymously—deeds done *matan-beseyter*. These were charitable acts of the highest order in Jewish ethics—good deeds that could bring no compensation in return. Such was the quality of the man the community buried in disgrace.

Needless to say, those in the Jewish community were stunned, but none more so than Rabbi Jehoshua ben Josef, who had decreed the burial in disgrace for what had emerged as a man more righteous than any in the community. A terrible pain of conscience tore at his spirit. He could find no solace for this injustice.

In his will, the rabbi wrote that upon his death, he, too, should be buried by the cemetery fence, next to this most righteous Jew who had never made known his acts of generosity and charity. The rabbi knew it would be seen as a great honor to be buried next to a distinguished rabbi, and the community would come to respect the man who had performed such selfless acts of charity.

He knew, too, that it would be a great honor for him to be buried next to one so righteous.

And so it was that my father, through his story, taught us the principles of Jewish ethics and, incidentally, explained that check for which there was no apparent bill.

Jew, Jew, Jew

The four hooligans stood outside the office of the Savings Bank and jeered, "Jew, Jew, Jew" at the black-coated Hasid trying to pass unnoticed. It was the day of the monthly meeting of the board of directors of the bank. Since the bank had both Jewish and Gentile customers, the board had representation from both groups. Four of Kolbuszowa's most prominent Jewish businessmen represented their community, and once each month, after the evening prayers, they would gather with their Polish counterparts to review the bank's activities. The occasion also provided the local hooligan community an opportunity for some activity. They would take the evening off for some recreational Jew baiting. "Zydzie, Zydzie, Zydzie . . . Jew, Jew, Jew," they taunted as the pale, bearded man averted his eyes and hurried past. He knew the good-natured abuse could quickly turn to something more ill-tempered—something more physical.

My father, Isak Saleschutz, who as one of the town's prominent merchants also served on the board of this bank, watched the activity from across the street. He had just finished his evening prayers and was on his way to attend the meeting as well.

Now my father was a man of many parts. While he looked to be a stern, humorless Jew, given only to his devotions and business, he was far from that. He was a resident wise counselor for the Jews of the town, learned in all manner of lore and willing, when asked, to offer insight and advice on topics ranging from talmudic interpretation to the best way to mix coffee beans. People came to call him Itche the Storyteller because the advice he gave often came in the form of a parable or story. He enjoyed the complexities of the human heart and the urges that motivated behavior, and his stories would often be touched with irony and humor. He rarely found the most direct route to a subject to be the most fruitful.

As he watched the hooligans taunting his colleague who preceded him into the bank he smiled and reached into his pocket and took out a few groschen. Then he approached the group boldly. Sure enough, as he approached, the youths turned their attention away from the door and toward him and began their derisive chant. "Zydzie, Zydzie, Zydzie," they jeered. "Jew, Jew, Jew."

Unlike his predecessor who attempted to slink past them, my father walked up directly to the leader of the group.

"Can't you shout any louder than that?" he asked. "I want to hear you shout louder than that." The boy looked at him with puzzlement, and my father added, "I'll tell you what. I want to see how loud you can yell. I will give you each a *grosch* (penny) if you will yell as loud as you can at the next Jew that goes into the building."

The boys thought they had died and gone to heaven. What could be better than to be paid for Jew baiting. They happily accepted the pennies, and my father stood by watching approvingly as the next Jew approached and was greeted by the raucous shouting he had inspired.

"Jew, Jew, Jew," these newly hired mercenaries shouted at the hapless subject hurrying by. It was clear they were intent on giving my father his money's worth, and they outdid themselves.

When the much-abused Jew had passed, the boys hurried over to my father and said with enthusiasm, "Give us another penny and we will shout even louder at the next Jew that comes along."

But my father only shook his head. "No I will not pay you any more. I paid you once. I will not pay you any more."

And the oldest of the boys glared back at my father, who he felt had betrayed him by refusing to pay to have more Jews taunted. He would show this Jew who was boss. "Okay," he said. "If you won't pay us any more, we won't shout any more."

This story just illustrates my father's ability to deal with people through his stories.

And so it was that this sometimes shrewd, sometimes ingenious, always devoted man found his way through the difficult relationships Jews had with their Polish neighbors. His stories revealed the foibles of human nature. He could create illusions and bring his adversaries to see and appreciate them. They would not only entertain, they would teach. There was a humorous gentleness to them.

And what became of my father, the storyteller? What was the fate of this storyteller under the Germans? I tell of it in my book *Against All Odds*. Let me repeat it in brief. My father had one more story to tell us.

"By now we could hear shooting and screaming coming from other parts of the ghetto; we knew a raid was on. My sister Matil came into the back yard again. Apparently she thought that my father would be safer somewhere else and she unlocked the outhouse. Just at this moment the Gestapo man who had come around the back saw them and told them to stop. . . . My sister Matil screamed and threw herself at my father and the Germans. . . . Then Rachel came out of the house, pleading with them to spare his life. They made no reply. . . . While one man was struggling with my sisters, the other was shoving my father into the shed, where he was no longer in view. I heard two shots. They were the loudest sounds I had ever heard. After the shots I heard screaming and shouting, then my father's voice. He was wounded but still alive. 'Pigs! Executioners!' he screamed. Then, '*Nekuma! Nekuma! Nemt Nekuma!* Revenge! Revenge! Take Revenge!' "

A son's duty is to obey his father. Sixty years later I still hear that anguished cry. And sixty years later, my remembering and my telling these stories to make sure that everyone else remembers what we had and what we were and what the Germans destroyed—that is my duty and that is the revenge available to me now.

A Drunkard, a Footstool, and a Son

My father was an observant Jew. His most fervent hope was that his children would follow in his Hasidic footsteps. It was a hope destined to be unrealized. My oldest brother, Avrum, was never very religious. Avrum became Albert when he left for America at nineteen, and the melting pot quickly absorbed him. Leibush, the second son, stayed home, but only in geographical terms. In religious matters. he traveled just as far as Avrum by the time he was in his teens. The third son, David, left home in 1933 when he was twenty and settled in Palestine, a pioneer. Civilizing the wilderness became his primary calling. Orthodox observance was well down the list. It fell to me, Naftali, the youngest, to carry tradition and observance forward. My father's dreams of father and son *davening* together required that I remain orthodox in appearance and behavior.

The appearance began to change first. My *payes* (sidelocks) grew shorter even as I became taller each day. I began to shave, contrary to religious dictate. Then the behavior: I began to ride a bicycle, and worst of all, I enjoyed the company of the girls in the neighborhood. My father realized his hold on me was slipping, and being the storyteller that he was, he translated his distress at this into two parables.

The first I call "The Drunkard and His Son." It seems that one day in Kolbuszowa a father and son were staggering down the street, both drunk. They could hardly walk, and while others gossiped and spoke of the disgrace they brought on their family, my father said, "quite to the contrary, I envy them."

And when asked how he could envy the father of a drunkard, my father wistfully replied, "I envy the father because the son is honoring him by following in his footsteps. The son respects the values and teachings of his father." Needless to say, such a story produced the desired quality of guilt in his fourth and youngest son. But the quantity wasn't sufficient to change my way.

A variation on the story came through his telling my mother that "he never thought the fourth leg of her footstool would start to rot." What did he mean by this? There is a Hasidic saying that if a Jewish woman, who has four sons, dies, she sits in a comfortable chair in heaven and keeps her feet on a footstool. The four sons are thought to be the legs of the footstool. She is comfortable as long as the sons reliably support the faith, but if they stray from strict orthodoxy, the footstool loses some of its stability. The legs loosen and the stool sways.

One by one the legs of my mother's footstool rotted away: first Avrum, then Leibush and David. But my father always looked on me to ultimately support the stool through my observance. When I started to stray, to think in a modern fashion, my father was led to his unhappy observation that the fourth leg of the footstool had started to rot.

And with the telling of these stories my father demonstrated that he could produce a tear in his listeners, as well as a smile.

The Audit

The day the auditors from the Internal Revenue Service came to see Simcha Gewirtz, they took him by surprise. Simcha was the president of the local *chevra kedusha*, the burial society for men. In our town as in most shtetls many activities that today would be organized on a commercial basis, were handled by volunteers and funded through charity. Charity was very important in the value system of the Jews. Even though they barely had enough money to get by, the poor Jews of the towns in Poland managed to scrape up a few pennies to help one another. Burial was almost always handled by a *chevra kedusha.* There was one for the women and one for the men. While the women's society washed the bodies of the women from the town who had just died and dressed them in the burial shroud, it fell to the men to build the coffins and carry them and their contents on their shoulders to the edge of the town where the coffins would be put on a wagon and taken to the cemetery. There, where the men had already prepared the grave, they would take the body out of the coffin, place earthenware shards over the eyes so they wouldn't look enviously in the new world, and inter it, armed with a knife if it had been the victim of foul play, for eternity.

Membership in the men's *chevra kedusha* was a much-cherished honor among the deeply religious. Burial of one's neighbors represented an opportunity to perform a *chesed shel emet*, a truly good deed. Why was it considered such? Normally, given human nature, while we perform good deeds for the betterment of others, we also perform them in the expectation that an opportunity will present itself where the good deed will be reciprocated. We will be rewarded for our virtue. Only in this act of final kindness, of burial, do we perform a good deed with no expectation of the beneficiary repaying us in any way. And so, while each of these pious men pursued other occupations in the community, when called on through the death of a fellow Jew, they were glad to respond to the opportunity it afforded for a truly good deed.

It was Monday morning and Simcha and his gravediggers were still tired from their efforts over the weekend. Saturday night was always a heavy day because anyone who died Friday afternoon or Saturday had to wait to be buried on Saturday night, after Shabbos. In the dead of winter it was cold, hard work digging in the frozen ground after dark, often by candlelight. Everyone knew the best time for a Jew to die was Friday morning. Then the society could perform its ritual of washing and dressing the corpse and getting it into the ground before the beginning of the Sabbath. If your soul got to heaven on Shabbos, which would be the case with burial just before, the heavenly court, it was widely believed, would be inclined to be lenient. Entrance to heaven would be easier than for someone whose burial didn't come until Shabbos had passed. And of course, from the burial society's point of view, entrance into the ground would also be easier.

On this particular weekend, business had been brisk and the work had been hard. The ground was frozen solid from many days of subfreezing temperatures. As Simcha and the burial society worked, their breath hung frozen in the air. Each man's beard was studded with droplets of ice, and against this bitter cold, each man fortified himself with the 192-proof alcohol that was the trademark of burial societies throughout Poland. In truth, this nearly pure alcohol was consumed in great quantities by the burial society, partly, I imagine, because of the depressing nature of the work and partly because of the need to keep warm. In fact, the members of the burial society were drunk most of the time.

So it was for that reason, as much as any other that Simcha Gewirtz was a little confused in greeting the agent from the tax bureau. Gradually, the agent's mission became clear through the alcoholic haze. He was asking for an accounting of the money raised from the citizens of the town. Every Jew gave money once a month, or once every two months, to the burial societies against the day they or their families would have need. Those who resisted giving the charity during their lifetimes were often denied burial until an appropriate sum was paid by the family. The burial society thus had a formidable weapon for collecting. It was recognized as the only charity that could get back at the uncharitable. In fact, there was one famous story told of a mean and most uncharitable Jew who died without ever having contributed. The society denied him burial and after several days the body began to smell. Members of the community came to prevail on the *chevra kedusha* to do the burial but they were adamant. At last they relented but said it was only on the condition that someone would come forward and speak on behalf of the dead man and indicate some redeeming quality in his character. But even this condition couldn't be met. No one would have a good word to say, until at last one little Jew stepped forward and offered, "Bad as he was, compared to his brother he was an angel." That was enough. The requirement was met. The Jew had been buried.

Despite the large sums handled, the society kept no books. Members knew who donated and who didn't. This was handled by traditional methods, not books. The neighbors gave money, and the society spent it—spent it largely on the 96 percent alcohol vodka that kept them going.

"No," he replied "there are no records. No, we don't keep books."

"Do you know how much money you have taken in?" he was asked.

Simcha looked offended. "Of course we know exactly how much money we took in. We don't need books."

"If you don't keep records, and you don't keep books," the agent asked, "how do you know how much money you have taken in?"

Simcha replied it was simple, and he showed the auditor the system of precise accounting that the society had been using for years. Taking the agent to the attic used by the burial society, Simcha Gewirtz opened the door and ushered the man inside. The room was about twenty feet square, filled with empty vodka bottles. Simcha pointed at the mountain of exhausted containers—testimony to burdens assumed and services rendered over the years.

"If you want to know how much money we have taken in and spent as a society," he said, "it is very simple. All you have to do is count the empty bottles and multiply by the price of vodka."

Four Women Who Were Left Behind

The United States has been a land of golden opportunity for tens of thousands of Poland's Jews. It certainly was for me. This story of America has been described many times. Passage is bought for a family member who gains a toehold in the New World. After some years of working and saving, enough is put aside to bring over other members of the family, and they, individually and collectively, have defined American culture. It is a glorious story, but not without tragic consequences for some.

Di Shtime was one of these. At least that's what we called her. I never knew her name. It means one who can't speak. We called her that because we never heard her utter a word. It was not as if we never saw her in a situation where speech might be expected. Once a week she would come to our store. As far as I know, this was the only time she went out of her windowless, single-room hovel. No one knew what she did while she was cooped up the rest of the time. Probably nothing. She just remained inside until the week had passed and then she put on a kerchief that covered her entire head and face and, wearing the same dress as the week before, she would appear at the door of the store and soundlessly wait. And just as soundlessly my mother would gather up the bundle of supplies she regularly gave her: a quarter liter of kerosene, a quarter kilo of sugar, a quarter kilo of salt, a kilo of flour, a kilo of cereal, two candles for the sabbath, a box of matches, and a package of chicory. No words were spoken. Certainly no money was exchanged. This was charity of the purest and most basic kind.

Di Shtime couldn't speak because she had been horribly disfigured by a fire when she was a child. The family house had caught fire, and while the others had been able to run out, she was caught and her face and body burned so badly that it was said it was hard to identify her as human. Without proper medical care, she had survived but had been robbed of her ability to speak, and for all we knew much of her ability to think as well. No one but my mother seemed to give her much thought. All we knew was that she lived alone and eventually died alone, her existence punctuated by weekly visits to our store.

I say Di Shtime's situation represents a tragic consequence of American immigration. That's because they had to leave her behind. When the family that had survived the fire went to America, they couldn't take their disfigured daughter. Oh, they could have brought her, but she wouldn't have been admitted by the medical authorities. They had a choice. They could stay in Poland and care for her, or they could leave and abandon her. And so, to compound the misfortune of the fire, she was left behind, abandoned to rely on charity, and evidently, completely forgotten by her family in the United States.

A second woman in our small town, Elka Guttenberg, had been similarly separated from her emigrating family. America didn't want her because she had cerebral palsy and could only barely control her movements. But her brothers and sisters were strong and welcome, and so they went, leaving Elka eventually to subsist on the charity of the Jewish community. She, too, was one of my mother's nonpaying customers, who would share the food we had eaten the day before. Elka was certainly more social than Di Shtime, and she lived in our neighborhood as part of the Jewish community. And the community supported her until the Germans came. They had less use for her than America did, and killed her shortly after the invasion.

There were other women who populated our little world, living out their lives in tragic and deprived circumstances. I think of how cruel fate was for them. One we called the Meshuggenah (crazy) Fradale because she had clearly lost her mind. Every day she walked about, talking continuously to no one in particular, describing her son. She told how he had been born and grown up and gone to *cheder* and been good to his mother and been handsome beyond compare. And she told how he had gone off to fight in the Great War. And how he had been killed. She wasn't always the Meshuggenah Fradale, but the loss of her son hurt her so deeply that she lost her mind as well. She and her two surviving daughters lived together in one room with a wash stand.

Let me chronicle a fourth poor soul, Golda Mirel who lived in the same house as Elka Guttenberg. Of the four, Golda Mirel is the most vivid in my mind because I saw her on a weekly basis for virtually my entire childhood. There was nothing wrong with Golda Mirel. She had no physical or mental impairment. She just suffered from that most basic of social handicaps: she had no money and no family. She was just a poor old Jewish woman with little means of providing for herself, so she, too, fell on the conscience of the Jewish community. And the community responded with wood for her fire, food for her table, and clothing for her survival. Every Friday morning for twenty years she came to our store and received the same package of survival necessities as Di Shtime got. Every Friday night and Saturday noontime, after we had eaten, she came, offered the greeting of "gut Shabbos," and received a plate of whatever food we had partaken of for the sabbath meal. She thanked my mother, finished the food, stood up, and went home. The Jews had little in material wealth, but they had the tradition of charity. This support of Golda Mirel went on as long as I can remember. Once again, the Germans had little use for a seventy-year-old woman. They killed her promptly after the invasion.

Fate plays strange tricks with people's lives. For these four, who all lived together along one alley, fate was not kind. Injury, illness, personal tragedy, and poverty mingled to add some bitterness to the sweet flavor of life in my childhood town of Kolbuszowa.

Strict Observance

Jewish law governs life among the Hasidim. Whenever one of my suburban neighbors chafes under the restrictions of *kashruth* or nibbles a little when he feels faint on Yom Kippur, or is otherwise inclined to bend the law, I think back to the meticulous observance practiced by my father and our neighbors in Kolbuszowa. There, the only deviation was to interpret its requirements more strictly.

Take the matter of fingernails. Hasidic fingernails grow just as reliably as everyone else's. However, cutting them was not a casual matter. And they were not disposed of like everyone else's. The law has its requirements, and these were closely observed. To begin with, you cannot simply throw away fingernail clippings. They are part of one's body, and the parts of the body cannot be casually disposed of. They must be buried or burned, and there must be witnesses to verify the fact that this requirement has been met. We would burn them.

Every Friday afternoon the male members of our family would go to the *mikvah* to take a purifying bath. There were two *mikvahs*, one cold and one warm, as well as a steam room with a large, wood-burning oven, lined with huge rocks. The rocks would be heated until they were red hot, and then water poured over them to create great clouds of steam. Each of us would carefully clip our nails over a sheet of paper, mindful that no small sliver escape unnoticed, and we would then put our nail clippings into a little package that also contained four tiny pieces of wood, about a quarter the size of a match. The little pieces of wood stood in as witnesses to the disposal of the nails. The package would be thrown into the fire burning in the oven in the steam room, and as the flames consumed it, we would meet the requirement for proper disposition of the nails.

The nails themselves would generally be clipped on Friday. One thing was certain. They would never be cut on Wednesday or before. It was held that once you clip nails short, it takes three days before they start growing again. I am not sure whether or not that is medically verifiable, but it was certainly held to be true among the Hasidim. If you clipped nails on Wednesday or before, they would be growing by Shabbat. That would violate two proscriptions of the law. First, the act of growing would constitute work, an activity that was prohibited by the law, and second, if the nails had resumed growing, they would cover part of the body that otherwise had to be immersed in the *mikvah*. The act of purification would be incomplete, and one's devotion to God consequently imperfect.

There were other traditions. In our suburban, Conservative temple in Springfield, New Jersey, the duties of the temple priests, the *Kohanim* are treated rather casually. However, my father was a *Kohen*—in our temple he was known as the *Kohen Gadol*, or high priest—and he knew he had both obligations and privileges that he took very seriously. For thirty-five hundred years, it has been the descendants of Aaron who have comprised the caste of Jewish priests. It is for them to bless the congregation each Saturday, Monday, Thursday, and Holiday; to be honored with the first *aliyah* (recitation of the prayers said before and after a reading of a part of the Torah portion) on these days; and to stand in for God when the father of a firstborn son buys his child back. Tradition has it that since God spared the firstborn of the Jews when he sent the angel of death to Egypt, the firstborn belongs to Him, and must be bought back by the parents. The usual purchase price was five shekels, to be paid to one of the priests in a traditional ceremony conducted in the temple thirty-one days after the birth. As both a Kohen and a prominent citizen in the community, my father was frequently selected from among the available *Kohanim* to officiate at *pidion habens* (redemption of first-born) in our community.

Since shekels weren't in broad circulation in our part of Poland, he chose to collect instead, eighteen Austrian kronen. (Eighteen is *chai* in Hebrew, which stands for life.) We had, at that time, recently belonged to Austria, and these large silver coins were in circulation and perfectly suited for this ceremonial purpose. Each time my father redeemed a child he recorded the name and date in a book he kept and put the coins into a box he had set aside for the purpose. Altogether, the book contained eighty-eight names when he was killed. My father was extremely proud that he had been chosen to redeem so many children. Perhaps one reason he was so often selected to participate in the *pidion haben* was because he always gave a barrel of beer, or some other item of comparable value for the feast, in return for the coins. Unlike others, he neither needed nor wished to profit from this activity.

But being a Kohen was not an unmixed blessing. There are prescribed laws on what they can and cannot do. For example, they are not allowed to touch a dead person, or for that matter, play a part in the preparation of the body for burial. They cannot enter a cemetery as others may. Special places are reserved for the *Kohanim* where they may walk, at least six yards from the nearest grave. They cannot enter the house where a dead body lies, and if a series of houses are connected by a common roof, the *Kohanim* are prohibited from entering any of the houses under the connected roof. Since Jews bury the dead within twenty-four hours the impact of these restrictions tended to be small.

It happened, however, that my father had a serious argument with a man in our town named Zanwell Landau, who had emigrated to America and then returned with enough money to establish a business in town. We learned that in America he had earned his living by tying one leg up inside his trousers so it appeared he had lost it. He would stand in this condition on the corner of Delancey and Allen Streets in New York and beg. Never underestimate the generosity of Americans. When Zanwell Landau returned, he not only had the new name of Kobylsky; he also had enough money to establish himself in business next door to our store.

Kobylsky was particularly angry with my father as a result of their quarrel and wanted to hurt him. How could he do so most effectively? "If my wife should die," he said, "I won't bury her right away. I will keep her laying in the house for a whole week if I have to." He knew that since our house and store were attached to his house and we shared a roof, this would in effect prevent my father from going to work. Kobylsky was particularly interested in preventing my father from entering his place of business on Tuesday, which was market day in Kolbuszowa, a day of major business activity. "Even if she dies on Wednesday, I will keep her past the market day," he vowed. And if he did, my father as a Kohen, would most certainly have avoided his store and apartment.

We had other manifestations of devotion to Judaic law and lore. Jews are told to be constantly on vigil for the coming of the messianic age. They know it will bring a raising up of all Jews who have died since the days of Abraham and their return, as well as the return of all living Jews, to Palestine. It will usher in an era of peace, when, it is written, "the wolf shall live with the lamb, and the leopard lie down with the kid." Although our people has been disappointed any number of times by any number of false messiahs, it maintains the conviction that the coming of this time of enlightened harmony is inevitable. Among those who didn't want to miss a minute of it was an extremely religious member of our community, whom we called Pinchas *Meshiekh* (Messiah) in place of his real name, Pinchas Goldberg. He was called by this name, not only to capture the dedication I am about to relate here, but also to distinguish him

Pinchas "Meshiekh" Goldberg is surrounded by his family in Jerusalem in 1947.

The house in Kolbuszowa in which Pinchas from Heaven lived. The second floor apartment was unusual and was said to bring him closer to heaven.

from another man named Pinchas who we called Pinchas from *Himmel* (heaven).

This latter Pinchas's name had nothing at all to do with religious zeal, despite the reference to heaven. Rather, he was called Pinchas from *Himmel* because the rooms he lived in happened to be up a small flight of stairs, and as a result, were located a little closer to heaven than the ground-level rooms in which most others dwelled. The poor man bore this memorable nickname for most of his days because of both the existence of the other Pinchas and the lofty locale of his rooms.

Pinchas Meshiekh, however, had sufficient religious devotion to cover both himself and his namesake. He truly believed that the Messiah was likely to arrive on earth any day and he truly believed that the children of Zion would be called home as a result. The words of the *ani maamim* prayer were his credo:

> *I believe with perfect faith in the coming of the Messiah, and though he tarry, I will wait daily for his coming*

Pinchas Meshiekh did not want to miss a moment of the messianic age. It was for that reason that when he went to bed every night, he wore his socks and his pants. He knew that at the time of the coming, he would be called to Jerusalem, and he didn't want to be delayed for a moment. His

Yechiel Teitelbaum, the Kolbuszowa rabbi, taken by the Gestapo in 1942. They forced him to put on the prayer shawl and *tefillin* (phylacteries). The rabbi was killed July 7, 1942 together with his two grandchildren, Malka (18), and Rachel (16), during the liquidation of the Rzeszow ghetto. This photo, which was used as propaganda by the Germans, was stolen by the author.

The synagogue in Kolbuszowa was built in the late eighteenth century. It was twice destroyed and twice rebuilt. During the time of the ghetto, over one hundred Jewish families lived in the building. After the ghetto was liquidated, the Germans used it as a stable. Today it is a museum.

boots were ready, his bag was packed with his *tallit* and *tefillin*, and his socks and pants were already on his body.

Despite his state of readiness, the Messiah never called Pinchas to the holy land. Some suggested that the problem was that there wouldn't be room for all of the returned Jews. To this, the cynical replied, "Don't worry. God saved us from Haman. Eventually he even saved us from Hitler. He will save us from Meshiekh too." Nevertheless, Pinchas did make the journey to Jerusalem. His children achieved sufficient success in business to be able to afford to move the old man, who by then had come to physically resemble the Michelangelo statue of Moses, to Jerusalem to live. There, he could relax a bit since his presence in the holy city relieved the potential need to suddenly pick up and go there. However, he would never sleep outside Jerusalem. For as long as he lived, he made sure to return each night, to the city the Messiah would surely visit first upon his arrival on earth. Now that is devotion.

While Pinchas's expectations led to behavior that was, perhaps, a little extreme, devotion to Meshiekh was by no means rare in Kolbuszowa. Our town had been pronounced by the famous Apter Rebbe to be the first in Poland to be visited by Meshiekh upon his return. The Apter, who lived from 1760 to 1831 had been the rabbi in Kolbuszowa, had written in his book, *The Ohev Shalom* (The Love of Israel), that the first steps to be taken by Meshiekh would be in the order of K.A.Y.M. These are the initials of the four towns, Kolbuszowa in Galicia, Apt, or Opatow in Poland, Yass in Rumania, and Mezibez in Ukraine. The cold *mikvah* in Kolbuszowa was built during the rebbe's time, and this same bathhouse, with its white tile walls and frigid water, was still in use, right up until the war. It was known as the Apter Mikvah, named for the famous rebbe, and my father would submerge himself in it every Friday along with the other Hasidim in Kolbuszowa. In fact, religious Jews were drawn to Kolbuszowa from a wide circle of surrounding towns so they could purify themselves in the *mikvah* of the illustrious Apter Rebbe.

I was there only once, on the day of my bar mitzvah. To this day, sixty-nine years later, when I remember the experience I always feel a shiver, not from the spirituality of the experience, but from the memory of the cold, deep water that covered me in the Apter Mikvah.

The Passovers of My Childhood

The Passover season always evokes happy memories of my childhood in Poland. Of all the holidays, it created the most lasting impressions. Then, as now, Passover lasts eight days, but preparation for the Passover of my childhood extended into the months before. My memories are filled with the images of the hectic and happy holiday celebrated by Jews in prewar Poland.

"You're getting warm," we giggled. "No, now you're cooling off." My sisters Rachel and Matil and I clapped our hands in glee, as our father, Isak Saleschutz probed behind the cushions and in the corners of the cupboard for the last of the *chumetz* (piece of bread). Each year, the night before Passover, when the house had been otherwise purged of all food impure for the holiday, our ritual was for my mother, Esther, to hide ten pieces of bread in ten secret places and for him, armed with a large wooden spoon and a feather from a goose wing, to find them. Since she tended to hide the *chumetz* in the same places each year, he generally had an easy time of it. However, occasionally she would forget one of her spots or improvise with another, and it was at these times that the annual ritual took on the character of a game. Our solemn and at times intimidating father, fully bearded and totally committed to the strictest traditions of Judaism, would dutifully move with his feather and spoon according to the directions of his delighted children. In the end the pieces of bread, the feather, and spoon would all be tied up and burned in the oven that heated the stones at the public bath.

Outside, at house after house along the street, the furniture, bedding, books—all possessions, spiritual and worldly, were piled at the curb. The need to remove every speck of *chumetz* from the house provided an excuse for a massive spring cleaning as well. The women hunted down the bedbugs just as avidly as they sought the *chumetz*. Sun and wind were called on to freshen the weary, well-worn belongings of the Jews.

If I were lucky, I could anticipate some new clothes to wear. All the children knew that anything new to wear during the year would come at Passover. Our family was relatively well-off, but for many Jews, clothing was worn day after day, year after year, until it literally fell apart. A new coat, or hat, or shoes for Passover was a major happening. We would proudly run to our friends to show off whatever we had gotten.

Then as now, the most visible manifestation of the holiday was the matzoh. Today, we go to the supermarket and find shelves stocked with several brands of several varieties of boxed matzoh, all marked with labels that assure us it is kosher for Passover. It was not as easy as a trip to the supermarket then. My mother and sisters would bring their own flour to the baker, who had fired up special ovens, used only during this holiday. There, they watched like hawks while he made dough from the flour. They carefully timed the process, knowing that if it took more than seven minutes, fermentation would begin and the dough would begin to rise. This would negate the whole significance of the matzoh, and the preparation would have to be discarded. When the dough was just right, he would form it, perforate it, and put it into the oven to bake for a minute or two, and out would come a batch of fresh, round matzohs, that were without a doubt, most definitely kosher for Passover. My mother and sisters would transport these fresh matzohs home in pillow cases, instead of boxes or bags. The danger with a box or bag was that some of the glue used to hold it together might come in contact with its precious contents and contaminate it. In this way, the family acquired its matzoh for the holiday and matzoh to give as presents to our Gentile friends. Everyone in the family, that is, but my father.

The purity of the flour and the process of making the dough were important elements in matzoh baking. They were so important that the truly observant, and my father was included among the truly observant, didn't trust third parties to oversee these activities. He planted his own wheat on a small patch of land owned by a cousin, Szymon Storch. in the nearby village of Przedborz. He personally monitored its growth and cutting, drying, and threshing. He inspected each kernel to be assured that there were no impurities. Our cousin would then grind it into a dark, whole wheat flour, and my father would send some of this wheat with my mother to be baked into his own special *shmira matzoh*. This matzoh would be okay for the last six days of the holiday. The first two days required something else—"super *shmira*," or *erev* (eve of) Passover matzohs. My father and his ultrareligious colleagues made their own dough from the specially grown grain, using water taken from the town well in special bottles, two weeks earlier, on the night of the new moon. They would bake it themselves, and while the matzoh dough was being kneaded, rolled, and punctured, they prayed and sang psalms to assure its purity. Only then did these dedicated men have something suitable for the seder nights.

And what a time those seder nights were. My father would be dressed in his white *kittle*, a garment worn only at one's wedding and burial, as well as each Yom Kippur and Passover seder. The table was graced with the holiday wine he had been preparing in our basement for months. All year my mother had been storing schmaltz (rendered fat) from the fattest geese we could find. There were chickens and turkeys, cookies and tarts made with potato flour, cakes made with matzoh meal, borscht, and eggs. Since I was the youngest, I asked the well-rehearsed Four Questions. As my father reclined against his pillows, he recited the tale of the exodus of Jews from enslavement in Egypt. The blessings were said, and the matzoh broken. The children sought out the *afikomen* (the middle of three matzohs used ritually during the seder ceremony), which we would later barter for presents. We watched as Elijah's cup subtly drained of a portion of its contents. We sang and we rejoiced and we prayed and we continued the traditions of our people as they had been observed in Poland for centuries.

We didn't know it, but we represented the final chapter in that long tradition of shtetl life. It is all gone now, except for the sweet, sweet memory that comes back each year at this time.

PART TWO   The War—Tales of Life,
            Death, Hope, and Despair

The Death of Rabinowicz

Our town, Kolbuszowa, was a little shtetl in southern central Poland. Half-Jewish and half-Polish, it was remarkable for its ordinariness. Ordinary in this case means poor, struggling Jews systematically abused by their even poorer Polish neighbors. It means a Polish central government whose policies ranged from grudging tolerance to overt hostility. It means a Jewish population of businessmen and tradesmen, of rabbis and teachers, of professionals and laymen, of beggars and laborers. Some were rich and some were poor, some smart and some stupid, some handsome and some ugly, some happy and some bitter, some devoutly Orthodox and some little more than Jewish in name only. And of course, it means that most fall in between.

This is the story of the life and death of Wilhelm Rabinowicz, a Jew who most definitely did not fall in between. (If it weren't such a bad pun, we would say he lay at the poles.) Possibly the smartest man in Kolbuszowa, he was also unchallenged as the ugliest. Almost a dwarf, Rabinowicz labored under a crippling hunchback. He would limp down the main street each day to court, and with a peculiar rasping voice, argue the most intricate legal issues with the most learned attorneys in the area. And inevitably, Rabinowicz would win, for he was acknowledged to be not only the ugliest, but also the most brilliant lawyer in the region.

Jews and Poles with legal problems were equally likely to seek him out, and he treated them all exactly alike: badly. For Rabinowicz let the burdens of his body overwhelm the brilliance of his mind when it came to defining his spirit. Bitter, scolding, sarcastic, if a Jew came to him with a case, he used to take out his pocket watch, put it on the table and tell them, *"Zydzie daj na stol piec ztotych*—Jew, put down five zloty on the table."* When a half hour passed, to the minute he repeated, "Jew. put down another five zloty." This is the kind of person he was. He never donated to charity, never spoke kindly to his neighbors, and didn't even live in the Jewish section of the town. He was completely unobservant in religious matters, not even bothering to have his sons circumcised (a detail that allowed them to survive the war, passing as Gentiles.)

Isn't it strange that before our tale ends, Wilhelm Rabinowicz will be singled out for a special blessing by God.

Before the war, as I mentioned, conditions for the Jews in Poland varied with who was in power, but generally were terrible. In the years before 1935, rather than terrible, they were only bad. We had only to put up with the basic anti-Semitism of the people. There was no organized governmental program of repression, and we knew that as long as Jozef Pilsudski, marshal of the army, was alive, our lives could remain bearable. He was not an enemy of the Jews. By contrast, Rydz Smigly, who succeeded Pilsudski, was not a friend to the Jews. When Germany demanded Danzig and the corridor from Poland in 1939 he became famous for saying, "We will not give the Germans a button from our coats." After the humiliating defeat of the Polish Army there was a joke among the Jews, who said, "he didn't want to give a button, but he gave the whole coat."

It was during this time that a young Jewish doctor named Marek Marienstrauss finished his medical studies in Czechoslovakia and came to our town to open an office. This young doctor was very poor. I remember when he came, the collar on his overcoat was completely worn out and he didn't have the money to buy a new one. Of course, he had no patients and rented a little room in a dingy house to start up a practice. As he attracted a few, the two other doctors in the town—one Jewish and the other Polish—did everything to discredit him. After all, he represented potential competition to them. The meager abilities of the citizens of Kolbuszowa to pay doctor bills would have to be divided three ways, instead of just two.

Actually the Polish doctor didn't have to worry about a livelihood. In addition to his practice, he had an official position as the county "physic." He was called on by the government to take care of everything in the county involving public health: inoculations, school examinations, and so on. This was a very good position, bringing with it a pension and an assured group of patients whose care would be paid for by the government. Although he didn't have to worry about Marienstrauss, the Polish doctor nevertheless did. He worried and plotted and might have permanently damaged the reputation of his young competitor had he not one day suddenly had a heart attack and dropped dead.

And so the position of county physic became open, and the *starosta,* or head of our county, came to Dr. Marienstrauss and pointed out that although he could bring another doctor in from another part of the country to take over the official duties, it would be much easier for him if Dr.

Members of the Kolbuszowa Red Cross, 1938. The local Red Cross contained only one Jewish member, Dr. Marek Marienstrauss *(front row sitting, far right)*

Marienstrauss would agree to become physic. Even as the young doctor was forming the words of gratitude with which to accompany his acceptance of the offer, the *starosta* added, "Of course, you realize, we could never appoint a Jew to a government job in our country. The position is yours, but you will have to become a Catholic to accept it. *You will have to leave Judaism and convert to Catholicism.*"

The Doctor wasn't shocked. He immediately understood the other's logic. Obviously, a Jew couldn't be part of the government. Only the relatively benign attitudes then prevailing would allow this offer to convert to be made. The temptation was great. He was being offered a chance to escape the uncertainty of building up a practice. A pension. Security and position. And what would he have to give up? His identity as a Jew.

Now Dr. Marienstrauss wasn't an observant Jew. He never went to *shul*. He didn't even mark the coming and going of the holidays. He wasn't an observant Jew, but nevertheless he was Jewish. He had been born a Jew and had carried the identity his entire life. He never questioned the idea that he was Jewish, and the idea of no longer being Jewish strangely troubled him. It troubled him so much that he told the *starosta* that he wished to take a few days to think it over.

Even as he walked away, he berated himself for not having accepted on the spot. What if they withdraw the offer? What if they find someone else? He realized what a rare opportunity it was for a Jew to gain an official position, and he needed only a little encouragement to accept. He needed someone to tell him it was the right thing to do, and so he approached the lawyer Rabinowicz, with whom he had some relationship, and asked his advice. Knowing that the lawyer's lack of Jewish observance exceeded even his own, Marienstrauss went more for ratification than for judgment. In fact, even as he unfolded the alternatives he felt foolish. Surely Rabinowicz would say, "Sure, grab the opportunity. Become something important in the town. Convert."

But the dwarf lawyer surprised Marienstrauss. Years before, he had thought through this very issue with regard to his own life. And he recognized that there is a very clear difference between nonobservance—even hostility toward one's religion, and abandonment of it through conversion. It was like the difference between illness and death. Illness is reversible. Death is a final parting of the ways. There is no going back. The continuity is broken. And as he looked at Marienstrauss, the lawyer pictured himself in a heavenly court of law trying to defend to a judge advice he might give that it was all right to convert for the sake of a job. It would be like murder. He would be condoning ridding the world of a Jew. Rabinowicz had long ago distinguished in his own mind the difference between the petty crime of nonobservance and what amounted to the felony murder of conversion, and he replied immediately to Marienstrauss in a voice that was hoarse like a rusted saw.

"Convert? What, are you crazy? What are you doing? What are you thinking?" And he pounded on the desk and shouted, *"Mosiek jest taki dobry jak Josiek"* (Moses is as good to me as Jesus). But in Polish it rhymes because Moses is "Mosiek" and Jesus, "Josiek." "Mosiek is as good as Josiek" and he said, "Don't do it. Don't change."

The young doctor, taken aback by the vigor of the lawyer's presentation, took his advice. Within the day, he went to the *starosta* and refused the job. This decision was received with a shrug of amazement. Naturally, they brought in somebody from a different town.

Little by little Marienstrauss improved his practice. His income gained, and he even became relatively affluent. He opened a nice office, could afford a better apartment. Before long he began courting a girl from a wealthy Jewish family. Things were looking up for the doctor.

And what of the lawyer? Nothing changed for him. At least, not for the better. His bitterness grew. His deformity worsened. He lived alone with his thoughts and his law books, and on the morning of September 1, 1939, as he sat listening to his radio, the news that the Germans had crossed over the Polish border was broadcast. Rabinowicz knew that it was only a matter of days before the Polish cavalry would fall before the German tanks. And as he listened and pictured the jackbooted Germans invading his town and his house, his frail chest suddenly felt a crushing fist tightening around his heart. Within minutes Wilhelm Rabinowicz was dead, killed instantly by a massive rupture of his coronary arteries.

Even though Rabinowicz was nonobservant, he was nevertheless a Jew. And when it was learned that he had died, the Jewish burial society came and made a ritual funeral for him, as they would for a religious Jew. They washed his body and placed it the burial shroud and in a simple wooden coffin; he was placed in the ground as ten mourners said Kaddish and a claque of the curious and a sprinkling of former clients looked on. Among the group looking on was Dr. Marienstrauss, now a highly regarded member of the community, and he related to several of those in attendance the story of his near conversion to Catholicism and the role of Rabinowicz in preventing that from occurring. And as some murmured mostly unflattering stories of the departed lawyer, others talked of the ominous and imminent invasion from the west.

As it turned out, Wilhelm Rabinowicz, was the last Jew buried in a marked grave in the Jewish cemetery at Kolbuszowa before the German occupation. Within days the Germans took over the town and began the systematic annihilation of our people. Jews were beaten, tortured, killed, burned, and buried in mass graves. Certainly, Rabinowicz would have been singled out for special early abuse by the Germans. They took delight in humiliating intellectuals. With his deformity as an added element, the invaders would have made a gruesome spectacle of his anguish. Instead, while the furies of the Holocaust were loosed on this suffering people, the body of Wilhelm Rabinowicz lay in peace in a marked grave, in a quiet spot, in the Jewish cemetery.

The biggest scholars from our town got together and they discussed why this had happened. Rabinowicz was buried as a Jew—this man who was never a part of the Jewish community. Why did God spare him the torture and humiliation that surely would have befallen him. As they debated, my cousin Shaul Saleschutz, the most prominent scholar in our town, pronounced that "God spared Rabinowicz because he saved Dr. Marienstrauss from conversion to Catholicism." And as some within the group demurred, my cousin went on to remind them that our sages wrote, "Whoever preserves a single soul of Israel, Scripture ascribes to him as though he had preserved a complete world."

Because Wilhelm Rabinowicz saved a soul, he was never to know the inhuman torture that surely would have been his fate.

A Piece of Cotton

During the darkest days of the Holocaust, every Jew's life hung by a thread. In most cases the thread was figurative—and it eventually snapped. In mine, I am convinced it was literal—a thread of cotton—and miraculously, it held. Let me tell you about this earliest of the miracle fibers and how I came to possess it.

Shortly after the Germans occupied our small town of Kolbuszowa I had to flee for my life. Ironically, my peril came, not directly from the Germans, but from the striving of a Jewish sycophant trying to curry favor with the German commandant. They turned up in every community: petty functionaries who hoped to improve their own condition by betraying their neighbors. Our town was no exception. A Jew who once was a friend of the family became the local German commandant's eyes and ears in the Jewish community.

Now we all know the Third Reich conquered Poland in a matter of weeks. It commanded legions. Every kind of war materiel poured from its factories from jackboots to dive-bombers, from railroad cars to Zyklon-B gas. The Germans could make everything needed to wage war, it seems, but coffee. The genius of German science synthesized rubber and manufactured gasoline. But fertile as it was, the German scientific mind just couldn't come up with a good cup of coffee that would satisfy the German taste. Any field commander who could ship real coffee back to the fatherland became an instant hero of the people.

As good luck would have it, my father, who ran a wholesale general store, had a few hundred kilos of green coffee beans. As bad luck would have it, our Jewish bootlicker knew this, and it is easy to anticipate the next part of the story. First, he implored my father to give him one kilo for the commandant; then, he suggested my father had best give two; then, demanded he give four; finally, he threatened violence unless eight additional kilos were forthcoming. My father told him, "Even a well will become dry if you take out too much water."

It quickly became evident to me that the laws of geometric progression would soon wipe out the coffee stores, and I intervened and told him we would give no more. Picture me, a nineteen-year-old yeshiva boy long on good intentions but short on experience beyond the study of Torah, telling him "this far, and no further." The traitor's response was two-fold. One, he told the Germans of the coffee warehouse, and they came and carted off, not only the coffee, but everything else as well. Two, he told them I was a communist and a subversive, and a danger to them. When I learned of this, I felt sure that I had to run away before they came to cart me off also, and so that night I left home and traveled, first to Cracow, and then from town to town, going east, and intending eventually to end up in Russia.

During the week before my planned illegal border crossing, I stayed with my brother-in-law's parents. His family was ultra, ultra-Orthodox, since his mother Rachel was the granddaughter of a very revered rabbi in Poland who had a major following: Chaim Halberstam, called the *Sanzer Rov*, the rabbi from the town of Sanz.

When the *Sanzer Rov* died, he didn't leave castles or estates. He was a poor Jew. He left mostly books (two of which he wrote, which are still highly thought of today, *Divrei Chaim,* [The sayings of Chaim] and *Darkey Chaim,* [The ways of Chaim]).To his granddaughter, Rachel, the *Sanzer Rov* left something very special.

The Rabbi of Sanz had a special *shpenzer*, a quilted jacket without sleeves. He used this quilted jacket for one purpose: every night at 12:00 midnight, he recited the special *chazot* prayer, a lamentation over the destruction of the Temple in Israel two thousand years ago. Each night, as a religious Jew, he put on his *tallit* and said this prayer. Because it was cold, he wore the quilted jacket when he prayed. The jacket was soaked through with his tears from all the years he wore it and wept as he prayed over the destruction of the Temple in Jerusalem. When he died, Rachel, my brother-in-law's mother, inherited the jacket.

For the disciples of the rabbi, the jacket was very important. For many years, whenever a woman in Cracow was to give birth, she would borrow the jacket and put it under her as a cushion. This, it was believed, would insure that both baby and mother would be healthy. Rachel gladly loaned the jacket, but it was such an important possession to her that she would go herself and stand waiting until the child was born, and then she would take it home. Thus, it never left her control.

After I had been there for a few days and told her that I was going to run away to Russia because of my problems, she said "I am going to give you something that I have never given to anyone before." I had no idea what this could be. She went and took out this quilted jacket, opened the lining, pulled out a piece of cotton and said, "Take this piece of cotton and as long as you have it, nothing will happen to you."

I laughed when she gave it to me. I thought it was a joke. But she was very solemn when she wrapped it in a piece of paper and handed it to me, and I accepted it and put it away.

From that time on, events conspired to threaten my life many times.

I had this piece of cotton with me when I went to Russia but was caught at the border by the Russians and arrested. I managed to escape from jail and remained in Russia for a few months before coming back to Poland. I had it with me when the Germans held me in labor camps. I had it when they forced me into the ghetto. I had it when they took my family away to be killed in the Belzec death camp, and I was put on a special detail to destroy the ghetto in Kolbuszowa after the Jews had been killed. I was able to run away from that labor camp into the woods, where I remained with partisan groups for two years. I was wounded seven times. I was given poison. I was caught and forced to dig my own grave. My best school friend, a Pole, shot me three times in the neck. I was liberated by the Russians, joined the Polish army, went to a Russian military school, and fought against the Germans. Throughout all of that I had that little piece of cotton with me.

I left Poland and went to Germany, intending to go to Palestine. I worked to smuggle Jews from Poland and Germany into Italy to go to Palestine. Eventually I came to America instead, established a home, a business, a family. Still, I have this piece of cotton with me. If someone came now and said, "Here is a hundred thousand dollars. Give me this piece of white cotton," I would refuse. Not that I am a believer, mind you, but there is something to it. I went through all those times and always had it with me. When I was shot by my friend I was dressed only in my underwear. Around my waist I wore a belt with my revolver and this piece of cotton in a little bag. I had it then and I still have it. This is one of my most precious possessions. Some people think I am crazy. Maybe I am. But that is how it is. And what of the rest of this tear-soaked *shpenzer*? If one thread could save me, how many would the jacket itself save?

Alas, all of its magic must have lain in the piece I wore. Rachel eventually was caught up with and killed by the Germans. Her family—killed. My family—killed. Our neighbors . . . you know the answer. The jacket, with the exception of the strands kept in a place of honor in my home, is gone, destroyed with the heart and soul of European Jewry. It was not without reason that it was soaked with tears.

So what's the point of this story about a few threads of cotton from a *shpenzer* that I claim saved my life but failed to save so many others? I'm not sure. Maybe the tear-soaked jacket is a metaphor for the whole of the Jewish people. A little was spared and the rest perished. Maybe the threads of cotton and I were both destined to be remnants of what was. Maybe it is all just chance. I don't know. All I know is I am here to bear witness. And the Jewish people are here, and both are unlikely outcomes, given the carnage directed at us.

In light of those odds, would you discard your faith in what seemed to work? I am like the person who ate chicken soup and then got well from an illness. I don't know if it helped or not, but it certainly didn't hurt.

The Cigarette

That day in 1939 when I decided to run away from the German-occupied part of Poland to the Russian side, I went to see my girlfriend, Rozia Susskind. She was two years younger than I, and I loved her very much.

Although I had first noticed her when I was twelve years old, the first time I spoke to her, I was eighteen. To me, she was like a holy object, an angel from heaven.

The day I ran away I went to visit her with two of our friends. She offered us German cigarettes, which were very hard to get. She gave each of us one.

Her family lived on the outskirts of town and had a very beautiful apartment; so beautiful that a German captain requisitioned one room and was staying with them. She had gotten the cigarettes from him.

When she gave them to us, our two friends smoked them, and that was it. But I knew that I would run away the next day, and I said, "I will have this cigarette when we meet again." I didn't know if this would be one, two or maybe five years, since I was running from the Germans. But because she gave it to me, it was too important for me to see it disappear up in smoke. I took a piece of cellophane, wrapped the cigarette, and put it together with my special piece of cotton.

Rozia Susskind and Naftali Saleschutz on August 17, 1941. This picture was taken in the rear yard of her house on the outskirts of Kolbuszowa. A German Captain, who was able to get her a supply of scarce cigarettes, had commandeered a room in the Susskind house.

At this time, the Germans had not yet created their Final Solution for the Jews, and they were glad to get rid of as many as possible by letting them flee to other countries. So they would not stop us from crossing the border.

The Russians were less predictable. They would sometimes allow the Jews to cross over and sometimes would detain and arrest them and send them to prison in Lwow. When enough prisoners were gathered, the Russians would send them to a gulag inside Siberia.

The next day I traveled in a big wagon, with others who were looking to escape, to the River San, which was on the German/Russian border, and proceeded to cross the river into the Russian zone. While we were crossing the river, the Russian border police spotted us and waited to catch us. As soon as we stepped onto the eastern riverbank in the Russian zone, they arrested us.

They put us in a nearby schoolhouse that served as an improvised jail and told us that we would be transported the next day to Brigitki, a major Polish penitentiary in Lwow, for illegally crossing the border. The whole school was full of detainees, and the police had posted guards around the perimeter of the building. During the night I managed to escape through a second-floor window onto the roof of the porch on the first floor. From there I climbed down the posts of the porch into the bushes and waited until I saw no guards. Then I ran away.

The next day I traveled to Lwow by train, since I did not believe anyone would suspect a train passenger of being an escapee. I stayed in Lwow for three months. Others whom I knew that crossed the river the same day and who did not manage to escape spent the entire war in the gulag. Seventy-five percent of them survived the gulag, compared to the paltry few who survived the German death camps.

While in Lwow I found out that Rozia's mother was gravely ill. Her father, brother, and sister had run away and were in Lwow, while she remained with her mother. The messenger who told us said we must not tell her family, because if they found out, they would return to the German side of Poland, and Rozia and her mother didn't want them to risk such a thing. But I decided right then that I was going back.

I found out that friends from my town had made arrangements with a smuggler to smuggle them back to the German side of Poland. These Jews were receiving word that, at that time, life in our town was almost normal. Jews were permitted to live in their houses and some even did business. Since they missed their families, they were anxious to go back. So I joined this group and we left Lwow by train and traveled to the last station near the border. It was now January of 1940, and the ground was covered with snow. So the smuggler gave each of us white sheets to wrap around ourselves and we proceeded to cross the border on the now frozen River San.

But when we got close to the river, a Russian patrol caught us and arrested us. After they took us to their headquarters, they searched everybody. They found that I had the piece of cotton and the cigarette wrapped in cellophane. The officer said to me, "You are a spy. Why do you have a cigarette wrapped in cellophane? In the cigarette there must be a secret message."

He was about to rip open the cigarette when I started to beg and plead, "Please don't do it," and I told him the story of why I had it.

He looked at me and said, "But I want to know what the message is."

I said, "You know what, I will take out the pieces of tobacco one by one and you will see there is nothing."

He agreed, thinking it was a joke. I took two pieces of wood—like toothpicks—and I started to pull out each shred of thin tobacco leaf. When it was all out, he saw that I had been telling the truth. I then had to put it back. I held this thin paper, and one by one, I pushed the shreds of tobacco back into the paper tube, tied its ends and asked if I could put it away. He said, "Yes," and I returned it to its place alongside my special piece of cotton.

They decided to take us to the railroad station, and in the morning, to transport us to Brigitki. At the railroad station, they posted two armed Russian soldiers to watch us during the night.

We knew we would be in trouble if they took us to Lwow, so we jumped the soldiers, took their guns and blankets, tied them down in the blankets and shoved them under the benches. Then we wrapped ourselves again in white sheets and crossed the river.

When I got back, Rozia was home with her mother. Her mother died two days after my return. Later, Rozia would be killed by the Germans. But I never smoked the cigarette. I saved it as one of the remembrances that I treasure because I had it all those times in all those different places.

It was something I always kept with me, and I still have to today.

In Memory of Four Unlikely Heroes

When the battle of Kolbuszowa was over on September 9, 1939, 65 German soldiers lay dead. So too did 148 members of the Polish army, 23 of whom were Jews. Separated in life by prejudice and hatred, these 213 fallen warriors had come together to share the ultimate experience of death on the battlefield. When this phase of the carnage had ended—we had no idea how much lay ahead—the Germans gathered up their dead and placed them in a common grave in Zwierzyniec only to dig them up again two weeks later and return the bodies for reburial in Germany.

The Poles too quickly buried the casualties suffered by their side. The bodies of the slain Jewish and Catholic soldiers were picked up indiscriminately by the Poles and buried together in a common grave located in the local Catholic cemetery.

Most of the Jews of Kolbuszowa concentrated on the business of survival. The battle was history. A few friends and family mourned for those killed, but for the most part the dead Jewish soldiers were strangers who had been drawn from other parts of the country. Kolbuszowa's Jews had more immediate concerns. Berysz Bilfeld was the exception. A short stocky man, Berysz before the war had been a scavenger who collected animal bones from the butchers, which he boiled to extract fat for sale to the soapmakers. He had a big, dilapidated storage shed for a house, and all kinds of junk that had escaped the scrap heap ended up there to await a buyer in need of just that item. Traveling Jews came to know Berysz well, for this good man unfailingly opened his house to anyone passing through Kolbuszowa and needing a bed in which to sleep. They found it among the heaps of old clothing and rags he collected and kept.

Long after the battle, Berysz worried about the Jews buried in the Catholic cemetery. He worried about the crosses casting their shadows across the common grave. He lamented that no Kaddish would be said over the grave. He worried that no Jewish soil lay beneath the dead Jews in the ground. He couldn't sleep. But what could be done? Berysz was not particularly a man of action. He was normally concerned with his fellow living Jews, but in this case, he was obsessed with the need to move the bodies of those killed in the battle to the Jewish cemetery. He spoke about it with everyone he knew. At length, by chance, he spoke to the right person.

Leib Lampel had been a sergeant in the Austrian Army during the First World War. A Jewish Prussian was certainly incongruous in Kolbus-

During the battle for Kolbuszowa on September 9, 1939, which lasted two hours, sixty-five German, 125 Polish, and twenty-three Jewish soldiers were killed. The Germans buried their fallen soldiers in a common grave and later exhumed them and sent the bodies to Germany. The Poles made a common grave on the Catholic cemetery in which they buried all Polish soldiers, including the twenty-three Jews. The cross and floral decorations erected by the Polish community are shown.

zowa, but Leib was one of those men who seemed born to wear a uniform and had done so with pride and distinction. Not only had Leib become a professional soldier, his three brothers also were *Feldwebels* or sergeants in the army. My father told me that during that war when Leib and his brothers came home for Passover, their father would proudly walk to *shul* with his four uniformed offspring. Rare as it was, the four served the Austrian forces well, and after the war they settled and prepared to live their lives out in Germany. But serving well and loyally wasn't enough if you were Jewish. The Germans threw all the Polish Jews out of the country, and Leib and his brother Jankel returned to live in our town. They weren't apart from the Germans long, however. The end of the battle of Kolbuszowa saw occupation of the area by a unit of the Wehrmacht, or regular German army.

It happened that the captain commanding this unit had served in Italy during the First World War with Leib Lampel. They recognized one another immediately, and this odd couple—the Wehrmacht officer and the exiled Jewish sergeant—found that as old comrades-in-arms, they could be of use to one another. The captain made Leib the procurement officer for his army unit and sent him out into the countryside to buy food from the peasants for the German soldiers stationed in Kolbuszowa. So, every day Leib would seek out fresh meat, potatoes, beans, cabbage, whatever was available, and return with a wagonload that few others could have produced. What had begun as an acquaintanceship between Leib Lampel and the captain blossomed into friendship, and because of that friendship the captain treated the Jews tolerably well and was available to help them when they found themselves in trouble. Thus, Leib was in a position to help when Berysz Bilfeld made his concern over the Jewish dead known to him.

"We must move the Jewish bodies from the Catholic Cemetery," Berysz explained. "It will be very difficult. First we will need the Germans' permission to do it, and then we have to get permission from the church to go into their cemetery. But worst of all, the 23 Jews are mixed in the same grave with the 125 dead Polish soldiers. We have to dig them all up after months of burial, identify, and separate the Jews out from the others."

Altogether there would be four involved. Leib went to the captain who, while thinking they were crazy, nevertheless gave permission. Then Berysz and Leib petitioned the Catholic authorities, and once again permission was obtained. They were joined by Moishe Kornfeld, who was my brother-in-law, and most importantly, by the *shochet* (Kosher slaughterer), Aszer Derschowitz who had performed circumcisions in Kolbuszowa. He was key because not all the dead Jews were to be identified by dogtags. Nor would they be recognized through their features, since many had traveled from other parts of Poland to be killed in the battle. What separated a Jew from a non-Jew in Poland was circumcision. Each of the 148 bodies sharing the mass grave from the battle of Kolbuszowa had to be exhumed, undressed, and examined. Those identified as Jews were separated from Catholics, and when the task was finally finished, the Polish soldiers were reburied in the Catholic graveyard and the Jews removed for proper preparation of their bodies and suitable interment in the Jewish cemetery.

All in all, it was a gruesome and dangerous task. And it was accomplished. I am telling this story because I think it is important to memorialize the handful of Jews who undertook this reburial and achieved it. None of them would personally benefit from performing the difficult task at hand. None wanted it. They did it because they had no choice. Jewish tradition required it.

As it was, there would eventually be three mass graves in the Jewish cemetery in our town. On May 6, 1919, a pogrom had occurred. The Polish peasants killed nine Jews on that occasion, and they were buried under a common marker. Later, on April 28, 1942, the Gestapo would kill twenty-two Jews and they would be buried together. My father was one of the twenty-two killed on that day. The twenty-three buried by Berysz Bilfeld, Leib Lampel, Moishe Kornfeld, and Aszer Derschowitz on that day in 1939 would be the third.

And so, through a rare combination of compassion on the part of the church, a coincidental relationship with the Wehrmacht captain, and a determination to see Jewish tradition observed on the part of the four— heroes all, in my mind—the twenty-three fallen Jewish soldiers were laid to rest at last.

There were many small acts of courage during those dark days, although no record of them exists. The Holocaust erased most of those who might have a memory of those deeds. This story is the exception. I sur-

Two restored common graves in the Jewish cemetery in 1995. One contains the twenty-three Jewish soldiers killed in the Battle of Kolbuszowa on September 9, 1939, and the second, twenty-two prominent Jews killed by the Gestapo on April 28, 1942.

vived the war and my memory for facts and names is good—sometimes painfully so. I choose to make the retelling of these events my monument to Berysz Bilfeld, Leib Lampel, Moishe Kornfeld, and Aszer Derschowitz for their act of kindness and courage performed in a Catholic cemetery so long ago.

The Jewish Woodchoppers of Kolbuszowa

By 1940 wood chopping had become a highly competitive business among the Jews in Kolbuszowa. Wood was the principal fuel that we used to heat our homes and to cook our food; we had no coal, electricity, or gas. The peasants harvested the woods surrounding the town, and each morning, summer or winter, a group of Jewish woodchoppers would go out to see if one of their Jewish neighbors had bought a wagonload of wood, or even a few logs that needed to be chopped up into pieces small enough to feed into their stoves. The more well-to-do could afford to buy and store wood until it had dried out and was suitable to be used as fuel. These were increasingly becoming the exception. Most Jews lived a hand-to-mouth existence, and they could afford just a few logs at a time, which they quickly burned while they were still green in a smoky and dirty fire.

The Jewish woodchoppers were an unlikely group. They included Naftali Nessel with his three sons, Pinchas Spielman and his two boys, as well as the two sons of the late Hersh Oster. Burdened with the saws, axes, and wooden sawhorses that were the tools of their newly acquired trade, the woodchoppers anxiously scoured the neighborhood for work. When they were fortunate enough to find it, it became obvious to anyone watching that they were not well suited for the heavy labor the task required. Nessel had the full beard and his sons wore the earlocks of Orthodox Jews. When they chopped the wood, sweat soaked through the *tallit katan*, the fringed undergarments they wore in keeping with biblical requirements. If their exertions knocked their hats off, they quickly made sure their heads didn't remain uncovered for long. Hands bled, arms and backs ached. The woodchoppers of Kolbuszowa were better suited to the study hall than to the woods, and that, indeed is where they had been until circumstance led them here.

In the end, the Germans would kill six million Jews. There were precursors to the end, however—a series of hardships and indignities to be endured. Property was confiscated, families relocated, the community ghettoized. Amidst all of this dislocation, it was still necessary to eat and be warm. A family had to earn enough, somehow, to feed and clothe itself while clinging to hope for survival.

Before the war, Naftali Nessel had been a grain trader. He wasn't a trader in the sense we associate with the Chicago Board of Trade. Rather, you should picture his small house, located a kilometer outside of Kolbuszowa on the road to Sedziszow. It consisted of a bedroom, a kitchen, and another room that he used as a storeroom. Each day his business was to wait for peasants who traveled from their villages to Kolbuszowa to sell their produce. If he saw containers holding grain destined for market, he stopped the wagon and tried to buy it from them. Some of the peasants knew him and sold to him. On other days he would walk to nearby villages and buy small portions of the grain the peasants had produced. All that he bought, he would keep in his storeroom, until he had enough to take to market and sell to a wholesaler, who in turn would feed it into the food supply of Poland or export it to England. Through hard work, Naftali earned, not a handsome living, but enough to sustain his wife and family of six sons and two daughters.

Livelihood was not his main focus, however. Scholarship occupies a principal place in the Jewish value system, and Naftali Nessel and his six sons were among the most learned, and hence, respected members of the community. Four of the boys went out of town to yeshivas. One of them, Yankel, whom we called Antele, even went to the famed Yeshiva Chachmey Lublin, which was the MIT of Jewish education. If not for the war, their lives would have consisted of study and debate over the subtleties of Talmud. There would have been hours devoted to prayer and personal communing with God, and as for a living—well, God would provide, as he had in the past.

When the Germans came, Naftali could no longer buy his grain. The yeshivas were closed. Life had changed from the centuries-old pattern. The oldest son, Yoshe Mayer and the second Shamai, responded by running away from home. In the end, only Yoshe Mayer would survive the war in Siberia; he lives in Israel today. A third son, Leibush was in the Polish army and was taken prisoner. He ran away and was eventually killed by Poles three days after he was liberated in August 1944. Yankel returned from Lublin and joined his brothers Leibush, Leizer, and the youngest, David, and they and their father contemplated how they could live. I don't know who thought of chopping wood for a living. Perhaps it was a divine inspiration. Whatever the source, the four of them became woodchoppers, going to Jewish houses early each morning to chop wood into fuel in order to earn a zloty or two to feed themselves.

The two other families of woodchoppers came to their new vocations through similar routes. Pinchas Spielman had lived in Karlsruhe, Germany, with his wife, three sons, and a daughter, long enough, he thought, to establish his loyalty to his adopted country. Still, in 1938, when the Jews were expelled, Pinchas was forced to leave everything behind and returned to Kolbuszowa. The family all moved into his mother's house that he had left twenty-five years earlier. He, too, chopped wood to earn a little money for the family. His son Laizer eventually was able to free them of this burden when, through his ability to speak fluent German, he found employment with the German police. I have described elsewhere the fate that befell my friend Laizer, or Lazarus, as the Germans called him. He was killed the night we escaped from the labor camp.

This third family, that of Hersh Oster was the least suited of the three to the wood-chopping ordeal. Hersh had been the *behelfer,* or assistant to the *melamid* (teacher) in the local *cheder.* When the *melamid* died, he took over the education of the children up to six years of age. Hersh died a month after the Germans came to Kolbuszowa. Naturally, the coming of the Germans marked the end of Hebrew education, and the Oster family needed another means to support itself. The two sons, Yosel and Naftali, turned to wood chopping. They had to support a very sick mother and two sisters. Nature had not intended these boys for physical toil. They were eighteen and sixteen years of age. Both were small and thin, almost fragile in build. The swinging of the heavy woodsman's ax took a severe toll on their health, and they produced little wood for their efforts.

Ultimately, the Germans solved the economic problems of these three families. Indeed they had the final solution for all of the Jews. Naftali Nessel was killed when he found himself chopping wood for the wrong party at the wrong time. On April 28, 1942, the Germans decided to kill the intellectual leadership of our community. They had a Ukranian detective named Wlodzimierz Halicki, who worked for the German criminal police, *Kripo,* draw up a list of the twenty most influential Jews in the town. Naftali Nessel's name was not on the list. However, my father's was, as was that of Mechel Feingold, a prominent Jew and member of the *Jundenrat* (administrative council of the Jewish community responsible to the Germans). It happens that on that fateful day, when the Germans came for Feingold, they found Naftali Nessel there also. Because he held the important position of buying agent for the Polish Count, Mechel received many special favors. That day a wagonload of wood was delivered to him. Naftali Nessel had seen the wagon filled with wood at Mechel's home and had come to inquire if he could do the chopping. Finding them together, the Germans shot them both. My father, and all the others on the list were hunted down and killed as well on that very same spring day. The list originally had twenty names on it. They killed twenty-two—two for good measure.

You already know what happened to Laizer. He was later killed as we made our escape from the labor camp in November 1942. One of Naftali Nessel's sons, Leibush succeeded in evading the Germans. He survived by hiding and fighting, deep in the woods for two years with me and my group. In the end, he was one of only 6, out of 125, that managed to do so. When the Germans were finally driven out of the region by the advancing Soviet army, he returned to Kolbuszowa to inhale the air of freedom. He inhaled for three days. The Polish Home Army, the AK (Armja Krajowa) took up where the Germans left off and killed him on the spot.

As for the others, they continued the struggle to survive and to feed their families through chopping wood until we were enclosed in the ghetto. Once there, there were no more logs to chop. Instead Jews burned their cabinets, tables, chairs, and other wooden possessions to gain warmth.

The Jewish woodchoppers of Kolbuszowa aren't even a footnote in the history of the Holocaust. Were it not for the brand they put on one man's memory—the memory of Naftali Saleschutz, now known as Norman Salsitz—their efforts and struggles would be now forgotten by all.

They Don't Give Change in the Concentration Camps

The old Jew had clearly been someone of importance. We heard he had owned one of the largest textile mills in the region, where he had employed thousands of people. There had been an air of importance in his manner when he came to the concentration camp in Pustkow. He had been used to giving orders. But now, a few weeks later, he was stooped, weary, nearly broken from the hard labor we all endured each day. The camp at Pustkow was designed to work its inmates to death. The diet, or rather, lack of diet, contributed. We toiled every day at heavy labor, substituting our brute force for any mechanical advantage machinery might have brought, in the building of roads, erecting of telephone poles, moving of materials. The camp was in the region where the Germans were undertaking their fledgling rocket program. Our efforts were required to build, but our observance of the launches, flights, and explosions that occurred daily was definitely unwelcome. The Germans didn't intend that we survive. Each day we worked, we grew hungrier and weaker. Eventually, I was fortunate enough to escape from that place. Most others didn't.

When people think of the camps today, they think of big concentration camps like Auschwitz, where tens of thousands of people at a time were moved in by railroad, stripped of belongings, gassed, or put into uniforms to work. In Pustkow it was different. We were a more regional camp, housing Jews from the surrounding area and also Lodz, the city with the largest Jewish population in Poland. Jews were brought there by truck without any belongings. Whatever they might have carried would have been confiscated anyway. Instead, they came only with the clothes on their backs. But having the clothes on their backs instead of uniforms offered some advantage. For one thing, they were warmer. For another, the more foresighted could hide jewelry, tobacco, items of clothing that might be bartered. Of course these were forbidden, and discovery would lead to severe punishment. But still, the possibility existed, and many did have minor items to trade.

One day our group was returning from the forest where we had been cutting down trees all day. We hadn't eaten since morning and the old Jew, the former textile mill owner was in desperate shape. Cold, tired, and hungry, he could hardly go on. A Polish peasant stood near the spot where we were stopped along the road and the Jew called to him, "Sell me bread."

The peasant looked the Jew and said, "I will sell you bread. Pay me dollars for the bread." The peasant in all likelihood had never seen a dollar. He didn't pronounce the word correctly. All he knew was that dollars were good money somewhere. His request for dollars was meant to mock the old Jew.

But the Jew, to the peasant's surprise, said, "Agreed. I have dollars. Bring me bread and I will pay you dollars."

The peasant went to his house, which was nearby, and we all watched, wondering how the transaction would work out. When the Pole returned and produced the loaf of bread, the Jew turned away and opened the lining of the torn coat he wore. He opened the lining and pulled out a thousand dollar bill. Before the old Jew had left Lodz, he had several of these thousand dollar bills sewn into the coat, thinking large sums would serve him well. So far he had not been able to use them for anything.

The peasant looked at the bill for a moment and then took it in exchange for the bread. I am sure he had no idea how much a thousand dollars was. No doubt he would have just as readily taken one dollar. But he accepted the money and the old Jew took the bread in exchange.Certainly, the peasant didn't know what a good deal he had transacted for himself, and perhaps left with second thoughts. The Jew knew exactly how well he had done. For his thousand dollars, he fended off starvation for another day or two. He had made the deal of a lifetime.

Violence in Pustkow

During the spring of 1999 Americans became aware of the impact of sadism in the police force. A prisoner in the custody of the New York police named Abner Louima was sodomized with a broken broomstick. The prosecutors in New York City vigorously moved to indict five policemen. The public's revulsion over the act was palpable. It was viewed as so extreme that the normal solidarity among policemen broke down and several officers did the unprecedented—they testified against one of their brothers in blue. The victim filed suit against the city. The convicted policemen were sentenced to prison terms.

The public outcry over this form of brutality and swift official action in the face of it offer an ironic contrast to the consequences of events I witnessed while an inmate of the labor camp in Pustkow in 1940. There, sadism was not only routine, it was encouraged. Brutal as the New York City policeman was, he was but a pale replica of the two German officers who controlled our lives in Pustkow, Camp Commandant Schmidt and Sharführer Miller.

Schmidt was an SS officer. My first encounter with him occurred the day I was conscripted to join the work force in Pustkow. Periodically, the Germans would conduct a *Kontrolle,* or roundup of the local labor force between ages twelve and sixty to select workers for different sites. We knew Pustkow was not a good destination. My interview for the job began with a blow from a rifle butt that sent me reeling across the room where I stumbled and split my head on a desk. I then received a series of slaps and kicks, and ended up on my knees, shining Schmidt's boots with a rag soaked in the blood from my cut. About two hundred of us were similarly selected and herded into open trucks for the forty-kilometer drive to the camp. We stood crowded into the back of the trucks, packed too solidly to sit or duck. That was too bad, because Schmidt made it a point to have his drivers swerve close to the edge of the road when we came to overhanging trees. The branches reached out and took their toll on the faces of those on the right side of the trucks. Two men, one a tailor I knew, lost eyes. Others arrived with their faces bloody and torn from the branches.

Life at the camp was surreal. Each day was marked with a hanging. While we stood in ranks for the morning roll call, one of the inmates was chosen randomly, called forward, and then another was chosen and ordered to hang him. When a young man from Tarnow, refused the participate in this sadistic ritual, Schmidt promptly hung him up by the arms and then stabbed his pleading victim in the neck. After this, the rest of us stood silently in ranks, praying to avoid the arbitrary terror that could follow an inadvertent glance or body movement that caught the commandant's eye.

Believe it or not, horrible as they were, these experiences in the camp eventually became routine. Remember that they took place in the context of people being shot, beaten, worked to death. One day, however, Scharführer Miller transcended the normal brutality of our daily lives with an act that was monumental in its cruelty. The young girl was from Mielec. I never learned what her name was. There were so many young people sent to the camp from that area, and none ever lasted long enough to establish much of an identity with us.

It was cold in Pustkow, and few of us ever wore enough to protect us from the weather. Some who had been conscripted from nearby had jackets. The ones who had been brought from a distance frequently wore only thin clothing, and they suffered from the cold during the long roll calls. On this morning the girl from Mielec stood shivering in front of an irate Miller. It seems the night before, she had taken a blanket she hadn't been issued, and he had found out. As Miller screamed abuse at her, she trembled from fright and cold. Then he ordered her to take off her clothing. When she just stood there, he ripped her clothing from her and there she remained, in front of the ranks of prisoners, naked, while the wind whistled through the area and we all tried to avert our eyes. It turned out that she had a brother in the camp as well, and Miller had the brother dragged in front of us, too.

"Rape her," he ordered. "Rape your sister." The brother remained inert. Again, Miller repeated the order, and when he did nothing to comply, Miller clubbed him to the ground where he lay still.

"Volunteers. I want volunteers to rape her." He now addressed us in the ranks, but no one came forward.

"Very well. I will show you how to do it," he said. And with that, he took a piece of jagged wood and jammed it into the screaming girl's vagina. While I and the other waiting members of the labor gang watched, a gush of blood spurted from the girl, and she fell to the ground and died within moments of the violation.

Death was common at Pustkow. A day didn't pass without one of us dying. But this killing was unusually brutal, even in those circles. It was so unusual that it came to the attention of the Camp commandant, Oberführer von Schelle, who was so impressed with this uniquely brutal act that he promoted Miller and, as a reward, sent him to Auschwitz, where his talents could really be put to good use.

As in the Louima case, we had an official violate a prisoner in his power. As in the Louima case, the action was so brutal it came to the attention of the authorities. But there the parallels stop. There was no indictment, no trial, no testimony. There was only a commendation for a job imaginatively done, and a promotion to a venue offering greater opportunity. That was Pustkow.

Surviving the morning hanging ritual was only the beginning of the risks. As we marched to our work sites, Schmidt and Miller delighted in randomly shooting into our ranks. One day, it was my turn. As we marched toward the woods to clear trees, I was shot in the hand. Moments before, the man marching next to me was killed with a bullet through his head. But even though he had been killed instantly, my wound also was a death sentence. If the guards learned I couldn't work, they would kill me as well. I had to escape.

Fortunately, escape from Pustkow was not too difficult if you had the right connections and a place to escape to. The Germans used representatives from the Judenrat to organize the prisoners. These representatives weren't themselves prisoners, but rather people of stature in the Jewish community who were assigned by the Judenrat to facilitate communications between the Jewish prisoners and their German captors. Two such representatives in Pustkow at the time I was there were men named Immerglick and Bittkower, from the town of Dembica. Another was Izio Kleinhandler, a gentleman from Tarnow who happened to be a cousin of my girlfriend, Rozia Susskind. Kleinhandler arranged work assignments for me that allowed me to survive despite my wounded hand. Eventually, on one trip to cut trees in the deep woods, I slipped away from the guards along with a fellow prisoner from Dembica.

The Jews in Poland had not yet been placed in ghettos. If you were from towns nearby, such as Tarnow, Dembica, or Kolbuszowa, and you escaped, you might find Jews to help you. If you had been sent from a distant city such as Lodz, the problem was greater, because you didn't know anyone. Once the area became *Judenrein*, or free of Jews, escape would be impossible for just this reason, but in 1940, conditions were still favorable. With help, I was able to get back to Kolbuszowa, where I hid in Rozia's attic and recovered from both the wounded hand and the pain of a disk in my back that I had ruptured on my last day of work.

That ended my personal experiences in Pustkow. Others were not as fortunate. Pustkow eventually evolved from a labor camp into a concentration camp. It subsequently became an *Industriehof*, or industrial center, where the Germans were secretly developing the V-1 and V-2 rockets. Once it became a concentration camp, Pustkow saw the commencement of a process of gassing Jews with truck exhaust fumes. Later when it was an *Industriehof*, the killing became more efficient. Since the work there was top secret, no one could be allowed to survive. Eventually, everyone who worked at Pustkow was killed. That included the Judenrat representatives who had helped the Germans deal with the Jews, Kleinhandler, Immerglick, and Bittkower. Every Jew, no matter how cooperative, no matter how useful, was targeted for eventual annihilation by the Germans. There are some famous stories of special concern being shown by SS for their favorite Jews. They killed them quickly with a bullet to the head.

Pustkow is not a familiar a name in Holocaust annals. Death camps like Chelmno, Treblinka, Belzec, Majdanek, Auschwitz, and Sobibor enjoy greater notoriety. That doesn't diminish the horrors experienced in Pustkow, and in places like it. Their victims are just as dead. Their pain was just as acute. People like Schmidt and Miller were there to make it a hell. Kleinhandler, Immerglick, Bittkower, the hanging victims, the girl from Mielec, her brother, the boys with their eyes gouged out by the trees, the man who was shot marching next to me—they were all victims of Pustkow. So were thousands more. Only I, and a few like me, are still here to tell their stories, sixty years later.

Due Process

German Style

Because it was bitter cold that day in the winter of 1940–41, I didn't take my bicycle to Mielec as I usually did. Instead I decided to ride with Chmielowiec, a Polish peasant who subsidized his living by ferrying Jews back and forth to Mielec twice a week in his wagon. Business was good for Chmielowiec. Jews had not yet been confined to the ghetto, and since their jobs had been taken and their businesses confiscated, all they could do was travel afield to try to buy food, some articles of clothing, soap, or any other item they might bring back to trade in order to better their condition. And so it was that I joined eight of my neighbors, two women and six men, from Kolbuszowa for the twenty-eight-kilometer trip to Mielec.

I was in a business similar to that of my neighbors but on a somewhat grander scale. Because I spoke accent-free Polish, and because of a broad face and small features, I could easily pass as a Pole. When I traveled I rarely wore my white armband with the blue Star of David required by the Germans of all Jews, and I frequently rode my bicycle to the surrounding communities to buy items on the black market. At age twenty, I was a major supplier of contraband to the besieged Jews of Kolbuszowa.

On this day I wanted to go to Mielec to smuggle back a quantity of saccharine. It happened that the condition of the Jews of Mielec was somewhat better than in Kolbuszowa and the other towns. The Germans who administered the town had lived nearby. The background of the mayor and the commandant of an area was important to the lives led by its residents. The people of Mielec had a relatively civil occupation, and as a result, had more goods than we. Jews from the region came there to buy supplies.

It was about four o'clock in the afternoon. The passengers in the wagon had completed their transactions, and we were heading back to Kolbuszowa. Eight Jews bounced along behind the two horses drawing the wagon. They sat huddled together for warmth, talking, praying, nodding off. It had been a long day, and as the sun went down the temperature fell with it. I sat along side Chmielowiec, the driver. As usual, I did not wear the armband required of Jews and worn by the others. I was dressed with a normal coat under a padded overcoat. It ballooned out, insulating me from the icy wind. It also hid the three kilos of saccharine I had strapped around my waist: three precious packages that were as valuable as they were illegal. In Poland, where the government had a sugar monopoly, saccharine had always been illegal. In Germany, where it was manufactured as a synthetic sugar, it was needed on the home front. There certainly was none for the Jews. In Germany there was nothing for the Jews. In Poland, very little.

Just as our wagon rounded a bend in the road about halfway back to Kolbuszowa, Chmielowiec snapping the reins with me at his side, looking for all the world like a Polish peasant and his son, a German automobile came along the other way. Our luck was bad that day. It was SS, and they pulled up, stopped the wagon, and commanded that the eight Jews get down and stand by the side of the road. The driver and I were ordered down and we stood next to the wagon.

What happened next I see as clearly as if it were yesterday. The Germans searched the wagon and with great excitement exclaimed over the treasures they discovered: a little soap, some flour, sugar, potatoes. It was a pitiful store of essentials being brought back by the Jews standing at the side of the road. It was pitiful, but it was fatal. The commandant barked an order and in a matter of seconds the eight mothers, fathers, uncles, nieces, people of Kolbuszowa, all of whom I had grown up with and knew intimately, lay dead in a ditch by the side of the road, shot down with a submachine gun. Eight bundles of blood-soaked rags in a ditch was all that remained of them.

The driver and I stood dumb. We were both dressed like Polish peasants. Except around my waist was that unusual accessory, three kilos of saccharine. If that were discovered, there would surely be a ninth body in the ditch. Neither of us spoke until the SS officer walked over to us and told us in German: "You are very foolish to give rides to Jews. It is against the rules. If there is a next time, we will deal with you very harshly. Don't travel with Jews."

Chmielowiec said nothing. What could he say? He understood no German. He looked blankly and shrugged. I, in contrast, understood German perfectly. Most Jews did, either from their experiences with the Austro-Hungarian Empire or from German's similarities to Yiddish, or from school, where German was a required subject. I understood, but I too just stood there, my face a blank, not showing fear, my eyes fixed directly on the German's. We stood there, looking at one another for a moment, a conqueror and a Jew masquerading as a Polish peasant. The SS commandant was seeking some sign of fear, some smell of guilt. *Yea though I walk through the valley of the shadow of death, I will fear no evil.* With a steady gaze, I betrayed no emotion. Abruptly the German turned, bid his companions to follow him back to the car, and in another moment they were gone. My apparent lack of concern with the dead Jews in the ditch must have made me all the more credible to the SS commandant as a Polish peasant.

The whole thing took just a few minutes. Arrest, trial, execution in a few minutes. The Germans were famous for their efficiency.

Whenever I think about that wintry day in Poland, I wonder about my escape from discovery. They had only to touch my back, only to open my coat to find the packages. But they didn't. My innocent face had fooled them. My eyes had betrayed nothing. My bearing was confident. God still had work for me to do.

The Kolbuszower Bunche Schwaig

Yitzhak Leibush Peretz, one of the best known Yiddish writers, once wrote a short story about a character named Bunche Schwaig. The character was so poignantly drawn by Peretz that one only had to say, "He's a real Bunche Schwaig," and others recognized the person's qualities with no further elaboration. The story went that Bunche was a poor man, a simple soul, who lived his life under extremely harsh conditions without ever complaining. Dressed in rags, he would do odd jobs for people. He drifted through the community, homeless and without family, gratefully accepting scraps of food from anyone who offered leftovers. His shelter was in the attic of the public bathhouse, where he was allowed to sleep when the weather was cold. His life was hard, but he never complained. In fact Schwaig wasn't his actual name. He acquired it because it indeed means "quiet." He was a quiet man who never had anything and who never asked for anything.

One harsh winter, the conditions were too much for Bunche. He became sick and died, and while his passing was scarcely noted on earth, his arrival in heaven caused quite a stir. The head of the Heavenly Court asked the bad angels to tell about Bunche's activities on earth. They described his activities in great detail, adding that despite the severity of his life, even they could find no bad thought he had ever held, nor any harm he had caused any man. Seeing this man of virtue who had never had anything in life on earth, the court told Bunche that here in heaven, he could have any wish he wanted granted. He could have anything he desired: wealth, immortality, palaces, anything.

Bunche blinked. He had never had anything before, let alone a choice among rich alternatives. He let his imagination roam over the possibilities, sampling in his mind the opportunities and their joys. At length he decided on his choice. He asked the Heavenly Court, "Maybe, maybe I could have a fresh baked warm roll and butter every day," he asked. "I have never had that before."

The entire Heavenly Court looked at Bunche and as one, all began to cry.

In Kolbuszowa we had a fellow named Yuku Leib. Yuku was a nickname too. Just as "Schwaig" meant quiet, "Yuku" meant *schlemiel.* His actual name was Leib Langweil, but to everyone in the town he was known as Yuku Leib—Yuku the Schlemiel. Not unlike Bunche in the story, Yuku was a simple man—a tailor by trade, who made underwear.

This picture of Leib Langweil was circulated by the Germans as propaganda to portray what a typical Jew looked like.

He never married and lived alone, but even at that, he never did enough to support himself. On Fridays he would go around begging a few pennies and challah to eat on Saturday.

Yuku Leib had a long, Semitic face and prominent, bony nose and looked like a caricature of the way anti-Semites had presented Jews for centuries. When the Germans came and they discovered Yuku Leib in the community they found a use for him that was far more important to them than any he had rendered prior to their arrival. They dressed him up in outlandish costumes, putting a tall, pointed, fur hat on his head with a cross painted in front on it, and made photographs of him. They sent these back to Germany as part of the propaganda war, characterizing his appearance as "typical of the Jews." He appeared in German newsreels and pamphlets. Yuku Leib, after a lifetime dwelling in obscurity, suddenly found himself of importance to the Germans in Kolbuszowa. Because of the hat, they called him "Bishop."

The Germans also found employment for their representative Jew. When he wasn't modeling he worked in the police station, cleaning up, shining boots, chopping wood, running errands, and performing a variety of menial tasks.

On one typical afternoon, while Yuku Leib was working around the station a detachment of police arrived with three of the most prominent Jewish businessmen in the community, Hirsch Kleinman, Akiva Schmidt and my father Isak Saleschutz. The Germans resented any shred of dignity possessed by Jews, and these three men, successful and scholarly, particularly bothered them for their self-confident demeanor. How to humiliate them?

The chief of the police detail announced that the three bearded and dignified Jews were to clean the outhouses of the police station. They would clean them with their bare hands and work to make them spotless. And as he was ordering the assignment, the police chief happened to spot Yuku Lieb and in a moment of inspiration declared that Yuku Leib would be the foreman. The tables would be turned. This hapless member of the community who had been on the bottom of the social heap for so many years would have command over these three men of wealth. They knew that Yuku Leib must have built up resentments over the years against men such as this.

"Make sure they clean it all, Bishop," they laughed. "You are in charge here." And with a last roar of laughter they left Yuku Leib and his charges to their dirty task.

Left in charge, Yuku Leib strode meaningfully up to the three leaders of the Jewish community, and as they unhappily prepared to bend to their task, he said, "Don't do a thing." They paused, and he added, "this is not work for gentlemen such as yourselves. You are not used to such work." They certainly weren't, but until that moment it hadn't looked as if there would be much choice. "Stand over there," Yuku said quietly. I will clean the outhouse. I am used to such work. This is not work for men such as you." And as the three prominent Jews from whom Yuku Leib had begged a few groschen and a piece of challah watched, their foreman, put in charge of them to make their lives miserable, proceeded to clean the outhouses until they were spotless.

Some hours later the German police returned. The Jews were standing along one wall. Yuku Leib, opposite them.

"So, Bishop," one of them said, "What do you think? Did they do a good job cleaning today?" Yuku Leib, normally without guile, smiled broadly.

"Yes." he said. "I gave them extra work to do. I think they did a very good job cleaning this place up."

When my father told us this story of Yuku Leib, who was granted an opportunity for power beyond his experience, but was bound by the humility of his life, he observed that Yuku Leib was our "Kolbuszower Bunche Schwaig."

And so he deserves to be remembered, while so many others have been forgotten.

A Mother's Grief

Six million is such a vast number that it frequently dulls our perception of the suffering produced by the Holocaust. Clearer insight often comes from individual stories such as the tale of what befell the Feuer brothers, and the heartbreak of their mother.

It was August 1942. The Judenrat of our town no longer served the needs of the Germans, and Landskomissar Twardon ordered them all arrested, including Dr. Anderman, who had been so important in providing leadership to the Jewish community. On the list of those to be arrested was a young man named Boaz Feuer, who was a member of he Judenrat.

As the Germans went from house to house to make their arrests, they didn't find Boaz. He was not at home when the Germans came for him so they went to ask his mother where he was. It happened that Boaz's younger brother Srulek was at the mother's house when the Germans came, and when they didn't find Boaz, they took Srulek to show them where Boaz lived. Srulek brought them to Boaz's house. Once again, he wasn't at home, but as chance would have it, his two other brothers, Yidd'l and Benjamin, along with his brother-in-law, Levi Glantz, were. The Germans took all four, Srulek, Yidd'l, Benjamin, and Levi to the police station, announcing that when Boaz turned himself in, the four would be released.

Concerned about his brothers and brother-in-law, Boaz did come to the police station to give himself up. They promptly arrested him, but instead of releasing the other four who hadn't been wanted in the first place, they bundled them all off to Rzeszow prison, where they were held for a few weeks pending shipment to Auschwitz.

This was before Auschwitz had acquired its identity as a death camp. It was simply known as a place where political prisoners were collected.

Frantic about her children, Dvora Feuer, their mother, implored everyone she could to intervene with Twardon. She went to anyone who might be able to approach him, and while she collected a full measure of promises, nothing was done to help. I know of this case because one of the people she contacted was my youngest sister Rachel, who spoke and wrote good German, to ask that she write a letter explaining that the police had come to seek one son but took all four along with her daughter's husband. Rachel wrote the letter, but the mother received no direct answer to her questions. Instead, she began to receive a series of telegrams.

"We are sorry to inform you that your son's TB worsened while in prison, and he died from it." "We regret to advise you that your son's chronic heart condition worsened, and he expired from a heart attack." And so on, for all five taken.

"But they hadn't been sick a day in their lives," she protested. "They were strong, healthy young men. Their father was a butcher and they carried sides of beef."

Oh yes, they were obviously sickly, wrote back the Germans, and if she wanted their ashes, she would have to sign a letter acknowledging that they were chronically ill.

Eventually jars containing ashes arrived at her house—along with a bill for the cremation.

The horror of it. The cruelty. I remember the change that took place in the old woman. Overnight, her face darkened. Her lips became black. Her spirit was broken by the cruel game played by the Germans.

Four sons and the husband of her married daughter. Dead. They came for one and took them all.

Cruel Remembrances

It has been more than sixty years since the events the world calls the Holocaust took place. I still dwell on the events of the time. At night the recollections come: images of cruelty seen, pain witnessed, suffering endured. Common events often trigger these memories. At night my dreams bear witness.

In New Jersey, the winter of 1994 was the coldest, most sustained siege of below-freezing temperatures and above-normal snowfall on record. After one particularly heavy storm, I bundled up in my warm sheepskin coat, gloves, and boots and took my snowblower to clean the driveway of my Springfield, New Jersey, house. That done, I came in and ate a bowl of hot soup and drowsed in the warmth of the house. As I relaxed after my efforts, my mind went back to another severe winter I had experienced—this one in 1942.

I lived in the Kolbuszowa ghetto, and when it snowed, a gang of Jews was rounded up to clear the roads to the next town. Typically two hundred Jews would take leave of home with their snow shovels early in the morning and work until dark. They ranged in age from very young to old. They wore whatever clothes had been salvaged when they moved to the ghetto. There were no meals. There was no warming tent. The Jews went out in the morning, worked all day, and trudged home at night to a cold house. The next day, we went out again.

The picture that came to my mind that evening in Springfield was of the pretty wife of Shaya Dreingel, a tailor in our town. When the gang was called to shovel the snows one day, he had some tailoring to do that would earn some needed zlotys for the family. While he discussed this with his wife, the call to assemble came, and she rushed off to join the gang in his place. The trouble was, she had no boots. Instead, she went out for the day's labor in a thin coat with a pair of summer shoes on her feet. We worked, as usual in the deep snow, and after a few hours she discovered that she only had a shoe on one of her feet. Somewhere along the way, she had lost the other shoe in the snow, but didn't realize it was gone. Her foot had become frozen, and she had no feeling in it. When we discovered her condition we rubbed her leg with snow, hoping to restore some circulation, but it was so cold that there was no response. We were

The Germans assigned a Jewish crew to clear the roads after each snow storm. The author is standing at the right of the German guards with the shovel on his shoulder. March 9, 1940.

eight kilometers from town. Two of her friends pleaded that she would die in the cold and somehow got permission from the guards to get her back. The friends made their way home, through the drifting snow, the wind tearing at their clothes while they carried the pretty, shivering wife of Shaya Dreingel the tailor.

They got her home; they worked to restore circulation in her legs. While Shaya Dreingel and their children lamented her condition and cried at her misfortune, her friends rubbed and bathed the frozen limbs. But it was too late. Her feet were frozen and gangrene set in to the one that had lost the shoe. We were fortunate to have a surviving doctor in Kolbuszowa. At least the amputation was properly done. As I thought of that experience, I realized that the cold winter of 1994 in Springfield, New Jersey, didn't seem to be so bad after all.

The winter brought another memory—a memory of another cold day when we were being lined up to go out on a work detail. Men, women, young, old—it didn't matter. We all worked until we fell. On this particular day, when we lined up, our group was missing two people: two women, the daughters of a teacher in town called Schwarzer Lehrer after his pitch-black beard. Schwarzer Lehrer's daughters had failed to appear for the work detail. I volunteered to go and get them.

Bundling against the wind, I made my way to Schwarzer Lehrer's house, knocked, and when there was no reply, I went in. It wasn't much of a house at best—one big room. As I went in, I realized that instead of feeling warmth from a stove, I found the temperature inside the house the same as outside. The two windows had broken glass panes, covered with cardboard. The room was dark, freezing cold, and stripped bare of all furniture. There wasn't a stick anyplace. There was just a bare, dirty floor, and as my eyes became accustomed to the darkness of the room, I saw that in the corner there were four women—a mother and her three daughters—huddled together on a straw mattress. They had a thin cover that they shared, and except for its meager comfort, they had only the body warmth of one another to ward off the cold. The room was empty with the exception of a pitcher of frozen water on a broken chair near the straw mattress. All the furniture had gradually been used as firewood. All their possessions had been sold for sustenance. Now on this bitter cold day in the winter they faced their bleak prospects together, cold, hungry, and without hope.

Before I could speak, the mother said, "I know why you have come. They want the girls to work. But look at them. They are so cold, so hungry. There is no way they can go out there. Go, tell them it is impossible." I looked again at these three, once beautifully vibrant girls who ranged in

Two of the three beautiful daughters, before the war, of the
teacher called Schwarzer Lehrer.

age from eighteen to twenty-two years. They were an age when energy
should be boundless and possibilities unlimited. Instead, their dull eyes
told a story of hopelessness. I felt my own fill with tears. I knew she was
right. The demands of the work gang would overwhelm them in a few
hours if they went out.

I returned to Mundt, the man in charge of the work detail and described what I had found at the house of the Schwarzer Lehrer. He didn't
force the issue. We left for our twelve-hour day of hungry labor on the
frozen highways of Poland. All of us came back that night. When I came
home, I told my mother about the widow of the Schwarzer Lehrer and her
three daughters. The widow and my mother had been childhood friends.
My mother had a pot of soup prepared for me and my brother-in-law, but
when she heard the story she told me to bring it, with a loaf of bread, to
the house where the four women were suffering.

Whenever it is cold and snowy, I see those big, black eyes looking out
from under the thin cloth in that unheated, large, empty room.

These were cruel episodes. But there was an aspect about them that
was impersonal. The cold of the winter is an act of nature. It affected people who had been made hopelessly vulnerable by the German occupation,
but there was no immediate act of cruelty. In fact, in each instance some
flickering of compassion manifested itself when the tailor's wife was sent

back and the girls were allowed to remain home. That is not the case in the next episode.

Israel Kleinman was a neighbor who was about fifteen years my senior. When he married a girl from Mielec, he moved there, but after his family was killed, he came back to live in Kolbuszowa. His status was uncertain, since he was not officially a member of our labor camp, but he lived in it anyway. However, rather than participate in its work details, he would slip in and out, visiting surrounding villages where peasants whom he had known during his years as a farm machinery salesman took him in and fed him. He would be away for a few days and then return, only to go off again. It was on one of these journeys that the German police arrested him and discovered that although he was in the camp, he didn't belong there. They could not account for his presence or activities at all, and they kept him in jail for a few days.

One afternoon, while I was on work detail chopping wood, two policemen brought Israel Kleinman from the jail into the prison yard. It was a bare earthen area, surrounded on three sides by a wire fence, with the building on the fourth. Israel stood in the yard, frail in his tattered overcoat, waiting to be told what to do, when the policemen opened the gate and let two barking German shepherd dogs in with him. The dogs immediately ran at Israel and began to terrorize him. Israel screamed and waved his arms trying to ward them off. But the dogs attacked the thin man and tore at his clothes while the German policemen laughed and shouted encouragement at the dogs. They jumped at him, catching his coat in their mouths and eventually tearing it off of him. And then their sharp teeth caught his flesh and tore bloody chunks of it from his arms and body. He fought them but it was futile. As they tore at him, he stumbled and fell. They were all over him biting his legs, face, shoulders. He screamed, but soon the screams stopped. For a half hour the dogs tore at him, and then he was dead.

The policemen told us to stop cutting wood. We had a wagon for stacking it, and they told us to bring it over and take the body out and bury it. They laughed as they patted their dogs and went back into the police station. And we were left to dispose of the remains of that horrible half hour.

Death was no stranger to us. We had seen our family members shot, our neighbors hanged. But that was death, quick and final. This had been protracted torture. This had been bestiality at a level we had not seen before. This had been cruelty at a level too stark to forget, yet too painful to recall.

A Close Encounter with Death

Bartelmus intended to kill me. I knew that because Laizer Spielman had told me so. Neither of us knew why. We just knew that Bartelmus had one day said to him, "Lazarus, there's a Jew I'm going to kill. His name is Naftali Saleschutz."

"Why are you going to kill Naftali? He's a friend of mine," Laizer pleaded.

"Never mind. I have my reasons. After he's dead, I'll tell you," was all he could get from Bartelmus.

When Laizer, told this to me, I was shocked. Why would Bartelmus want to harm me? I had never spoken two words to him. Could it be true? When a member of the Schutzpolizei decided to kill a Jew, there was very little to stop him. If he killed a dog, he had to write a report to get replacement bullets. When he killed a Jew no report was required. My life was in grave danger, and I didn't know why.

Western Poland had been conquered and reconquered so many times across the centuries that there were regions called *Niemiecka Colonia* (German colonies), where the Polish citizens, to all intents and purposes were *Volksdeutschen*, or ethnic Germans, speaking German, dressing like Germans, behaving like Germans. These enclaves of German culture were to become very valuable to the occupying German forces because they provided a natural resource for police work. The people were bilingual, speaking Polish and German. Other Poles who wanted to inform on the Jews, but couldn't speak German, could bring their information to this Schutzpolizei, as they were called. Similarly, the occupying Germans could rely on them to communicate with the Polish citizens. It was a bad situation for the Jews because these Schutzpolizei were constantly proving to the Germans through acts of cruelty that they could be relied on.

The Bartelmus who wanted to kill me was one of the Schutzpolizei. He was a strapping, good-looking German who had lived in Bielsko, Poland, on the Czechoslovakian border before the Germans drafted him into the Schutzpolizei. In Kolbuszowa he always carried a submachine gun and a revolver and was well known for his brutality toward Jews. The one exception was my friend Lazarus Spielman, alias Laizer, a Jew who dressed and had the mannerisms of a German and who seemed to get along well with everyone—Jew, German, and Pole alike. He was particularly useful to Bartelmus because he spoke German fluently—more fluently, in fact, than Bartelmus—and more importantly, could write German as well.

Lazarus Spielman had been born in Karlsruhe, Germany, but in 1938 the Germans threw all Polish Jews who were not citizens of Germany, adults and children alike, out of the country, even though they might have been born there and lived there for their entire lives. And so Lazarus found himself in Poland, where the Jews called him Laizer. A year later, when the Germans invaded Poland, he worked for the German police, cleaning boots, straightening their rooms, doing whatever odd jobs he could find. The Germans became fond of this willing Jew, who was useful to them in many ways. For Bartelmus, Laizer's ability to write German proved particularly helpful because, while Bartelmus could speak German, his writing in the language was extremely limited. Laizer became a familiar figure around the German police station, and he was a good go-between for the Judenrat's efforts to get Jewish prisoners released through the passing of bribes.

Thus it was that in his situation as an aide and confidant to Bartelmus he received the shocking news that he passed on. Bartelmus intended to kill me. Kolbuszowa is a small town. I made it my business to avoid Bartelmus, going out of my way if I thought I might encounter him. However, it was inevitable that sooner or later, he would have his opportunity, and I would learn if he was joking or serious about his threat. It came one day when a load of furniture arrived for the Germans to use, and Laizer was sent to get two men who would unload it. I went, along with another Jew, and while Laizer supervised, we struggled with the heavy burdens. As I was carrying the headboard for a bed we were unloading, I suddenly saw the wood shatter about six inches from my head. A shot had whizzed past my ear and lodged in the headboard. I dropped the headboard and remained trembling while Laizer ran over. There, about a hundred yards away, Bartelmus stood laughing, holding his revolver over his head. He laughed and waved his gun, and when Laizer ran over to him to beg him not to shoot again, he only said, "I told you I would shoot him, didn't I. I missed. I never missed before."

Laizer said, "Now that you have shot at him, tell me. Why do you want to kill him? Pretend you succeeded. You said you would tell me after you killed him."

And Bartelmus, still laughing and shaking his head over the improbable occurrence of his having missed me said, "Okay, I will tell you. I saw Saleschutz one day in town with his girlfriend. She is too pretty for him. I think any Jew with such a pretty girlfriend should be killed."

Outrageous as this was, Laizer treated it matter-of-factly, and sug-

gested that now that he had frightened me, it should be enough. Bartelmus, still enormously amused by the whole thing, considered this over-
ture and said, "Perhaps. Let me talk to him." Laizer beckoned me to come
over, and still shaking, I approached. Bartelmus roared with laughter
again. "You are lucky, Saleschutz. I never miss. I don't know how I
missed you today." He repeated the story. "Rozia is too pretty a girl for
you. One day, I may decide to kill you after all. We'll see."

And so it was that I survived this brush with the random possibility
of dying in that dangerous time. If I had been killed, it wouldn't have been
for any offense. None of the Jews who died during the Holocaust committed any offense to be killed for. It would just be on a whim. A caprice. We
would live or die according to the whim of the Germans who occupied
our country. That day, I lived.

A Tale of Two Heroines

Part I

Some people are naturally acquisitive. I am one of them. I have always
been a collector. When I was part of the labor detail assigned to going
through the houses of the ghetto, I made it my business to collect any
family photos I could find and save them. I still have the report cards from
my childhood school days. I have the little megillah I took from the German looting of Jewish possessions. Whether it is pictures of Jewish life, or
religious art objects, or coins, or correspondences carried on over the
years—I have collected and saved them all. My house is filled with these
items, some of museum quality and some of interest only to me and my
family.

I also collect stamps. I have done this since I was a child, and I continue to collect them to this day. Stamps were my first geography and history lessons, my first window into the world outside Kolbuszowa. I am
particularly interested today when announcements are made of new issues of commemorative stamps marking events and people. Sometimes
they are of passing, and sometimes of permanent significance. Regardless, I collect them all.

On March 25, 1975, the United States Postal Service began issuing a
series of stamps honoring heroes of the American Revolution called
"Contributors to the Cause." One stamp of natural interest to me was the

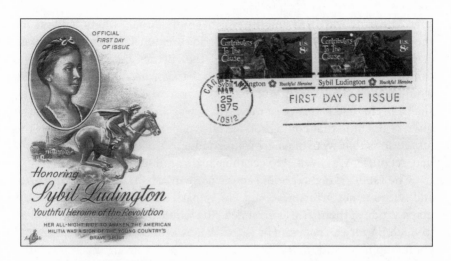

The Sybil Ludington stamp issued by the U.S. post office honors a youthful heroine whom the author compare to a young Jewish girl from Rzeszow killed by the Germans.

commemoration of Haym Salomon, a Jewish immigrant from Poland who raised money to finance the Revolutionary War and played a hero's role in our War of Independence. Naturally, I felt pride from the knowledge of the active role played by this Polish Jew in America's history. That pride, however, didn't begin to compare with the emotion that came to me through the stamp honoring a sixteen-year-old girl named Sybil Ludington, who on a dark night in April 1777 rode her horse Starr through the Connecticut countryside to warn her father's militia of a flanking movement by the British army. Her act saved the lives of her father and his force, and they in turn went on to fight and ultimately to help win American independence.

This is certainly an inspiring story, but you may well ask why it produced the emotional reaction I experienced as I read this background. Actually, my feelings had nothing to do directly with Sybil Ludington, but rather with another girl from another time, who made an equally perilous journey, and whose story came to a less happy ending. There is no stamp for her—no memorial of any kind. Perhaps those who read this story will, in their own minds, make the Sybil Ludington stamp a commemorative for this authentic Jewish heroine as well.

Her name was Sonia Halberstam. She, too, was sixteen years old, and she was the daughter of one of the prominent rabbinical families in Rzeszow. The time was 1942 and life was becoming increasingly tenuous for the Jews in Rzeszow. Indeed, all of Poland threatened to become one vast cemetery for Jews, and many thought that if they could get out of the country, perhaps to Hungary where conditions were better in 1942, they would have a chance to survive. Passports were the key to even beginning such a flight, and it turned out that there was an underground unit in the town of Bochnia that could produce false papers good enough to pass the inspections that were made by train conductors and German railroad police. A courier was needed to get the papers produced in Bochnia.

The rabbi's daughter Sonia spoke perfect Polish, had Aryan features, and without her armband could easily pass among the Poles and Germans as one of them. It was arranged. She would be the one who would go to Bochnia for the papers. For security, she would carry the names and photographs of no more than forty residents from Rzeszow, stay overnight while the forty false passports were prepared, and then, carrying the incriminating documents hidden among her hand luggage, she would take the perilous trip back on the train to Rzeszow.

It went as planned. As she went from station to train, Sonia was routinely questioned by the German authorities, and this pretty sixteen-year-old Polish girl with the innocent smile would explain where she was going and why. And just as routinely, she passed through and brought the precious documents to the desperate Jews.

Sonia Halberstam made this round trip safely four times. She brought 160 passports back with her over the span of two months. In October 1942 she set out on a fateful fifth trip. Her luck didn't hold. On the way back the German authorities questioned her, and dissatisfied with some detail, they searched and arrested her. What a triumph for them when they discovered in Sonia's bag, among the items she carried, the forty passports made out to forty separate people, Jewish citizens of the Rzeszow ghetto. Forty passports that were to be tickets to freedom turned out instead to be death warrants.

Who can imagine what agonies the girl suffered as the Germans tortured her to reveal the sources of the documents and the names of others involved. That is better left to the imagination. We don't have to imagine what befell the forty whose passports the Germans now held. I know personally what happened to them. It was the second day of Rosh Hashanah, a day for celebrating the arrival of a new year that none of them would live to enjoy. As I describe in the next story, they were taken by the Germans to the woods in Nowa-Wies, near Kolbuszowa, and shot dead.

The similarities between the two sixteen-year-old heroines are so great that when I first saw the Sybil Ludington stamp, the story of Sonia

Halberstam, long since forgotten, returned immediately to my mind. Sonia Halberstam, an authentic Jewish heroine, was every bit as courageous as Sybil and every bit as deserving of a commemorative stamp. One heroine was recognized; the other was forgotten, except in the memories of her sister Leah and two uncles who survived, and of course, in mine.

A Tale of Two Heroines
Part II

When the Germans captured Sonia Halberstam while she was carrying forty forged passports to Rzeszow a tragic series of events began. The passports would have saved forty Jews by allowing their exodus from Poland to Hungary. She had been the courier who had made four previous trips between Bochnia and Rzeszow over a two-month period. Her luck ended when, on the fifth trip, the German police stopped and questioned the pretty sixteen-year-old girl. A search of her luggage revealed that she was not the carefree Polish teenager she pretended to be. It doomed, not only Sonia—she was tortured to death by the Germans seeking to learn who had prepared the passports—but the forty Jews whose names and pictures appeared on the passports.

Within two days, they had been rounded up by the Germans and sent from Rzeszow, where the Jews were concentrated, to Kolbuszowa. There, they were held in the makeshift jail in the basement of the magistrate's building. We didn't know what plans the Germans had for these forty. What we had learned from the Polish workers, called the *Baudienst,* or *junaki* (teenage laborers) who were conscripted into labor, was that they had been digging a series of ditches outside of the neighboring village of Nowa-Wies. That usually meant a mass execution would soon take place and in all likelihood, they would be among the victims. The Germans had used this method before. They would march masses of Jews to the edge of the ditches, have them strip off their clothing, and then they would turn the machine guns on them. The naked bodies would fall back under the impact of the bullets, gradually filling the ditch as rank after rank of men, women, and children repeated the ritual.

At the time of Sonia's capture I was a member of the labor gang that had been drafted to dismantle the remains of the Kolbuszowa ghetto. The Jews who had crowded its streets had long since been moved to Rzeszow for transport to the Belzec extermination camp. For the moment I was secure. The Landskommisar had found that having me around was useful, and he regularly had me drive a horse-drawn wagon to truck salvage items from the ghetto to the Germans' warehouse in Rzeszow. I was in the habit of making two or three such journeys each week and could come and go from the camp without challenge.

Knowledge of the ditches that had been dug in Nowa-Wies for burial clarified another matter for me. A few days earlier, Landkomissar Walter Twardon, the commandant of the region, had brought twenty-five emaciated and lice-ridden Jews to our camp. He told us that he had found them in a hospital in the Biesiadka labor camp, too sick to work, and he wanted us to take care of them so they could contribute to our work effort. There were fifteen girls in their teens and ten young men. All had boils and running sores on their legs. All were filthy and emaciated. We had deloused them, boiled their clothes, put salve on their sores, and given them the first full meals they had had in recent memory. Their gratitude was boundless. We were the first people to treat them as human beings in a long while, and their tears flowed generously as they thanked us over and over again. I knew that kindness and consideration were entirely foreign to Twardon's behavior pattern. It saddened me to realize that in all likelihood, whenever the shooting of Jews commenced in Nova-Wies, these twenty-five young people, so thrilled at their evident deliverance, would be among them. There was no way we could warn them. Twardon had threatened reprisals of ten of us for any one of them that escaped. Besides, they had no place to go. Even if they tried, their condition would have marked them as escaped Jewish prisoners.

When the news came that forty prisoners were being held in the magistrate's building basement, I went to see what else I could learn. Security was not tight, and I could speak with the prisoners through a basement window. To my surprise, I found my cousin Birman, who had owned a hardware store in Rzeszow, was among the prisoners, and he was extremely agitated by the thought that the Germans would gain access to the names of others who were scheduled to receive counterfeit passports. They were still in Rzeszow, and Birman was certain that the Germans would go for them in the morning. It was imperative, he felt, that they be warned of their danger before the next day.

Avigdor Polimer, another of the labor gang, usually accompanied me on the wagon. He had worked with horses before the war, and Landkomissar Twardon valued his skill with them. Twardon had several beautiful horses for riding, and Avigdor took care of them. He would water and groom them and would often accompany Twardon as he galloped across the local countryside. Since we also had dray horses to pull the wagon, Avigdor took care of these as well. Therefore, it was only natural that he become part of the party going back and forth. I roused Avigdor and told him to hitch up the team of horses to the wagon. We had to get to Rzeszow that night.

When we made these trips back and forth to Rzeszow, we took the opportunity to conduct a little illicit commerce as well. We had fixed the wagon so it had a false bottom. Between the internal floor of the wagon and its actual bottom was a space in which we would hide items we took to Rzeszow to sell as well as contraband we brought back to the camp. One of the activities that took place within the labor camp was the baking of bread for the local Polish town people. Before the war, most of the bakers had been Jewish, and a number of them were held as inmates in the camp. The Germans brought in flour and assigned them the task of preparing bread to be distributed each day to the Poles holding ration cards. This suited us. Each time the bakers finished a batch we would manage to steal forty or fifty loaves, some of which we ate ourselves, and the rest we smuggled out in the wagon for the few Kolbuszowa people still being held in Rzeszow.

It was the middle of the night. We loaded the hidden compartment with bread. The wagon itself always stood ready to go, loaded with paper, brass, bottles, candlesticks, plates, and other items retrieved from the ghetto demolition. Our

SS Obersturmbann-Fuhrer Heinz Ehaus, Kreisshauptman. Acquired by the author from the German War Crimes Office.

German commandant of the Kolbuszowa area, Walter Twardon, Landkomisar. Acquired by the author from the German War Crimes Office.

two-and-a-half-hour journey through the Polish countryside was uneventful, and we arrived at about four in the morning. It was the second day of Rosh Hashanah, 1942, and we woke people up with the warning that anyone who was involved in the passport plans to go to Hungary should hide. The Germans would be coming for them. Heeding our advice, the forty vanished into the night. We later learned that our victory was short-lived. The next morning, when the Germans found the forty people they sought missing, they did what we should have anticipated them doing. After all, this wasn't the first time the Jewish community experienced the consequences of German logic. They rounded up a different forty Jews and trucked them back to Kolbuszowa for execution. One Jew was as good as another when it came to meeting a quota for killing.

Meanwhile, we had to get back to Kolbuszowa ourselves. By the time we completed the round trip, daylight had arrived over the Polish landscape. We rode into the camp at about 7:00 in the morning, just in time to find the Gestapo loading prisoners into two trucks with mounted machine guns on the back. There was the usual shouting and barking of dogs and pushing and punching. As we came upon the scene, the Gestapo commander pulled us off of the wagon, and told us to get into the truck too.

"No. No. We don't belong with those people," we protested.

A Jew was a Jew to the Gestapo, and they pushed us up onto the truck along with the other condemned people. We had committed the worst crime a Jew could commit in those days: being in the wrong place at the wrong time, and I confess I felt certain that I wouldn't survive this day. I had a feeling of acceptance, having struggled so long and so hard to survive. It was ironic that I should finally be taken off to be killed as a result of going to save the others.

But fate plays strange tricks. Twardon had come to watch the proceedings, and I when I saw him, called to him from the back of the truck, "Herr Landskommisar, Herr Landskommisar."

He strode over and saw his errand boy and his stable boy about to be trucked off for massacre.

"What are you doing up there? You don't belong there."

"They just grabbed us and put us here," we cried.

Twardon told the officer in charge of the detail to free us.

"I need these two," he said.

An obviously unhappy Gestapo officer waved us down from the truck, and it rumbled off moments later. What irony. Just before the trucks left for the killing fields of Nova-Wies that morning, my life was saved by the butcher who had annihilated the entire Kolbuszowa ghetto, including my father, my mother, my sisters, and all of my nieces and nephews still living in Poland. At his whim, Avigdor Polimer and I were allowed to step away to live another day.

All in all, over four hundred Jews were machine gunned before the day was over. They included the forty who were identified by the capture of Sonia Halberstam, the forty who took the place of those who got away, the twenty-five young people who had been transported from the Biesiadka labor camp a few days before, and three hundred others who were rounded up to fill the ditches of Nova-Wies.

I knew my days were numbered. The number just didn't come up that day.

Perfect Aryans

The *Appell*, or roll call was taking an unusual amount of time. Normally roll call for the Kolbuszowa *Arbeitslager*, the Kolbuszowa forced labor camp, was over quickly, and we were sent out to our day's labor. Our assignment was to tear apart the buildings of the old ghetto, vacant since all the Jews had been taken to be gassed at Belzec. About a hundred of us had been sent back to Kolbuszowa, where we were housed at the Beth Midrashim. We lined up each morning and marched off to knock the old houses apart, salvaging anything that might be of value to the Germans.

It was 1942, and on this morning we were held in our ranks waiting. At length, the Landskomissar, Walter Twardon, came out accompanied by two Gestapo officers. We didn't know what the presence of the Gestapo men meant, but we knew it wouldn't be good for us. As we stood in the ranks, now, the three worked their way slowly down the line, stopping and looking long and hard directly into the face of each of us. I stared straight ahead, past the inquisitive stare of the Gestapo men. One by one they worked their way along.

At length, they picked five of us out of the line-up: Moishe Weichselbaum and his younger brother Arek, Lazarus (Laizer) Spielman, Milek Golstein, and me, Naftali Saleschutz. "Step forward," they commanded, and the five of us did. Of the five, four of us were blond. Moishe and Arek Weichselbaum also had blue eyes, straight noses and could easily pass as perfect Aryans. Milek was also blond, but he had a more round, Slavic face with freckles. Lazarus, who had been born in Germany, also looked like a German soldier. With a stern expression and the breeches and boots of a policeman, he certainly appeared to be more German than Jewish. Of the five, I was the only one who was not blonde or Teutonic in aspect. They asked us to look to the right, to the left, straight ahead. They took pictures in profile from both sides and in full face. And then, without

The author and six of his friends who before the war belonged to the Zionist organization, Hanoar Hatzioni, took this picture November 10, 1940 to have a remembrance of the German's requirement that they wear an armband with the Star of David. Sitting to the left is Schmuel Weichselbaum and standing in the middle is Naftali Saleschutz, both of whom the Germans selected, among others, as "perfect Aryans."

comment or command, the three left, we were returned to the ranks and marched off to our duties obliterating the memory of the vibrant Jewish community of Kolbuszowa.

Two days later, the two Gestapo men, accompanied by Twardon and the commandant of the German police again confronted the roll call. Once again, they had the five of us step forward. This time, though they had brought with them a variety of instruments to measure facial characteristics. Our skulls, faces, chins, noses, and foreheads were all measured with tapes and calipers, the figures dutifully recorded, and new pictures taken. Again, following this odd ritual we were dismissed and sent back to our duties.

About a week later they were back. However, rather than having the five of us again step forward, they selected only the Weichselbaum brothers, bundled them into the car and drove off with them to Rzeszow. Who knew why? We thought they, like so many others, would simply be wiped out as a matter of random procedure. The Germans rarely explained their activities to Jews. We thought we had seen the last of the brothers, but we were wrong. Two days later, the Germans returned with them.

What had happened? What had it been about? The Weichselbaums explained that for the entire two days they had been at Gestapo headquarters. They had been completely undressed, and photographed, and measured again. Hair samples had been taken, ratios calculated, and records meticulously noted.

We all knew how methodical the Germans were about science. So, too, about the pseudoscience of race. The Germans were obsessively documenting these two Jewish boys whose ancestry dated back a thousand years but who looked so Aryan. They were looking for some means of explaining these Aryan characteristics in Jews. No doubt the pictures and records of the Weichselbaum brothers found their way back to Berlin—two Jewish boys who played their small role in establishing the base for good eugenic behavior in purifying the race.

As it turned out, the exercise was harmless to us. We survived none the worse, and what is more, five days later fifty-five of us managed to escape from the labor camp.

But that was when luck ran out for the Weichselbaum brothers. German faces, but Jewish luck. They were among those of us who escaped, and afterward, they hid in the attic of the flour mill that had belonged to their family. Pruchnik, who used to be a machinist in the mill had moved into the Weichselbaum house, next door to the mill. They contacted him, and Pruchnik expressed his joy at seeing them and agreed to bring them food and water each night. After a few nights of this, however, Pruchnik evidently rethought this arrangement and informed the German police that Jews were hiding in the attic of the mill. The police came and took Moishe and Arek to the *Kolejowka* (the unfinished railroad station), and there they executed them.

The Weichselbaum brothers are long gone, but for all we know, they and their measurements still gather dust in some archive labeled "Aryan Studies"—put there by those most meticulous of scientists, the German racial specialists.

My Five Sisters

Once upon a time there were five sisters. How many fairy tales have we been read in childhood that began with this memorable phrase? Don't be deceived. This story is no fairy tale, and, unlike most tales that begin this way, this one does not have a happy ending. These sisters do not live happily ever after. In fact, they, and their husbands, and their children, and their nieces and nephews do not live past July 1942. You see, the five sisters were my sisters, and they, along with my mother and my girlfriend, and many of the Jews I had known during my childhood were taken from the ghetto in Rzeszow to the Belzec death camp, where they were gassed and their bodies burned and their ashes scattered on that warm summer day. The German bookkeepers dutifully entered in their ledgers the numbers that eventually would add up to six million. Let me personalize some of those numbers by telling you about the lives of my five sisters.

The oldest was Gela, born in 1903 while we were still in Galicia under Austrian rule. My parents, Isak and Esther Saleschutz already had one son, Avrum, when their daughter, whom they named Bluma-Gela was born. Since she was seventeen years older than I, I have no recollection of her childhood. Instead, I thought of her as my mother since she

The five Saleschutz sisters *(left to right: Matel, Lieba, Rachel, Gela and Malcia)* and the four Saleschutz brothers *(left to right: Albert, David, Leibush and Naftali)*, 1934, in Kolbuszowa during the visit of Albert from America. David was already in Palestine at this time and his picture has been inserted to have all nine siblings together. Albert was the oldest and Naftali the youngest.

and my sister Malcia were responsible for raising their little brother Naftali in that family of nine children. Perhaps it was the responsibility of being the oldest daughter that gave Gela her quiet, direct demeanor. A pretty girl with a small, non-Semitic nose, blue eyes, and round face, she could have easily been mistaken for a Polish woman, particularly since she spoke perfect Polish.

When Gela was nineteen a matchmaker brought to my father the prospect of her marrying Ruven Weinstein from Cracow. He was the grandson of the sexton, or *gabai*, to the renowned Sanzer rabbi, Chaim Halberstam. This lineage meant a great deal to my father. Rabbi Halberstam was nearly a legend, and if Jews had saints, I guess he might have qualified. He at least had the reputation of being a miracle worker. Ruven's grandfather, Rafael Zimetbaum as *gabai* to the Sanzer rabbi, was cloaked in the rabbi's prestige. Moreover, Ruven himself was reported to be more than just the descendant of a pious person. He had already attained a significant reputation as a scholar and had been able to recite long passages of the Talmud from memory since he was a boy. Ruven Weinstein was a scholarly prodigy, and the prospect of Gela marrying him produced enough excitement in the Saleschutz household to generate a hearty acceptance accompanied by a significant dowry. That's the way things were done in the Orthodox community then, and in some circles, now as well.

Ruven moved to Kolbuszowa after the wedding, and he and Gela temporarily set up housekeeping in part of our parents' house. It was intended to be just for a few months, until they found a suitable place for themselves. In fact, however, Ruven and Gela would remain as part of our household for the twenty more years they were destined to live. Ruven met every expectation for learning and teaching. He was unusually tall, perhaps the tallest man in Kolbuszowa, dark and distinguished. Graced with a beautiful voice, he led the prayers on the holidays, and as a child I would often sing with him in the *shul*. With part of the dowry my father had given them, they opened a textile store that prospered, and Ruven and Gela settled in for a life of pious obser-

Gela Saleschutz

vance, distracted, but not too seriously, by the requirements of commercial life in the textile business. Gela became involved in the local *Bikur Cholim*, an organization whose task it was to support members of the community who were ill, or who had just given birth. Eventually she assumed major responsibility in the *Bikur Cholim*, and the women in the community looked to her to assign them each day to their tasks, ranging from merely keeping the patient company to maintaining the family until health was restored.

It wasn't long before Gela became pregnant, and in 1924, four years after I was born, she had a girl whom they named Matil Szandel and whom the family called Szandel. Since Szandel was only four years younger than I, and since we all lived under the same roof, she in effect became like a little sister to me. Szandel was gifted with a beautiful voice inherited, I imagine, from both her father and the same strain of the Saleschutz family that gave me my musical abilities.

The household was a mixture of piety—Gela being just as religious as my father and mother—and gaiety. All of my sisters sang, and the evening prayers at our meals were rendered with perfect harmonizing. My sisters also sang the latest show tunes, which they picked up when traveling shows came through town. Sometimes they would take me with them. If not, they brought these songs home and taught them to me. Our house was filled with music, and that is how it remained until the Germans came in 1939. By then I was nineteen and Szandel, fifteen.

While Gela was quiet, her sister Malka, who we called "Malcia" was vivacious. Since she was named after my mother's sister who had died as a young woman in childbirth, her formal name was Alte Malka. Whenever someone was named for a person who had died at an early age, their name included "Alte" which meant "old," or "Chaia" which meant "life." Either way, the implication is clear. The intent is to ward off a repeat of early demise. The name Malka means queen in Hebrew, and naming her that was prescient. She was the prettiest of my sisters, with large, dark eyes, black hair, rosy cheeks and a delightful smile. In fact, there is a song called "Tayere Malkele" (Dear Malkele) that

Malcia Saleschutz

was written by a man named Nokhem Sternheim in 1922 for Malcia. Sternheim was a traveling performer, going from town to town in Poland playing and singing the equivalent of what today are called one-night stands. My father knew him very well, and whenever he came through Kolbuszowa, perhaps every other year, he would stay at our house. He was very much taken with Malcia and on one visit, when Malcia was six-teen, he laughingly promised to write a song about her. He was true to his word. He wrote "Tayere Malkele," which he performed that week for the people of the town. It made Malcia quite a temporary celebrity. Interest-ingly enough, the song can be found today in a book of Yiddish music col-lected by Chana Mlotek, called *Pearls of Yiddish Songs*. The lyrics translated by Mlotek are the following:

> Whoever has not seen Malkele
> Does not know what beauty and charm are.
> Dear Malkele.
> When she raises her brows
> The sun may feel ashamed.
> Dear Malkele
> When her eyes blaze
> A whole world bows to her.
> There is nothing more beautiful than
> Dear Malkele.
> Her joy brings paradise
> Dear Malkele.
> When her eyes sparkle
> It seems like seraphs are gazing.
> Dear Malkele.
> She is more lovely than Shulamis,
> Hotter than the month of Tamuz,
> Dear Malkele.
> Do other people have such *shabes-tsimes*
> Such Sabbath feasts
> Dear Malkele?
> Passover after the seder
> In festive clothes, in spite of our enemies,
> Who has such satisfaction,
> Dear Malkele, as we?

Malcia was just four years younger than Gela, and the two essentially took over my child rearing. In fact, until I was four years old, I always called Malcia "Mama."

Perhaps because she was so pretty, the family rebuffed the proposals made by the matchmaker until Malcia was twenty-nine years old, which was considered relatively old among Hasidic women for settling down to marriage. She had taken over much of the buying for my father's business after our brother Leibush married and established his own business. She would travel to surrounding cities such as Rzeszow and Cracow to visit our suppliers and order merchandise. She was quite an independent young woman when eventually, Szaya David Lische from Dembica was presented by the matchmaker. He was found to be of good lineage and acceptable by all parties, for he was the grandson of a famous rabbi. My father gave his new son-in-law the same handsome dowry of two thousand dollars that he had given Ruven Weinstein, bought him a house next to ours in the marketplace, and set him up in a flour-wholesaling business that had originally been part of his own expending business activities.

Szaya David did not disappoint. He proved to be an acute business-man, expanding the flour business and prospering. More importantly, he proved to be an excellent scholar. He became a *gabai* in the *shul* and was active in town and religious functions. In 1938, a year before the war, Malcia delivered an angelic child who was named Blimcia, after our grandmother Bluma Gela. Then in 1940 she had a second girl, Dobcia.

What a cruel time it was for these two beautiful little girls to come into the world. Much of their brief lives were lived out in the ghetto, where, once the Germans came, we all shared quarters. This intimate ghetto contact has proven cruel for me too. I became very attached to both girls, and when I brought them little treats from my journeys outside the ghetto walls, they would laugh and throw their arms around me and hug me. They were blond and blue-eyed, with golden hair, filled with laughter and play; it is their complete innocence and trust in the world, even as the Germans prepared to gas them, that haunts me most when I lie awake at night sixty years later.

In 1909, my sister Lieba Ryfka was born. The family was growing. With Gela and Malcia looking after me, Lieba turned toward helping my mother in other ways. She involved herself with the household and grad-ually took over responsibility for the daily kitchen activities. She was a wonderful cook, and the rich smell of challah or bread baking in the oven was constantly a part of the atmosphere we shared. And so it went until 1937 when the matchmaker presented Moses Kornfeld, a scholar who had attended the finest talmudic school in Europe, the Yeshiva Chachmey Lublin. Entry to this school was highly competitive, and the fact that Moses had been accepted spoke highly of his abilities. I knew one other person who went there, my childhood friend whom we called

Charlie, and Charlie was probably the only true genius I ever encountered. Moishe, as we called him, was a perfect match for Lieba, for while he wasn't officially ordained a rabbi, he like she, was intensely religious. In fact all of my sisters were.

Lieba Saleschutz

Moishe moved to Kolbuszowa from his hometown of Radomysl-Wielki after a gala wedding attended by virtually everyone in the Jewish community. Like the other sons-in-law, he received a two-thousand-dollar dowry, was set up in business, and moved into a house my father had bought for the newlyweds. His was a wholesale textile business, selling fabric to clothing manufacturers and the like.

Lieba soon brought two sons into the troubled world gathering about us. In 1938, Henoch was born and in 1940, after the Germans had arrived, Yossel began his short, and troubled life.

Yossel's life would have been troubled even without the Germans. He had been severely jaundiced after his circumcision.. This cleared up, but when he was a few months old we noticed that he had a problem. Unlike other children's eyes, which followed their mothers' fingers when they moved them, his eyes just stared straight ahead. This was during the early period in the occupation, and the German authority bent somewhat and gave us permission to travel by rail to Cracow, where an eye specialist could be consulted. There, the family received the devastating news that in all likelihood the yellow jaundice had damaged Yossel's optic nerve. He would be blind for life. His parents returned from Cracow with Yossel, burdened with knowledge of the doctor's verdict and determined to give everything to him that love could provide. Poor Yossel. As he became a toddler, he naturally waddled around, bumping into things he couldn't see. Little did his brother realize as he unknowingly challenged him, "What's the matter, are you blind?" that indeed he was. Even less could any of us imagine at the time that Yossel, just like the rest of the family, had but two years to live. In that respect, we were all blind.

Meanwhile, as the German grip tightened, its impact was felt everywhere, even in the children's play. Little Henoch and his friends used to act out in games, scenes that they saw about them. One day I came upon them imitating one of the more notorious German police officers we had, a man named Hafenbier. In the game Henoch pointed a piece of wood at his little friends, pretending it was a rifle.

"*Bist du Jude!*" he asked in a harsh voice. "*Jawohl*—Yes, we are Jews," they answered.

"Bang, bang, bang," Henoch yelled. "If you are a Jew, you are dead."

As the other children played out their roles by falling down, Henoch said, "*Ich bin Fafenbier.*" His mispronunciation of the villain's name provided the only light moment in this tragic reenactment. Perhaps Yossel was fortunate in being spared the sight of some of the ugliest moments in mankind's history.

By a twist of fate, Lieba became the breadwinner for the family once we had been moved into the ghetto. As with every unnatural division, the area that was declared ghetto was separated from that which was not ghetto by a boundary. In this case, there was a row of houses that faced inside the ghetto on one side and outside on the opposite side. The Germans had us put up bricks inside the house to wall off the portion facing outside the ghetto, thus sealing us in. However, in the house at the corner of the ghetto area, there was a gap in the brick work through which one could pass in and out of the ghetto without going through the formal gate.

Matil Saleschutz *(left)*

It happened that Lieba lived in that corner house, and the gap was recognized as a portal through which trade could be conducted. The Jews inside, pressed for survival, gradually sold off whatever assets they possessed to Poles on the outside. The Poles didn't offer much, but whatever it was, it helped keep life going inside the walls. Lieba acted as the agent, the go-between in these transactions, and for her trouble she was granted a small commission by all parties. As a result, our family, too, was able to survive with a little less hardship than would otherwise have occurred.

In 1911, my fourth sister Matil Szandel was born. She grew into a very different type of woman than her older sisters. Her interests extended outside the boundaries of our small community. She very early joined a local Zionist organization, Hanoar Hatzioni (Young Zionists), and she, like all of its members, learned to speak fluent Hebrew. Instead of becoming involved with the household as Lieba did, Matil turned to our father's business. He taught her the subtleties of the trade, and before long she was doing all of the billing, bookkeeping, dealing with customers, and taking responsibility for more and more of the daily activity. Matil was part of the "women's movement" before such a thing existed.

The matchmaker's failure to come up with anyone suitable or acceptable for her only extended her opportunity for involvement in the business, and ultimately my father decided that she would inherit and run it. None of my brothers showed any inclination toward it, and I made it known that my interests lay in going to Palestine. So by the time the war broke out, Matil, at age twenty-eight, was a poised young woman, fluent in Hebrew and more importantly for the moment, Polish. With her Slavic features, she could easily have passed in the general community as a Pole. She chose, instead, to remain with the family, identified as a Jew, and on that July day in 1942, joined her family and neighbors in the Belzec gas chamber.

My youngest sister, Reisel Rachel, was born in 1917, only three years before I was, so my childhood years coincided with hers to a greater extent than with those of any of the others. Rachel was special in the family, not only because she was the youngest girl, but also because she was the smartest student in the school. Everyone was attracted to her quick intelligence. She, too, joined the Zionist organization, Hanoar Hatzioni and before long became its local head. Her plan was to go to Palestine, so even though she worked in the store like her older sister Matil, and like her, acquired good language skills in Hebrew, English, German, and Polish, there was never any thought on her part that she would remain in Kolbuszowa. Rachel was open to all kinds of ideas that were seen as radical in the Orthodox world of our childhood. The doings of the birds and the bees were not readily available to Hasidic youth, but somehow Rachel had acquired a book that made it all clear. She shared her treasure, a book called *Tajemnica Zycia Pow-*

Rachel Saleschutz

stajacego or *The Secrets of the Beginning of Life* with me. I, in turn, shared its contents, including the pictures of naked men and women, with my friends, who I am afraid shared information about its existence with so many that the knowledge eventually found its way to the leaders of the Talmud Torah we attended. They dismissed me from the school.

Part of Rachel's free spirit included her rejection of the notion of a matchmaker arranging her future for her. Instead, she came home one day and announced that she was interested in a young man who was a student in the local gymnasium named Chaim Lieber. When he left for Palestine as a student in the Hebrew University in Jerusalem, she soon found another romantic interest named Avrum Leidner. This time it was true love and they planned to be married. The only rift that divided them was Rachel's desire to go to Palestine, while Avrum wanted to go to America. They argued over this, and eventually Avrum prevailed. It was decided. He would go to America and Rachel would follow.

While my three older sisters had had large wedding parties, Rachel had an engagement party two weeks before Avrum left. We bought him a gold watch as an engagement present. The wedding, it was clear, would be in America at some time in the future. The plan turned out to have a fatal flaw. A week after Avrum's departure, the Germans invaded Poland, and Rachel's opportunity to follow her fiancé was lost.

Still, she could have saved herself from the fate that she and her sisters met. Because she spoke fluent German, Rachel became secretary to a German who was the head of the labor office, *Arbeitsamt*. She was so intelligent and independent that it is not surprising she became invaluable to her boss, and he offered her a job outside the ghetto when the family was evacuated from Kolbuszowa to Rzeszow. Rachel said she would take the position, if he could assure her that her mother and sisters would be allowed to remain in the Rzeszow ghetto and not moved again for "resettlement." He was unable to provide those assurances, so Rachel didn't take the job that might have saved her life alone.

Later on, she started to get forged papers that would have allowed her to live outside the ghetto in a distant town. She wanted my girl friend, Rozia Susskind, to go with her, but Rozia didn't have the self-confidence that Rachel possessed. She was afraid she could not sustain the masquerade on the outside, and once again, Rachel passed up an opportunity to extricate herself from the trap that was closing down on all of us.

These then, were my five sisters. Not a day goes by that I don't think of them. I think of how the high-spirited Matil and Rachel used to smuggle me out of *cheder* to take me to the movies. They knew I loved the musicals with gypsies dancing and playing and wanted me to share the shows with them. Of course, the movies was no place for a Hasidic boy. They would tuck my curls up under my hat and walk close to me on either side so anyone seeing us might think they were with Szandel. My father would roar with displeasure when he learned I had abandoned my studies, even for a day, for something so frivolous as the movies.

I remember Lieba taking dancing lessons from Josef Haar, an itinerant dance teacher and then coming home to teach us all the shimmy, the one step, and of course, the Charleston, which we spelled "Czarlston." I went to watch the dancing lessons being given, and since we had no Victrola in the house, I would provide the music by singing the songs Josef Haar had played from his records. In my mind, I hear the music that was constantly in the house.

I hear Rachel, with her strong, clear voice singing with fervor the Zionist songs that she knew would be part of her destiny. I hear Matil and Lieba humming the show tunes they were so fond of.

There is not a day that the criss-crossed threads that tied our lives together don't appear in one form or another in my dreams. Little Blimcia's blond curls are as clear today as they were sixty years ago. Henoch, Yossel, my brother Leibush's children, Szulim, Szlomo and Rozia; my sister Gela's daughter Szandel, my brothers-in-law Ruven Weinstein, Szaya David Lische, and Moses Kornfeld, my mother Esther, my father Isak. All but my father were killed on the same day; he, two months earlier in the Kolbuszowa ghetto.

Whenever I am in *shul*, and the mourners rise to say Kaddish, I rise with them. I rise because I am in perpetual mourning. As I recite the words of the Kaddish, I visualize the face of one of those who perished during the Holocaust, and I say the Kaddish for that particular person at that particular time. I do this because there is no one else left to do it. They are all gone, like so many dried leaves that blow along the ground before the autumn wind. By the spring, they have vanished without a memory or a trace. The dead, as well as those who would mourn them, have lived and died and, except for me, and a few like me, no one in the world knows their names, what they did, who they loved, or for that matter, that they were ever here at all.

A Letter by an Inmate of the Ghetto
Recounts the Struggle to Survive

Following is an authentic translation of an original letter in Polish sent by an inmate of the Lubaczow Ghetto in Poland to his cousin, who saved it in spite of untold hardships. The letter was translated and made available to the *Jewish News* by Norman Salsitz, of Springfield, who is himself a survivor of several German labor camps and who during the war was also active in the Jewish and Polish underground.

Lubaczaw, Oct. 10, 1942
My dear and loved ones:

As you can see, I survived another few months, waiting with fear for death. But, so far, we still live. During these months I lost many of my family and friends. It does not matter. We have grown calloused and egotistical. We only think of ourselves, we even can no longer cry over the loss of a dear one because in our hearts we know we will go there too and then there will be no one left to cry for us.

The High Holidays have passed and we all lived in the illusion that the war will end. But now, we see that after all that is happening that we are lost and that there is no longer any hope.

We passed the *Yahrzeit* [anniversary of death] for our dear mother, God rest her soul. I did everything possible under the circumstances to observe the day. It does not matter if the cemetery was destroyed or not, but I am glad to know that our parents were buried in their own plot instead of having been sent to Belzec to be cremated and the remains to be used as fertilizer or made into soap.

It is unbelievable that our children are being killed and what is left is being processed for canned food. Their clothing is being stripped off their backs to be sent to Germany to be used.

In fourteen days we observe *Yahrzeit* for our dear father. Will we live until then? We don't know.

We do know that our "action" [the term "action" (*Aktion*) was a euphemism for deportation of the Jews to a death camp] must be near because they are gathering Jews from surrounding villages, and as soon as they have rounded up about six thousand Jews a transport will be ready for Belzec.

I cannot tell you how poor we are. It is now eight months since we were forced to leave our house. Part of our furniture was sold. The rest was confiscated and a little bit we still have. But we don't have a chance at all to run away. We cannot hide because the Gentiles would not hide us because of the risk to themselves if they are caught hiding Jews.

I will leave here a few souvenirs that belonged to my parents. Maybe you will be able to get them. At any rate, write a letter to the enclosed address in Lubaczow [the address of a Gentile friend] to claim these souvenirs.

These are not expensive things, but dear and important mementoes to me, and some photos and documents. I also do not want my house to fall in the hands of [names deleted] because they refused to help us. Therefore, if someone of the family should by chance survive and remain in Europe, they can sell the house, or should they wish, live there as long as they want.

There is a jar filled with souvenirs buried in the cellar, to which I have added some of my own.

Anyway, should we be able to survive the next transport and the war would go on, it would be impossible for us to exist much longer because all our belongings are gone and sooner or later we shall die from hunger.

As it is, I looked death in the eye. They were going to shoot me. I was already tied to a telephone pole but a miracle saved me.

My crime was that on a very hot day I carried a pail of water to a waiting transport filled with people from Cracow and Wieliczka who begged for water for the small children.

There were a hundred people in sealed freight cars jammed together. My heart was filled with pity so I got some water for them. Of course, I got caught by an SS man. I did not beg for my life. I did not care any more.

I thought it was better to end it all right here then to go by train like that to Belzec. I live near the station, and I can see the trains passing by. My heart bursts with every passing train.

One more thing I would like to find out before I die: Are Saul and his family still living? Since Shavuot I did not hear from his wife, and it is over a year since I heard from him.

If I had a few thousand zlotys, I would try what others are doing because with my non-Jewish features it would be very easy. Barefoot and penniless, it is impossible to try something like that.

This is the third letter I have written to you to let you know at what time the end for us will come.

There are a few Gentile families who treat us well, especially the owner of our building. I only pray to God I should be able to repay her kindness. If we shall not be around, I beg of you to do this for us because when we were thrown out from our house, she took us in and treated us like human beings. So much for today. Maybe 1 will be able to write another letter.

Many kisses,
Lola

The Escape

By 2:00 A.M. everyone but Laizer and I had slipped away from the labor camp. I had planned the escape for weeks, because I knew it was only a matter of time before the Germans would decide we had outlived our usefulness and kill us all. Convincing my fellow inmates had not been easy. I was asking them to trade the temporary security of the camp for the risks of being on the run in a hostile countryside. Had we been in Denmark, Bulgaria, France, or Italy, we might have expected support from the general population. Not in Poland. Most of the peasants could be expected to be every bit as eager to kill us as were their German occupiers. For that reason, those willing to attempt the escape were limited to people who had personal contacts among the peasants from before the war, and who had enough money to buy their help. Altogether, fifty-five of the labor camp inmates would make the run for freedom. Within one week, only twenty-five would still be alive. Most of the rest would be killed or turned over to the Germans by Poles.

I turned to Laizer and said, "Everyone else that I was able to persuade to escape is gone. It is our turn. You cross the road first, and I will follow."

Laizer said, "I can't go first. What if something happens to you and you cannot follow me. I can't even speak Polish. You go, and I will follow as soon as I see you have made it."

I knew he was right. The fellow I called Laizer had been born Lazarus Spielman in Karlsruhe, Germany. He was more German than Polish, dressing, looking, acting, and speaking like the German he was. His only problem was that he was also Jewish, and when the Nazis took power and expelled the Jews, his family had no choice but to return to Kolbuszowa, the town his parents had left for Germany some twenty-five years earlier. The Spielman family had to leave everything behind. When they returned to Poland they were penniless and were fortunate to move in with the grandmother. Laizer's father now eked out a living by chopping firewood for the Jews in Kolbuszowa. At the time, Laizer was my age, nine-

The author *(right)* with Lazarus "Laizer" Spielman. This photograph was taken a week before the planned escape from the labor camp in anticipation of using it later on identification documents. Spielman was killed during the escape attempt.

teen, and we became good friends. It turned out that he was distantly related to me, his mother being my mother's cousin.

That he spoke no Polish did not affect his relationships with the Jews of the community. Yiddish was the language we all used. Since Jewish children attended the public school, we all had to study the language. But the only time after childhood that a Jew spoke Polish was if he had to deal with a Pole in business or on some governmental matter. The result was that many Jews whose families had lived in Poland for generations nevertheless spoke the language poorly and with a heavy accent. Since our family had an active business in town, and we dealt with Poles daily, I spoke the language like a native, a skill that would allow me to survive.

The arrival of the Germans proved to be a boon to the fortunes of the Spielman family. The Judenrat was required to send a quota of Jews each day to work for them. Laizer was assigned to work at the police station, and when he showed up in his German clothes, (the only ones he owned) with his German bearing and his fluency in the language, the Germans immediately put him to work dealing with the Judenrat and with the Jewish prisoners who had been arrested. It became apparent to both the Germans and the Judenrat that Laizer was valuable as a go-between, and after a while, the Judenrat paid him a wage to remain in the employ of the German police. He reported to the police station every day, and pretty soon the Polish peasants also began to think of this very German-looking civilian youth as someone who could be in a position to do them favors should they need one. They paid him in produce such as eggs, chickens, and meat, and he in turn interceded on behalf of both Jews and Gentiles if he could.

Since I was recognized as his friend, they would sometimes approach me to ask him to help. Laizer would take nothing from the Jews beyond what the Judenrat paid him. He had no hesitation, however, in accepting whatever the Poles offered, and as a result, his family lived far better under the occupation than they had before. Laizer had a pass from the police to come and go at will, and I would often have him accompany me on my trips to Rzeszow. While I, too, had approval to go, I did not have the cloak of official protection that he bore.

When the Jews were moved into the ghetto, he and his family were moved in as well, and when the ghetto was emptied and the Jews moved to Rzeszow, Laizer and his brother were chosen to join the group that remained in the labor camp to dismantle the ghetto. Meanwhile, he retained his employment by the police and kept his odd dual identity of Jewish prisoner and police functionary in our labor camp.

I was the principal agitator among the labor camp group for mounting an escape. Because of my relative freedom of movement in and out of the camp, I had a sense that conditions for Jews were worsening in occupied Poland. The ghetto in Rzeszow had been emptied and its occupants, including the Jews from Kolbuszowa had been sent to Belzec in July. The massacre at Nowa-Wies had taken place in September. I knew it was only a matter of time before our turn would come.

It was easy to go in and out of the camp. Normally the gate wasn't guarded. Escaping permanently, however, required planning. You had to have some place to go and someone who would hide you. I arranged to get papers for myself and my brother Leibush through a woman I knew. I had her contact her priest with the request that he provide me with the birth certificate of a Polish school friend of mine, a boy named Tadeusz Jadach, who had been born about the same time as I was, but who was killed in September 1939 in the army. I requested papers with a similar history for Leibush. The priest complied, and the same woman agreed to hide me in her attic for a few days, should I escape. Others whom I persuaded to flee made similar arrangements. Some would prove reliable; others, tragically less so.

I had gone around to all of the occupants of the camp with the message that liquidation of the camp was imminent. Our work dismantling the ghetto was finished. They were sure to kill us. Nearly half rebuffed me, offering various reasons. I remember going to Motel Kornbluth, a handsome, blue-eyed, blond youth who shrugged and said, "God will do with me what He will do." Chaim Josef Offen, a sixteen-year-old scholar whose family had been friendly with my father, said, "I will stay. If I am killed, then I will join my mother and father and brothers and sisters." I went to Hirsh Gewirtz, who had been a prominent member of the community and secretary of the Judenrat. He was in the camp with his brother and two sons.

Jadzia Burkiewicz was the non-Jewish telephone operator in Kolbuszowa. She allowed the author to maintain contact with the Jews in Rzeszow and anticipate events, since any action taken by the Gestapo in Rzeszow would soon take place in the Kolbuszowa labor camp.

"I can't run," he said. "If I do, I will be caught and killed. This way, maybe they will let me live out the war in Rzeszow."

The common problem faced by most of those who stayed was that they had nowhere to go; no one who would hide them; no money to buy protection.

Two Jews had been put in charge of the camp, Henry Mund and Yossel Rappaport. Naturally, they opposed my plans for escape. They called me a troublemaker and threatened to turn me over to the Germans if I kept on instigating the others. When I told them that it didn't matter, that I would be gone in the morning, they posted guards at the gate. The guards they selected, Laizer and another fellow, named Binnim Rosenbaum, had already decided to escape, however, and in the end Mund and Rappaport were persuaded to simply look the other way. The night of our escape, they got drunk.

Laizer, like so many of the others, argued that he had no money. Worse, he didn't speak Polish and had no reliable contacts on the outside. I told him not to worry. I thought of him as a special friend; and because of that, I would provide all the money we needed, and he would be with me and my brother Leibush. He argued that he would be protected by his friends in the police department, but I told him I had seen too many Jews used by the Germans until their usefulness was over, and then they were the last to be executed. No German, it seemed, wanted to protect even his "favorite Jew." We all had to perish.

By the time Laizer and I lay by the fence preparing to make a break for it, the German presence in the area had become pronounced. They did plan to evacuate the camp in the morning and were securing the surrounding area. We had to go now, because the next morning it would be too late. Yet the odds of making it had been substantially reduced with the Germans and the Polish police on high alert. As we debated who should go first, reflectors roamed the road outside the compound. These guided searchlights, and the Germans moved them from place to place, suddenly lighting up an area in hope of catching someone in the beam.

I consented to Laizer's logic that if I didn't make it, he didn't stand a chance and agreed that I should make the attempt first. I had loosened two boards on the fence earlier in the evening, and now I raised them and wriggled through. Once outside, I had to make it across a road to get to an outhouse on the opposite side. From there, we would exit the back and cross the fields to the attic that would shelter us. My brother was already out, and in his hiding place in the neighboring village.

I lay for a moment at the side of road, and when the light had moved on, I got onto my hands and knees to minimize my profile, and crawled across the street to the shelter of the outhouse. Breathless, even though the distance had been short, I huddled in the darkness and waited for Laizer.

Suddenly, I heard a fusillade of shots. The street was lit up by the German searchlight. There were men running, shouting in German. Dogs barked. I lay quietly in the outhouse. Ten minutes went by. I realized that Laizer wasn't going to keep the rendezvous we had planned.

I slipped out of the back and made my way across the field to the attic.

The Overcrowding of the Lifeboat

It was clear to me that Twardon would not keep us alive over the winter of 1942–43. Our crew in the Kolbuszowa labor camp had just about completed its task of dismantling the remains of the ghetto after the Jews had been shipped off and there was little more need for us. We would either be sent to one of the death camps or we would be shot right here. Twardon, the regional Landskomissar, was a cruel and ruthless tyrant. We expected no mercy from him.

This set of circumstances made escape essential. Escaping from the camp itself would be relatively easy. Security was lax. Surviving for a long period after escape was something else. One had to plan ahead of time and arrange a hiding place. For the most part the Poles would not hide Jews; quite the contrary. The average Pole felt it his duty—indeed his joy, to turn in escaped Jews to the Germans. One had to locate one of the select group of Poles who, either because of past relationships or because of substantial payments, would run the risk of sheltering Jews. And it was a risk. If they were caught, they would be shot along with the Jews they harbored.

I approached several likely prospects whom I knew to see if they would shelter my brother Leibush and me. We had hidden a great deal of wealth with which to bribe them. We could offer clothing, quilts, linens, household items, silver. We had my sisters' jewelry and fur coats. We could offer all this because, sadly, our five sisters and entire family had either already been killed or were in Belzec death camp. Their owners would not be using them again.

These items had all been hidden in Rzeszow. I offered them to Vichta Starzec, a poor woman who, before the war, had worked as a maid for several Jewish families, mine and Leibush's among them. Vichta and her twelve-year-old daughter Wladka lived in a two-room house close to the Rzeszow-Kolbuszowa road. Her husband was in Argentina. In exchange for these possessions, she agreed to hide me, my brother Leibush, and also Moishe and Arek Weichselbaum and Laizer Spielman and Noah Hutner, my best friends. Moishe, Arek, Laizer, and Noah had no money to pay Vichta. But, it was clear that we had enough to pay her to shelter all of us for a long time. She could sell the clothing and use the money to feed us. And so it was arranged that Vichta would take in the six of us.

We escaped on November 18, 1942. I had been informed by Patyk, the commandant of the Polish police, that the Germans had scheduled our liquidation for that evening. Leibush and I tried to convince as many of our companions as possible to join in the break. Unfortunately, Noah changed his mind and decided to stay in the camp with his younger brother. While seeking to organize others in the effort, Leibush spoke to his neighbor, Froim Brodt, who in despair said that he would gladly run away from the camp, but he had no place to hide and no money with which to bribe a Pole to hide him. Impulsively, Leibush told him, "You can stay with us and take Noah's place." And so as Brodt prepared to leave the camp in response to this unexpected good fortune, he sought out two of his friends to tell them he was leaving with Leibush to be hidden by Vichta. These two, Israel Meyer Stub and his brother Itche, who also had no place to hide and no money, wished Brodt good luck, but began to brood on his good luck and their own fate.

We began slipping out of the camp at 8:00 P.M. Leibush and Froim went directly to Vichta's house. Next, the Weichselbaums left, but before going to Vichta, they decided that they wanted to retrieve some of their possessions being held by a Polish machinist named Pruchnik, who had worked for their father's lumber and flour mill, and who had moved into their house and taken over all of their furniture. Pruchnik took them in and they hid in his attic for two days before moving on to Vichta's house. By the time Laizer and I left the camp at 3:00 A.M. a total of fifty-three of us had already escaped.

Tragedy struck at the last minute. The guards spotted Laizer running. He was shot and killed. I managed to get away, but rather than going to Vichta, I decided to hide out with another friendly Pole, and I remained in her attic for the next three days. Of the fifty-five who escaped, thirty were caught by Poles in the first three days and given over to the German police, who shot them on the spot.

And so the scene right after the break saw Froim and Leibush at Vichta's house. The Weichselbaums were hiding with Pruchnik. Laizer was dead and I was in hiding elsewhere in the town. It was at this point the same night that the Stub brothers appeared at Vichta's door. Vichta knew they were not part of our plan and refused to let them in. However, they told her they had a message from me for Leibush, and she let them in to learn what the message was. Once inside, they greeted their friend Froim, and the group began to talk about the events of the night. As dawn approached, Vichta told them they had best get to their hiding place or they would be seen, whereupon, the Stub brothers announced that they had no place to go and they intended to remain right where they were in Vichta's house. "If you force us to leave, and we are caught, we will inform the Germans that you are here, and they will catch you as well."

Vichta and Leibush had no choice. The Stubs would remain, but that raised the number to eight: Leibush and me, Froim and Laizer (they didn't know he had been killed), the two Weichselbaums, and now the Stub brothers. Eight Jews, six of whom had no money, in a tiny cottage attic near the main road. Impossible.

Two nights later, the Weichselbaums arrived to claim the spot planned for them. Vichta, however, saw that the Stub brothers had taken over their spot, and with tears in her eyes refused to let them in. They pleaded with her, but she said that no, there was no room and they would have to find someplace else. They made no threats. They did not say they would expose the others if they were caught. They just left.

Fearfully, they returned to Pruchnik the machinist, who once again took them in and hid them in the attic. However, Pruchnik realized that he had no interest in protecting Moishe and Arek. After all, he was living in their family's house, enjoying their family's things. Why should he jeopardize any of that? The next morning, he went to the police station and turned in Moishe and Arek Weichselbaum. The police came, took the brothers from the attic down to the unfinished railroad station, Kolejowka, stood them against the wall, and shot them.

Three days later when I arrived at Vichta's house, I learned of the tragic turn of events. Froim and the two Stub brothers were safe in Vichta's house. Laizer was dead. Moishe was dead. Arek was dead. Of our original group of boyhood friends who planned to escape together, only Leibush and I had made it.

After three weeks, Leibush and I were forced to leave Vichta's house and joined a group living in the forest. Froim and the Stub brothers remained at Vichta's house until the liberation. They all survived the war. My store of goods had been sufficient to sustain them in relative comfort.

I often reflect on the irony of what happened that November of 1942. The Stub brothers behaved brutishly, bullying their way into the security of Vichta's home. The Weichselbaums behaved in a gentle, yielding fashion and were killed for their gentleness. Chance held them up for two days while their place was taken at Vichta's house. The decision of Noah to remain at the camp had opened the conversation between Leibush and Froim. Such little things determined who would live and who would die in that dreadful period in history.

Tarzan

There were about a hundred of us hiding out in the woods in the spring of 1943. Because we were Jews, the Poles considered us to be their enemies, and we were hated as much as the Germans. During the winter of 1942–43, we had one bunker that could hold up to twenty people. This bunker hid the women, the elderly, the sick, and "Tarzan."

"Tarzan" was the nickname we had given to the energetic eighteen-month-old boy who had been born in the woods. He, like all the Jewish children of Poland, was considered an enemy of the state because his parents, "Langer" Avrum Seiden and his wife, were Jewish. We called the child "Tarzan" because he always ran around naked. When it was cold, he was wrapped in a blanket.

Tarzan endeared himself to all of us with his innocent joy of living.

His happiness was infectious. We would have forgotten how to laugh were it not for Tarzan.

Tarzan loved to roam about naked. If someone attempted to bundle him for warmth, he would indignantly kick his little legs fiercely and twist his tiny, sturdy body until he was free. Once, an elderly woman in our group managed to get enough yarn together to knit him a sweater. She was proud of her achievement. It kept the woman happily employed whenever conditions allowed her to spend a few hours outdoors.

Alas, the child was totally unappreciative. When his mother put it on him, he screamed with such intensity that she quickly removed it, lest someone hear him. Tarzan's contempt for clothes served him well. He was the only one among us to escape the torment of lice, because on him they had no place to hide.

Tarzan was affectionately raised by all of us.

When we returned to the bunker after a day or a week of bone-wearying work building another bunker, Tarzan would entertain us with his baby jabber and funny faces. He used to call us all "Dada."

While those unable to work spent their days in anxiety and boredom in the dark dampness of the bunker, the rest of us hid in the protective brush of the forest. In the evenings we slept near the bunker or with the few friendly peasants who lived near the forest. I had adopted the name Tadeusz "Tadek" Jadach for my excursions into the outside world. Only a handful of us were able to impersonate Catholic Poles.

I spoke perfect Polish and had Slavic features so I could easily pass. Most of my fellow Jews were not as fortunate.

The winter was the worst time for us in the forest. Whenever it snowed we had to stay in one place for days and sometimes weeks, because we did not dare disturb the smooth snow with our footprints. If the snowfall was wet and mixed with rain, our wet clothing

Tadeusz Jadach, a Catholic classmate of the author, went into the Polish army and was killed in September 1939. Being aware of this and recognizing that he bore him some physical resemblance, the author arranged to get his birth certificate for ID purposes. This picture was provided after the war by Jadach's sister.

quickly froze onto our bodies and became stiff, like sheets of ice. We walked like mannequins.

The clothes on our backs were all we owned, and thus, we had to wait for them to dry on our bodies. Sometimes this took days. We would sleep on spruce branches during nights of heavy snowfall in temperatures reaching twenty degrees below zero. Then we would wake up under two or three feet of snowfall which covered us completely.

Despite these hardships, I had vowed never to spend a day in a bunker. I would rather kill myself than have to spend another day underground. I had once been forced to stay in a bunker after I had escaped from the labor camp. The experience was dreadful, and it still haunts me to this day. I felt as if I was being buried alive. The bunker was pitch black and coolly damp. The air was heavy with the stench of manure. We were helpless to protect ourselves from the lice that thrived on our moist clothes. Now and then some brackish water that had a peculiar odor would drip down. I later learned where it came from. The cows put to pasture above us had to urinate.

I remembered vividly not being able to stand up; not being able to see, to breathe. Time stood still. This was death. I couldn't believe I was there for only one day—no more than twenty-four hours.

That March our group decided to build a second bunker. We had thought it would be safer for us to be in a bunker than outdoors in the winter. I threw myself into the work although I knew I would never use the bunker.

Building a bunker in total secrecy was backbreaking labor. First, we dug a hole about fifteen by twenty feet and five feet deep. We had to dig at night to avoid being seen. We would place the dirt in sacks, which we carried on our backs a few kilometers in several directions and then carefully disposed of so there would be no signs of fresh dirt. Next, we cut young trees, being careful to select trees located several kilometers away and spaced a good distance apart. The trees were used to support the ceiling, which was com-

Monsignor Antoni Dunajecki, head of the Catholic church in Kolbuszowa, provided the birth certificate of Tadeusz Jadach to the author. He did this as an act of conscience when informed by a Catholic parishoner of the need.

posed of logs. On top of the logs we placed about a foot of dirt. In the dirt we planted trees.

A passerby would never guess that living quarters were situated here. The "door" to our bunker was a tree that could be removed to reveal a two-foot by two-foot entrance. Our new bunker would be an exact replica of the old one.

Inside the bunker we built a brick stove with a small chimney that disappeared between the moss and leaves. We did an excellent job. Our bunker was completely camouflaged.

Who could have imagined that we, mainly yeshiva scholars, merchants, and storekeepers, could have adapted so well to the wilderness? We, who were forbidden even to serve as Boy Scouts, were now living in the woods like primitive tribesmen. Necessity is a good teacher, I thought.

While we were working on the new bunker, every few nights some of us would go to the old bunker to check on the others, bring them food, change tools, and find out the news.

Avrum Seiden, Eli Katz, Leiba Leibowicz and I went on such a routine visit on March 19, 1943, when the first stage of our work was almost completed. The three women, the elderly men, and the infirm would be glad to hear how far we had progressed.

When we reached the section of the forest that hid the old bunker, we knew right away that something was wrong. There was no guard posted at the usual place. Broken branches could be seen throughout the vicinity of the bunker. My heart was gripped with fear as we entered the area of the bunker with our guns drawn. Then we halted in shocked silence when we saw what had happened.

It was a massacre. The ground was strewn with naked bodies, ripped open and mutilated. Little Tarzan lay next to his mother. Both their heads were split open. All together there were eighteen bodies. Eighteen defenseless people savagely killed. It looked as if wild animals had attacked them.

I was horrified. I watched in despair as "Langer" Avrum picked up his dead infant and knelt to kiss his lifeless wife.

Someone mentioned that we had better go. The murderers might be waiting for us. We put the bodies in the open bunker and covered them with branches. We then returned to the nearly completed bunker that we would never use, to tell our comrades the grisly news. We knew who was responsible for the murders. There was no doubt in our minds that our fellow countrymen, the neighboring Poles, had committed this deed. By the way the bodies were destroyed, we knew they had been killed, not with guns, but with the crude tools of the Polish peasants—axes, knives, and pitchforks. And for what reason? Just to get rid of a few Jews and to confiscate the meager clothes and shoes the helpless Jews wore? It was common knowledge that the acquisition of rags was sufficient cause for Polish peasants to kill Jews. It happened often.

But we had to learn what happened. Leiba and I visited a friendly peasant, Jan Chodor, to find out. Jan told us. The *wojt* (mayor) of the village Kupno had called the villagers together to inform them that he had learned that Jews were hiding in the woods in an underground shelter they had built. It was their duty to kill them. As an incentive he told the people that each participant in this effort could take whatever clothing, footwear, and money he found as a reward.

There was no shortage of volunteers. One hundred Poles from two villages, Kupno and Poremby-Kupienskie, joined in the raid under the leadership of the *wojt*. The surprise attack was launched at 6 A.M. One by one the captives were taken out and slaughtered.

Jan broke into tears. "I knew them all, they were my friends," he said.

It was as we suspected. Three days later we returned to our fellow partisans and discussed how to inter the bodies of our loved ones.

We returned to the bunker where they lay. We dug one deep grave next to the bunker and buried them together. The brief funeral service was recited by my brother Leibush.

We decided not to bury them in the bunker. They had spent many long months underground in the dark, praying and hoping to survive the war. It wasn't fair that they should be locked forever in the hole where they had spent their unhappiest hours, their only escape —death. No. We would leave the bunker open and empty as an eternal monument to our friends and relatives who were murdered in cold blood, not by their wartime enemy, the Germans, but by their age old enemy—their Polish neighbors.

The Kielbasa Pusher

Try it. Everybody is doing it now." I heard these very words that tempt our children with drugs nowadays during the darkest days of the war. What was being pushed? Not crack, not heroin, but kielbasa.

I came from an extremely religious family. My father was a devoted Hasid, and until the age of seventeen I attended yeshiva. The laws of *kashruth* were strictly observed in our household, and none more strictly than the prohibition against pork products. The thought of pork made me gag. To touch or smell pork products was forbidden; to taste it unthinkable.

Since my father had a store and dealt with a Gentile clientele, however, we certainly came in contact with customers who themselves had no such prohibitions. In fact, when the Gentile peasants came to Kolbuszowa to stock up on supplies, they inevitably bought pork products along with everything else. It was not unusual for them to want to leave those things they had already acquired with us while they went on to do the rest of their shopping. We set up a special pork room in which they could leave their sausages and other pork products. We never went in the room, but the peasants regularly availed themselves of the opportunity. On one occasion, I remember, I did go into the room and smelled, for the first time, smoked pork sausage. I threw up.

After the ghetto was liquidated, I shared a room with twenty-five other young men who had been conscripted into a labor gang. Our job was to destroy the buildings that remained in the ghetto. Unlike most other Jews held in camps, we were comparatively well fed. We had bakers in our camp who baked bread for the Polish population. Each day, they would hold out a hundred loaves for the camp inmates before making delivery. We also had constant contact with the countryside and could trade with the peasants.

One of the items that could be obtained was kielbasa, the Polish pork sausage. Naturally it held no interest for me—only revulsion. However, not all Polish Jews had been raised in Hasidic households, and one of the less observant roommates offered to share some kielbasa with me.

I refused to touch it. The next day, it was offered again, and I again rejected it. He persisted. "Come on," he would say. "It is wartime. The rules are different. You don't lay *tefillin* like you used to, do you? Just touch it."

Day after day, in friendly prodding he got me to weaken my almost visceral rejection. The repetition of the exposure to the pork sausage held in his hand gradually desensitized me to its implications. One day, I tentatively touched it. Another day I held it in my hand for a brief period. He induced me to smell it, to lick it, to put it in my mouth. But, like a good teenage girl, I would go so far and no further. I would even chew it, but I never swallowed the kielbasa. I remained a virgin.

Things were different after we escaped to the woods. There was no bakery. There were no hundred loaves. There was only cold and hunger. We ran constantly to avoid discovery.

I guess I should thank my persistent kielbasa pusher from the camp. There came a time when I was offered kielbasa, not as a joke or a temptation, but as a means to survive. I put it into my mouth, I chewed, and for the first time, I went all the way—I swallowed.

That day is vivid in my memory for all it represents. Exigency had battered down the walls of tradition. The fabric had finally torn. After that, I stayed alive by eating, among other regular staples in my diet, the dreaded pork kielbasa.

A Justified Revenge

It was October 1942 and our work in the labor camp was nearly completed. We had been assigned the task of dismantling the houses of the ghetto in Kolbuszowa after the Jews had been evacuated to Rzeszow. Room by room we had progressed through the houses of our neighbors and friends of a lifetime, warehousing anything of value for the Germans and destroying the rest. It was heartbreaking as well as backbreaking work, and now it was just about over. When it was, we were sure, we would no longer be needed by Landskomissar Twardon. We would be killed.

It was with that inevitability in mind that we planned our escape from the camp into the countryside. Such an escape was not particularly difficult to execute. We were loosely guarded and able to enter and leave the camp easily. More difficult would be survival after we escaped. The countryside was populated by a generally hostile Polish nation, long on anti-Semitism and not likely to be given to hiding or supporting Jews fleeing the Germans. There were a few, however, who might be induced to help if financial reward could be arranged. A few others had prior relationships through business and felt a loyalty or a guilt that could be converted to our advantage.

There were a hundred of us in the camp by early November 1942. Of that number, on November 18, fifty-five fled one evening, just ahead of the German and Polish police, into the countryside. I want to tell you here, the story of two of the families that fled: Moshe Rosenbaum, his son, Binnim, and son-in-law, David Feit, and two brothers, Archie Glazel and Moshek Glazel, who were close friends of the Rosenbaums. The Glazel brothers and the Rosenbaums had been butchers before the war, and they had had an employee of more than twenty years duration, a man named Posluszny, who lived in Nowa-Wies. An arrangement had been made before the escape for Posluszny to prepare a bunker under his barn where Moshe Rosenbaum and Binnim and the Glazel brothers would hide. David Feit had made arrangements to be hidden by a Polish family who lived in Werynia, the next village, some four kilometers to the north. Naturally, Posluszny wasn't hiding his employers of twenty years out of friendship or a sense of loyalty. They paid him an agreed-upon sum in return for the shelter.

For six months after the escape the four hid out in the bunker during the day. At night they would walk around a bit inside the barn. Never did they venture outside. For six months Moshe made his regular payment and Posluszny provided security and sustenance. David Feit, meanwhile, was living in the neighboring village, and each Saturday night and Sunday, when the German and Polish police were least active, he would journey to the bunker to visit his father and brother-in-law.

The arrangement went smoothly until Moshe reached the end of his money. When he told Posluszny that he had no more money with him, but would make it up to him after the war, Posluszny avowed that that would be fine with him. After all, what are friends for?

As it turned out, one needn't seek out enemies with Posluszny for a friend. Realizing that there was no foreseeable gain in sheltering the Jews, he went to the Polish police, disclosed the location of the bunker, and invited them to come and seize the Jews and kill them. It was necessary that he go to the Polish police, for if the Germans knew that he had sheltered the Jews, they would kill him along with the Jews. The Polish police knew this too, so they agreed that the Germans needn't learn of this. They would simply capture and execute the Jews. Good riddance, and it was reasonable to spare Posluszny. After all, wasn't he turning in the Jews?

As luck would have it, the Polish police came to the bunker on a Sunday morning when David Feit was visiting. They surrounded the barn and shouted for the Jews to come out. "We know there are four of you in there," they shouted, for Posluszny had told them how many were being harbored. And as the Poles pounded on the bunker, four Jews emerged: Moshe Rosenbaum, the Glazel brothers, and David Feit, who was unlucky to be in the wrong place at

David Feit, 1936.

the wrong time. Four Jews expected. Four Jews captured. The Polish police marched the group to the nearest wall and unceremoniously shot all four dead. Neighbors were ordered to bury the Jews. Posluszny had absented himself that day; but when he received the report that four Jews had been killed and buried he was satisfied that it was the group he had betrayed and went about his business, unconcerned.

But, that day, there had of course, been five in the bunker. Binnim, the fifth Jew, remained in the bunker, unnoticed, until nightfall, when he came out and ran to their maid, Karolka, in Kolbuszowa Gorna, some three kilometers to the east—a maid who had worked for the family and had, indeed, raised Binnim from childhood. He told her the tale of what had just befallen the family, and she took him in and fed and sheltered him for a few weeks.

Not many Poles were as sympathetic, however; quite the contrary. One day Binnim went out to get food from some of the other friendly peasants of the area, and he was recognized by a Pole named Miska, who was the brother of Landskomissar Twardon's chauffeur: small world. Miska grabbed Binnim and shouted for others to bring the German police. "I have caught a Jew."

Binnim Rosenbaum was a member of the Ordnungsdienst, the Jewish Police in the ghetto. Here he is seen at the far right, with his fellow officers, *(left to right)* Jankel Leibowicz, Josel Rapaport (the commandant), and Mendel Bilfeld.

Under interrogation by the German police, Binnim told the story of where he had been during the time since his escape. He told how Posluszny had harbored the Jews, how he had turned them over to the Polish police, and how they had shot the Jews. There was story enough to satisfy the Germans. There was no need to tell them about the maid in the next village. She would be spared involvement.

Posluszny was not so fortunate. The Germans arrested him, charged him with harboring Jews, sentenced him to be shot for his crime, and summarily carried out the execution—at the same time they shot Binnim. The very handsome Binnim was then nineteen years old. And so, the Rosenbaum family, the Glazel family—five young men, and the betrayer Posluszny were gone. The Polish peasants clucked about the perfidy of the Jews. "See what happens? We hide the Jews and they turn on us." And so we did, in bitter vengeance.

But the story is not quite over. At the end of the war I was part of the Polish State Security stationed in Legnica in Lower Silesia, and fate delivered Miska to me. I recognized him on the street and had him arrested. There was no trouble finding witnesses to his turning in Binnim. Everyone in the town knew he had done it. Thus it happened that two years later the final actor in this tragic play met his end.

A Day in Treblinka

*P*avel *Leleko was a Ukrainian guard at Treblinka. He gave the following account, discovered in Russian archives:*

There were large posters reading "Palestine awaits you," "The Ukraine will give you work and bread," and other slogans and appeals.

Two to three trainloads of doomed prisoners arrived daily at the Treblinka railroad station. Each train consisted of sixty cars.

The sight of the camp, the enormous flaming pyre burning at one end, the suffocating stench from decomposing bodies that spread from some ten kilometers around, and was particularly strong within the camp itself, made it clear what it really was. The people chased out of the cars with whips guessed immediately where they had been brought; some attempted to climb over the barbed wire of the fencing, got caught in it, and we opened fire on those who were trying to escape.

In March 1943 there arrived a train in which half the prisoners cut their throats and hands with razors. While unloading was going on, the prisoners cut themselves with knives and razors before our eyes.

Undressed, the women were sent in batches to the gas chamber. Many women were not quite sure they would be exterminated and in order to have some means of subsistence in the future, they hid some valuables on their persons. When a women walked along the path holding her legs close together, she was stopped at once and examined, and if anything was found on her, she was beaten almost to death. On occasions I would hear the men as they walked quietly to their deaths say to one another, "Why are you weeping? Do you believe you can arouse compassion in those Ukrainians?" I also heard the men sometimes say "Today you exterminate us, and tomorrow the Germans will kill you."

Franz, the camp commander, would order his dog to attack the naked people. Being trained for this, it grabbed them by their genitals.

With whips and clubs they chased people into the passage of the gas chamber building and then into the gas chambers. The Ukrainian motor operators then competed as to atrocities with regard to the people to be killed. One of the motorists was the Ukrainian Marchenko. He had a sword with which he mutilated people. He cut off the breasts of women.

Seven hundred to eight hundred people could be crowded into the not-so-large chambers. When the chambers were filled to the very limit, the Germans and the Ukrainians started to throw in the children left by the women, either in the undressing place or, more frequently, outside the gas chamber building. As the ceiling of the gas chamber was very low, the children thrown into the chamber hit the ceiling and then, disfigured, sometimes with broken heads, fell on the heads of the prisoners.

When asked what they saw through special portholes, the motorists answered that the people were writhing, crushing each other. Gradually the noise in the chambers died down. Some fifteen minutes later the motors were stopped and there was an unusual silence.

While the Ghetto Burned

The following was written by Jadwiga Manys'-Lobman of Warsaw and translated from Polish by H. Hirshaut

Every year on the 19 of April, I visit the plaza named for the Ghetto Fighters, and I place a small bouquet of flowers at the foot of the monument of the heroes. I do it to honor the memory of the thirty-three thousand Jews who fought, not only defending their own lives, but also the dignity and the honor of a people targeted for annihilation by Hitler's Nazi henchmen.

One flower, the most beautiful, I dedicate always to Jadzia Wieczorek, a young woman with whom I shared a floor mattress in cell 22, in the Pawiak prison in Warsaw. Just as no one knows the millions who fought during World War II, so, too, has no one preserved this girl's silhouette on canvas, nor in sculpture, nor written about her. She simply disappeared from this earth. But she didn't disappear from my memory, nor did the events that occurred during the time we were together: the Uprising in the Warsaw ghetto.

It was the week before Easter, the most joyful holiday in the Catholic faith, that I learned the tragic story of my friend Jadzia, and I can't erase this girl from my aging memory.

Before dawn I was awakened by the sound of heavy military trucks rolling on the pavement. This was rather unusual because Pawia Street and all the adjoining streets, where the ghetto used to be, had been deserted for months. Being curious to see what was happening, I got up quietly, in order not to wake my cellmates. I reached the wall, which had a small, barred window at the top, in the recess of the wall, which we called our "balcony."

I saw tanks and heavy armored cars passing by, the German soldiers holding machine guns at the ready. Meanwhile one SS-man spotted my head in the window and immediately pulled the trigger of his weapon. In a split second I turned my head away, let go of the bars, and dropped to the cement floor. The bullet shattered the glass and the plaster around the window. It came exactly on the mark where my head had been a second before.

The explosion woke up the "tenants" of my cell. There was still time until the morning *Appel,* and we began to guess what was happening. Being completely isolated from the rest of the city, we fantasized that probably the underground AK or AL organization, was launching an attack in order to liberate us.

The block eldest, the "duckling" who poked her head into our cell was visibly nervous. Later we learned from the orderly who dispensed the morning coffee that the Germans were going to liquidate the ghetto. The more informed prisoners, among them a few Jewish women who wound up in our cell, told us that several Jewish groups in the underground are ready to confront the Germans and, if necessary, to give up their lives, but not without fight. They were amassing whatever arms they could get;

they had built bunkers and were placing women, children, and the sick in the safety of basements. And now this moment had arrived.

When a new "action" of deportation was ordered, the Jews refused to go to the *Umschlagplatz* [the gathering place for deportation]. The enraged Germans decided to "teach" the stubborn Jews a lesson. I was thinking, "There are only thirty-three thousand Jewish souls still alive in the ghetto, and they will all be murdered: Jewish people who for hundreds of years coexisted with us and helped build this city and this country."

Exactly at 7:00 A.M. the battle began. The next day we found out that the invaders were "greeted" with grenades and Molotov cocktails. The shooting was sparse because the freedom fighters tried to save their ammunition, keeping the last bullets for themselves, in case they would have to surrender. This heroic fight was the loneliest and the most painful that was undertaken in defense of survival, freedom, and honor during World War II. The murderers paid a heavy price, which they didn't expect. Crowded in our cell, we got on our knees and prayed intensely, imploring God to help the Jewish fighters and to punish the oppressors. Even the most hardened inmates of the Gestapo prisons couldn't control their emotions and sobbing. It was as if we had raised our voices to God asking for help for his "Chosen People."

At 2:00 P.M. it got quiet, and only sporadic shooting was heard. The workers from the kitchen and the laundry brought news, that many dead and wounded SS men were brought from the battleground to the men's section of Pawiak.

That night, laying by my side, Jadzia Wieczorek told me her sad story: She came from a very fine, affluent Jewish family. As the only child, she was pampered and surrounded by love. She faced poverty for the first time when the family was forced to relocate to the ghetto. When the mass deportations began she decided to save her parents and herself, planning an escape from the ghetto. She had a Polish friend on the "Aryan" side, with whom she was in love and intimately involved, even before the war started. So it seemed only natural that she turned to him for help. He didn't refuse and agreed to help with the escape. He volunteered to safeguard their valuables, and took away a small suitcase filled with money and jewelry. This was supposed to sustain the family until the end of the war. But when the time came for him to turn over the suitcase to the family, he refused to return it. When Jadzia demanded the money, he threatened to denounce her to the Gestapo. She didn't believe he would do it, but as a precaution she moved her parents to a new hiding place, keeping the address secret. She kept on seeing him occasionally, hoping that somehow she would be able to convince him to return the valuables.

Then one day, when they met on Aleje Ujazdowskie, she was sure they could reach a compromise. They kept on walking and talking, and at some point it became a heated argument. Suddenly she realized that they were on Shuha Street near the headquarters of the Gestapo.

"I am taking you right there," he said furiously, she still didn't believe he was serious, but he grabbed her hand and pulled her inside the building. To the SS man on duty he reported, "This woman is a Jewess."

It was clear while she was telling me her tragic story that Jadzia was resigned to the fact that she would die soon; but she worried about her parents. Her quiet sobs tore my heart to pieces. I was ashamed for the deeds of my compatriot and felt like choking.

The next morning on Pawia Street, the armored vehicles rolled again. The skies were filled with airplanes, searching from above, looking for pockets of resistance, and bombing without mercy. We knew that the liquidation of the ghetto would be swift and brutal. All through the following weeks the attacks continued. At times they subsided, then again intensified, but they never really ceased, even during the nights.

It is not my purpose to describe here the events of the Uprising in the Warsaw Ghetto. Historians, psychologists, writers and film makers are dealing with that. I only want to convey a small fragment and the reaction of women prisoners, trapped inside the walls of Pawiak, who though helpless, felt united with the Jewish ghetto fighters.

During the methodical burning of the buildings the acrid smell and the heavy smoke seeped through every crevice of the prison walls and windows. We began to choke. Disregarding the strict rules, we pounded with our fists on the doors, begging to be let out into the corridor. We got away with it because the Germans were preoccupied with their own defeat.

And the ghetto looked now like a battlefield over which even birds didn't fly. . . .

In the second part of May 1943 Jadzia Wieczorek was taken away with a group of other Jewish women. She was shot and buried in the ruins, in that huge cemetery, which is what remained of the Warsaw ghetto. The man who denounced her didn't enjoy his loot for too long. The AK sentenced him to death because he was a traitor working for the Gestapo. He was killed on Kazimierzowska Street in front of his house.

Jadzia's parents survived the war, as did I, but before we were finally liberated we experienced many forms of hell.

"Charlie"
The American Who Never Made It

Charlie loved this country. He loved everything about America. What a pity he never lived to set foot on it. With the opportunities that abound here, he would have thrived.

His real name, of course, wasn't Charlie. It was Kalman Kernweiss. He lived in the small village of Kupno, just outside of our own town, Kolbuszowa. We called him Charlie because he wanted us to, and he wanted us to call him that because he thought it was the most American-sounding name he could think of. As I said, Charlie loved the idea of being an American and read everything about the United States that he could lay his hands on. He had even written a letter to Eleanor Roosevelt telling her how much he admired the country, and to his astonishment and great joy, she had answered him and told him she would like to help him come to America. His intelligent black eyes took on a particularly brightness whenever he spoke of his plans. He carried Mrs. Roosevelt's letter with him wherever he went.

Most of the village Jews in rural Poland were poor. Charlie's family was exceptional. They were one of the poorest. His father, Mordechai, eked out a livelihood by buying chickens and eggs in Kupno and selling them in Kolbuszowa for a few groschen more than he had paid. With no capital to work with, the day's transactions involved only a chicken or two and a few dozen eggs at a time. My father would give him merchandise on credit to sell in Kupno so he made a little on each leg of the trip, but there was never much to spare in the Kernweiss household.

While financially, Charlie was the poorest of my friends, intellectually, he was by far the most gifted. Everything interested him. It was not unusual that he read all about America. He read all about

Kalman Kernweiss was known as Charlie because of his desire to be all things American. He was killed by a Pole for a pair of boots before he could realize his dream of going to the U.S.

everything. His teachers in the local Talmud Torah recognized his brilliance and arranged for him to attend a yeshiva in Cracow.

His teachers in Cracow also saw that he was extraordinary and arranged for him to receive a full scholarship, tuition, room, and board—the whole works—to the prestigious Yeshiva Chachmey Lubin, one of the best Jewish centers of higher education in Europe. He was seventeen years old then. Normally this school could be attended by only the wealthy, and among them, only the most brilliant students. My father thought I should go to Yeshiva Chachmey Lubin, and he could well afford to send me. I knew I had neither the interest nor the talent for such a school. Charlie, by contrast, received a full-tuition scholarship and left home to attend.

Charlie's brilliance, unfortunately, was his undoing. The curriculum at the yeshiva, while rigorous and demanding, wasn't enough to consume all of Charlie's energies. As part of his anticipation of some day going to America, he undertook to teach himself English by means of reading newspapers with a dictionary at hand. Each night, when he had finished the assigned studies, he would work on his English. He taught himself, and what he learned he offered to teach others. When the scholars at the yeshiva found that he was "wasting his time" in this manner, they became indignant. Since they were paying all of his expenses, they felt that he certainly should give them all of his time. They abruptly terminated his scholarship and expelled him from the school.

What could he do? Charlie returned to the Cracow yeshiva but made the same mistake with the same result. His fascination with America was so strong that he continued to study English and teach the language to his fellow students. He was expelled from Cracow as well. Charlie returned to Kupno.

With little else to divert him, he continued his self-taught English studies and actually became an English teacher, using the newspapers as his text. I know this because I became one of his students. My early English studies provided me with some basic grammar and vocabulary. My father would sometimes listen in to Charlie's explanations of things such as the infinitive to me, and whenever he spoke about him, he referred to him as "the impinitive." Like everyone else, he was charmed by Charlie's intensity and would ask, "When is the impinitive coming?"

Needless to say, teaching English to a few of his fellow teenagers did not add much wealth to the family. Their poverty deepened. One of the most vivid memories I have is a mental picture of him dressed in a shabby jacket worn over his shirt and tie. He had developed the peculiar habit of carrying his right arm, bent at the elbow, across the front of the jacket. I remarked on it one day, and when I took his arm away was shocked to find that his shirt consisted only of a collar and shirt front. The rest of it had worn out, but he could not afford to replace it. The cover provided by his arm allowed him to continue the pretense of owning a shirt. I gave him one of my own to offer a semblance of dignity and a little warmth.

When the war came, Charlie's family moved from Kupno to Kolbuszowa. Well, they didn't exactly move to the town. Rather, they occupied a cold shack on the outskirts of the town. There were a lot of children in the Kernweiss family, and the move worsened their living standard considerably. They were crowded together in cramped quarters, cold and poorly nourished. Illness is a common visitor in circumstances such as this, and before that first winter was very old Charlie came down with typhus.

I recognized the gravity of the situation. Typhus is highly contagious and could spread throughout his household and beyond. The Germans were always concerned about disease spreading, not because of its impact on us, but because they realized that they could catch it as well. Their usual policy was to eliminate the illness by eliminating the ill. If they knew Charlie had typhus, they would have killed him, and in all probability, his family as well.

My girlfriend, Rozia Susskind, who was also being taught English by Charlie, was as concerned about his situation as I. Fortunately, she was able to help. Since her brother was away in Russia, with no probable date of return, she took the liberty of bringing a few of his shirts and pants to Charlie. I went to a doctor we knew to find out if there was anything we could do for him, particularly what he should eat. The doctor advised us that boiled rice would be best for him, so I got the rice from our store, Rozia boiled it, and we brought it to the woodshed where Charlie lay isolated from the others. Little by little he gained strength. This in spite of the fact, as we later learned, that all of the children in the family were sharing in the rice we had brought for Charlie.

At length, the typhus passed, and Charlie went to work for the German police. He didn't exactly seek them out. The Germans would assign the local Judenrat a daily quota of forced labor requirements to be provided to do the dirty and menial tasks around their offices. These would usually turn over on a daily, or at most a weekly, basis. In Charlie's case, the police found his intelligence and his ability to speak German and English as well as Polish, Yiddish, and Russian extremely useful. He cleaned up, shined the Germans' boots, translated when the Germans interrogated prisoners held in the jail cells in the headquarters basement, and for his trouble got more to eat in the form of table scraps than he had been accustomed to at home.

One day Charlie was sent to the basement prison cells with instruction to identify who, among a group of prisoners crowded in there, was Jewish. As he looked about, he was shocked to find his mother among those held. One by one, Charlie spoke to each prisoner in Polish. Half way through, he came to his mother. Neither of them gave even a flicker of recognition. Charlie spoke to her in Polish and she answered in kind. He spoke in Yiddish and she feigned incomprehension. Polish peasants didn't speak Yiddish, and when taken, she had told the Germans that she was a Polish peasant. Charlie confirmed this for them, even adding with a flourish, that he had bought a chicken from her in the past. The Germans released her, and Charlie returned to his janitorial duties.

In July 1942 a series of *Aktionen* began. The Germans, instead of picking workers for the day, selected Jews for deportation. They had emptied the ghettos of the neighboring towns and collected the Jews in the regional center of Rzeszow. They then began a series of deportations to the east, to Belzec death camp, that removed all but two thousand Jews. It was during this period that my mother, sisters, and girlfriend, Rozia, were all taken from me. Both Charlie and I were among those left, and we soon learned why.

The ghetto Jews had been evacuated from the small towns to Rzeszow, but the buildings still stood, filled with their belongings, collected and handed down from generation to generation over three hundred years. They contained pictures and furniture and jewelry and menorahs and candlesticks and silver and countless other items of value. The Germans wanted the wealth, and then they wanted the buildings destroyed. This time the selection was to form the work gangs that would be sent to each town to go through the ghetto, room by room, to collect these remnants of its soul, and then to destroy the body. As fortune willed, I was selected for the Kolbuszowa ghetto. Charlie was sent to Glogow, sixteen kilometers away.

It turned out that the Polish peasants had beaten us to much of the ghetto contents. They had looted and vandalized the synagogue. Torah scrolls were strewn about. Hebrew books had been burned, or worse, desecrated. Still, there was plenty for the Germans to ship back to Germany.

By the fall season, the Kolbuszowa ghetto was no more. The German warehouse brimmed with loot, and it was evident from both rumors and logic that we would soon be killed. There was simply no reason to keep us alive. We desperately devised a plan that we thought gave most of us at the Kolbuszowa labor camp a pretty good chance of escaping. When one night a friendly guard warned me that the camp was to be liquidated the following day, I knew we had to make the attempt. But I also knew that if we escaped, the labor force at the two other camps, Sokolow and Glogow, would be killed. I bribed the sympathetic Polish guard to go to warn the Jews at these camps. I had no way of knowing if he would. But I tried.

On the night of November 18, 1942, fifty-five of us attempted to escape the labor camp. Some had money, some didn't. Some had forged papers, some didn't. Some spoke Polish, some didn't. Some made it. And some didn't.

I was hidden, for a time, by a woman who had been our maid before the war. Eventually, however, she threatened to betray me, and I left before she could. I found myself living outdoors, deep in the woods with a group of Jews. We lived that way, without shelter, for over two years. One by one, we would be picked up by the Germans or picked off by the Poles. We would be promised help and find treachery. As some died or wandered off, others came, and that is how I was advised by a girl who came to look for us in the woods that she was sheltering a Jewish boy in her barn and we should come to get him to stay with us. I went with her, and to my great surprise, found that it was Charlie.

It turned out that my messenger had gotten through to the camp at Glogow in time for some of its inmates to escape. Charlie had known this girl from before the war and had gone to her in desperation. He was one of the lucky ones. She took him only because she was fond of him, since, as before, Charlie had no money. She didn't tell her parents that she was hiding an escaped Jew in the barn, and the danger, that any day they would discover and turn him in, was great.

The fact that he had no money made him reluctant, at first, to join our group. "I can't pay for anything," he said. I had to laugh. None of our group, with the exception of me and my brother Leibush, had any money. Our family had had the foresight to bury six hundred American dollars when the Germans came, and I had gone to dig that up after fleeing the labor camp. That was what sustained our group in terms of buying food and protection from the peasants.

Charlie joined us and proved to be a valuable member of the community hiding and fighting in the woods. He had come to know a lot of Polish peasants during his and his father's dealings with them. And Charlie was likable. So, we would send him on missions to buy supplies for us around the countryside, and inevitably he came back with a purchase none of us could have made without his contacts. Believe it or not, Charlie also resumed our English lessons deep in the woods. We were all preparing for America.

One particularly valuable contact that Charlie had was with a village shoemaker. Shoes were an essential to our survival, and we would send him with our shoes to have them fixed. Sometimes I went with him. Sometimes he went alone. On Charlie's last trip to pick up a pair of shoes and a pair of relatively new boots that were being fixed, I went along for protection. When we came to the shoemaker's house, Charlie went ahead, and I waited at the edge of the woods, about 150 feet away. I don't know why I didn't go with him. I just waited.

Charlie wasn't gone more than five minutes before I realized something was wrong. I heard him cry out the name I went by in the woods. "Tadek, Tadek, help me." I drew my revolver and ran to the house. I entered and found him laying in blood, with a pitchfork standing up vertically from his stomach where he had been impaled. The shoemaker ran out before I could take any action against him. Charlie could hardly speak, but he gasped out, "Do something." I pulled the pitchfork out and the blood poured out.

"Can you walk?" I asked. "Barely, " he said. And so I half-dragged, half-carried him back across the opening, to the woods and back to our hiding place. The trip cost Charlie most of his blood and all of his strength. I tried to staunch the bleeding with rags, but it was hopeless, and Charlie died the next day. Charlie had been betrayed, in all likelihood, because the shoemaker liked the boots he had fixed and didn't want to return them.

So, that's the story of the American who never made it. Who knows what he might have become: the movie industry in America was founded by people just like Charlie a generation before. Holocaust survivors have flourished in business, in the arts, in science, in philanthropy.

Charlie's potential was limitless, but instead, it all ended in a snowy field in Poland. Charlie—student, teacher, and scholar—had been killed for a pair of boots. He was twenty-three years old and destined never to see the land of his dreams, America.

A Tale of Survival

Part I

There were as many as 125 of us Jews living in the woods outside of Kolbuszowa after the town became *Judenrein* in 1942. By the time the war was over, six of us had survived. Jews in the northeastern parts of Poland survived the war living in woods where they organized partisan groups. For the most part they had help from Russian partisans, who supported them with food and supplies. We, in southern Poland, were isolated. Alone. We lived underground in bunkers. We lived in swampland and the deep forest. We hid out in attics and in barns. Lice infested us. Mosquitos tormented us. Our clothes were rags. We bribed, begged, hunted, fought, and ran to survive. We desperately wanted to outlast the war. In the end, six of 125 did. What happened to the rest? Our enemies killed them.

Who were our enemies? Everyone was, it seemed. Where were they? They seemed to be everywhere. Certainly the German army and the police were our enemy. We knew that and avoided them. If it were only the Germans, survival in the woods would have been relatively simple. The German army didn't venture into the deep woods. Others did, however. The Polish police made it a practice to hunt down Jews wherever they could. They rewarded informants in the Polish peasantry with one kilo of salt or sugar per Jew, and when they learned of someone hiding in a barn or an attic or a bunker, they would dispatch a detail to flush out and kill the Jews. The informants were frequently Polish peasants who one of us had trusted to hide him. Usually, the shelter was provided as long as, and until, the Jew ran out of money. Then the Jew became a danger and a burden, best exposed to the police. This happened to Yankel Lampl, David Feit, the Glasel brothers, the Rosenbaum family and many others. Oftentimes, the peasants would save the police the trouble. When one of our bunkers was discovered by a band of Polish peasants wielding axes and picks, eighteen of our group were hacked to pieces. That led us to abandon bunkers as a viable shelter and forced us deeper into the woods in the dead of winter.

And then there was the AK, or Armja Krajowa (Home Army). This was the official nationalist Polish underground, headquartered in London. It was the AK whom the allies supported with flights dropping supplies, arms, and food. The AK who operated to harass the Germans and interrupt their supplies and operations should have been the natural allies of the Jews in the woods. We, too, were armed. We, too, wanted nothing more than to attack the Germans. But the AK was violently anti-Semitic. We didn't know at the time, but the AK operated under a central directive issued by General Bor Komorowski, commanding the AK in Poland to eliminate the "bands of Jewish Bolshevik bandits" that were roaming the woods. Two of the six survivors in our group from the woods were killed in Kolbuszowa by the AK within four days of their liberation by the Russian army. So between the activities of the Germans, the police, the peasantry, and the AK, our existence was reduced to scurrying to remain out of sight, and when necessary putting our lives in the hands of people we believed to be trustworthy, but who all too often proved otherwise.

We were just about at the end of our rope in November 1943 when I learned that the AK in our region was commanded by a man whom I had known since childhood. We had gone to school, sat next to one another in the classroom, sang in the same chorus, played, and grown up together. The link went further. His father and mine had been business associates. They sat on the board of the bank together. I was overjoyed when I learned that Stashek Augustin and his brother Yashek were in command. As commandant of our group, I felt that they represented our best opportunity to come out of the woods, to unite and join up with the Polish resistance, and to contribute to the harassment of the German army. By this time, the Russians were advancing from the east and there would be at most only about six more months before the Germans were driven out. Jews were certainly not ordinarily welcomed by the AK, but the relationship with the Augustin brothers went back too far and was too deep for us to be identified as Bolshevik bandits.

Reaching our friends was quite another matter. The AK operated

Stashka Chodor, *(far left)* a Polish Catholic, and her family played major roles in helping the author survive during his time in the woods. Stashka was sixteen years old at the time. Also shown are Jozek and Zoska, her brother and sister. This photo was taken in 1948.

with the same degree of security we needed, since they, too, were hunted by the German occupiers. As it turned out, the daughter of Jan Chodor, a Polish peasant who over the years had been a steadfast and loyal friend— one of the truly righteous Gentiles—was a member of the AK cell. Her name was Stashka, and through her intercession, we contacted and were escorted to the AK hideout.

My reunion with Stashek was everything I had imagined. He could not have been happier to see me and my brother Leibush, to learn that we had survived, and he told me he wanted my Jewish group to work with him and his unit. Leibush had known him and his father through our family business, and he, too, was welcomed to change out of the rags we wore for clothes and eat and drink the first food of substance we had had in a year.

Friendly and warm as the reunion was, I knew better than to place my entire trust in the goodwill of the AK commander. I continued to wear my gun, carry my hand grenades and the 120 rounds of ammunition I kept with me at all times. The next day I found my caution might be well founded. Stashek came in from a trip to talk and throughout the entire time, he kept his hand in his right pocket. Even when he had to awkwardly reach across the room to get something, his hand never left his pocket. It made me wonder what was in that pocket. A day later we were to find out.

While Leibush and I were sitting in the room assigned us between the stable and the barn, the Augustin brothers came in and again began to chat about the advancing Russian lines. Leibush and I were dressed in our underwear. Boots and possessions were piled up in the attic. Stashek stood in front of me and embraced me. He put his hands on my shoulders and said, "After the war Naftali, you and I are going to be very important around here." He then asked to see my flashlight, which I handed over to him.

Suddenly the lantern that was lighting the room was blown out. Pitch blackness enveloped the small room and a series of shots rang out. I went weak. My head spun, and instinctively I knew I had been shot and would probably die on the spot. I fell down. Blood ran down my back and arm, and in the split second that followed, I took out my gun, which I had in my belt, and fired a shot wildly in the room. The bullet hit the wall, but the flash illuminated the scene of Yashek aiming his gun at my brother Leibush. I turned and despite a dead finger where I had been wounded, managed to get off a second shot that killed Yashek. I turned and shot Stashek as well, but he was only wounded and managed to get out of the room.

Nr 482

GEN. KOMOROWSKI DO N.W.: MELDUNEK PÓŁROCZNY
O SPRAWACH AK I POŁOŻENIU W KRAJU

O.VI L. dz. 3214/tjn/43
Dnia 31 sierpnia 1943 r.   Dnia 24 kwietnia 1944 r.
Poczta Lawiny [1]

MELDUNEK ORGANIZACYJNY Nr 220
za czas od 1. III. 43 do 31. VIII. 43

Naczelny Wódz
Przedstawiam meldunek organizacyjny Nr 220 za czas od
1. III. 43 do 31. VIII. 43 w ślad za meld. org. nr 190 [1].

---

4. Bandytyzm. Silnie uzbrojone bandy grasują nieustannie w miastach i po wsiach napadając na dwory, banki, firmy handlowe i przemysłowe, domy i mieszkania, większe gospodarstwa chłopskie. Napady rabunkowe połączone często z morderstwami, dokonywane przez ukrywające się w lesie oddziały partyzantów sowieckich wzgl. przez zwykłe bandy rabunkowe.

Te ostatnie rekrutują się z przeróżnego elementu zbrodniczego i wywrotowego. W napadach biorą udział mężczyźni i kobiety, szczególnie Żydówki. Niecna ta akcja zdemoralizowanych jednostek przyczynia się w znacznym stopniu do zupełnego wyniszczenia wielu obywateli, znękanych już i tak czteroletnim zmaganiem się z wrogiem.

Okupant nie przeciwdziała zasadniczo temu stanowi rzeczy, wzywane niekiedy w poważniejszych wypadkach na pomoc niemieckie organa bezpieczeństwa odmawiają pomocy, unikając z reguły interwencji i nie walcząc z bandytami, często wręcz przeciwnie. większa akcja bandytyzmu wywołuje represje w stosunku do niewinnej ludności polskiej. Aby dać pewną pomoc i osłonę bezbronnej ludności wydałem, w porozumieniu z Gł. Del. Rządu, komendantom ·Okręgów i Obwodów instrukcję. dotyczącą bezpieczeństwa terenowego, w której nakazałem kmdtom Okr. i Obw., w razie potrzeby, występować zbrojnie przeciwko elementom plądrującym, bądź wywrotowo-bandyckim. Położyłem nacisk na konieczność likwidacji przywódców band i na usiłowanie zniszczenia całych band. Poleciłem komendantom terenowym zapewnienie sobie współudziału miejscowej ludności i agend Del. Rządu w zorganizowaniu samoobrony i służby alarmowej.

This proclamation, order Number 482, was issued August 31, 1943 by the commandant of the AK (Armja Krajowa-Home Army), General Bor Komorowski. It called upon the Polish underground to kill the Jews hiding in the countryside, whom he labeled Jewish Bolshevik bandits. The headquarters of the AK was in London, England.

It was clear that the welcome had been nothing more than an act designed to disarm us mentally so we could be easily taken. I was shot four times—three times in the neck and once in the hand. My boyhood playmate found his loyalty to the AK directive to kill Jewish Bolshevik bandits more compelling than any loyalty or warmth he might have retained from the old days.

Leibush and I didn't have time to gather our things. I left behind my boots, clothing, and the diary I had been keeping since the start of the war. We fled into the snowy night, barefoot, dressed only in underwear, and trailing a telltale stream of blood from the wound in my neck. Once again, Leibush and I were alone in the countryside, trying to find our way through a hostile Polish landscape to safety. Only this time, the odds were longer than ever.

(to be continued)

A Tale of Survival

Part II

As my brother Leibush and I fled into the winter night our prospects for escape were bleak. I had just shot Stashek and Yashek Augustin, two brothers who commanded the local unit of the Armja Krajowa (AK), or Home Army. Yashek was dead. Stashek was wounded, and the Gestapo arrested him and killed him a few days later. The AK desperately wanted to kill us.

My first thought was to get away. The second was to wonder where. Our friend Franek Zawisza lived in the same village (Kolbuszowa Gorna), and he would shelter us if we could get there. But could we? God must have been guiding us that night, as we stumbled through the frozen field, traveling by dead reckoning in the direction I thought would lead to his house. We plunged ahead, falling into ditches and holes, breath rasping in the cold night, bloodstream marking our meandering path. Then I saw two moving lights in the distance. I realized that they were the headlights of the bus that ran between Rzeszow and Kolbuszowa. That was our salvation. The lights marked the location of the road and oriented me to direction. With this new reference point, we were able to find our way through the snow-covered fields.

At last we arrived, across the road from Franek's house, staggered to the other side, and into his barn. Soon we realized, however, that we couldn't stay there. The path of blood and footsteps through the snow led right to our location. We would have to move on.

During the run through the fields I had remembered Jan Shitosh, a self-taught medicine man who functioned as the village veterinarian. He could stop the blood, if only he wouldn't turn us away. Shitosh was aghast at my appearance; I was wet, dirty, barefoot, wearing only under-wear, and blood-soaked underwear at that. He was more upset when I told him we had run into some Germans whom we had killed, and he noted that the trail of blood would lead them to the house. "Quickly," he said, "hide in the barn. The quicker I fix your wound, the quicker you will be out of here." We went to the barn, and in a few minutes Shitosh joined us. He washed my wounds and bandaged them. I learned that I was bleeding from the neck, palm, and index finger, but it did not look life-threatening.

Shitosh also did us the great favor of providing some old clothes to put on and offered each of us a pair of shoes. I was able to put mine on, but Leibush's feet were much too big for anything available. He would have to go on barefoot. It was clear that Shitosh was anxious to see us gone. If the Germans came after we left, he would say he knew nothing of us. If we had been in his barn, it was without his knowledge.

Already in his debt, we wanted to do nothing that would further en-danger the man. I told him that I had a friend in Przedborz who I knew would hide us for a longer time, and who might be able to get me a real doctor to treat my wounds. Shitosh directed us on how to reach that vil-lage through the woods, warning that the snow would be deep. What nei-ther he nor we realized was that beneath the snow was a thin layer of ice that we kept breaking through as we made our way. Leibush's feet quickly became cut in a hundred places. He staggered on in agony. This time it was he, and not I, who left the bloody trail behind.

At last we arrived at Jan Chodor's house in Przedborz, a refuge we had used many times during the past two years. Before the war, Chodor had bought from us and had many times been extended credit or charity by my family between harvests. He was desperately poor, and he hadn't for-gotten how we had supported him. Chodor could be relied on to help when he could, and he often did. There, in his barn, we found hiding another of our comrades from the woods, the most resourceful Leiba Leibowicz.

Leiba had been raised as a woodsman, and illiterate though he was, his knowledge of camping, hunting, and survival techniques had fre-quently been the difference for all of us between freedom and capture. Leiba's experience again helped us when he saw what a mess Leibush's feet were. He bound them up in bags he made of torn sheets and filled them with soft oat skins that he found in the barn. While he couldn't go any distance, Leibush was at least able to stand with the oat skins on his feet.

Chodor's daughter Stashka was a member of the same AK group as the Augustin brothers. Fortunately she shared her father's appreciation for our family's past relationship and felt more loyalty to us than to the AK. She and her mother, Stefka, brought me to Doctor Lechowski in Sedziszow, a neighboring town, and presented me as an AK member of Stashka's group wounded in a firefight with the Germans. He washed and bandaged my wounds and told me, "You were miraculously lucky. You were hit in the neck three times, but none of the bullets lodged there. You may have put your hand up to your neck, because it looks as if the fourth bullet passed through the length of your finger without breaking the bone."

I returned to Chodor's house. Within two weeks, I headed east to join another AK group, only this time I presented myself as a Catholic partisan, Tadeusz Jadach. I learned the joy of striking back at our tormentors. Seven months later, the Russian army liber-

When the Jewish escapees lived deep in the woods, they were fortunate to have a professional trapper in their midst, Leiba Leibowicz *(left)*. His contacts among the peasants as well as his knowledge of the forest proved invaluable. He survived the war, but six months after the liberation was poisoned. Shown on the right is Jozek Chodor.

ated Kolbuszowa and the surrounding area, and I joined the Polish army to continue fighting the Germans.

For the few remaining Jews in Poland, this turn of events in the war should have brought peace and security. But it was not to be. Unfortunately, the war between the Poles and the returning Jews would continue long after the Germans were gone. In 1945, 1946, and 1947, the Poles murdered over twenty-five hundred Jews who had survived the death camps, the partisan attacks, the hiding in cellars and attics, the exile to Siberia, and the masquerading under false Aryan documents. They had survived the German invaders only to ultimately fall at the hands of their Polish neighbors.

My Last Day in the AK

I knew my days in the Polish Resistance were over when the report came in that a family in the next village was hiding Jews. There was no way the local underground leadership would ignore this information. Although the AK existed to fight the German occupiers, its members shared with their enemy a common hatred of Jews. For the most part, this hatred found few targets. By 1944 the Germans had cleared the region of its Jewish inhabitants, and while the Poles railed against Jews, they rarely saw one. Every now and then, however, one or another stray Jew who had eluded the German purge by hiding or joining a Jewish partisan group would be discovered. When this occurred, the Polish partisans would rush to get ahead of their German occupiers to reveal the existence of the Jews and, more likely than not, kill them.

That's certainly what they would have done to me if they knew I was a Jew. But they didn't. They thought I was a Pole named Tadeusz Jadach, and they welcomed the ferocity with which I participated in their raids on German supplies, the derailment of their trains, the cutting of their communications, and the ambushing of their patrols. Having witnessed the killing of my friends and family by the Germans, I was more than willing to strike back in every way I could. Membership in the AK gave me the opportunity. It also gave me the opportunity to live indoors, under shelter, with the support of the peasantry, and the appreciation of the people—both genders. We were warm and well fed, a welcome contrast to what I had been enduring while hiding out in the woods with my Jewish group.

I had joined the AK group located near Huta Komorowska, home of one of the notorious concentration camps in Poland. It was far enough from Kolbuszowa to minimize the odds that I would meet anyone who would recognize me. We covered the towns of Baranow, Tarnobrzeg, and Sandomierz, north of Kolbuszowa. Because of my willingness to participate in all kinds of missions to disrupt the Germans, I quickly became a favorite of the unit leader, a giant of a man called Wysoki Zbyszek, or Tall Zbyszek.

On this particular night in June 1944 one of our men had returned from visiting his village and reported that his villagers knew of a family that had been hiding Jews in an underground bunker under his barn. The neighbors had heard them when they had come out for air or to stretch and pinpointed the exact location for him. It didn't take much discussion before Wysoki Zbyszek concluded that the proper thing to do was to have the informer go back to his village with another AK man, go to the house where the Jews were hidden, and shoot them.

"Oh yes, shoot the peasants hiding them, too."

He had picked the man to go back when I interrupted and said, "Let me go on this one. You know it is the type of job I like to do." The commandant knew I liked to go on every job and supposed this was just like the others.

"Okay, Tadek, you are right," he said. "Tadek will go to take care of the Jews."

We left within the hour, and walked through the dark woods to the outskirts of the village in which the Jews were said to be hiding. It took us about two hours. "Come, I will show you which house the Jews are hiding in," my companion whispered, and we crept forward. From a distance, he pointed out the barn, and we formulated a plan for him to knock on the front door of the house. "They will recognize me and open the door." We made our plans for the disposal of the Jews. That done, we checked our guns and moved toward the house, he a few paces in front of me.

It was then that I resigned from the AK. I shot my companion in the back of the head and he pitched forward, dead.

Our training had been always to gather up the weapon of a fallen comrade, so I took his gun and proceeded as before to the front door of the house and knocked. I knew the peasant's name. I knocked again and called out, "I know you are hiding Jews. I have come to save the Jews."

"What are you talking about? There are no Jews here. Why should I save Jews? I hate Jews. It is against the law. I would be killed if the Germans found Jews in my house."

"The AK knows you have Jews hidden here. They want to kill them and you." I tried again and again to convince him of my purpose, but he clung to his story with the desperation of one whose life is suddenly in serious jeopardy. He refused to let me in.

Unable to convince him, I too took a desperate chance. I began to shout in Yiddish, in our local accent, "I am a Jew who has come to save you. You must leave this place. Our group came to kill you, and it will unless you leave." I continued in this vein for what seemed like an eternity.

I was losing hope of convincing them, when the door to their house opened and they revealed themselves. There were three, a man about twenty-eight years of age, his girlfriend, and her brother. The girl was about twenty-three, and the brother in the neighborhood of eighteen.

After literally years of hiding, the three were understandably frightened, undecided whether to continue what had been successful for them so far, or to trust themselves to the assurances offered by this unknown voice. It must have been the local accent that persuaded them. I am not sure how I would have responded were I in their position. I am sure I helped establish my credibility when I immediately handed over the gun of my slain companion.

They could not stay here. That was certain, I said. I didn't care where they went, but told them they were welcome to join my group at Poremby Kupienskie, outside Kolbuszowa. I would be returning there. Since I had killed my companion, I couldn't go back to my unit. With mixed emotions, I realized that this had been my last day as a member of the AK.

After some debate, they decided to go with me, and we rejoined my old group in the woods outside Kolbuszowa. I was glad I had saved them from the Polish vigilantes. They were grateful.

By the end of the war, only 6 survivors remained from my group. Two of the group who had been with me two years in the forest went back to Kolbuszowa, our home town. After all, the war was over. Three days after the liberation by the Russians, these 2 were shot in Kolbuszowa by the AK. Of our Jewish group of 125, only 4 survived the war.

The young man, his girlfriend, and her brother were not among them.

The War Ends

The Killing Continues

We were still hiding in the woods when we were liberated by the Russians. There were six of us—my brother Leibush and myself, Leibush Nessel, Naftali Kaner, Leiba and Hershel Leibowicz. It was July 29, 1944, and the last elements of the German army had packed up and fled the advancing Russian forces. For our part of Poland, the war was over. We knew that much, but we weren't sure where we should go in response to these changed circumstances. "Let's go to Kolbuszowa and show them we're alive," suggested Leibush Nessel. Naftali Kaner agreed. We had grown up together in Kolbuszowa and been driven out by the Germans. What would be more logical than to return and reclaim whatever property remained?

I didn't think much of that plan. The "Armja Krajowa," (AK) would be taking over, at least until the Russians established an administrative presence in the area. I had worked with the AK as Tadeusz Jadach, a Polish Catholic. I knew them to be a bunch of violent anti-Semites and wasn't convinced that the killing of Jews would end with the departure of the Germans. In the small towns, Jews would be at risk.

"At least," I argued, "let's go to Rzeszow." Rzeszow was a bigger, better organized town than Kolbuszowa. I reasoned it would be more difficult for a group of the AK to take over there. My brother Leibush agreed with me, and we pleaded with the others not to go back to Kolbuszowa.

"But the Germans are gone. Thank God we have survived. We will be treated as heroes because we are alive." Leibush Nessel and Naftali Kaner were thrilled by the defeat of the Germans and anxious to return home to resume their lives. They left the woods and headed back to Kolbuszowa. Leiba and Hershel Leibowicz had already gone. My brother Leibush and I went, traveling cautiously and by night, to Rzeszow.

As it turned out, our friends Leibush and Naftali weren't the only surviving Jews to return to Kolbuszowa. There were eight others, six of whom had been hidden by friendly Poles, and who had now come out in the open for the first time in years. I knew them all well: Pasiek Rappaport, Josel Rappaport, Israel Stub, Itche Stub, Froim Brodt, Mayer Orgel, Leiba Leibowicz, and Hershel Leibowicz. The first six had paid their Polish benefactors well and been sheltered during the years of the occupation. The other two had been in the woods with us.

Their celebration of freedom was short-lived. Within three or four days, the AK learned that the eight had survived and in a few hours had them rounded up and imprisoned in a barn belonging to the count of Kolbuszowa. Their intent, as I had feared, was to kill any surviving Jews they found. This eight would be held until nightfall to be executed.

Guards were posted at the barn by the AK and changed every two hours to be sure the Jews didn't escape death a second time. It was this rotation of guards that would prove to be the salvation for the eight imprisoned Jews, however.

One of those coming off his tour of guard duty was struck with the injustice of killing the Jews. His name was Stepien, and he was the son of a man who had worked for the Jewish owner of the local flour and lumber mill. His father, thought Stepien, had always been treated well by the Jews. Killing them, he was sure, was something his father would disapprove of. And so he decided to act.

He sought out a Russian army officer and told him that eight Jews were being held prisoner and would be killed that evening. By coincidence the Russian was also a Jew, and he demanded he be taken to the barn where the prisoners were held. The Russian surprised the guards, disarmed them, and let the bewildered Jews out of their captivity. But this turn of fortune wasn't yet complete. The Russian handed his revolver to the Jews and told them they had best kill the guards as a suitable revenge.

Killing the guards or anyone else was not part of the nature of these eight. None of them lusted for blood. They just wanted salvation, and they asked the Russian if instead he could help them get away. They, too, decided that the bigger towns such as Rzeszow would be safer for them, and they asked if he could arrange for them to make the thirty-kilometer trip under Russian security. He agreed, and it was in Rzeszow that we met the eight and heard this story from them.

Naturally, the AK leadership was furious that the Jews had eluded them. They vowed to kill any additional Jews they could get their hands on. And onto this scene of smoldering hate and resentment came our two remaining companions from the woods, Leibush Nessel and Naftali Kaner. Euphoric over their survival, they announced their presence so everyone would be aware of it. In a matter of hours, the AK seized our friends. This time there would be no barn, no waiting. They were marched down to the river, shot, and killed on the spot.

Perhaps this was an aberration, you may be thinking. It should be expected from ignorant peasants. No, this was no aberration. More than twenty-five hundred surviving Jews would be killed by Poles in the first three years after the war. In Lezansk, a small town near Kolbuszowa, a group of Jews were living together. An AK member threw a hand grenade into their house, blowing them up. In the case of Leibush Nessel and Naftali Kaner, I know exactly who shot them. One was Wladyslaw Kisiel, who was former director of Internal Revenue before the war. The other was Stanislaw Zielinski, who owned a bus company. These were not peasants. These were intelligent, educated men who belonged to the AK and who wanted to remove any surviving remnants of the Jewish community.

The only way to survive as a Jew in a small town in Poland after the war was the way Jankel Plafker did. That was to convert. After returning to Kolbuszowa, Jankel announced his intention of marrying a Catholic girl, and he soon did so. He changed his name to John Plaszczynski, and he and his bride moved into the building that was formerly the ritual Jewish slaughterhouse. Jankel became a devoted Catholic and eventually was made the caretaker of the church, carrying the keys and opening the door for those who would enter. Jankel remained in Kolbuszowa, not only accepted, but popular among the Catholics as a result of his conversion. He died in 1998.

As for myself, it is clear to me that I would have been one of the first to have been killed had I returned to Kolbuszowa. Instead, I remained at Rzeszow, but even there I knew the future for Jews in Poland was to be a dismal one. The hatreds were too deep, the history too long. I knew I had to move on or be killed. In a short while, I slipped out of my Jewish

After leaving the AK, the author joined a Russian partisan group as Tadeusz Jadach.

identity and joined the Polish army, beginning my masquerade as Tadeusz Zaleski, a Catholic and an officer in the postwar establishment. But that is another story.

Belzec Described by an Engineer Who Worked There for the Germans

Following is a statement made by a Polish Gentile who was an engineer for the Germans at Belzec. This statement was made to Tadeusz Zaleski (now Norman Salsitz) during interrogation in January 1945. This report with the name of the engineer was sent to the Yad Vashem, the documentation center in Jersualem, by Norman Salsitz of Springfield, N.J.

In 1940, Jewish prisoners were brought to Belzec to make antitank traps for the Germans. These traps were twelve kilometers long, nine meters wide and two and a half meters deep. One wall of the trench was perpendicular and the other side sloped. These fortifications ran from Belzec to Narol and Cieszanow and from there to Dzikow.

Cieszanow was located thirty kilometers from Belzec. From Cieszanow to Dzikow is twelve kilometers. Belzec is also three kilometers from Tomaszow-Lubelski, right on the German-Russian border during the period 1939 to 1941.

There are tremendous forests surrounding this area. The assembly point for those who were transported there was the flour mill in Belzec. The roads were so primitive and so cluttered with stones that Jews had to build the roads.

There is one witness, Jacob Gutman, who was born Aug. 12 1919, in Radom. He lived in Radom on the First of May Street 85. His prisoner number was 25759. He was one of the workers on the tank traps.

After finishing the roads and the tank traps, Belzec was designated as an extermination camp for the transportees of the Jewish population of East Poland and the provinces of Lublin and Lwow (Lemberg).

The trains with the transportees came close to the town of Belzec. The victims then had to march on foot, in ranks of five, the four-kilometer road from the flour mill where the train had let them off to the tank traps. If the assembly points were full and there was no room for more, the excess transporters were sent to Narol and Cieszanow. The commandant of the Belzec camp and of Cieszanow was a Major Dof. He was also one of the founders of the Dachau concentration camp.

Since the layer of dirt in the tank traps was quite thin or light, soon part of the bodies began sticking up above ground. Because of the stench, the people who lived in the surrounding areas left their homes. The stench was so great that even at a distance one could vomit from it.

After a few weeks, the ground settled down even more and in the whole district you could feel the smell of death.

The Germans wanted to hide the knowledge of these events. They collected workers from surrounding villages and they collected stones and gravel and covered the entire surface with cement so that one smooth slab covered the whole section.

After a short while, the slabs cracked. So they brought bulldozers and ripped up the slabs, poured in gasoline and set the whole thing on fire.

The First and Last Jews in Kolbuszowa

I was born in 1920, in the town of Kolbuszowa, located in the section of Poland, known as Galicia, in Polish Malopolska—Minor Poland. At the time of my birth, roughly two thousand Jews and two thousand Christians populated the town, living and working together in a strained, but serviceable, relationship. Twenty-four years later, by 1944, only nine Jews were left. The Holocaust had taken the rest. By 1946, there was but one, a former slaughterhouse worker I had grown up with and known as Jankel Plafker.

When the war ended, Jankel came out of hiding and surveyed his prospects. The Jewish community was, to all intents and purposes, gone. Two Jews who had survived the war with me in the woods returned to Kolbuszowa only to be killed on the day of their arrival by two highly respected Polish townspeople working with the AK. Plafker returned to the village of Kolbuszowa Dolna, married a Catholic girl named Kusik, converted to Catholicism, and faced the world from that time on as John Plaszczynski. So thorough was the conversion that the former Jankel Plafker became the sexton of the church, maintaining the keys and opening and closing its doors each day for the clergy and worshipers.

When John Plaszczynski died in 1998, Kolbuszowa lost the last member of a Jewish population that traced its presence in the town back to 1700 when an invitation extended by Count Josef Karol Lubomirski brought three Jewish families to settle there. Lubomirski, having been given outright ownership of the town by King Jan Sobieski in recognition of his military services after Poland's victory over the Turks in Vienna in 1683, maintained it as a fiefdom, with landless peasants tilling the soil in return for a share of the harvest.

Jews had been in Poland since the eleventh century, when they began to migrate from Germany and settle principally in Cracow. It wasn't until the fourteenth century, however, in the time of King Kazimierz Wielki, or Kazimier the Great, that the community in Cracow began to flourish. It was then that the first synagogue, bathhouse, and cemetery were built, and Jews established themselves as bankers and administrators for the king and nobles. Pressure from the church, however, generated waves of anti-Semitism, and a series of pogroms took place during the late fifteenth century. In 1495, King Jan Olbrecht decreed that the Jews leave Cracow, and they established Kazimierz just outside of the city as a center for Jewish activities. Despite the hostility, Jews continued to come from Czech and Germany and the surrounding region, and by the early sixteenth century the Cracow area had become a talmudic center, with Rabbi Moshe Isserles, known as the Remuh, its spiritual leader.

Count Lubomirski wanted the original Jews in Kolbuszowa for their skills as tradesmen and craftsmen. The most notable of these pioneering Jewish families were the Geldzahlers, who served their patron as goldsmiths. Their gold jewelry was unrivaled in its workmanship and was exported to other cities in minor Poland, and then to Russia and Germany, and eventually throughout Europe. The Geldzahler family established branches in France, Germany, and Belgium to facilitate this trade. Indeed, the family exists in Belgium to this day.

Just as Plafker should be noted the last Jew to inhabit Kolbuszowa, Geldzahler warrants recognition as the first. This is a story about Jews in Poland and some of the history surrounding the arrival of the first Jew and the departure of the last.

History records that by 1773, there were eighty-six Jewish and ninety-six Christian families in Kolbuszowa. The two groups lived harmoniously enough for a city coat-of-arms to have been created in 1775 that showed a Jew and a Pole shaking hands between a Polish eagle and crusader cross on top and a Star of David underneath. The colors of the coat-of-arms (Herb) were red and white, the Polish colors, and blue and white, symbolic of the Jews. But lest this spirit of brotherhood be carried too far, we note that the right sleeve, which was on the Polish arm, was longer and wider than the left, which was worn by the Jewish arm.

This coat of arms for Kolbuszowa was adopted in 1775 and is unique among Polish coats of arms in that it includes an expression of friendship between Poles and Jews. Today it is on display at the entrance to the town.

The eighty-six Jewish families in early Kolbuszowa included—in addition to the goldsmith—tailors, butchers, tanners, soap manufacturers and bakers, as well as financiers and exporters. The local inn, or *Karczma*, belonged to the landowning nobleman but, as in most villages, was run by a Jew as his agent. Here, travelers could stay and find food and drink. Since the Polish peasants were serfs (known as *Pan-szczyzna*) who owned neither the land they worked nor the buildings they lived in, and who received no money wages but rather shared in the harvest, the need for the skill and industry brought by the Jews

was clear. So, too, however, was the jealousy and resentment these activities generated, and the Jews often found themselves to be the necessary
but detested lubricant that allowed Polish society to function.

In the 1770s the first synagogue and bathhouse were built in Kolbuszowa. It remained for a sign from heaven to guide them to the establishment of a cemetery. The Jews of Kolbuszowa normally took their dead by
wagon over dirt roads to the town of Zochow, some thirty kilometers
away, for burial. On one such journey, however, legend has it that the
horses stopped at a point one and a half kilometers outside of the town,
and refused to go on no matter how much they were coaxed. The Jews
took this as a sign from heaven that a cemetery should be built in this
spot. The presence of these traditional facilities attracted more and more
Jewish families from Rzeszow, Sokolow, and other neighboring towns.

As Kolbuszowa grew it evolved into a center for manufacturing wood
products. It was located in the midst of vast forests called Puszcza San-
domierska (wilderness of Sandomierz) yielding a variety of wood suitable
for things as varied as furniture, violins, butter churns, toys, wagon
wheels, and containers of various sorts. The name "Kolbuszowa Furniture" became recognized throughout Europe. The violins made in six-
teenth-century Kolbuszowa were every bit as sought after in their time as
the more famous Stradivarius. Wagon-wheel manufacture was a craft
taught by father to son. The *Tokarz*, as the woodworking craftsmen were
known, produced the products, and the Jews distributed them throughout Europe. The Jews were also instrumental in establishing shoemaking
as a cottage industry in the Nowe Miasto section of the town. They
would supply the Poles with the leather and other required raw materials
to be fashioned at home into shoes for local use as well as export.

For some two hundred years Jews and Poles coexisted in this small
corner of Galicia. As long as the region was under Austrian control, life
was relatively easier. Since most Jews spoke German, and even if they
didn't, Yiddish was close enough, they could more easily make themselves understood to the Austrians than could the Poles. They even coexisted with a regiment of *Husary*, or Hungarian cavalry, that was stationed
in Kolbuszowa. By the early twentieth century, five of the six lawyers in
town and two of the three doctors were Jewish. But mostly, Jews excelled
in business.

My father, who was called the sugar king before and during World
War I, because he had a distributorship of sugar given him by the Austrian
government, was a prime example. Sugar at the time was so scarce it was
rationed; so from his position as the one who controlled availability to
this highly valued commodity, he gained many influential friends from

among those he favored, and of course, his share of enemies from among those he didn't.

After World War I things began to deteriorate for the Jews. The Austrian occupation ended in 1918, and the Jews felt more anti-Semitism. In 1935, Josef Pilsudski, who had been marshal of Poland, died, and when Rydz Smigly took his place as marshal, things grew decidedly worse. The German influence at this time exacerbated the long-smoldering Polish anti-Semitism. Then came the German invasion in 1939, the building of six German death camps on Polish soil, and the June 7, 1942, liquidation of the Kolbuszowa ghetto and transportation of the remaining Jews to Belzec, where they were killed.

The Jewish cemetery is a microcosm of the history of our lives in Kolbuszowa. Today, it is overgrown and abandoned. No stones mark recent visits to grave sites. (It is Jewish custom to mark one's visit to a grave by placing a stone there rather than flowers.) No Jews are left to visit the thousands whose remains are buried there. Amidst the weeds and tipped stones of this abandoned cemetery are three common grave sites that tell the tale of the decline of Jewish prospects in Poland. In each of these is buried a cluster of Jews who died at the same time in a common event.

The first dates from the independence of Poland from Austria. It was a time of great rejoicing in Catholic Poland. On May 6, 1919, this landmark event generated such enthusiasm that it was celebrated with a pogrom launched against the Jews in which nine were killed, forty girls raped, and hundreds wounded. The nine are buried together in one of the common plots in the cemetery.

A second common burial site dates from an incident, described elsewhere among these stories, that took place on September 9, 1939, when the Germans invaded. Jews and Poles fought together in the Polish army in an attempt to resist the German force. By the time the outcome had been determined, 148 had died on the Polish side and 65 on the German. The German graves detail gathered up their dead and shipped them back to their families in Germany. The Poles, too, performed the melancholy task of burying their dead in a common grave in the Catholic cemetery. However carefully Gentiles were separated from Jews in daily life, in death they were joined. Twenty-three of the dead Poles buried in the Catholic cemetery were Jews. No Jewish soul could rest in such ground. In the dead of night a few weeks later, four unlikely Jewish heroes performed the grisly task of digging up the bodies in the Catholic common grave, identifying the twenty-three Jewish soldiers by inspecting for circumcision, and reburying them in the Jewish cemetery. This became our second common grave.

The third I know all too well. It was created when, on April 28, 1942, my father, along with nineteen other prominent Jews in our town, was marked by the Gestapo for execution. In their zeal, the Germans managed to kill twenty-two that day. When the slaughter was ended, that day, these, too, were placed in a common grave in the cemetery at Kolbuszowa.

And so there in the abandoned Jewish graveyard in Kolbuszowa a discerning eye can trace a great deal of history. Men, women, children, rich men, paupers, rabbis, and the non-observant—all are buried within the crumbling walls. Pogrom victims, soldiers, and the murdered—they are all there. All that is missing are the first and last Jews in Kolbuszowa. The first, Geldzahler, died a hundred years before the miracle of the horse led to the establishment of the cemetery. The last won't be found there either. Rather, he lies in the Catholic cemetery under a cross-bearing headstone marked Plaszczynski. The last Jew in Kolbuszowa was the sexton of the Catholic church.

PART THREE Surviving the Holocaust

The Photographs

The Germans knew a picture was worth a thousand words. That was why they forbade us to take photographs. They didn't want one word, let alone a thousand, or a thousand thousand, of Jewish culture surviving the Holocaust. They certainly didn't want anyone to see a photographic record of what they had done to the Jews, unless it was one of their own making. Silence was their ally, and the absence of pictures would help make historians mute and the world deaf. It was my personal destiny to break that silence. I preserved nearly five hundred pictures of Jewish life in Poland, taken both before and during the war.

Somehow, even as a child I valued photographs. In our town of Kolbuszowa, only three people had cameras: two official photographers and a Jew named Shmuel Berl, who brought one with him when he returned after living in Vienna for a period. I attached myself to Shmuel like a pest, followed him wherever he went, watched and asked and learned about taking pictures. Of course I had nothing to do with what I learned from him. I had no camera. But that was remedied when, as fate would have it, in 1934 my brother Albert, who had gone to America fifteen years before as Avrum, announced that he was coming for a visit. I wrote to him begging that he bring me a "photographic apparat." A what? Eventually he realized I meant a camera, and when he appeared he had with him an old Kodak box camera.

I was fourteen years old at the time, and I began snapping pictures of family, friends, scenes of life in the town. I took pictures of everything I encountered—except girls. Naturally there were no girls in my pictures. As a fourteen-year-old yeshiva boy complete with side curls and long *kapota*, I rarely encountered, and certainly didn't look at girls. Besides, there were plenty of things to photograph without girls.

Gradually, both my skill and my collection grew. I recorded many people and scenes during the next few years. But this was during the 1930s in Poland, and events would soon close down my photographic efforts, as the Germans conquered our land and took control of our lives. Eventually, they would prohibit ownership of cameras. Anyone caught with one would be shot. Yet, because I was still young enough to be infused with feelings of immortality, I continued to take my pictures secretly, even after we had been sent to the ghetto. I maintained this clandestine recording of our life and times until it was announced that the ghetto was to be liquidated and its residents relocated. Recognizing that the dangers involved in carrying the camera during the move were simply too great, I did the unthinkable. I smashed my beloved camera into a thousand pieces. I certainly wasn't going to give it over to the Germans. As I broke it, I felt as if I were breaking with a part of my life. I loved that camera as I have loved few worldly goods. It was gone.

But I still had my pictures. Hundreds of them. Of course, we didn't know it then, but the Germans were moving the Jews of Kolbuszowa to the larger ghetto at Rzeszow as part of an effort to gather the Jews of the region into one place to be more conveniently transported to death camps or concentration camps. We would be forced to leave most of our possessions behind. We could take only what we could carry. I knew that one thing I would take with me were my pictures, whatever else had to be jettisoned. And so when we moved from our small ghetto in Kolbuszowa to the larger one in Rzeszow, I took with me the chronicle of our town and time, under wraps, hidden among my possessions.

Within a few days of arrival at Rzeszow, the Germans began to ship out transports to Belzec. This was in June 1942. It was to be a relocation, they claimed. Jews were going to be resettled to work in the fields in the east. And they went. No one knew then that resettlement meant the gas chambers, the death camps. No one knew, so they went.

In due course, my mother, my five sisters, their husbands, and their children were all sent on a transport to Belzec. (My father had already been shot.) I didn't go because two weeks before, I was selected as one of a hundred young, strong boys to be taken back to the empty ghetto in Kolbuszowa to destroy it. They set up a makeshift labor camp in the old synagogue and each morning marched us out to work.

The Germans were intent on wiping out all remnants of the Jewish community. One by one, we attacked with hammers and axes the houses that we had lived with. The rooms where we had been born, where we ate, slept, prayed, loved—these rooms were knocked apart by our small band of conscripted destroyers. The wood produced by our efforts went to the Poles to burn for fuel for the winter. The valuables went to the Germans as plunder. The tears remained with us. Goaded by the Germans, we worked tirelessly to destroy our past.

The German commandant ordering this destruction was a vicious, sadistic Gestapo man named Walter Twardon. We all knew him. During the years he was Landskomissar of our region he killed hundreds of people. Two years before, when the Germans first came, he had commandeered all of the merchandise my father had in his store. Twardon still had much of this booty stored in its original packaging with my father's name on it, and he wanted to repackage it and send it back to his home in Germany. Since he knew that I had intimate familiarity with the merchandise, he assigned me to work making packages for shipment. Coffee, sugar, soap, oil, all kinds of things were packaged and shipped off.

Meanwhile, the valuables from the destroyed ghetto were also piling up. Twardon widened my responsibilities to include taking them to Rzeszow and while there, picking up coffee to bring back. It wasn't long before he had me running a regular route from Kolbuszowa to Rzeszow carrying brass and iron there and bringing back coffee beans to be shipped to Germany. In such a way was I able to get a pass that allowed me almost free run, back and forth, three times a week from Kolbuszowa to Rzeszow. I made the trip with an old horse and wagon. So it wouldn't be a total loss, we built a false bottom into the wagon for a little smuggling as well.

This wagon thus became more than just a means of transporting merchandise for Twardon. It also became a conduit for my bringing bread stolen from bakeries in our camp to the few Jews remaining in Rzeszow, and most significantly for purposes of this story, it enabled me to recover and bring back the photographs I had taken with me when we were moved out of the ghetto originally.

Once in Rzeszow I checked the place where my family had been housed before the deportation east. It was an old coal bin, and when I returned to it, I found it still contained all the things my family had brought with them, including my pictures. While working to demolish the ghetto, I had come upon additional photographs and documents that others had. I had gathered these up as I worked so that, combined with my own collection, there were nearly five hundred pictures of life in our town, and a comparable number of documents. I suspected that our families had been killed, and I decided that I had to preserve the pictures in order to perpetuate their memory. These images of the faces of the Jews of Kolbuszowa would assure that their lives and times would not be forgotten. What to do with them? Where to keep them?

I bought a roll of wax paper and made packages—twenty-five photographs and documents to a package. I wrapped them tightly, and into each one I put a letter in Polish that said, "If this package is found by anybody

A typical Polish peasant's dwelling with its barn. The author hid and preserved many of the photographs and documents in this book in the thatched roofs of these houses.

and I am not alive, send it to Albert Salsitz, 2070 72nd Street, Brooklyn, N. Y. *and you will be rewarded."*

Altogether there were about forty packages. Since I had a pass to go out from our camp and town I was able to take them after work in the dark to the homes of friendly peasants in villages near our town. Their barns had roofs made of thick, thatched straw. Unbeknownst to these peasants I would go to the attic of the barns or stables and shove a packet of twenty-five photos and documents into the straw and leave it. I always put the packet in the same place in the roof: the tenth patch from the left and fifth row from the bottom. In the last roof I left a list of the houses where all the packets had been put. Thus, I left my pictures to remain, until the war ended, or until they were discovered, or possibly, until they turned to dust in the highly likely event that no one found them and I was killed before the war ended. That was 1942.

Two years later, I had not only survived the war, I had ended it as a high-ranking officer in the Polish army. When the shooting had stopped, I went back to these same forty barns—this time in broad daylight in my uniform and in my military car. None of the houses had been destroyed. None of the packages had been disturbed. The tightly thatched straw and wax paper had preserved these pictures and documents despite the passing of the seasons and the tyranny of the occupation. When I told the curious peasants what I was retrieving from their roofs they were justifiably shocked. Had the pictures been discovered by the Germans, their unwitting guardians would have no doubt shared the fate of their Jewish subjects.

The story is almost ended. There is one final episode. There came a time for me to flee Poland altogether. When I did, my wife was arrested and held for a while. I wrote her from Germany, once she was released, to leave whatever she had to in order to get out of the country. Leave everything, but bring the photographs.

Nearly sixty years have passed since they made it safely out of the ghetto, the coal bin, the labor camp, the peasants' roofs, and Poland itself. The irony hasn't escaped me. Because I was sent to destroy the last remnants of Jewish life in the ghetto I was able to preserve a major record of that life.

The author found this Kodak box camera, which is just like the one he had in Poland, at a flea market in Buenos Aires, Argentina. With no bargaining, he bought it for fifty cents.

The pictures I took as a child have been widely viewed. They were given to survivors I have met who had no other record of their families. They were published in a Yiskor Memorial Book of our town in 1965. They appear in the three books I have published, *Against All Odds: A Tale of Two Survivors* (Holocaust Library, 1990), *A Jewish Boyhood in Poland—Remembering Kolbuszowa* (Syracuse University Press, 1992), and *In a World Gone Mad: A Heroic Story of Love, Faith, and Survival* (Abingdon Press, 2001). They appeared in the Holocaust Memorial Council publication *Fifty Years Ago: In the Depths of Darkness*, published in 1992. Now I am working with the U.S. Holocaust Museum in Washington, where they are making five albums from the five hundred photographs that I saved.

What a gift that old Kodak box camera was from my brother Albert! (In 1992, I found a replica of the camera, which I bought, in an antique store.) What a gift it turned out to be to the memory of those who perished. What a gift it was to me each time I take the yellowing photos out of their wrappings in the comfortable study in my well-to-do suburban community, and slowly go from face to face, from scene to scene and remember what was . . . and think of what might have been.

My Brief Career as a Pilot

By now, readers are aware that by the time the war was over, I was no longer Naftali Saleschutz. Instead, I was known as Tadeusz Zaleski and I was a Catholic security officer in the Polish army. What I haven't told is how I got to that position. It is such a bizarre story that to this day, I am not sure I understand it.

The advancing Russian army liberated Kolbuszowa the night of July 28. When the sun came up on the twenty-ninth the Germans were gone. By then, there were just six of us left alive in the woods from the original 125, and with varying degrees of caution, we emerged. It turned out that caution was well advised. In many instances, the Poles took over as the enemy of the Jews, and it didn't take long to realize that there would be no such thing as a "normal" existence for the survivors.

Everything and everyone Jews had known and loved were gone. Their old houses were in the hands of Poles, who now added this practical fact to their traditional anti-Semitism as reasons to eliminate the surviving Jews. My father's dying words had never left me. When the Germans shot him down in our back yard and he lay there, he had shouted, *"Nekuma! Nekuma! Nemt Nekuma!* Revenge, Revenge. Take Revenge!"* I had sworn that I would, and two weeks after emerging from the woods, I joined the Polish army.

At that time, the Poles were drafting young men to join the fight against the Germans. Notable among the exceptions to who was eligible for the draft were the Jewish survivors. Even if they had wanted to draft Jews, there were no records of who had survived. That didn't matter to me. I wanted to fight the Germans, so I volunteered. Besides, volunteers were offered the opportunity to pick the branch of service they would go into, and I had decided that I wanted to be in the air force so I could bomb the German fatherland. I wanted to go into training to become a pilot.

They sent the volunteers who had applied for air force training to undergo a series of extremely rigorous mental and physical tests. I was the only Jew who had volunteered for the air force, and after the tests were completed, I was chosen to join the small group of Polish soldiers who also were selected for pilot training. When I asked the Russian Jewish doctor who had examined us, how, after all of the neglect and abuse I had suffered in the woods, I was in good enough shape to be eligible for this select service, he said the fact that I had survived at all proved my intelligence, and the hardship had built my endurance. When I told my friends what I was doing, they gave me the nickname of Lotczyk, which means pilot in Russian. Even today, I meet people who call me Lotczyk, and I know I knew them in those days.

Pilot training for the Polish air force took place under the auspices of the Russians at a base in Kujbushev, Siberia. I received my orders to report to the railroad station in Lublin, the capital of Poland at the time, for transport to Siberia. When I arrived with my knapsack I found about two hundred soldiers who had also been selected for the air force had already gathered to await the train. No one seemed to know when the train would be coming. Rumors ranged from five minutes to five days. All we knew was that we would put our belongings on the station platform, and wait.

Our spirits were high. We were young, in the army, going off to pilot school. I made friends with those waiting in my immediate area, and pretty soon, we were joking, swapping stories, ogling the girls, and, perhaps a few even sipped a little vodka. I hadn't taken the trouble to identify myself to my new comrades as a Jew, as I was the only one.

We had been waiting a few days in this state of expectation, when a young, and most attractive female lieutenant walked through our area. The whistles and flirtatious comments came instantly. "Hey, lieutenant, are you here to take us to Russia?" "Wait for me, lieutenant. I'll follow you anywhere."

She laughed good-naturedly and stopped to talk to the boys. As she did, she looked around at our group and, still smiling, pointed at me and said, "Do you have a few minutes? I'd like to talk to you."

"To me? Sure, I have time for you." I winked at my buddies and left my knapsack. "Watch this and call me if the train comes," I said. And as they all called after me to watch myself, and to not do anything they wouldn't do, and the things young men in the army say to one of their buddies going off with a pretty girl, the young lieutenant led me away.

She led me around the corner of the station where we were outside the view of the others. We stopped and she asked, "Are you *amchu?*"

I looked more closely at this beautiful lieutenant. "Are you *amchu?*" means, "Are you from our nation?" Among Jews, "*amchu*" was a signal we used to ask new acquaintances if they, too, were Jewish. It was the way those who were passing as Gentiles could discover one another. To a non-Jew, this Hebrew word was meaningless and passed without understanding. We had found it to be an important communication tool in dangerous times. I nodded yes.

She asked me, "What are you doing with that bunch of *chamy.*" "*Chamy*" is a Polish term that the townspeople used to refer to the peasants. It means something akin to ignoramuses and is not intended to be a compliment.

I told her, "Those are my buddies. I joined the Polish army to take revenge on the Germans. We are going to Russia to learn to be pilots and then we will bomb the Germans."

She looked at me and smiled. "Maybe you belong with the *chamy* because you are not very smart. How long does air training school take?"

"Two years," I said.

"And do you think the war will still be on in two years. We are already throwing them out of Poland. How long do you think it will take before the war is over? No more than six months. Then you will be stuck in Siberia. Why are you so anxious to take revenge anyway?"

I told her that I had lost my parents and five sisters, friends, and relatives during the war.

"Get your knapsack and come with me." she said. "If its revenge you want, I will arrange for you to get revenge."

"How can I go with you? I will miss my train. I have orders for the air force."

Again, she told me to follow her. She would arrange everything. I stood there, weighing what had just happened to me during the last few minutes. I had passed a competitive physical and mental examination to qualify for the air force. I was on my way to invest two years of my life in training. My plans were made and complete, and suddenly this woman lieutenant singles me out at the train station and tells me to abandon all that and go with her.

I had to admit, her argument about the war soon being over made sense. I decided to go with her to see what it was she was talking about. I figured the train probably wouldn't be along within the next hour. Against a loud chorus of envious whistles and catcalls from my buddies, I went back, took my knapsack, and left with the lieutenant. I led them all to believe we were going to have a brief romantic interlude.

Instead of a place where we could have our tryst, the lieutenant led me to the army base. She walked briskly, returning salutes and greetings from everyone we met. I began to think that perhaps there was more to my lieutenant than a pretty face. Finally, we went into one of the buildings, down the corridor, and entered a huge office. Seated behind the appropriately large desk was a well-decorated colonel in the Polish army. I learned that his name was Grosz.

"What do you think of this guy," she began to tell the colonel. "He wants to take revenge on the Germans so he joins the air force. I told him we could do better for him."

"Perhaps we can," said the colonel. "Let's see what his story is."

And with some prompting, I told them the story of the ghetto, the labor camps, the escape to the woods, the service with the AK, the betrayals at the hands of old friends, the loyalty from unexpected quarters. By the time I was finishing, several hours had passed, and I was concerned that I would miss the train.

When I had finished, the colonel looked at me for a long while. Then he said, "We can use you. I am in charge of army intelligence, and I think a man like you would be excellent for our purposes."

I said, "What are you talking about? I have orders to go to Kujbushev."

He said, "Let me see your orders," and when I handed them to him, he tore them up. I was in shock. I knew I would be in a great deal of trouble if I didn't show up where I had been ordered to go.

He told me not to worry. He would write me new orders. He asked where I had been staying before joining the army, and I told him Rzeszow.

"Good, the chief of security in Rzeszow is a friend of mine, I will send you there."

He then asked what my name was, and I told him Naftali Saleschutz, but I was known as Tadeusz Jadach in the underground.

"No, neither of those will do. Saleschutz is too Jewish, and you can't use the same name you used in the underground. We need a good Polish name for you. Tadeusz is okay, but we need a Polish second name." After trying out a few on me, he said, "What about Zaleski? That sounds like Saleschutz and it is a good Polish name." And so I became Tadeusz Zaleski.

My head was swimming. New orders, new assignment, new name. I barely heard him say to his secretary, "Make out orders for Tadeusz Zaleski sending him to Rzeszow." The secretary wrote, along with official orders assigning me to Informacja, or military intelligence, a letter to the commandant of intelligence activities in Rzeszow indicating that the colonel had known me and vouched for me as an honorable and effective officer. The female lieutenant took me back to the railroad station where my buddies were still waiting for the train to take them to Siberia, and to their utter disbelief, they learned that I was not going with them. My days as Lotczyk were over. Instead, I boarded the train to Rzeszow, where I was welcomed into the intelligence service by the commandant, put on his staff, and assured with a wink.

"Don't worry Zaleski. We will give you a chance for revenge."

I never saw the female lieutenant again. To this day, I don't know her name, nor why she selected me. I did see Colonel Wiktor Grosz on several occasions on official business. And most importantly, just as they had promised, I had many opportunities for the acts of revenge I desperately wanted.

A "Kol Nidre" Memorial

More than seventy years pass between the time of the beginning of this story and the time of its end. And the story is not over. It is a work in progress.

The year is 1928. Life in the Jewish community in Kolbuszowa is as I described it in my book *A Jewish Boyhood in Poland.* The *shul* was the dominant institution among the Hasidic population—which included me and my family. Intense as the involvement with the synagogue was, day in and day out throughout the year, the coming of the fall season signaled great focus on God and his covenant with us, the Jewish people. The series of High Holidays that marks the season was upon us.

Naturally, my father was a pillar of the synagogue community, and I, at age eight, sang in the choir and continued my studies. I have always had a natural musical talent and could easily learn and repeat a song after one or two hearings, so my pure, unaltered soprano voice was welcomed to blend with the choir and cantoral recitations.

Kolbuszowa was particularly fortunate because it counted among its native sons Israel Hillel Bakon, who upon reaching adulthood, had journeyed to Berlin, where he became a world famous cantor. Since he had married a local girl, Chaya Aidel Elfond, before fame overtook him, he would return to Kolbuszowa from time to time and participate in the service and frequently perform original arrangements of the liturgy, so otherwise well known to all in the Orthodox community. And when he did, I would sing with him, so it was in that way that I came to know him and he, me.

We fast forward the picture to the rise of Hitler and Nazism in Germany, *Kristallnacht,* the burning of the synagogues and holy books. There was no longer much calling for a cantor in Berlin, no matter how talented, so Cantor Bakon returned to Kolbuszowa with his wife and small child, Hersh.

We needn't dwell on the turning pages of the calendar and what they brought. The invasion of Poland was complete in days, Kolbuszowa occupied, and eventually the Jews were walled off into a ghetto.

And so, once again, Cantor Bakon was largely unemployed. Jewish services were forbidden, and he turned his talents in other directions. There in the ghetto, Israel Bakon found the ingredients to manufacture soap. He used lard and caustic acid that he procured from the Polish peasants along with the other materials and produced a harsh, but effective cleanser. It found a ready market in the ghetto, and it was in that way that this man of music eked out an existence making and selling soap.

He also worked for the German police, since he spoke perfect German from his years in Berlin. He did odd jobs, cleaning shoes, toilets, the barracks, and doing repairs wherever they were needed. He would translate for the Germans and act as an intermediary between them and the Poles and Jews. Soon the Germans became aware of his musical talents, so the representatives of the land of Wagner, Beethoven, and Brahms would have their sometime translator, sometime boot polisher, perform grand opera and German show tunes for them in the evening. For this they gave him a little food that he could take to his family, and between the soap and the handouts he survived.

As time went on, it was clear that the Germans intended to liquidate the ghetto and its occupants. On the final Yom Kippur in the ghetto, in 1941, Israel Bakon went to the leaders in the Jewish community and proposed that a last Yom Kippur service be held in secret in a private house. I remember the excitement because it had been some time since services on this scale had been held in Kolbuszowa. The community got itself ready, and at the *Kol Nidre* service, held the night before Yom Kippur, much of the Orthodox Jewish community was in attendance. And they were in for a treat, for Chazan (cantor) Bakon had composed a special melody for the *"Yaaleh,"* a prayer in which the Jews implore God to accept their prayers, with such hopeful passages such as:

> May our knocking at Your gates be heard at nightfall,
> Our joy come to us in the morning
> And our petition be granted at dusk.

He taught this to me, and we harmonized his haunting notes artfully crafted to match the spirit of the passage. Cantor Bakon and I had sung many of his compositions together before. But this was different. This one carried the beauty of a master composer at the peak, and tragically, also at the end of his career.

Within nine months the ghetto was liquidated by the Germans and its occupants exiled and subsequently exterminated in the gas chambers of Belzec. Cantor Bakon, his wife Chaya, and their four-year-old son

Hersh in the end were no different from the rest: killed. The final verse of the Yaaleh had ultimately been rejected.

> May our cry rise up to You at nightfall,
> Our plea reach Your presence in the morning,
> And your mercy be shown to us at dusk.

My own life took a few peculiar turns, bits and pieces of which are described in different stories in this collection. I was conscripted to be part of a labor gang that was sent back to strip the by-then empty ghetto of anything of possible value to the Germans. I lived in a labor camp from which a few of us escaped, I was hidden for a short time by Polish peasants, but ultimately betrayed and forced to live in the woods for almost two years, surviving on the land.

During this time, my brother Leibush and I had contact with the Resistance, and in August 1944, in the chaos of advancing Russians and fleeing Germans, I joined the Polish army, masquerading as a Catholic Pole, Tadeuz Zaleski. Stationed in Rzeszow, a bigger city near Kolbuszowa, I had frequent opportunity to intervene secretly on behalf of Jewish groups that found themselves in the clutches of the authorities. The Polish peasants had lost none of the hatred of the Jews that we felt had to be a part of their genetic endowment. Nothing had changed for the Jews. We went from Polish hatred, to German hatred and back to Polish hatred. It was essential that my secret identity as a Hasidic Jewish boy from Kolbuszowa remain a secret, and I was largely successful. There were a few other Jews in high positions in the army, however, and we shared our secret with one another.

Given the generally hostile environment for returning Jews—they frequently found Polish people occupying their houses, and this was a constant source of conflict—many found it too dangerous to live in the small towns that dotted the Polish landscape and assembled in the bigger towns. Rzeszow was one of these points of concentration, so as an officer of security in the Polish army, my opportunities to help were abundant.

The first fall after the liberation, when the temperatures were changing, a group of Jews led by a former *shochet*, or ritual slaughterer, came to me with a request. They understood they were making their request of Tadeusz Zaleski, Catholic, who, while an army officer and representative of government authority, had acquired a reputation for behaving decently toward the Jews. I should hope so.

Their request was to hold High Holy Days services in the ancient synagogue of Rzeszow, which somehow had survived the war. It had been many years since such a happening had occurred in this building, but it stood intact. The surviving Jews were concerned that if they all gathered together in one place for the service, the Poles might seize the opportunity for a pogrom. They wanted government protection while the services were to be conducted. Behind my cold military exterior that I presented to them, I was delighted. I pressed them for details, but it was my immediate intention to give them this protection and to dispatch a squad of troops to secure the area.

In fact, I had a wild idea that went far beyond protection. I wanted to participate in the *Kol Nidre* service just as I had so many years ago with Cantor Bakon. But how? I was Tadeuz Zaleski, a Catholic officer of the State Security.

I sent one of my Jewish confidants to talk to the *shochet*. My messenger was in uniform, and he informed the organizers of the service that at a particular point during the *Kol Nidre* service, they would have a visit from a guest participant in the service. They should expect him to approach the ark from the side and should step aside to allow him to perform this element. It was certainly mysterious, but they readily agreed. They assumed it would be someone coming through from out of town who my lieutenant wanted to favor, and they certainly wanted to accommodate him.

At precisely the moment for the chanting of the Yaaleh, shrouded in a large wool prayer shawl, I entered the main hall, walked to the ark, faced it, with my back to the congregation, and I began to sing. It was Bakon's melody that I sang that night. It remained with me over the years, and its ability to inspire had lost nothing. The notes went out from the prayer shawl and hung over the congregation. And then it was over, and I was gone. I don't know if anyone suspected it had been me who chanted. I had preserved the work of my wonderful teacher, and once again the world could enjoy that which would have been lost, had not he taught it to me in the ghetto in Kolbuszowa.

It is six decades later, and as this is being written, the seasons are again changing and again the High Holidays are upon us. I no longer live in Kolbuszowa. I no longer live in Rzeszow. I left Poland and traveled to Germany, to the United States, to Brooklyn, and eventually to Springfield, New Jersey, where I have lived in comfort for forty-five years.

Worship is much easier to come by than it was in the ghetto or in Rzeszow. No overt threat hangs over the Conservative congregation to which I belong. The congregation has a choir and a cantor, and I have sung in that choir since coming to Springfield. And although the cantors have come and gone over the years, I have taught to each of them the Yaaleh composed so long ago in the ghetto by Israel Hillel Bakon.

Each *Kol Nidre* night for the past forty-five years I have chanted that melody. And somewhere, I am sure, the souls of Cantor Bakon and of countless other slaughtered Jews from the ghetto stir to its timeless notes. You are invited to *Kol Nidre* services at my synagogue next year. You will see that I don't exaggerate the beauty of that melody.

Another Surviving Jew Is Found

By 1945, to all outward appearances, the war had claimed one more Jew: me. While I wasn't lying in a pit and hadn't gone up a chimney, I nevertheless was unrecognizable as a Jew. Naftali Saleschutz was gone. Instead, I was known as Tadeusz Zaleski, Captain in the Polish liberation forces, stationed in Cracow. When I looked in the mirror to shave each morning I was reminded how far I had gone. My skin was scraped clean, sidecurls gone, and hair closely cropped. In place of the Hasidic cap, I wore a peaked officer's hat. Instead of an unadorned black caftan, I sported the brass and ribbons of a military uniform. I had worked with the Polish underground and security forces for the past two years and was an accepted and trusted member of Poland's military.

It is hard to believe that this picture taken in 1933 at the time of the Bar Mitzvah of Naftali Saleschutz is of the same person photographed in 1944, Tadeusz Zaleski.

During the spring of that year a commission came to Poland to investigate war crimes. It was made up of leading legal, academic, and religious figures of the day drawn from all over the world and headed by the Archbishop of Canterbury, Hewlett Johnson, known as the Red Dean. The commission would tour the sites of the Polish death camps to gather information. Since my records showed that I spoke English (it wasn't until two years later, when I came to America, that I realized I didn't) and had no small measure of personal initiative, I was assigned to be one of two Poles who took the group around. My job was to schedule the tour from day to day.

Our first visit was to Auschwitz, where thousands of sick and dying Jews were lingering in the camps. These were the ones that had been too weak for the Germans to herd away in the death march ahead of the advancing Russian armies. I made sure that each of the death camps was visited and in each there were vestiges of the recent horror. Each visit was marked by my reliving the tragic destinies of so many of my family and friends. It was heartbreaking for me but devastatingly instructive for the commission. These were scenes none of them would easily forget.

As the time we spent together on this grim tour extended I developed a good working relationship with the archbishop. I felt we were close enough that I could ask a favor of him. What was it? Would he be kind enough to carry four letters for me to be mailed when he returned to a part of the world where there was postal service? In Poland, at the time, there was none, and ordinary people had no way to communicate with anyone outside their immediate area. I explained that these were letters written by my girlfriend to friends in America and to the relatives of Jewish neighbors who had gone to Palestine before the war. She wanted to tell them that she was alive and, just as the commission was going to do, tell the people in Palestine what had happened to their families.

This was nearly true. Actually, my girlfriend of the time was Amalie Petranker from Stanislawow—she later became my wife; she was herself a surviving Jew who had masqueraded during the war as a Christian. She had unquestioned acceptance of her identity as Felicia Milaszewska and had in fact worked for German industry during the occupation—in Poland as a Roman Catholic Pole and also as a *Volksdeutch* (ethnic German). She, like me, had led a double life, and now we would use the archbishop to mail letters to our families telling them that we had survived the war.

Naturally, the letters wouldn't be from the Jews Naftali Saleschutz and Amalie Petranker, but rather about them. One letter was addressed to Amalie's grandmother, Rivka Genger, in Tel Aviv, Palestine; another to my brother David in Ramat Gan; another to her sister, also in Palestine; and a fourth to my brother Albert in America. The letters were written in English by my girlfriend, who spoke perfect English, sealed, and given to the archbishop to act as courier and to mail. And he was true to his word. The letters were mailed, received, and, in fact, brought the first news to many that there were Jews who had survived the Holocaust. The letter sent to my brother in America was subsequently reprinted in the *New York Times.*

But this isn't to be the story of the letter sent to America, but rather of those sent to my brother David and to Amalie's grandmother in Palestine. Both, as it turned out, arrived at about the same time. David received the news with unmitigated joy and relief that two of his brothers—Leibush and I—had survived the war. You can well imagine how it is to have such a message drop in on you, written by a stranger whom you do not know, yet filled with detail that could assure the authenticity of the message. He celebrated and thanked God, and as he reread the letter, he realized that the writer had mentioned that she had written to another person in Palestine, Rivka Genger, of Tel Aviv. My brother decided to visit this Rivka Genger to share the experience of getting such a letter the same day.

He made the journey, high in expectation, but when he met her, he found her strangely subdued. Where his own joy had been uninhibited at learning of the survival of a brother, hers was restrained—not what one would expect from a grandmother learning that her granddaughter had survived the Holocaust and was alive and well.

He soon learned the reason for Rivka's restraint. Yes, she was happy that Amalie had survived where so many had died. Yes, it was wonderful news. Yes, but. What had she survived for? To marry a Pole? And Rivka poured out her disappointment and heartbreak that after learning of her granddaughter's survival, she would be in mourning for her because she was marrying a non-Jew. Why couldn't she wait to come to Palestine? There were so many Jewish boys for her to give herself to. Why was she planning to marry a Polish army officer, probably an anti-Semite? And with this cry and lament, she showed my brother the photograph that had been sent her showing Amalie and me, arm in arm, smiling with the bright light of love and life on our faces. There was Amalie in her new dress and me in my Polish army dress uniform, handsome, dashing, and looking for all the world like the Cossack marauder she knew from youthful pogroms.

Seeing the photo, David recognized me immediately. He bid her to wait. He would be back. Perhaps the situation wasn't as bad as it appeared. He was of small consolation to her, but she put on a brave front as David promised to return in two hours.

Back home, David had another picture of me that had been taken in a different uniform on another occasion. It was the uniform of the Hasid taken at the yeshiva. I still wore my side curls. In place of the military tunic and brass buttons, my body was covered with the homely caftan worn by the Orthodox. I had the black velvet Hassidic cap and the knee-length pants. I looked exactly like what I was at the time, a yeshiva boy following in the tradition of generations of forebears.

David returned to 6 Avodah Street in Tel Aviv to show Rivka the picture of me. Clearly it was the same boy. "Here is your Cossack," he said. "It is my brother Naftali that your granddaughter plans to marry." And to Rivka Genger's disbelieving eyes, there swam into focus through the tears of despair, a figure dressed in the unrelieved drabness of the Hasidic garb. When Rivka recognized the face, she realized she was looking at the most beautiful sight she had ever beheld in her long and eventful life.

The Hundred Children

One night, my wife Amalie and I settled down for a quiet night at home, watching television. The newspapers had advertised an NBC movie called "My Hundred Children." We looked for motion pictures related to the Holocaust, and the network's promotion indicated that this story took place in Poland immediately after the war. Since we both had been there during this time, we made sure that we tuned in to the program. As the story unfolded, I was dumbfounded. I realized that not only did I know much of the story being told, I had played a principal role in its outcome.

The story opened in Cracow. A woman named Lena Kuchler is looking for information on her sister. The refugee center posted the names of known Jewish survivors, and each day Lena came to scan the list. The number of names listed were pitifully few, and it turns out that they would never include the name of her sister, Fela. We learn that Lena had survived the war by passing as a Catholic, but that her sister, fearing that she looked too Jewish, had left the home that had been sheltering them both. Lena's situation was not very different from that of Amalie, who also survived the war masquerading as a Polish Catholic. She too had a sister, Celia, but in her case, there had been no point in searching. She knew that her sister had been taken away by the Germans in 1941.

In the course of going to the Jewish Refugee Center each day, Lena learns that a hundred abandoned Jewish children are living on the third floor of the building. They had been brought there, but owing to the lack of resources at the center, had been virtually abandoned. The story involves her heroic effort to save these children from the hunger, the disease, and the Polish anti-Semitism that would otherwise doom them.

As I watched the picture unfold, I realized that I knew this story. In fact, a long time ago, I had been a principal player in its outcome.

"Commandant Zaleski, there is a Jewish woman waiting to see you," my secretary informed me. As the war was ending I had joined the Polish army, and by 1945 I found myself in Cracow in charge of security. I, too, was masquerading as a Polish Catholic, but it was increasingly recognized in Jewish circles that I was extremely sympathetic to the needs of the survivors. Perhaps they suspected I was a Jew. There were a number of other army officers in situations similar to mine, and it was not unusual for a representative of some Jewish group with a problem to come to my office seeking help. For my part, I found myself in a powerful position to give it and did so whenever I could.

After introducing herself, the woman before me revealed the astonishing news that there were a hundred Jewish children who were survivors of the camps, the alleys, the woods; some had been abandoned by their Catholic protectors after it became obvious that their Jewish parents would not be returning to make the payment promised to them at the beginning of the war. These children were in dire need of help, but there was no money or food at the center for them.

"Mister Stulbach and Lady Markowiecka of the Jewish Committee," she told me, "had suggested that I might help."

I stared at her. One hundred Jewish children. I couldn't believe it. I had to help her, but how? I had no money or food to give her either. But I did have one thing. I had control over the stores of supplies and loot that the Germans had left behind.

While she watched, I wrote out an order and gave it to her.

"A thousand kilos of sugar. Our children can't eat sugar. What on earth can I do with a thousand kilos of sugar?" she asked when she had read the order.

"What you can do," I told her, "is sell it on the black market. Sugar is worth its weight in gold on the black market."

The Germans had left behind many things looted from the Poles. The sugar was just part of it. I told her that she would have to arrange for the transport of the sugar herself, but if she could do so, my order instructed the warehouse guards to transfer it to her. A few days later, the Jewish

Committee sent a truck to take delivery of the bags of sugar. These would be sold and bartered and would buy what she needed to save the hundred lives for which she had taken responsibility.

A week later she was back in my office.

"The children need soap."

Once again, I wrote an order for bundles of soap to be delivered to Lena Kuchler from the German warehouse, and this time I added clothing and blankets to the requisition. She thanked me and returned to her mission, and I returned to my duties as chief of security in postwar Cracow.

I lost track of Miss Kuchler and the children at that point in 1945; there was great chaos, and my duties were demanding. I had heard that she had left Cracow with the children, but was unaware of the outcome. The NBC program updated me that night, fifty years later, on what had happened subsequently.

Part of the money from the sugar was used to rent a country house in the town of Zakopane, which was located in the Carpathian Mountains. The children lived there with Lena Kuchler and gradually grew stronger and more healthy. But Zakopane was not immune from the anti-Semitism that infected Poland. She couldn't get a doctor who was willing to treat Jewish children, and when she tried to enroll them in the public school system, they were at first shunned by the teachers and later abused and beaten by their Polish classmates. Eventually, after an aborted attempt by the local Polish Jew haters to burn their house down, she saw that there would be no place for them to live in peace in Poland.

She arranged with the Jewish Committee in Cracow to smuggle the children to Palestine, and, traveling with falsified passports, bundles of currency, and bottles of vodka, they bribed and begged their way out of Poland, through Czechoslovakia, and eventually to France. In 1948, after Israel achieved independence, Lena Kuchler brought her brood of a hundred children to the promised land, where they joined the tens of thousands of other displaced persons who found refuge at last in the Jewish homeland. And so, the film ends.

I sat still for a long time as the credits for the picture ran. Most people will tell you that I am a pretty tough old man. I have been beaten, shot, starved, frozen. I have killed, and I have seen people I loved killed. I have had to be tough in business to get from the state of penniless immigrant to that of prosperous suburbanite. I became tough because I had to. Still, as I watched the film that night my eyes filled with tears. They do each time I watch it over again and see those wretched children restored and saved through the actions of this courageous woman. Perhaps, had I not been there at the time, her drive and initiative would have shown her another way to gain the needed money. Or perhaps not. Who knows? We can't rewrite history.

The fact is, I was there, and I am pleased that my help was instrumental in allowing Lena Kuchler to rescue those abandoned children who wanted nothing more than to be Jewish and to live.

Yad Vashem in Israel has a voluminous file documenting people's personal experiences in the Holocaust. These have been gathered through testimony of survivors and witnesses to the events of that time. The names of those mentioned have been catalogued on a variety of bases. One can look up people classified as friends, enemies, Jews, Gentiles, criminals, saviors, people of all nationalities and roles. The quiet of the library belies the turmoil of the lives methodically collected and catalogued in those files. I have looked through them, seeking to learn what happened to friends, relatives, acquaintances.

One time, as I was browsing through the records, I looked for the name Tadeusz Zaleski, my Polish Catholic alter ego. First, I automatically looked among the Jews, but couldn't find a reference. Eventually, I found that I was listed among the Gentiles who had helped survivors, the righteous Gentiles. There in the records of Yad Vashem is the narration given by Lena Kuchler acknowledging the debt of the hundred children to this Polish officer who gave them the sugar and other items that contributed to their survival and eventual escape to Israel.

Save the Child

•

The war was still grinding on, an insatiable monster, feeding on human lives. But by March 19 the monster had moved on to German soil. Now German towns and villages were being destroyed and German blood shed on the immaculate fatherland. How, I wondered, would the "superior" German citizens cope with the disorder that death and destruction bring?

While the battles of war, heralded daily in newspaper headlines, continued, I was fighting a personal battle within myself. It was one in which the stakes were high for all those involved. At risk was my own conscience—and the soul of a little boy. As the Talmud says, "He who saves a single life is considered to have saved the entire world."

I was stationed in Cracow, where I served in the military intelligence. Each day, news arrived of yet another concentration camp liberated; and

yet another set of horror stories revealed for all to see. At first each reve-
lation caused me to gasp in shock, as if I had been punched in the gut. But
then a numbness set in, brought on by the relentless statistics of death. A
portion of my mind had just seemed to shut down, an overloaded system
refusing to react. I was unable to feel anything.

In my role as a high-ranking Polish military officer, I could at last
contemplate some punitive action against the hated Germans. I could
now settle some scores. The Polish uniform I wore gave me power. For
higher authority, I needed nothing more than what I had seen, what my
people had endured.

I watched as Jewish survivors of the German killing machine returned home and began searching for remaining family members. Mostly
they found no one, nothing. In some towns, such as my own, out of thousands, only a handful survived.

One day one of these survivors, a young woman, came to see me. I
could tell she was nervous because she kept biting her lips. Seeing my
secretary sitting in my office, she asked if we could be alone. Always on
guard to protect my assumed identity as a Polish officer, I said the proce-
durally correct thing: "We have no secrets here. My secretary knows
everything that goes on in this room."

The woman was not intimidated. She must speak to me alone, she insisted. My curiosity aroused, I asked my secretary to leave.

When we were alone, I became aware of the woman's sweet face, lus-
trous black hair, and dark brown eyes that looked directly at me as
though trying to penetrate my innermost thoughts.

I'll have to be careful with this one, I thought.

As soon as my secretary closed the door, she apologized for coming to
me with a personal problem. She told me she was sent by Rabbi Moshe
Steinberg, then chief rabbi of Cracow, one of only a handful of people who
knew that I was Jewish.

"You are the only one who can help me," the young woman said,
grabbing my hands and kissing them profusely. I pulled my hands away,
embarrassed.

"I just returned from Auschwitz and a number of other concentration
camps. It's a miracle I'm alive. I still don't believe what I have lived
through. Me, a girl from a respectable middle-class family. I am a graduate
of a gymnasium. I know three languages. I can sew, play piano, write letters. We were good citizens. We worked hard. What did we do to deserve
this? The world has gone mad!"

I interrupted her. "Did you come here to tell me your personal history? I'm a busy man. Please get to the point," I said impatiently, afraid that if I wasn't extremely stern with her, she would become hysterical.

There were tears in her eyes as she begged me to listen to her story.

"My husband and I managed to avoid being deported for a long time. We worked hard, were strong, saved our food. But one day an order came for three thousand able-bodied men to work in a labor camp in the east." She spoke softly, but clearly. "After he left, I was alone with only my two-year-old son. I knew that soon I, too, would be taken away. There weren't many of us left in the ghetto. I had heard stories about what happened to the children, especially the little ones," she sobbed.

"I knew I had to find a place for my boy to stay that would be safe. So I gave him to a Polish woman, the maid of my sister. I gave Maryna, the maid, all the money and jewelry I had left, begged her to take care of my baby. She promised to take him to her village, where he would stay with the other children in her family. She said he would be safe there. Two days later, the S.S. came and sent me to Auschwitz," she said, clenching her hands in her lap.

"I won't bother you with what happened to me there. So many died there. So many. I wanted to die too, but I would think of my baby, and knew he was safe, and that kept me going. I knew he needed me." She looked up. "I was so glad that I had him with somebody. I saw what happened to the other children." She paused. Her skin was white where she dug her nails into her hands. She drew in her lips and looked down for a minute, closing her eyes and shaking her head.

"After I was liberated, I came straight here to look for my child. Maryna was no longer here. I was told she had moved. A week later I found my husband. He told me that he had survived because he hoped that our son and I would be waiting for him.

"We both searched for this Polish woman. When we finally found her, she didn't have the boy." The woman grimaced, shaking her head. "She gave us all sorts of stories, none of which made sense. We knew she was lying. We begged her to tell us where the boy was. We offered to give her our house in Cracow if she would tell us. We were desperate. I felt like wringing her neck, like slapping her dumb, empty face."

Finally, she told us the truth. She had given the boy to a Catholic monastery. We located the monastery a few days later, but our troubles weren't over. The child was now four years old. He had been baptized and given the Christian name Christopher.

We spoke to the priest in charge. He, of course, denied the whole story and refused to let us see our child." She paused again to collect her composure. "Every few days we went to the monastery to look through the fence, to see if we could still recognize our son. One day during a religious procession we saw him. I knew my child, right away. Of course, he didn't see us. We went to the government authorities, to the police, to Catholic priests, to everyone we could think of, begging for help. They couldn't care less," she said. "We finally went to the Jewish Council in Cracow. They were sympathetic, but said there was nothing they could do. Finally the president of the Jewish Council told me to see Rabbi Steinberg, that he could help us. And that is how I am here. He told me to be discrete," she added, looking around. She was silent, looking at me with great expectation.

But in the mechanically sympathetic manner that I had developed, I told her I was powerless to help.

I explained in fluent bureaucratese that this was not a matter for military intelligence, and that as an army officer, I could not involve myself in such matters.

I yearned to be able to help this desperate woman. In her I could see the same fierce, determined spirit that helped many women to survive for years in the woods and in the concentration camps. But I cloaked my feelings behind a facade of institutional indifference. How, I wondered, could I help this woman without giving away my identity as a Jew?

The woman left my office with tears in her eyes, bitterly disappointed. I, too, was greatly distressed, unable now to concentrate on my duties. Her face kept haunting me, her voice insisting, "You must help me." That night I could not sleep; I had heard her cry but had done nothing.

Even as the days passed, I couldn't shake her from my thoughts. Still I felt powerless. I could not ignore the risks of assisting her. Were I to help a Jew, I would without doubt be revealed as a Jew. Patriotic Poles certainly had no use for Jews.

A week later I saw the president of the Jewish Council on official business. He told me he had sent the young woman to see Rabbi Steinberg again. "She had nowhere else to turn," he added. "Can you see her again?"

I did not answer. I could not look the man in the eyes. But I wasn't surprised when the next day she returned and requested to see me. I was happy she had returned. My mind was made up; I had a plan.

"I am going to help you," I stated, without expression or explanation. "I have a plan to retrieve the child. But you must follow my instructions exactly. Do you understand?"

Suddenly her attractive face radiated joy. She nodded her head vigorously.

"It will take at least two weeks for me to put this plan into action. You are not to come here anymore. If I need you, you are to meet me at this address," I said, handing her a paper. "Now give me a complete description of the boy."

I assigned two of my most trustworthy officers, Henry Konikowski and Karol Krol, to make the necessary investigations and preparations. Now I was excited and happy at least to be able finally to do something.

Two weeks later, everything was ready. I contacted the parents of the boy with instructions to wait at the address I had given to the mother—a private apartment in the center of town. The boy would be delivered to them that night.

At midnight we drove to the monastery in Mogila. Our convoy consisted of a truck filled with soldiers and an official squad car. I rode with Krol and Konikowski in the car. They both understood the reason for this "raid"—both were Jewish. Henry Konikowski's real name was Heniek Reichwald from Rzeszow, Karol Krol's real name was Karol Kruger from Zakopane.

First, we surrounded the main building of the monastery. Then I knocked on the door and addressed the caretaker. I ordered him to open the gate and to call the priest in charge. The frightened man ran quickly down the hall and summoned the priest, who came, accompanied by several other priests.

I told them we had knowledge that a large cache of weapons and ammunition was being hidden in the monastery (not an uncommon practice).

Naturally, they denied this, but we said we had orders to search.

Once our search was under way, I had Konikowski, who was an electrician, short the electrical circuits so that all the lights went out. In the darkness, Krol and I located the boy, placed him in a knapsack, and hurried to the waiting car. Meanwhile, we continued our "search," our flashlights probing the darkness. In a short time, the lights went back on, and Konikowski, back at the car, drove away.

We were finished. I apologized to the priests for the disturbance. There was, I explained, probably some mistake with our intelligence, but that in time of war chances cannot be taken.

When I returned to headquarters, word arrived that everything had gone smoothly, and that the family had been reunited. The frightened boy, when taken out of the knapsack, had all along been clutching in his hands . . . a cross.

ADDENDUM

No subsequent complaint was made by the monastery to the authorities. My own explanation for this is that the administrators of the monastery were quite well aware that they had basically been party to a kidnapping by virtue of holding a child against the will of his parents. They must have known that they were in no position to make a complaint.

As Natural as Breathing In and Out

By the time the war ended I had a good deal of authority as an officer in the Polish Army. I was stationed in Cracow under an assumed name as a Polish Catholic, and to the extent I could, I used that authority to help Jews reunite with members of their families, or at least to learn what had become of them. As I traveled in the region around Cracow stories of some Gentiles who helped Jews during the war came to my ears, as well as stories of people who committed atrocities against the Jews. One tale concerning an incident that had occurred in Bochnia, a town in the Cracow area, was told to me by several survivors from that area.

The story concerned a young Jewish couple who had a beautiful two-year-old child. As the roundups of people to be sent to the death camps became more frequent, the mother, hoping to save her child, approached a neighboring Polish family whom she knew, with a proposition. She would give them all of her valuables if the Polish couple would take in their little boy and raise him as their own. After the war, if she survived, she would come back to claim the child. If not, the couple would raise him as their own. The Polish couple was childless, knew and liked the little boy, and agreed to take him in. Their story would be that this child belonged to a cousin from a distant town who had been arrested for serving in the Polish underground.

Heartbreaking for the Jewish couple as the separation was, keeping the child would have been worse. They were deported within a few days, and a mother with a child would certainly be the first to be gassed upon arrival at the camps.

The Polish couple took good care of the baby and treated it as if it were their own. For several months they lived as a family, as normally as possible under the occupation. After the week's work, every Sunday they went to church, and the child was being brought up in the Catholic tradition. On one of these Sundays a Polish woman from the neighborhood recognized the child and confronted the couple.

"Why do you take a Jewish child into the church?" she asked. The couple told her that she was mistaken. This was not a Jewish child, but the son of their cousin who was in Auschwitz for fighting for the underground. The Polish woman began to shout at the couple that no, the baby was Jewish and shouldn't be taken into the church, and as she did, she spotted two German policemen across the street. She ran over to them, gesturing. While she spoke no German she did know one word. "Jude, Jude," she shouted, pointing to the child. The Germans approached the couple, dressed for church with their beautiful child, and asked, in German, "What is going on?" The wife spoke German and explained that this woman had mistakenly identified the child as Jewish. The child belonged to her cousin, and she was taking care of it.

The Germans were satisfied with that, and were content to walk away when the Polish woman ran up to them, again screaming, "Jude, Jude". This time she added in Polish, "I will prove that the child is Jewish." With that, she grabbed the child away from the couple and pulled his pants down. Triumphantly she pointed at child's tiny penis with its revealing circumcision. At that time, only the Jewish boys were circumcised. It was damning and conclusive evidence. As the Polish woman gleefully exclaimed over her exciting victory to all in her hearing, the German police took the two-and-a-half-year-old child into an alley and there, on a Sunday morning, next to the church, they shot him in the head and left him.

When this story came to my attention, I sent two of my men to Bochnia to find this woman and bring her to Cracow. I asked her about the incident. Was it true that she had identified this Jewish child by pulling his pants down as I had heard? This strapping, red-faced daughter of the Polish soil stood before me, ostensibly a fellow Pole, and acknowledged that it was. "Tell me," I asked, "Why did you do this? What did it matter to you if this child lived, and was loved by the family? Why did you have to prove to the Germans he was Jewish?"

The woman looked at me for a moment. She seemed genuinely confused that she had been brought to Cracow to answer such a question from so long ago. Then she shrugged and answered me in Polish, "What else could I do? It was a Jewish child."

"Kol Nidre" in Cracow

*K*ol Nidre, we all know, is the holy prayer Jews have chanted for centuries on the eve of Yom Kippur, making vows to be kept for the coming year. Yom Kippur, we also know, comes in the autumn of the year. Finally, Poland is notorious for its anti-Semitism. Why then, in the middle of March, was the public address system in Cracow, Poland, playing *Kol Nidre* over its loudspeakers?

It is 1945. The Germans have been pushed out of Cracow by the advancing Russian forces, and in the wake of the battle, the Polish people are struggling to piece together lives that have been distorted, first by the German invasion, and now by its reversal. Amidst this turmoil, a handful of Jews eke out hand-to-mouth existences. Of the two thousand Jews in my town of Kolbuszowa before the war, only nine remained alive at its end. Across Poland, barely fifty thousand of its 3.5 million prewar Jews had survived. Those in Cracow have just returned from the concentration camps, come out of hiding, returned with the Russian army, or like me, been masquerading as Polish Catholics.

My fellow members of the Polish security forces know me as Tadeusz Zaleski. In the personal desolation I experienced from the loss of my entire family, I have turned to my work here as a source of distraction. Since joining the security force, I have risen in rank and responsibility and have been sent on a special assignment to liberate and help institute security in Cracow.

It was no coincidence that the loudspeakers were playing *Kol Nidre* on that March day. Here is how it happened.

In December of 1944 our special Polish security forces task force of a hundred was ordered to go from Rzeszow, where we were stationed, to Cracow, which had to be liberated. At this time, we were just behind the Russian forces, and our assignment was to be there to establish local authority once the Russians had liberated the town. Bouncing over the rutted roads in trucks and jeeps, shivering in the January cold, we were fortunate to be able to stop and spend a night in a flour mill formerly owned by a Jew and recently abandoned by the Germans.

Once in the mill, we began to look for souvenirs, and found an old Victrola and a stack of records. One by one, we played the records, and since we were young and free, we sang along with some, and danced to others. We were warm and happy for the first time in several days. At length, one record stopped, and the next one was put on; I was stunned to hear a familiar sound that I hadn't heard for many years: the *Kol Nidre* prayer.

"That's terrible," said my Polish companions. "Throw that one away." None of them knew what it was. They only knew you couldn't sing and dance to it.

"Don't you recognize it?" I countered. "It's a classical Spanish opera, an ancient Castillian aria. Don't throw it out." Some of my more cultured companions were embarrassed that they hadn't recognized it immediately, but now that I mentioned it, they did recall it as a Spanish opera, and they took it off the turntable and gave it to me. I casually put it among my belongings, in that way saving what was probably the last copy of the *Kol Nidre* recording performed by this cantor.

In Cracow, by March, we had established some semblance of government. I was the commander of local security, and I had made a friend of another masquerading Jew named Lieutenant Schorr. Schorr was in charge of Polish radio in Cracow and as part of the morale program, they played music over the loudspeaker system. I had shared the story of my saving the *Kol Nidre* record with him, and out of that, with a wink and a smile, one day, he played the aria from the mysterious Spanish opera for all to hear across Cracow.

The few Jews remaining in Cracow naturally recognized the prayer as soon as they heard it. And they were thrilled. Their morale soared as Lieutenant Schorr played *Kol Nidre* over the loudspeaker at least once each week.

At last, they thought, the official Polish government's attitude has changed to favor us.

Like a Cat, I Seem to Have Nine Lives

Cats are said to have nine lives. Through agility, alertness, and sheer luck, they often manage to survive falls, drownings, fires, near-death experiences of every variety, and live, if not to tell about it, at least to be wiser for the experience. Our family's cat, Ryfka, was born the same week I was and lived with us for twenty-one years. Her kittens populated half the homes in Kolbuszowa. Like most cats, Ryfka offered us a fascinating blend of aloof independence and affection, hunting mice, rubbing against our legs, and going out for days at a time. When the family moved into the ghetto, Ryfka stayed but one night. The next morning she went out and never returned. After twenty-one years of sharing our lives, she evidently didn't care to share our stay in the ghetto. Who can blame her!

At times I feel as if I must have absorbed some of our family cat's genes. In recollecting the events of my life, I count at least eight occasions, several of which are described elsewhere in this volume, when I found myself at death's door. Any one of them could have claimed me, but I am still here, not only wiser, but also, unlike the cat, able to tell about them.

The first occurred when I was but six weeks old. In 1920 Poland was in the grips of a smallpox epidemic, and the burial societies were busy. Many people, Jew and Gentile alike, had died from the disease, and the hospitals that had established systems of quarantine to separate those with the disease from their neighbors, were filled. My cousin, Regina Rothbard, whose family lived in a little village some distance from us, had come down with smallpox. They came to our town to seek medical aid for her, and while they stayed with us, she had shared a cradle with me. A few days later I, too, was stricken.

The hospital was full, and the family kept a vigil over me, but it was not long before the infant Naftali, the youngest of the nine Saleschutz children, had stopped breathing. My mother and sister covered my body with a sheet, and the next day, the burial society sent its representative to take the latest tiny victim of the epidemic away. Because I was but an infant, my father gave him a yeast box. He put me into this makeshift coffin, and as he sighed over the lamentations his work produced, my father offered him a glass of vodka to ease the burden.

The two unhappy men sat talking and sipping, and as they did so, they heard a sound the representative took to be mice scampering across the floor. "No," my father assured him. "We don't have mice. Our cat is very effective at keeping their population in check." As both men listened, they heard the sound again, and this time it was evident that it was coming from the yeast box. I was alive and sneezing from the dust that remained in the box. I hadn't stopped breathing after all, but if not for that pause for a drink, and the dust from the yeast, no one would have known. (see "The Yeastbox")

While I am aware of that earliest experience only through family folklore, I know the events that occurred during the war very personally. The Germans invaded Kolbuszowa in September 1939, and during the spring of 1940 I was selected for the concentration camp in Pustkow. There, whether I lived or died was simply a matter of chance. Or, more accurately, I should say, when I died was a matter of chance. That sooner or later we all would be killed was a certainty. One of the camp commandants, each morning and evening, randomly selected two men from our ranks to be hanged. It was at his whim. Then, as the rest of us marched to our daily work detail, he amused himself by firing his revolver into our ranks. On one such march, the man next to me was shot through the head. I was hit in the hand, which meant I would not be able to use an ax to cut trees. I knew that once the Germans learned of my injury they would have no reason to keep me alive. Others shielded me from exposure of my injury, and a few days later, I escaped.

I returned to Kolbuszowa where I found myself once again in a situation where my fate was in the hands of a reckless sadist. I learned through a friend who worked for the German police that a policeman named Bartelmus had announced that he wanted to kill me. I didn't know why; only that he intended to shoot me. My strategy to avoid him was successful for a time, but there came a day when the police needed some labor to unload a shipment of furniture that had come for the police station.

As I lifted my end of a headboard from the bed of the truck, it was shattered by two bullets smacking into it. I looked up in shock and saw Bartelmus holding his pistol and laughing. So, it was true. He did want to kill me. "You were lucky that time, Saleschutz. I missed. I will shoot you another day." He laughed. I later learned why he wanted to kill me. It seems he thought my girlfriend Rozia Susskind was too pretty for me, and this was enough reason to kill me. Well, Bartelmus evidently found more immediate causes to pursue, and he didn't harass me after that. But a few inches to the left, that day, and the bullets would have found me instead of the headboard. (See "A Close Encounter with Death")

Death from another source—illness—nearly claimed me in January 1942. We had been confined to the ghetto already when I developed a severe infection in my right ear. As it progressed the pain mounted and my hearing diminished. There were no Jewish doctors left in the Kolbuszowa ghetto, so my brother Leibush bundled me up and took me through the snow to Rzeszow on a sled.

There, I was examined by Dr. Heller, who pronounced that I was gravely ill. My ear was filled with pus, and the infection had reached the lining of the brain. He prescribed immediate surgery to clean out the infection. Even then, the prognosis was uncertain, but without the surgery, I would surely die. There was, however, no Jewish hospital left in Rzeszow. The operation required a highly specialized expert, and he advised we go to Cracow for the surgery. Easier said than done.

Jews were prohibited from traveling on the trains. My brother went to the Jewish police, who went to the Polish police, who went to German headquarters to explain my dire condition and need to seek medical service in Cracow. Leibush brought with him a large amount of money that was passed among the various officials involved. Ultimately, he obtained a rail pass that permitted our transport.

The family decided that I should be accompanied by two of my sisters, and the three of us boarded the train for Cracow. We were the only Jews on the train, and despite our documents giving us official permission to travel, our armbands made us immediate targets of the other passengers on board. One Pole in particular radicalized a number of the other passengers, and they hurled abuse at us. They petitioned the German railroad police to throw us off the train, but he told them that we had permits to travel. That only infuriated the mob more and ultimately, the railroad policeman told us, that despite our permits, we would have to get off the train at the next stop. My head was splitting and my sisters despairing as we disembarked in the city of Tarnow, many miles short of our destination, Cracow.

We had relatives who lived in Tarnow, and my sisters brought me to their house for want of any alternative action. They, in turn, told us that the Jewish hospital was still functioning in Tarnow and, after looking at me, decided that we should go there at once. By a miracle, Dr. David Rabinovich, a wonderfully skilled surgeon, was available at the hospital. He examined me, said I required immediate surgery, and pronounced my chances of survival to be one in ten; even at that I would probably be deaf, blind, or paralyzed.

Against all odds, against all expectations, I survived the operation. It took two months of convalescence in Tarnow to get me to a condition of minimal ability to travel. Dr. Rabinovich, whom they called *zlote raczki,* or golden hands, certainly deserved the nickname. I not only survived, but my hearing was unimpaired. He, alas, was killed by the Germans two months later when they learned that he had performed an operation on a Polish patient against the rules.

In January 1942 a severe middle-ear infection nearly claimed the author's life. He underwent an operation in February and is here seen on March 15, 1942 in a picture taken by his sister Rachel.

I was literally delivered from the grave on another occasion. As two German soldiers guarded me, I was in the process of digging a hole that was to be my burial site. It seems I had inadvertently made an enemy of a woman who was a friend of a friend of Landskomissar Walter Twardon, the beast who controlled our living and our dying in Kolbuszowa. That is all it took to get one killed. Jews were among the most expendable of things in Poland.

My problem occurred while I was assigned to the labor camp. My family had already been killed in Belzec. One of my tasks was to walk to the dairy to pick up the twenty-five liters of skimmed milk used by the workers in the camp. While the dairy prepared butter and cheese for the Germans, the Poles got only the mostly watery residue. The round trip took about a half hour, and since I only had an hour for lunch, to come and go with the milk, the authorities had given me permission to go to the head of the line whenever I got there. Unfortunately, while I had the permission of the authorities, I didn't necessarily have the sympathies to the others whom I jumped ahead of in the line.

One Polish woman, Skowronska, one day took particular exception to my doing so and, despite my explanation to her, cursed me and refused to let me ahead of her. When I persisted and got my milk, she proceeded to spill out the entire twenty-five liters on the ground. Worse, she denounced me to her boyfriend, who was the postmaster in Kolbuszowa, and who happened be a good friend of Twardon. On the basis of the boyfriend's report, Twardon ordered that I be shot. Jewish life was that cheap.

That night Patyk, a Polish policeman whom I knew, warned me that I was to be shot the next day. "Run, and save yourself," he advised, but I knew that if I did, the Germans would shoot ten in my place. I couldn't do that, so I remained and sure enough, as predicted, the next day the Polish police came for me, handed me a shovel, and commanded that I start digging. I knew it was to be my grave, and as I dug the hole, first knee deep and soon waist high, I reflected on my parents and my sisters and all of the friends who had been killed since the occupation. And now I was to join them. Then, I said to my guards, "Before you kill me, you must call Twardon. I have important information for him." They scoffed and I said, "If you won't call Twardon, call his secretary. Let her judge. You will be sorry if you kill me before I can give him this information." While I kept digging, the guards called his secretary, and when I told her I had information for Twardon, she thought it would do no harm to delay my end a few minutes, and told the guards to bring me to the commandant.

"What are you doing here?" he barked. "It better be worth my time."

I think he thought I would divulge information about Jews who were in hiding, but instead I offered him something more valuable. I offered to get him coffee beans.

Now, you might think this was a trivial offer, but coffee was extremely scarce in Poland at that time. My father had hidden a large inventory of coffee before he was killed, but I didn't tell Twardon that. I only said that I would get him a continuous supply of coffee beans. I told him I would gather it, a few decograms at a time from Polish shopkeepers I knew in Rzeszow. I would buy it. It would cost a fortune. "Fifty kilos," he demanded. Despite my tenuous situation I bargained him down to twenty-five kilos. He asked how he could be sure I wouldn't run away, and I informed him I could have run the day before, but didn't because he would kill ten others in my place. This information surprised him. I know he thought I had been a fool, but it gave him some assurance that his bargain was a sound one. He spared me that day.

Vinyarski, the sausage maker wasn't that fortunate. Here, the Germans had a freshly dug grave on their hands. The waste of something so useful went against their grain. Twardon settled another grudge by commanding that Vinyarski be shot in my place, but once again, I had narrowly escaped death.

By the winter of 1944, I was living deep in the Polish woods, leading a band of some sixty-five Jewish survivors. Our existence was little better than that of animals. We lived outdoors, in makeshift shelters under the trees. Our clothes consisted of what we wore, and the food we had was bought at high price from a few friendly Polish peasants in the countryside. Each time we had contact with them, however, we ran the risk of betrayal, capture, or murder. Life seemed unsustainable under those conditions. Something had to be done, and I decided to risk making contact with the Polish underground to offer to join forces with them.

One would think this would be a natural alliance, since we were fighting a common enemy, the Germans. However, the Home Army, or AK as it was known, was notoriously anti-Semitic and would be just as likely to turn us in as help us. They were led locally, however, by two brothers—the Augustin brothers—one of whom I had gone to school with. So I arranged for my brother Leibush and I to meet with them to discuss the possibilities.

They couldn't have been more gracious when we met them. They fed us, offered a dry place to sleep for one night, and when we were lulled into a false sense of security, shot me four times—three times in the neck and once in the hand. I surely thought I would die on that occasion but found the resourcefulness to draw my own revolver in the darkened room where this happened. I shot once and in the flash of the gunfire was able to see the man who had shot me. I fired in his direction and the bullet hit him in the heart and killed him. Leibush and I managed to escape from that trap. I had my wounds treated and survived yet another near-death encounter. (see "A Tale of Survival, 1 and 2")

On July 28, 1944, I was one day away from liberation. The Russian army was sweeping through Poland, and the Germans were in retreat. I found myself with my friend Leiba in the woods in the middle of this very fluid situation. We couldn't tell where the Russians or the Germans were at any particular moment. When we started to cross a clearing in an effort to get from the German-held territory to the Russian, both sides began to fire at us. We fell into a creek and hid out in a haystack, trying to assess our next move. A few hundred yards in the distance we spied two figures mounted on a horse.

Leiba, who was a village Jew, said, "I know those two. They are from my village. I recognize the horse. In fact, I sold it to one of them years ago." He told me I could go ask them what was going on. He would go, but they would recognize him as a Jew. Since I was dressed like a Polish peasant, they would not know I was Jewish and would talk to me. So, I came out of the haystack and approached these two.

Too late, I realized that Leiba had made a mistake. These were not Poles but German SS officers riding together on a horse. They saw me, and I couldn't retreat from them. Immediately, the Germans pointed their weapons at me and began to question me. "Who are you? What are you doing here?" I began to answer them in Polish and one of the Germans translated for the other. It was obvious that the one who spoke some Polish didn't speak very fluently. I didn't want to indicate that I spoke German, because then they would be more likely to suspect I was a Jew. So, I stood there, in my padded peasant's coat babbling a story at them that one lamely translated to the other. The one who spoke only German said, "Let's take him to our headquarters. There, we will find out what is going on here." And they mounted up on the horse and told me to walk in front of them.

I turned and began to walk. Underneath my peasant's coat I was wearing my usual arsenal of weapons: a revolver, two hand grenades, a bayonet and a hatchet. The grenades, bayonet, and hatchet were attached to my belt. The revolver was stuffed into the belt in front of me. I knew that once they got me back to the headquarters they would discover these arms, and I would be exposed. I had to take care of matters before then. As we walked along, me in front and the two of them on the horse, I reached into my belt, withdrew my revolver, turned and fired seven bullets into the two of them, killing both on the spot. I took their guns from their bodies, and using the horse as a shield, made my way back toward Leiba.

Meanwhile, the sound of my shots had attracted volleys of bullets from both sides. As I made my way forward, I came upon a Russian patrol. The Russians searched me, and when they found the three revolvers and the grenades and the hatchet, questioned who I was. I showed them where I had killed the Germans, and they cheered me as a partisan and allowed me to join them. That was an extremely close call. The last night of the war and I was nearly captured and killed by the Germans.

You would think the end of the war for me would have brought an end to this series of near-death experiences. Yet there was one more, extremely harrowing episode in store for me. This happened after I had become a security officer in the Polish army. I was the commandant of police in the Cracow region. The town of Wieliczka was in the region under our jurisdiction, and a report came in that there were some German soldiers holed up in a house there.

The main force of the German army had long since retreated, so I took a truck and fifteen of my men to Wieliczka to take them into custody. We stopped in the local police station and confirmed the information. As we were leaving, the police chief noticed that I was armed only with my revolver and he suggested I take a submachine gun with me. I agreed. If the Germans offered resistance, a submachine gun would be useful. It was an Italian model, one I wasn't familiar with, but nevertheless I took it gratefully.

We went to the house where the Germans were reported to be hiding. Not surprisingly, the owner of the house denied that there were Germans hiding, so I ordered him to stand aside while we searched the place. Two of my men climbed up to look into the attic of the house, and as they did, the Germans who were hiding there opened fire, killing them. I was furious. My two men had just been killed because the owner of the house had lied to us. I took the butt of the submachine gun and hit him in the head with it. As I struck him with the butt, the gun began to fire. It was on automatic, and in two seconds forty-two bullets sprayed out of the barrel. As I stood there in shock, all forty-two bullets flew between my legs, shredding my coat that hung down, and blasting a large hole out of the wall. What a close call! Any movement of my gun or leg would have meant its being blasted from my body. Instead I emerged unscathed. We flushed the Germans out of the attic and killed them and the owner of the house on the spot.

These then are my eight brushes with death. I am now eighty-two years of age. If a cat has nine lives, and I mimic that path, I guess my ninth encounter with death will come along one of these days. I am not too sure how I will fare on this next encounter. Frankly, I am not too worried about it, either.

Courting My Wife

My courtship of Amalie, my wife now of some fifty-seven years, was unconventional, to say the least. In fact, I don't think I even realized it was a courtship at the time. It began more as one Jew, who happened to be in a good position, doing favors for another Jew, who deserved them.

Our book, *Against All Odds,* describes how we met. I was an officer in the Polish army who entered Cracow just behind the retreating Germans. She was the employee of the M&K Construction Company who had been left in charge when the managers had fled, and in her possession was a set of plans that showed where explosives had been planted all over the city to destroy it. We both were Jews masquerading as Poles, and fate had brought us together in the closing days of the war.

As the chaotic first days of my unit's entry into Cracow passed, I settled into my position as the Polish officer in charge of enforcing security in the area. We had the complex task of presiding over the often conflicting interests of the Russians who had liberated the area, the AK or Polish Home Army, the civilian population, and the occasional Jews who were returning after spending the war in hiding or with the Russians.

Meanwhile, Felicia Milaszewska, the name adopted by Amalie Petranker during the years she passed as a Pole, continued to live in the luxurious apartment she had moved into when the M&K management had abruptly left. It was on Juljusza Lea Street, one of the most elegant neighborhoods in the city, and it had been furnished extravagantly with paintings, crystal chandeliers, a Persian carpet, and the finest of furniture. It was certainly too fine an apartment to be left in the hands of a woman who was a secretary in a German construction company. The government gave her a notice to move out. It was more appropriate for a dignitary high in the military or governmental hierarchy.

Felicia came to my office, which happened to be located on the same street, and advised me that she had been dispossessed. She told me she had no other place to go and asked if I could somehow help her keep the apartment. She was a beautiful woman. She had saved the city of Cracow from being blown up. She was Jewish, and she, like me, had lost her entire family. Yes, I would help. I drafted an official document that stated that this apartment had been seized by the office of Tadeusz Zaleski for his use. "Put this notice on the door," I told her. "When they come to take over the apartment, they will see that it already belongs to me, and they will leave you alone."

My notice did the trick. The military bureau of housing took the notice to be official and never came to evict her from her comfortable apartment.

Two weeks later she came to me with another problem. Before the war, she had planned on becoming a doctor and intended to study medicine. Now that she had the opportunity, she wished to attend University Jagielonski, which was one of the prestigious schools in the country and which was located in Cracow. However, there were several problems. She had no papers showing that she had finished gymnasium. In fact, she had no legitimate papers at all. She was still masquerading as Felicia Milaszewska, and Amalie Petranker's papers, if they still existed, were buried among the records in her hometown of Stanislawow. Worse, she had been told that even if she had the documents, there was a backlog of two thousand students who had applied for the two hundred spaces available, and they were being given on a priority basis to students who had had their education interrupted. Since I had been so successful with the apartment, she wondered, could I help in this matter as well?

Once again, I made myself available to this beautiful lady. I went to

Six weeks after their first encounter, the romance of Felicia Milaszewska and Tadeusz Zaleski is progressing nicely.

the dean of the school wearing my full dress uniform and introduced myself as the fiancé of Felicia Milaszewski. Despite the apartment episode, this was entirely untrue at the time. At that time I was so driven to succeed in my military career that I had no time for girls. Nevertheless, I told him I would take it as a personal favor if he could find some way to admit my fiancé to the school.

He smiled and assured me that he understood that documents had been lost and records misplaced because of the war. He would be willing to accept her despite the lack of documents if he had room. The class, however, was full, and there were only a few days before school began. There was nothing he could do, unless—and this he added as an afterthought—she had the sponsorship of the local Communist Party, the Polska Partia Robotnicza, known as the PPR. The school was obliged to hold forty spaces for students who would attend under the auspices of the party, and there were openings in that quota. If I could get a letter stating that she was attending under their sponsorship, he would accept her.

I knew the woman who was the secretary (the highest position in the PPR) of the party in Cracow. She had been in Lublin when I was there, and I had done favors for her in the past. I went to renew our acquaintanceship, and when I told her that I wanted my fiancé to enter the medical school under the party quota, she asked me to have her stop by to pick up the letter.

The next day, Felicia and I returned and discussed our needs with the party head. She agreed that she could be part of the party quota and passed several documents across the table to be signed. As she examined them, a frown formed on Felicia's face. "I cannot sign this," she said. The document she rejected was an application to join the Communist Party or in the alternative, a certification that she already belonged. Felicia wanted nothing to do with the communists because, I later learned, her family had been dispossessed from its comfortable home in Stanislawow and her father stripped of his property during the 1939 to 1941 period when Hitler and Stalin had agreed that that part of Poland would come under Russian control.

However, if one were to attend under the party quota, membership in the party was essential. These students weren't being sent to the school because of their academic qualifications. They were being sent there to spy on the others. If they weren't loyal party members, they couldn't be trusted to perform that duty.

I had been resisting membership in the party as well. It was unusual for someone to rise as high in the army as I had without this formal political endorsement. Of course, the army didn't know I was the son of a rich Orthodox Jewish family. My family had always considered communism to be an anathema. Each time the 150-question application had been presented to me, I had kept it, never turning it in. "This is too important," I would explain. "I do not yet know enough about communism. I want to study more, and later, when I am ready, I will join."

While Felicia's refusal preserved her integrity and character, it did nothing to advance her entrance into medical school. We returned to the dean empty-handed and explained that one of the requirements was membership in the Communist Party, which she was not prepared to commit to at this time.

"Isn't there some way I can do this?" Felicia pleaded. "It is my dream."

The dean said as a means of placating her, "If a high governmental official ordered me to accept you, I would have to allow you into the class. There is only one man with the authority to order me to accept you into the school. That is the Polish Minister of Education, Stefan Skrzeszewski, and he is in Warsaw." He said this knowing full well that reaching a man as important as Skrzeszewski with a matter such as this was absurd, and doing it in the remaining two days was impossible. It was a generous but empty gesture.

However, one should never underestimate the importance of personal contacts and the value of the currency of favors done and reciprocated. As with the head of the party, I knew Skrzeszewski too, and I was certain that if I could get to see him, he would write the needed letter. Warsaw, however, was five hundred kilometers away. Getting there by car would be impossible. There were no trains running.

Perhaps I could get a flight to Warsaw. I knew the Russian military commander in the area. I worked with him every day. Could he get me to Warsaw by tomorrow, I asked him? It was a matter of great urgency. He got on the phone and arranged for a pilot and a plane to fly me to the capital. The plane was an old-fashioned biplane that used to fly battlefield reconnaissance. It looked as if it belonged in World War I, and the Russians called it a Kukuryznik. *Kukurydza* means corn, and the plane got this name because it could barely fly higher than the corn stalks that grew in the fields.

The next day I flew from Cracow to Warsaw. Skrzeszewski embraced me as a long-lost comrade, and I told him about Felicia as we sipped vodka together. I told him that she deserved to be a national hero for saving Cracow; that she had ignored the German order to have the city blown up, but instead had turned the plans over to me. I told him that he had the power to reward this patriot with a directive to the dean of the medical school to admit her.

"Of course, of course, Tadeusz. I am happy to be of help."

With the letter secured and a few more vodkas under my belt, I flew back to Cracow, to Felicia, and to an amazed and somewhat bewildered dean of the medical school, who promptly admitted her to begin her studies.

And she would, I am certain, have been an excellent physician today if our relationship had not evolved into a romantic one. Within a few months it had, and when I received orders to transfer to Legnica and then to Breslau, she decided to move with me. By then, I had gotten her an engagement ring, and we had decided that our future together lay outside of Poland. After one semester at the medical school, she dropped out. To this day, she regrets not having become a doctor, although I like to think her decision to become my wife continues to outweigh those regrets.

The ring that I got for her to seal our engagement is one she wears all the time today. It doesn't only represent our more than half-century bond. It also reminds us of the chaotic times we experienced together during those days when I was a Polish officer and she a medical student in a world emerging from madness.

The ring was purchased from a Jewish merchant in a black market area near the Sukienice in Cracow. It wasn't, however, purchased by me, but by a Captain Szczerbakow of the Russian KGB. He bought it and then traded it to me for the full-length, black leather coat with a white, polar-bear-fur lining that I wore as part of my uniform every day. I was literally able to tell my wife that I had given the coat off my back for her ring. We still laugh about it.

Captain Szczerbakow came into my life when he was assigned to our unit as a Sovietnik, an officer assigned to indoctrinate us Poles in the Russian way of doing things. Each Polish unit had such a KGB-sponsored training officer attached. We became fairly good friends while we worked together, and during that time, he let me know on many occasions that he coveted my coat.

I had gotten it in the usual way. It had been given to me by an officer in the quartermaster corps in Rzeszow, for whom I had done numerous favors. Through my contacts, I had always been able to help him make up shortages in his supplies, when he needed to, in order to pass inspection. He was grateful for this, and when a dozen of these beautiful leather coats, intended for high-ranking officers, arrived at his depot, he gladly offered one to me. The coat was extremely warm, with its zip-out fur lining, and very stylishly made. Ironically, the buttons gave away the fact that the coat had actually been made in the United States and sent in a lend-lease shipment to the Russians. The outside buttons had a hammer and sickle embossed on them, but the inner white buttons that held them on were inscribed "Made in USA." The intended destination of the coat, and others like it, was the Russian army. My friend in Rzeszow had "liberated" this one, and I now happily wore it.

"Sell it to me," Szczerbakow implored. I wouldn't. I was as proud of that coat as he was envious.

The need for a ring changed all of that. Despite my important military position, I had no money. Certainly I could have used my power for personal gain, but I never did. I used it to help Jews deal with the bureaucracy whenever I could, but I never accepted bribes or extorted money. As a result, a lot of people owed me favors, but no one owed me money. I went to Captain Szczerbakow with the proposition that if he would get me an engagement ring, I would trade it for the coat. By then, I knew I would soon be leaving Poland and the army and would have little use for such a garment anyway.

So, one sunny afternoon in August 1945 he and I went to the market near the Sukienice, located in the "Rynek" marketplace, in the shadow of the Cathedral of St. Mary. There, the Jews traded gold pieces and exchanged money. As we pulled up in our military jeep, all of the traders began to scatter. Other army officers on other days had no doubt come in a similar vehicle, only to bully the Jews and confiscate their wares. We, however, wanted to do business, but it would be difficult if all the traders ran away. I recognized one of the running merchants, Izzy Miller, and called out to him.

Izzy had been a boyfriend of Amalie's (by then I was calling her by her Jewish name) sister before the war, and he came warily back to see who I was and what I wanted. I told him that I wanted to buy my girlfriend a ring, and he showed disbelief when I told him who my girlfriend was. Perhaps, I asked, he knew someone with a ring to sell. Indeed he did, and the captain and I entered into spirited bargaining until a price was agreed on. Captain Szczerbakow happily paid for the ring, handed it to me, and became the proud owner of a black leather coat with a zip-out, white, polar-bear lining and buttons emblazoned with the hammer and sickle on one side and "Made in the USA" on the other.

I became the owner of the one-and-a-half-carat ring that my wife wears without fail, every day.

The Lord "in" My Shepherd

It was one of those scenes that would have been unimaginable before the war. Now it was a commonplace. Who in their most lurid nightmare could imagine columns of women and children, lightly dressed, stumbling along a snowy road, breathless, fearful, falling and being goaded forward again? Dogs barking, helmeted soldiers yelling, bullying, brutalizing—it was a scene from hell. Who could imagine it? We didn't have to. This scene was repeated every time the Germans emptied a ghetto. People would be herded from the town to the railroad siding. Just so, it happened when this small town was made Judenrein.

This story was told to me by a Czechoslovakian woman of one of those horrific journeys. That she survived is a miracle. How she survived may be a greater one. Here is the story as she told it to me many years later.

"They lined us up in the town square. We didn't have any warning. They just got us out of our houses and lined us up and told us to march. There was no pretense. We weren't told we were going to be relocated to a better place. We weren't told anything. There was just brutality. There were rifle butts. There was the shouting. And mostly there were the dogs: the German shepherds, barking, running, biting. And there we were. One minute secure, or at least as secure as a Jew could be in the ghetto, and the next minute outside, in the cold, terrified. It happened so fast. They lined us up and we were forced to march up the road to the railroad crossing. One man yelled that it was impossible. They shot him. Another pleaded to be left. They shot him. With that, we did as they ordered. We marched along the sides of the road, out of the town, toward the railroad crossing two kilometers away.

"For the Germans it was a sport. Warm in their trench coats, red-faced, some a little drunk, shouting for us to hurry, they added to our panic by shooting randomly into our ranks. Sometimes they hit one of us. Sometimes they didn't. It wasn't serious to them. It was sport. A rifle would give its sharp crack and a Jew would fall. Sometimes they would be killed, sometimes only wounded. The Germans didn't want to leave alive anyone along the roadside, so when one of us fell to a shot, one of the German shepherds would be dispatched to examine the victim for life. If the fallen one still breathed, the shepherd would bark and jump around to signal his master that another bullet was required. It would be provided. If, by contrast, the victim lay still, and the dog's investigation produced no evidence of life, the dogs would generally, after a few sniffs bound off. And so it was hopeless. Be shot along the road or be killed at the end of the journey. Either way we knew it was the end. For the moment we desperately wanted to live.

"But in my case, it apparently wasn't to be. One of the random shots fired into the column . . . one of the devil-may-care, laughingly fired shots from one of the German troopers, one of the casually offered rounds . . . found me. One minute I was hurrying along the road, eyes on the feet of the man ahead of me, struggling to get to the station, and the next I was on the ground, with a searing pain in my thigh where the bullet had struck me. The shock was immense. The bullet hit like a blow that at once alerted me to the danger and at the same time stunned me, paralyzed me. I couldn't move.

"And then I heard the barking grow louder as the inevitable German shepherd came to investigate. I lay perfectly still. I knew that if the shepherd barked and raised a fuss after finding me alive, a German soldier would fire another, final shot into my body. If the dog found me dead, he would leave. I lay still but of course I could not fool the dog. They could detect breathing. They could detect warmth. They could detect life and give the signal that would end it.

"As I lay there, shivering on the ground with the dog standing over me, I was suddenly aware that the dog wasn't barking. He wasn't jumping around. Nor was he smelling me for life. No, the dog was crying. Out from behind the great teeth of this trained attack dog came the whimpering of a baby, the way dogs will when they have been hurt or shamed. And he nuzzled me and began to lick my leg where it was wounded. The whimpering continued for perhaps half a minute. And then he was gone. His master called, and he bounded off without another sound, signaling that I was dead. I lay crumpled where I had fallen without moving. The line passed me by. The shooting, the shouting, the barking, the dying moved off up the road. I lay there until they were gone, and I crawled, and then got up and limped off into the forest to find shelter, help, and ultimately survival. But as I did, I remembered.

"It had been two years before. We weren't yet moved into the ghetto, when a company of German soldiers arrived at our little town to commandeer food, warm clothes, tools, whatever might be of use to them. And they commandeered all the dogs of any size in the town, particularly German shepherds. They were training them for camp duty. I had a shepherd that I had raised from a puppy. It lived with us in the house and often slept with me in my bed. I was heartbroken when the Germans took him, and I hugged him and buried my face in his fur and cried when he left.

"And I never saw my dog again until that day along the side of the road when he saved my life."

When I heard this story from the woman I was struck with the humanity displayed by the dog and the inhumanity of his masters. It was a tale of beautiful irony that reminded me of another German shepherd—oddly enough, one that I had commandeered from a German commander when the roles were reversed.

I was in charge of a unit of the Polish army just after the war. I was stationed in Breslau, and we were in charge of rounding up former Nazis and administering the return of the city from German to Polish hands. In that capacity, one day, I drove with my chauffeur out to the countryside to a farm where we had been told a former Gestapo officer lived. A blonde woman who identified herself as his wife came to the door, and when she learned that I was looking for her husband advised me that he had left about a week before. She didn't deny his identity. "He knew you would be coming for him," she said, "and he certainly didn't wait for you." I was disappointed but not surprised. We would catch up with him sooner or later.

As she stood in the door of the farmhouse, arms crossed, blocking the entrance, I looked over her shoulder into the room and saw crouched under the table—alert, teeth bared, eyes blazing—a beautiful German shepherd dog. I said that if I couldn't take in the Nazi, at least I could take his dog. I had always valued dogs and recognized in this one a beast of good breeding. I would have him for my own.

She laughed and advised me that this was an attack dog, and I would lose a few fingers or a hand if I tried. The Germans, I knew, always used dogs in their concentration camps, and they were well trained in obedience as well as violence. For a while it looked as if she was right about the difficulty of the task, but at last the chauffeur and I managed to get a muzzle on the dog—his name was Lux—and we got him into the car.

I turned him over to a German dog trainer to be reprogrammed. We worked with the dog for a month redirecting his loyalties and responses to me; by the end of the period I was his master, and he reveled in his role as my protector. Checking the bushes, checking the car, he preceded me into every room, and all day he lay obediently under my desk, missing nothing, ever alert and ready to pounce should danger be sensed.

One day I was visited by a Russian colonel who admired the shepherd and offered to buy it. When I rejected the offer, he thought I was simply bargaining and raised the bid. Once again, I told him no and added, "besides this is a one-man dog. His loyalties are to me, and he would do you no good even if you owned him." The Russian scoffed, and he, as I had a few months ago, assured me he could take care of it.

"Try," I said, "to take out your gun and point it at me. You will see." Smiling, the Russian reached for his holster. It was over in seconds. The dog bolted from his spot beneath my desk, leapt, and threw his weight through his paws against the Russian. He toppled over and fell with the dog at his throat, gripping but not biting, waiting my instruction. I gave the command in German to retreat and the dog released his victim and returned to his spot. Even I was impressed. The Russian was enthralled and offered still more in money and favors if I would only sell him the dog. Yet I refused. Loyalty such as that should not be lightly sold.

One day about a month later we got an order to take a census of how many Germans and how many Poles there were in Breslau. With so many people in migration throughout Europe, it would be impossible to get an accurate count, but at least an approximation would be possible. I issued an order that for the next week, every German would wear a white armband. At least we could get a sense from the proportion of people wearing armbands to those who weren't.

The day in which the order went into effect I went out with the shepherd on a leash to have lunch. We hadn't gone more than a block when the dog bolted free, jerking the leash from my hand, and in the same lightninglike motion that I had seen a few days before, he jumped on a German in the street, knocked him over, and with fangs bared at his throat, waited for me to give the next order. I was horrified and called the dog off, apologizing to the citizen for his fright. As a member of a defeated people in an occupied city, he shakily accepted my apologies and protestations that nothing like this had ever happened before. What else could he do?

Nothing like it had happened before. But it wasn't much time before the episode was repeated again. The bolting, the jumping and the pinning down of the victim. Another German lay victimized with the dog at his throat.

And then I realized what had happened. Of course! The dog was responding to training from an earlier time: the armbands. The dog thought these Germans in the armbands were Jews. This had been a dog trained to run down and attack ghetto Jews wearing armbands. With a shudder, I realized that the order before probably had not been to release the victim, but to kill him. For the next week I kept the German shepherd inside, away from the armband-wearing Germans whom he mistook for Jews.

So, there is my story. Two German shepherds, giving out ironic justice. One trained from birth with love, saving a Jew. The other trained to kill, attacking a German. The Lord, I thought, is truly present in all of his creatures.

A Friend in High Places

The war was an ocean wave. It crashed over the landscape, flooding every corner and crevice with its effects, and when it receded, it left a transformed landscape, familiar yet blurred, with elements dislodged by the forces that had acted upon it. Wroclaw, the capital of lower Silesia was a case in point. It had been called Breslau and was part of Germany before the war. As the Russians advanced, driving the Germans back, the armies fought a bloody, house-to-house battle for control of the city. For days the battle raged, and when it was over, Breslau was in ruins. The Russians moved on, leaving a city with 80 percent of the buildings destroyed and governmental control changed. This was in 1945, and the city went from being Breslau, a part of Germany, to being Wroclaw, a part of Poland.

The Polish government, in annexing Breslau, acquired a city with two hundred thousand German civilians still living there. This was at a time when I, known as Tadeusz Zaleski, was the chief of the security forces for the town. Official policy was to move the Germans out of their apartments and move Poles in. If Breslau was to become a Polish city, it needed Polish citizens. We didn't much care what happened to the Germans. The militia's practice was to seize the apartments, force their German residents to vacate them, and then to give them to Poles so they could move in. The Germans, having lost all property rights, were simply told to pack up and leave.

As is so often the case, this housing policy of the Polish government had some unintended outcomes. Its effects were felt by all the Germans of Wroclaw, and this included the handful of German Jews who had survived the war and were drifting back to the city to claim their apartments. For the most part, these were *mischlings*, Jews who had intermarried with Germans and who, along with their children, had been hidden by their German relatives. Their lives had been spared, but they had shared much of the suffering that Jews of Europe experienced at the hands of the Germans during those years: families annihilated and property taken. They were victims of the Germans, but now that the war was over, the Polish government saw them as being German first. They had no status. Their apartments were being seized and taken over by Poles just as were those of the German residents.

The surviving *mischlings* were in despair. Having suffered at the hands of the Germans because they were Jews, they were now suffering at the hands of the Poles because they were Germans. The few Jews who came back selected as a spokesman a Dr. Hada, who had been a leading citizen of Breslau before the war and who had survived by being hidden. On behalf of the Jewish committee, Dr. Hada appealed to the Polish militia to see the injustice that was being done to his group. Having been persecuted during they war, they were again being robbed and pillaged, this time by the Polish regime.

Dr. Hada might as well have talked to the wall if he expected Poles to be sympathetic to the plight of German Jews. Being both German and Jewish put a double curse on these people in the eyes of the Poles. And so it was in some desperation that the Jewish Committee decided to appeal beyond the militia to the chief of the State Security, Tadeusz Zaleski.

It wasn't easy for a German to see me. He had first to submit a written request, explaining the reason to my secretary. If my secretary thought it worthy of my attention, she brought it to me; and if I thought it warranted consideration, I saw the petitioner.

One day, a delegation consisting of Dr. Hada, a Mr. Wulkan, Mr. Mendel Asch, and a Mrs. Kowalska, secretary to the committee, approached the police station with a written request for an audience. They gave the request to the sentry, who in turn brought it to Zaleski's secretary, who screened it and immediately recognized the request as something Zaleski would have an interest in and brought it in.

When the group came before Zaleski, Dr. Hada thanked him for allowing them to present their petition and commenced to outline for the Polish commander the tale of the experiences of Jews at the hands of the Germans during the previous decade. He spoke in German which was to be translated into Polish by Mrs. Kowalska for my benefit. As he told of the selections, the killing of families, the destruction of communities, I found myself on the verge of tears, for the story was a mirror of what had happened to my own family and to so many like it. I held up my hand and told him he needn't continue with his narrative because I myself was Jewish and I spoke German and I knew all too well that what he told me was true.

From then on, I became the protector of the *mischling* Jewish community. We arranged that Mendel Asch, who had been a reporter for the Jewish newspaper in Warsaw, would be a liaison between the committee and me, advising me of any problems the surviving Jews might be having.

In the meantime, I would see to it that a distinction was made in the re-settlement practices between Germans and German Jews.

Asch came to my home several times a week from then on; and I was able to protect the Jews in Wroclaw from the harassment of the militia, and they were able to establish a more secure existence.

The *mischlings* weren't the only Jews who were finding life after the war difficult. The surviving Polish Jews found little had changed in the attitudes of their Gentile countrymen. The anti-Semitism that seemed to come with the mothers' milk flowed among the Poles unabated.

After Silesia had been liberated, the economy of the region was in chaos. Normal commerce had all but disappeared, but people will find a way to survive. Out of the chaos an informal black market arose around the Wroclaw railroad station. Since Wroclaw was the biggest city in the region, Poles and Jewish survivors from the small towns in western Poland began coming each morning with pork, butter, cheese, beans, vegetables, and the like, which they exchanged with the Germans for clothing, jewelry, household items, and other manufactured necessities. These black market goods were called *shaber* and the traders *shaberowtze*. In the evening, after a day of trading, the *shaberowtze* would take their bags of merchandise back on the train to return to their communities to resell to the peasants.

For the most part, the railroad police looked the other way, even though black market trading of this sort was officially illegal. For the most part, they looked the other way, but not entirely. One group was singled out by the colonel in charge of the railroad police for special attention. That was the small number of Jewish *shaberowtze*. Each day between four and five in the afternoon, as the traders waited at the railroad station for the train to take them back to the Polish interior, the colonel of police would arrive with a group of his officers. The Jews were huddled at one end of the station, trying to avoid scrutiny and seeking security through numbers from being robbed by their Polish neighbors. The colonel strolled through the crowds on the station platform, and as the train approached, he and his officers confronted the groups of Jews, accused them of illegal black market trading, and confiscated their *shaber*. The protesting Jews were then pushed, empty-handed, onto the train as it left the station.

The anti-Semitic police colonel had been continuing this harassing practice for several weeks when it was brought to my attention. The Polish government, in the days after the war, had a most ambivalent relationship with the Jewish survivors. By tradition, as I noted, Poles despised Jews. Yet, the government recognized that the Jewish population contained many of the most able administrators in the community. One of these was a Jew named Jerzy Kluska, who had been a member of the illegal Communist Party before 1939 and who had been appointed deputy mayor for a district of Wroclaw. My true identity was known also to a few top Polish administrators, and Kluska and I became good friends. As chief of security, I was able to do a number of favors for him, and he, in turn, had reciprocated in several ways, not the least of which was finding me an apartment on the centrally located Hansa Strasse.

Kluska learned of the exploitation that was taking place at the railroad station and brought the situation to me. Officially, we could do nothing because *shaber* in itself was illegal. We knew we wanted to do something to protect the Jewish *shaberowtze,* but it would have to be something unofficial.

And so it was, that one afternoon a group of about twenty Jews stood waiting on the railroad platform. Their trading completed, they were carrying their bundles of clothing and pots and pans, waiting with the Polish *shaberowtze* for the train. Just as punctual as the train, however, was the colonel of the railroad police. He appeared, and just as reliably, he assembled the Jews to seize their *shaber.* Among the Jews this day were Kluska, me, and five of my most trusted men in disguise. Today, they would call it a sting operation. The twenty-eight-year-old colonel confronted us, along with the other Jews, opened our bundles, declared their contents to be the result of illegal trading, confiscated them, and had his men move us into the station. When he returned to push us onto the train, we were waiting. I announced to him that I was the chief of security and that he and his men were under arrest for illegally confiscating our belongings. Before they could react, my men had disarmed them and sent for a truck to take them back to the police station.

It was a scene I hold dear in my memory. One moment the Jews were being robbed at the hands of the police. The next they were being delivered by the police. We told the Jews to recover their merchandise from the platform and go back on the train with the others to their communities. They would be safe from persecution from then on. Many of them believed an angel must have descended from heaven, and as the story spread that Wroclaw was safe for *shaber,* its importance as a market center grew among the Jewish survivors of western Poland.

The colonel was charged with theft and discrimination, a practice that was against the law in official Poland, although it was unofficially regularly practiced. He lost his position and was in jail, scheduled to stand trial.

I never learned what the outcome of the trial was, however. While my actions made the Jews more secure, my personal insecurity in my dual existence was growing. It was hard for me to see a future for myself in postwar communist Poland.

One night, I disappeared into East Germany to find my way to the West. Mendel Asch, his wife, and her sister accompanied me to seek freedom.

Working for the Communists

The Communist government in Poland after the war was scrupulously neutral as far as the Jews were concerned. They turned a blind eye toward religious affiliation. What mattered was loyalty to the country and loyalty to the party. I wasn't naïve about believing such official neutrality would cause neutral behavior from those executing the policy, but after the horrors Jews had experienced at the hands of earlier governments, I was willing to give it the benefit of the doubt. Indeed, I was working for the government in State Security, but because of my skepticism over the manner in which the same old Polish mentality would execute the new policy, I was working for them under the assumed identity of Tadeusz Zaleski, a Catholic Pole.

In 1945 I received an assignment to go to the new Polish city of Wroclaw, formerly Breslau, when it was considered to be in Germany. I had been transferred from my position as chief of state security of Cracow County to a similar job in this, the largest city in Silesia. I hadn't been in the position very long when an official from Warsaw came into my office one day and revealed that he was in Wroclaw to investigate a report that had been received by his agency that there was embezzlement and theft occurring at a major factory in the nearby city of Walbrzych, which fell under our jurisdiction. He was here to investigate.

This man was from the highest chamber of control of the state, an extremely important central government agency known by its initials, NIK. It operated independently of controls from the army, the secret police, all of the normal arms of government. We might liken it to a mix of our General Accounting Office and the FBI in Washington. I assured this official from NIK that I would support his project in every way I could and that he would have my fullest cooperation. It wasn't more than three or four days later that he returned to my office and told me he had completed his investigation to his great satisfaction. Three of four days didn't seem like a long time for an investigation of such importance, and I questioned him about this.

"Oh, it was simple," he said. The factory director, a good Polish Catholic, had stolen the money. There was no question about that. "The good news is," he said, "there is a Jewish assistant director. I have worked it out with the director that we will blame his Jewish assistant for everything." That way, he explained, the director won't have to go to jail. After all, he is a good Pole. "The Jew bastard can take the blame."

I told him his plan was ingenious. I was certainly impressed, as would be everyone who heard it. I suggested we should create an official record that I could send on so he could get full credit for his creativity. Would he mind, I asked, repeating his plan while my secretary was present. "Absolutely," he said proudly. "I will put it on the record."

And so, I called in my secretary, and with him in the office, the government man repeated the whole story. I just sat and heard for a second time how he planned to blame the Jew for the crimes being committed while he protected the Polish factory director. At length, every detail had been covered. The agent sat back and asked if that was all right. I assured him it was, because based on his account, I was placing him under arrest.

He didn't know what I was talking about. Arrest? For what? For protecting a Pole and getting a Jew? That made no sense to him. I immediately called his superior in Warsaw and explained that his representative had planned to help an embezzler escape responsibilities while shifting blame to his assistant. I never indicated that my interest or my call originated because I was Jewish. No, I was simply a good security man doing his duty. The NIK superior in Warsaw had no choice but to agree that these activities were contrary to the interests of the state, and he gave me permission to place his agent under arrest and return him to Warsaw for prosecution.

I am happy to report that both the plant director who was embezzling the money and the NIK agent who would have shifted the blame to his Jewish assistant were tried, convicted, and imprisoned. God knows what would have happened if Tadeusz Zaleski really were a Polish Catholic rather than a Jew masquerading. Most likely he, too, would have joined the conspiracy, as well as the merriment that would arise from "sticking it to the Jew bastard."

Living in the Land of Babel

I have always found my ability to speak several languages to be extremely useful. This ability can be even more useful when others don't know you have it. For example, there was the incident that occurred the night before the Germans were driven from Kolbuszowa.

The Russians were advancing on our area, and we didn't know which territory they had taken and which was still held by the Germans. In the darkness, I mistook two men whom I saw in the distance to be Poles, and in the hope of gaining information, I called out to them. They waited, and as I approached, I realized to my dismay that they weren't Poles at all, but two German SS men. They addressed me in German, but I answered them in Polish. Since one of the Germans spoke a smattering of Polish, and the other one didn't speak any, the Polish-speaking one translated for the other. Because I also spoke German, (along with Yiddish, Hebrew, Russian, and a little English,) I could understand their conversation.

It began to lead in a direction that wasn't in my best interests when they discussed taking me to their headquarters to question me. I was carrying, under my peasant's coat, my usual arsenal of grenades, a hatchet, a bayonet, and a revolver, so I could ill afford to go with them. They treated me like a simple Polish peasant, and when their attention was diverted elsewhere, I was able to get out my revolver and kill both of them. I describe the incident in some detail in *Against All Odds*.

A considerably more benign language incident occurred in Cracow around April 1945. By then I was well established in the Polish army. Most of the world knew me as Tadeusz Zaleski and believed I was Catholic. A few of my friends knew I was a Jew. Several of them were playing similar parts. Others may have suspected, because I had made it a point to ease the lives of Jews who ran afoul of the authorities.

As Passover approached that year, a delegation of Jews came to see me to announce that they planned a commemoration of the uprising of the Warsaw ghetto that had started on the first day of Passover two years earlier and lasted for twenty-seven days. This would be the first such commemoration to take place after the war had ended. My visitors knew that such a ceremony would attract a good deal of attention, and given the climate, a good deal of hostility from the surrounding Polish community. What they wanted was protection from disruption that could range from shouted insults to a full-blown pogrom.

I knew that if they went through formal governmental channels, they would be met with indifference. The Communists were not hostile to the Jews. They just had matters they considered more urgent to concern themselves with. I said, "Yes, I will provide you with protection and make sure the commemoration is not interrupted."

The plan was to have two outstanding Jewish actors take part. One was Yonas Turkoff, who had been a member of the Wilne Trupe, a well-established group of actors before the war. The other was his wife, Diana Blumenfeld, who was a popular singer of Jewish songs. Also they had a number of survivors who would participate. Some of these spoke only Polish and Yiddish. It was decided that my future wife, then known as Felicia Milaszewska, would also participate and speak in Hebrew. The performances by Yonas Turkoff and Diana Blumenfeld would take place in a moviehouse named "Skala" on Karmelicka Street in Cracow.

As a final preliminary activity, all relevant parties got together to plan the event. I was invited to come to meet Turkoff and Blumenfeld, and I was introduced to them as Tadeusz Zaleski, commandant of the Security. They smiled at me, and I smiled at them.

While we were smiling at one another, Diana Blumenfeld turned to her husband and said to him in Yiddish, "Look at that anti-Semitic, Polish face. I wonder how many Jews he has tortured. How can they possibly expect this Pole to protect Jews. I don't trust putting our welfare into his hands."

To which her husband answered in Yiddish, "They say he is all right. And what choice do we have?"

They, of course, had no idea that I understood their Yiddish perfectly. I should. It was my native language. I didn't reply to what I wasn't supposed to have heard. What I did do was arrange to have a squad of my troops guard their house and the Skala Theater. The commemoration took place without a hitch, and I am sure the Polish army's reputation for sympathy to Jews got an ill-deserved boost because of my actions.

Language played a major role in my first encounter with my wife. I was Tadeusz Zaleski and she was Felicia Milaszewska. We were both Jewish, but neither of us knew the other was. In fact, I thought she was a German, and she was trying to convince me that she was a Pole. Finally, driven to desperation, she claimed that not only was she a Pole, but she was also a Jew. I scoffed at that idea and challenged her to prove it.

"I can speak Hebrew," she said, but added, "even if I did, you couldn't understand it since it is clear you have no love for Jews."

I told her to say something in Hebrew, regardless. With perfect diction and with obvious scorn she told me in Hebrew, "You are a fool, and I wish you would stop questioning me." She convinced me, and she has been questioning me in English, Polish, Hebrew, and Yiddish ever since.

Sometimes it is not even the whole language, but an inflection, a nuance, even a melody. On another occasion when I was with the Polish army I came upon a girl in a social situation. She was blonde and blue-eyed, and looked like a typical Pole, but something about her attitude subtly seemed to set her aside from the others in her group. I thought that perhaps she, like me, might be a Jew passing as a Catholic. But it would be important for her to deny it if I were to ask. Instead, I quietly began to whistle "Hatikvah," the song that would become the Israeli national anthem. If she recognized it, she could acknowledge it. If not, she would simply be hearing a Polish soldier aimlessly whistling a pretty tune. Sure enough, before the evening was over, we had a chance to share with one another the knowledge that at least two more had survived.

Because I spoke perfect, unaccented Polish, I was able to join the AK (the Polish Home Army). This notoriously anti-Semitic underground group had no use for Jews, but I remained with them because together we fought the Germans. Ultimately, however, I was sent on a mission to flush out a Jew who had been reported to be hiding in a Polish farmhouse. The AK had little more love for Jews than they did for Germans, and my orders were to kill the Jew.

Instead, I decided to use the opportunity to warn him that his enemies knew where he was hiding. But when I approached the house, the Polish farmers denied he was there, and there was no way he would come out to be warned. Finally, I called out in the local dialect of Yiddish, and he understood that only a Jew from the region would speak like this. He heeded my warning, and that night, he fled from his hiding place. In the process, however, I, too, had gained a need to flee from my home with the AK, for in order to warn the Jew, I first had to kill the Polish partisan who had been assigned to accompany me on our mission.

And so it was that because I was multilingual, I was able to survive the war, join the AK Home Army, the Russian partisans, and the Polish army, and then move to Germany and eventually to America, where I became a peddler, selling to ethnic Poles, Russians, and Germans. I love to give lectures to groups in Yiddish, and to this day, I am amused when someone delivers an off-color remark behind my back in a language they do not realize I understand. I am at home in the land of Babel.

The Kielce Pogrom

Our nation celebrates the Fourth of July, with fireworks and small town parades. The date signifies independence, liberty, and the right to pursue happiness. It is ironic that this date also marks the anniversary of an event that snuffed out for an entire people any hope that happiness, if pursued, might be caught. I refer to the Kielce Pogrom, a massacre of members of the Polish Jewish community who, through grit or luck had survived the German Holocaust only to perish, fourteen months after the war ended, at the hands of a crazed Polish mob. It seems fitting that Americans, while celebrating the enjoyment of rights too often taken for granted, become aware of another people in another time at another place who weren't as fortunate.

The story could begin on July 4, 1946, the day of the pogrom. Or it could begin in 1939 with the German invasion of Poland. More appropriately, however, we must look back through the misty centuries to the ecclesiastical demonizing of Jews as dirty, blood-drinking, Christ-killers. Fueled by the Crusades and then reinforced by the dislocations created by the expulsion, anti-Semitism took root and flourished during the Middle Ages, surviving in various strains of intensity into modern times. In few places was it more intense than in Poland.

It was not by accident that Hitler built his most infamous death camps on Polish soil. Compliant sympathizers to the Final Solution could be found in the general neighborhood for the asking. The fate of Polish Jewry at the hands of the Germans is well documented: Auschwitz, Treblinka, Chelmno, Majdanek, Sobibor, Belzec, and the liquidation of the Warsaw ghetto are familiar landmarks in the desolation. Of 3.3 million Jews living in Poland before the war, all but a handful perished in the Holocaust. But what of that remnant? What became of them when the war was over? One would hope that such a benighted people would be sympathetically welcomed home like a sick invalid returning from a long hospitalization, and nursed back to health. That's the way the Danes and the Dutch greeted their surviving Jews. That's not the way it happened in Poland.

The surviving Jews coming out of the woods, coming back from the Russian gulag, coming out of the death camps, who returned to the homes from which they were uprooted a decade earlier, were not welcome. Here and there, particularly in the more cosmopolitan centers, perceptions may have altered a bit, but in the countryside, sites of the small shtetls, the mood of the Polish peasantry was no more receptive. Lone survivors of extensive Jewish families, returning because they had nowhere else to go, would find their homes either destroyed or occupied by new tenants. Now these returning Jews were not only members of a scorned race. They were weakened members, few in number, who nevertheless posed a threat to property that had long since been absorbed into the worldly assets of the Gentile community. Even when they made no claim, their presence posed the threat of a future attempt at repossession. Documents show that over twenty-five hundred surviving Jews were killed at the hands of the Poles between 1945 and 1947.

Because of these incidents, the returning Jews tended to avoid the small rural communities and instead herded together in the larger regional centers. One of these centers was Kielce, located south of Warsaw. Here two hundred Jews—there had been twenty-five thousand in Kielce before the war—lived and prayed together in a former Jewish Community Center and tried to piece together their lives. It was like playing with fire in a tinderbox.

One night early in July, eight-year-old Henry Blaszczyk disappeared for three days. When he returned home, Henry said he had been kidnapped by Jews and held in a basement. Further inquiry added the detail that he had seen several dead Christian children in the basement as well. The news spread like wildfire. Some went to the house in question, but a search failed to turn up any sign of what had been reported. Indeed, it later turned out that the house didn't have a basement at all. It didn't matter. What had been dredged up was worse—a canard as old as anti-Semitism itself, the blood libel.

Jews, it was held, used the blood of Christian children to bake into their matzohs. It gave them strength. These children had been kidnapped to be killed for their blood. Never mind that it wasn't Passover, the traditional season for baking matzoh. The Jews needed the blood more desperately than ever because of their weakened state resulting from the war. Drinking the blood would help them become strong once again.

Once begun, this story could not be stopped. A mob of workmen from a nearby steel mill armed themselves with their tools and marched to the Jewish home. They went in and proceeded to systematically bash each Jew they encountered with their wrenches and hammers. They threw Jewish children off the balcony of the building. One child was reported by witnesses to have been swung by the feet into a wall, crushing his head. Jews who fled were stoned.

Alarmed, the Jews called the police to come to protect them. The police arrived with arms drawn, but then they turned them on the hapless

Jews. One of those shot was the leader of the Jewish community, Dr. Severyn Kahane, who called the police to report the pogrom in action. Official testimony at the trials that took place afterwards documented that he was shot to death by two of the policemen who responded to that call. Witnesses to the event reported "the streets ran with blood"; "people threw stones until they were tired"; "in the end there was no more hatred, only the mechanical beating of more Jews."

Altogether forty-three Jews were killed and fifty injured in Kielce on July 4, 1946. Thirty more who were taken from trains running between Lublin, Czestochowa, Kielce, and Radom were questioned, and when identified as Jewish, killed on the spot. Men were stripped and examined and shot when their bodies revealed them to be Jews. And all of these victims were people who had just survived a decade of horror at the hands of the Germans.

Eventually the rage subsided. The Polish government convened a court of inquiry and to its credit, convicted and condemned nine leaders of the pogrom. It is unclear whether the executions were carried out because a program of systematic disinformation over the incident was soon

On July 4, 1946, forty-three Jewish survivors of the war were killed by Poles in the Kielce pogrom. Their funeral was conducted by the Polish government and they were buried in a mass grave.

undertaken. The Communist government, which controlled the media, decided shortly after the trial to suppress this stain on Polish humanity. Various versions of the events were propagated, the most popular being that the whole thing had been engineered by the Jews themselves to build a case to put before world opinion to allow them to emigrate to Palestine. And go to Palestine they did. As a result of the Kielce Pogrom any lingering doubts about Polish anti-Semitism were dispelled. Fifty-thousand Polish Jews had survived the German killing machine. Another 250,000 survived internment in Russian camps and returned after the war. Fully a third of these 300,000 fled the country during the next few months.

It wasn't until forty years later that the veil of deception began to be lifted. The Jewish cemetery was rebuilt. In 1989 a film was made in which Polish witnesses testified about the events of that time. Eventually, in 1996, Dariusz Rosati, Polish minister of foreign affairs, acknowledged that this pogrom had indeed occurred. Rosati went on to say that it hadn't been a Communist plot; it hadn't been a nationalist plot; it hadn't been a Jewish plot. No, it was an entirely spontaneous Polish event, born of the hatred Poles felt against Jews, who for so many years had lived among them but apart. Hated and despised, envied for their material success and feared for their claim on expropriated properties, the Jews of Poland were an inevitable target.

It took but an eight-year-old boy's lie to produce this tragedy that Jews should mark each Independence Day, even while they celebrate the birth of the United States of America.

At the Martyrs' Grave

This sermon was given in Kielce on July 7, 1946, over the open grave of forty-three victims of the Kielce Pogrom by the chief rabbi of the Polish armed forces, Lt. Col. Dr. Dawid Kahane.

In large and small towns, in villages and townships, often even in an open field, there are graves standing in a row, surrounded by picket fences. At spring time, when the fields and the forests become green, on the Holy Souls' Day or another solemn day, flags would lower over those graves, somebody's hand would throw flowers, a lone tear would flow.

It is different with us Jews. We, Polish Jews, know other graves,

graves detected by a not expectant passerby. Graves spread all over the world, like field stones thrown by an inconsiderate hand of fate.

Those who lie in those graves knew, when they met their deaths, that nobody would erect a tombstone over their graves, nobody would recite the Kaddish, nobody would sing the "El Mole Rahamim."

These graves are joined today by another one, a grave of the Kielce Jews massacred in the Revived Poland. People who by miracle escaped from the hands of the German murderers met their cruel deaths by the hands of Polish fascists. It is not our role at this time to analyze who organized this odious pogrom. But I want to say one thing at this solemn moment, in the presence of the victims of the Kielce Pogrom: There is one category of people, one class in Poland, that could possibly prevent this, to oppose this disaster. They are the clergy, the officials of the Catholic Church in Poland.

In Deuteronomy 21, we read:

> If in the land that the Lord your God is giving you to possess, someone slain is found lying in the open, the identity of the slayer not being known, your elders and magistrates shall go out and measure the distance from the corpse to the nearby towns. The elders of the town nearest to the corpse shall then take a heifer which has never been worked, which has never pulled in a yoke; and the elders of that town shall bring the heifer down to a rugged wadi, which is not tilled or sown. There, in the wadi, they shall break the heifer's neck. The priests, sons of Levi, shall come forward; for the Lord your God has chosen them to minister to Him and to pronounce blessing in the name of the Lord, and every lawsuit and case of assault is subject to their ruling. Then all the elders of the town nearest to the corpse shall wash their hands over the heifer whose neck was broken in the wadi. And they shall make this declaration: "Our hands did not shed this blood, nor did our eyes see it done. Absolve, O Lord, Your people Israel whom You redeemed, and do not let guilt for the blood of the innocent remain among Your people Israel." And they will be absolved of blood guilt. Thus you will remove from your midst guilt for the blood of the innocent, for you will be doing what is right in the sight of the Lord.

Priests of the Polish people! Polish intelligentsia! Polish people! When you leave this place, can you say with clean conscience: "Our hands did not spill this innocent blood, our eyes did not see it?" What have you done since regaining the independence to enlighten the masses of the society that were poisoned for five years with the venom of Hitlerism? Polish Bishops, where is your pastoral letter in this matter?

Dr. Rabbi Dawid Kahana, Lieutenant Colonel in the Polish army, gave the eulogy during the official ceremony held at the gravesite of the victims of the Kielce Pogrom.

Aren't known to you the papal encyclicals clearly denying all nonsense about ritual murder? Is it that the Commandment "Thou shalt not murder" does not pertain to Jews?

AT THE TIME OF THIS NEW TRAGEDY WE TURN TO YOU TO USE YOUR WEIGHTY AND VENERABLE WORDS TO CRUSH THE STONE-TURNED HEARTS AND CONTRIBUTE TO COMMON AND HARMONIOUS WORK OF ALL CITIZENS OF OUR COUNTRY FOR THE GENERAL GOOD AND HAPPINESS OF ALL.

In the name of the Head Religious Council of Polish Jews and of the Organizational Committee of Jewish Religious Congregations in Poland, I bid farewell to you, our brothers, victims of the Kielce Pogrom. I bid you farewell with the words of the Holy Scripture: "YOU ARE LEAVING US FOR THE BEYOND, BUT YOUR MEMORY WILL STAY WITH US FOR ETERNITY. AMEN."

(Translated from the Polish)

PART FOUR　Getting a Foothold
in the Golden Land

Our First Day in America

W e had been at sea for two weeks. The stormy North Atlantic is usually rough to cross in winter, and January 1947 was no exception.
The old liberty ship *Ernie Pyle* was pitching and yawing and staggering its
way from Bremerhaven to New York. It was the last trip the wartime
freighter would make, and on this occasion it was bringing a cargo of Jewish refugees and displaced persons from the Old World that had treated
them with such scorn to the golden promise of America. My wife,
Amalie, and I were among them. We gave no heed to the discomforts of
the trip. We had experienced much worse. Our only discontent was impa-
tience—we were impatient to get started on our new lives in our new
land.

On January 18, 1947, the captain announced that we would be sailing
into New York Harbor in a matter of hours. New York. I remember

A two week voyage to America on the Liberty Ship, *Ernie Pyle*,
ended on January 18, 1947.

vividly that each of the Jewish passengers went below, and we dressed in our best suits and dresses. We wanted to make a good impression on Miss Liberty. And then she was there, as we had seen her in pictures and on postage stamps. The first glimpse of the Statue of Liberty made an impression on me that was so strong and so lasting that I choke up when I think of it. We had come to America. It is an emotional memory for all immigrants and an incomparable one for survivors of the Holocaust.

We steamed into the harbor, past the statue, past Ellis Island, which was no longer in use for processing America's new citizens, and the *Ernie Pyle* was towed into position along the dock in New York. America's newest residents watched from along the rail as the gangplank was put in place, and at last I was able to walk the last steps of that long journey from Kolbuszowa to New York, from Jewish shtetl to the greatest city in the world.

The disembarkation point was chaos. The immense hall into which we were ushered had signs with the letters of the alphabet laid out. We assembled at our letter *S* awaiting our luggage, as did the dozens of others. Eventually it came. We waited then for the customs inspector to process us and our possessions. Dressed in our best clothes, nervous, anxious to do nothing that would offend the uniformed inspectors, we waited. Down the line some were asked to open their luggage and let the inspectors rummage through their belongings. Others were allowed to go after a cursory inquiry. We were all too familiar with the arbitrariness of government officials. We had seen a glance, a snap judgment on acceptance or rejection save some and doom others. The significance of the moment was not lost on those of us waiting at the letter *S*.

A heavyset man shouldered his way through the crowd. He wore a worker's jacket and walked with the self-confidence and sense of belonging that could only belong to a governmental official looking for contraband being smuggled. He brusquely spoke to a few people in the hall and then approached my wife and asked her if she spoke English. Singled out in this manner, she nervously acknowledged that she did, and he announced, "I am looking for two people named Saleschutz. Do you know people named Saleschutz?" This was serious. Here was this government official looking for us. What to tell him?

She grabbed my arm and announced, "We are Saleschutz. My husband, Naftali and I are named Saleschutz. What do you want? What's wrong." I tensed, anticipating the worst.

"Wrong? Nothing is wrong. Welcome to America." The heavyset man with the worker's jacket reached out and hugged Amalie and hugged me and repeated. "Nothing is wrong. I am Yankel, the son of Raisel Rothbard."

Raisel Rothbard was my father's sister. I knew about her and I knew about her son Jack, the American name given to people named Yankel. This man had gone from an imagined threat to a welcoming relative with this simple declaration of blood tie. As the other passengers looked on, wondering who this American official was and what made us so important, Jack said, "You don't have to wait." He pulled us out of line and had two men bring a luggage cart and an inspector over to clear us. Within moments, the inspector had slapped stamps on our baggage, and we were on our way out of the hall. There, parked at the curb, in an otherwise illegal spot, my brother Al sat waiting in his car. We got in and were whisked away.

Jack, I thought, must be awfully well connected in the government hierarchy to have gotten us such favored treatment. I was just as impressed as our fellow passengers, who by now regarded us as sharing all of the power and influence he had demonstrated. I had no idea what his position was, but I was impressed.

As it turned out, Jack was not in the government service at all. Jack Rothbard owned a luncheonette across from the piers. Everyone who worked there, the baggage handlers, the inspectors, the longshoremen ate in his luncheonette and knew and liked Jack Rothbard. They were happy to do him a favor, and when he had heard from Al we were coming in, he had gone along to greet us.

It was our first lesson about democracy in America and a very welcome first experience. Here, we had discovered, a Jew could live and be accepted like everyone else. America was truly a golden land.

"Relatively" Speaking, We Were Not Well Off

Like so many before me, when I came to the golden land of America on January 18, 1947, my assets were mostly what the accountants would call intangible. I had the benefits of a Hasidic education in Poland, the strength and shrewdness that came from surviving the Holocaust, the experience of being a state security officer in postwar Communist Poland, and the will to succeed in America and to support my beautiful bride, Amalie.

I said "mostly intangible." My one tangible asset was an extensive family already established in America since the 1880s. My father, one of seven brothers and sisters, had, over the years, seen all of them depart for the New World. Indeed, the main reason he had remained behind was because of his religious lifestyle and great commercial success in Poland. They had gone to seek their fortunes elsewhere. He had succeeded so well in the old country that he was tied by his properties, responsibilities as a businessman, and social activities to Kolbuszowa. And because of it, he perished. But they had gone ahead and become successful in America, and it was to them and their children that I turned for help.

I did so with the help of my Uncle Shulim. Shulim, or Sam Salis as he had become known here, was one of the kindest, most thoughtful people I have known, then or since. If there was a family member in need, Shulim made it his business to try to help. Shulim was kindness itself. The trouble was, Shulim had devoted so much of his time and energies to others that he had little to show himself in the form of material wealth. Shulim was a go-between, an arranger. So it was in this capacity that he brought me, one day shortly after my immigrating, to the impressive home of one of my uncles, where he and another uncle, my oldest brother Albert, who came to America in 1921, and several of my cousins had been called together to discuss my prospects and to see if a job could be arranged for me.

They were gathered in the sumptuous living room of my uncle's home, talking, for all I know, about baseball or where their children were going to summer camp, or some other topic not concerning me, when Shulim and I arrived. I was wearing my best—and only—suit, cut a little too wide for contemporary American styles, a hat cut a little too narrow, a tie a little too old-fashioned, shoes a little too heavy. My English, while passable if one listened attentively, clearly marked me as recently arrived from central Europe. But they knew that, of course. Shulim had explained it.

When the formalities had been completed and inquiries made and responded to, and we had exhausted who knew whom, and what had happened to them, or was happening, or would be happening, we turned to the purpose of the meeting: my future.

"So tell me, Naftali," my uncle asked. "Have you bought a cemetery plot yet?"

"A cemetery plot? Why did I need a cemetery plot? I am only twenty-seven years old."

"In America, there is a saying that it is better to have it and not need it, than to need it and not have it. In America, everyone has a cemetery plot for himself and his family." And he went on to say first things should be done first. Before spending another night in the New World, I should be sure I had arranged for eternity here by owning a family plot. As it turned out, they all belonged to a burial society, and before the conversation progressed a step further, I had agreed to purchase four plots (I had no children) for seventy-five dollars each, which I was assured I would be able to pay off to the cemetery over time. And so I did. I have them to this day.

With eternity thus assured, it seemed time to turn to the business of the present: a job. But first, there was the matter of my name.

"Naftali . . . that's not a name for America," one said. My name, Naftali, was taken from my grandfather. Everyone in our family had named children after him.

"No, let's think of a better name." The names Nathan, Nat, Noel, Norbert, Nolan, and eventually, Norman were put forward.

"Ah, Norman. Now that's a name. With a name like Nathan or Nat you could make maybe thirty-five dollars a week. But Norman. That's a name they would pay up to sixty-five dollars a week."

I did some rapid mental arithmetic, calculating how the difference of thirty dollars a week would add up over a lifetime to let me die a millionaire, and quickly agreed that my name would be Norman. Then came the last name. Saleschutz, everyone agreed was too long. It needed something more American—maybe Sanders, Sales, Salz; maybe Salis, like my Uncle Shulim. I told them that my brother in 1921 had shortened it to Salsitz, and the group agreed that would be acceptable, although not ideal.

Now, perhaps, we would be able to get to the business of the day— that of a job for me in America. One cousin owned a garment factory, and we began to explore how I might fit in to his operation.

An uncle suggested I be a salesman.

"No," said another. "His English isn't good enough. As a salesmen he would represent the company, and with that English it will be an embarrassment to the company."

Another suggested I be a sewing-machine operator.

"No, there would be union problems," was the quick reply.

Another said, "a cutter." Again, the idea was rejected because of the union.

Anxious to get something, I suggested helpfully, "Perhaps I can be a shipping clerk. I would like to do that." I knew already what a shipping clerk was.

"A shipping clerk?" my cousin the owner jumped up. "No! No cousin of mine will be a shipping clerk. He suffered enough in the concentration camps. He deserves something better."

When I asked how much a shipping clerk could earn, they said, "Shipping clerks get about forty-five dollars a week."

"Forty-five dollars a week!" I exclaimed. "That's a fortune. I'll be glad to be a shipping clerk."

"Absolutely not. Shipping clerks have to sweep the floor as part of the job. My cousin who survived the war is not going to sweep the floor in my place," he announced with a sensitivity for my feelings that I didn't share. Forty-five a week sounded okay to me, but it was growing more and more clear that I was not going to be helped by these people.

At length I was asked if I could fix machines. Perhaps I could be a repairman in the factory. I could work as an independent contractor and avoid the union.

I replied, "I am an expert at fixing machines. There is a machine I have a lot of experience taking apart and putting together. I did it so often I can do it blindfolded."

"Really, what kind of machine is that? Is it a Singer?" I was asked.

"The machine I know best," I told them, "is the machine gun."

The room grew very quiet after that. None of them liked the implications of that remark, but by then I had come to feel a resentment toward my rich relatives.

I said, "Uncle Shulim, let's go. There is nothing for me here." I left with a new name, four cemetery plots, and a realization that I could count on no one but myself if I was to make it in America.

What I didn't know at the time was that some members of my family resented the fact that I had come to America with a wife. Instead of being proud that I had married an exceptionally beautiful young, very intelligent, educated woman from a good family who spoke seven languages (Hebrew, Polish, German, English, Russian, Yiddish, and Latin), they thought I had been stupid to do so. They later would say to me, "You are a young fellow, and not bad looking. If you would have arrived alone, you could have found a rich wife. Maybe she wouldn't have been so young, so pretty, so bright, but you could have found a widow or a divorcee with a few children, maybe a business and some property. You could marry rich and not have to start from scratch."

The exception to this cynical welcome we received was my cousin Esther Rothbard with her three children, Regina, Frances, and Berl. They had been saved by Uncle Shulim, who brought them in 1938 from Kolbuszowa, my home town in Poland, to America. It was Esther who found us an apartment in the Williamsburg section of Brooklyn in the same house in which she lived. It was Regina who put me in my first job in the ink factory. It was Zigi, Regina's husband, who corrected my use of English letters. It was Frances, with her husband Irving, who took us to our first baseball game in Ebbets Field and explained the rules of the game to us. It was Berl who took me to Ripley's Clothing store on Delancey Street, where he bought me a new suit, coat, three shirts, and three ties and told me, "Now you look like a real 'Yenkee.' " My wife and I never forgot their help and kindness. So too, we never forgot the others, as well.

It wasn't long before I began to make a small, and then somewhat bigger living as an installment peddler in the Polish neighborhoods in New Jersey. My wife became a Hebrew teacher, and we worked hard and saved and gradually pulled ourselves up economically. Later I became a builder and developer and had quite a successful career.

But, at the time, we knew very few people and were hungry to establish some social contact with others. We counted on our cousins, who were our contemporaries, to embrace us, and help us meet people. One Sunday afternoon I called another of my cousins and told her I had been here for six months and wanted to visit with her family. In truth, I had another reason. Since my selling was with the Polish immigrants, I got very little chance to speak English. While it was getting better, I wanted to practice.

When I told her I wanted to visit, she heartily agreed and said, "Call me sometime and we will make an appointment and you will visit us."

Well, I already had a nickel invested in the call and didn't care to invest another, so I said "Why should we wait? Why sometime? My wife and I will come see you today."

There was a silence on the phone, and then she replied. "No," that won't work. "I already have invited some guests."

How chilly it became in that phone booth. This remark hurt me terribly. Clearly, she was ashamed of us and didn't want to expose what in Yiddish is called "the *greena chayas*" (the greenhorn animals) to her other friends. We had survived the war; we had survived economically on our own. We had lost our families. We wanted kinship. We wanted warmth. We wanted new ties. But these were not the family members we hoped to find. These were Americans, born in America, insiders, and they saw us as different, inferior, outsiders.

We embarrassed them.

I hung up the phone, and it was a very, very long time before I called again.

Many years later, we were comfortably established and prospering in our new lives; they saw us differently. Not surprisingly, they saw themselves differently as well.

"Well, we really did a good job with the 'greena' cousins," they bragged. 'We really helped them in the beginning and put them on their feet."

Revisionist history has always altered our views of the world.

Looking for a Job in America

When I came to America I didn't expect to find the streets paved with gold. I didn't know much about my new adopted country, but I at least knew that much. What I did hope to find was hospitality. I had a very large extended family of uncles and cousins who had left Europe before the war, and many of them had succeeded fabulously well in business. I expected them to welcome me to their world. I hoped for a little help in getting started. With a few exceptions, I was destined to be disappointed in seeing those wishes come true.

The major exception was my Uncle Shulim. Shulim Salis was the good uncle in our family. He was gracious and sensitive to our needs as new Americans. He was that way with everyone—a sincerely good man—and I owe him a debt of gratitude. However, in the all important area of getting established financially, he couldn't be of direct help. Uncle Shulim was one of those people to whom money never seemed important, and as a result he never earned much. He was, however, in constant motion trying to arrange meetings for me with one relative or another. I confess I was reluctant at first. I wasn't ready. Before leaving Poland I had been a high-ranking officer in the Polish army. Here, I was without a usable trade, not speaking the language with any skill, married with responsibilities, but entirely without money. It was quite a comedown, and I was frankly depressed about it.

At length Uncle Shulim suggested we go visit my father's first cousin Shaul Zaleschutz, who was very wealthy. He had a few mills and was considered the king of the silk lining business. I agreed to go, and one Sunday morning we went to their house. As his wife Esther gave us coffee and some cookies to eat, Uncle Shulim introduced me, and Cousin Shaul said, "Yes, I heard about you. You were a general in Poland."

"Well," I said, "Don't give me a higher rank than I had. I wasn't a general, only a lieutenant colonel."

We chatted about family matters and then Uncle Shulim got to the point of our visit: I was in need of a job.

Shaul said, "I cannot do anything about a job. I retired and gave the business to my two sons. You know what—tomorrow, go over to my son and tell him I sent you. We have a lot of people working for us. I am sure he will see to it that you get a job."

The next day I went over to the plant. I put on my good suit with its European-design high shoulder pads and my coat, and went to the address on Seventh Avenue. When the attractive receptionist in the front office asked, "Who do you want to see?" I said, "I want to see Mr. Zaleschutz."

"Who should I say is calling?"

"Please tell him it is his cousin. We have the same name, and his father sent me over." Of course the English in which I said all this left a lot to be desired. I spoke Polish, German, Yiddish, Hebrew, and some Russian. They all accented my English. She told me to go in.

Seated at a large desk was an unsmiling man, a few years older than I. He didn't get up. He didn't extend his hand. He just looked at me curtly and said, "What do you want?"

I didn't want to ask if he knew Yiddish, so in my best broken English I said, "I saw your father yesterday, and he told me to see you. I survived the war and am looking for a job. Your father said you would find something for me to do."

He looked at me for a few moments. Then he took his wallet out of his pocket and took out a hundred-dollar bill. He put it on the table and said, "Take it and get off my back."

It is hard to find words to describe my feelings when I heard these words. It was not unlike the sensation of hitting yourself on the hand with a hammer and waiting for the pain to arrive. You want to cry, but you cannot breathe. Nothing comes out.

I just stared at him, and then tears started to fill me eyes. I couldn't speak, but I could think of how I would have answered him if he had come to see me while I was military commandant in the second largest city in Poland. I saw myself standing in a review stand, and by my side was my cousin, an honored guest. The music would play and I would introduce him: "Look, this is my cousin from America." This flashed through my mind in an instant. Still, I hadn't uttered a word.

He must have seen the look on my face because he abruptly took the hundred dollars back. "Well, on second thought, I am going to send it to the United Jewish Appeal. Let them do what they want with it."

I had survived so much—come so far, to be treated like this. I ran out of the office, past the receptionist, my breath coming in convulsed gasps. I still couldn't talk. I could barely breathe. I left the building and began to cry. I stood on the sidewalk sobbing.

I was twenty-seven years old at the time. The last time I had cried was when I saw my father killed on April 28, 1942. I hadn't even cried when I lost my entire family. My tears had dried out with my father's death.

While I was standing there a man a few years older than I walked by and asked why I was crying.

I asked him, "Are you Jewish?" and he said he was.

I asked a question, born from the bitterness I felt. "Why did we all have to be killed in Auschwitz while you lived here in America." It was an irrational thing to ask, but the events of the preceding few minutes had robbed me for the moment of my reason.

As I continued crying, he said, "I have to find out what happened to you. I must hear your story." I protested that I didn't want to talk to anyone, but little by little, he calmed me down and suggested we go for lunch where we could talk.

After a meal of sour cream and pot cheese with vegetables—I had never eaten in a cafeteria before, and simply imitated my companion in placing the order—he prodded me to tell him what had just happened.

As I repeated the events he became angry. "That sonofabitch," he said. "I know the bastard because I buy materials from him. He deserves a punch in the nose. Come on back with me. Don't be afraid. We'll teach the bastard a lesson."

"No", I said. "I don't want to do that. I only want to tell you one thing. As far as I am concerned, he is dead. As long as I am alive, I will never speak to this man again. I don't want to know him."

He gave me his card and invited me to come to see him when I felt better. I remember his name, Louis Segal, and I did go back to see him. This total stranger was very helpful to me, although he periodically would urge me to go back with him and "hit the bastard."

I never saw my cousin again. His father subsequently died, as did his mother, and eventually, he did too. It was just formality. As far as I was concerned he had died on that day back in 1947.

There are many stories like this. Stories I will never forget. With the exception of Uncle Shulim, family that could have smoothed the way for me in the new world I found myself in turned their backs. Strangers were frequently more helpful. Then later, when I started to make a living, and then to make more than just a living, all of the family who never did anything for me came up to me and said, "You did all right for a greenhorn."

And to strangers they would say, "We put him on his feet."

My First Job in America
The Ink Factory

Ever since the Germans marched into Poland I had survived by taking charge of events. When they were going to shoot me, and I dug my own grave, I talked myself out of it by offering to find coffee beans for the German commandant. When I was nearly caught smuggling food back to the ghetto I pretended to be a Catholic wagon driver and not a Jew who could understand German. When the underground was going to betray me I seized the initiative and shot the two assassins. When the war was ending I managed to manipulate events so I could become part of the emerging Polish army, pretending to be Gentile and rising to the rank of lieutenant colonel. No matter what the odds, I didn't let events dictate the outcome. I shaped it.

Given that history, you can imagine the frustration and depression I felt upon coming to America to seek a new life and finding myself without work, without family support, and floundering financially. People whom I certainly would have welcomed with open arms were the roles reversed, rebuffed me. Some offered me charity, but none could give a hand up onto the economic ladder.

Finally, I landed a factory job doing menial labor in the Liberty Ink Company on Montrose Avenue in the Williamsburg section of Brooklyn. For a take-home pay of twenty-one dollars per week, my job was to fill twenty-four bottles at a time with ink from a huge vat. I held a device all day long in each hand, and by pressing a lever, I allowed ink to flow into twelve bottles on the right and twelve on the left. At the right time, I released the lever, stacked the bottles of ink, and repeated the operation again—and again for eight hours a day, five days a week.

It was mindless, unchallenging work, and because it required no mental effort whatsover, my mind was free to play over the events of the war; over my family, my father's death before my eyes, the fate of my sisters, death, and despair. Never during the long years had my mind dwelled over and over again on these images. Given the frustration of the situation and my inability to change it, I despaired, grew melancholy, and began to fear for my mental health. My concern was confirmed when an old friend from Poland, Dr. Adam Penzer, who was a psychiatrist and director of Greystone Hospital in New Jersey, told me I had to find a job that would keep my mind busy. But I didn't. I seemed to have lost control over the events of my life.

To compound my unhappiness, the European Jewish owner of the factory, who had been in the United States perhaps twenty-five years at that time, took particular pleasure from giving me a hard time. He addressed me, when he spoke to me, as "Greener Tuchas" or Greenhorn Ass. Most of the time, he wouldn't talk to me directly at all. The work force consisted of ten of us: nine blacks, or Negroes, as they were called then, and myself. I got along beautifully with my black coworkers. I could well identify with them as second-class citizens in this country. After all, it had not been so long ago that the Jews were not second-class, but fifth-class citizens in Poland. Who knew better than we how it is to be social victims? We got on very well. It was just the boss, who compounded the dullness of the job with an abrasive level of abuse, that made the job go from bad to worse.

"Greener Tuchas," he shouted one day. "Stir the pot from left to right, not right to left." In addition to ink, the factory occasionally made a batch of mucilage, or glue. We did this by filling a large container with water and as it boiled, stirring it round and round until the powder we added dissolved into a sticky, taffylike paste. The constant stirring was needed to keep the mucilage from caking or getting lumpy. It was hot, dirty work, but I didn't particularly mind that. It was a break from filling the ink bottles.

I even composed a song that I would sing while stirring the mucilage, and as I sang, my black coworkers began to hum along and then to imitate my singing the Polish lyrics to the melody of a popular Polish folk song.

> *Mieszaj, mieszaj, mieszaj na calego,*
> *Mieszaj tu, mieszaj tam, mieszaj na calego,*
> *A jak juz bedzie wymieszane*
> *Moj boss. Ten skurwy sun, bedzie mial wygrane*
> *To mieszaj, mieszaj, mieszaj na calego.*

Which meant,

> Mix it, Mix it, Mix it, all the way.
> Mix it here, mix it there, mix it all the way
> And when it will be completely mixed,
> My boss, the son of a whore, will be the winner.
> So mix it, mix it, mix it all the way.

Seeing that I was comfortably stirring the pot counterclockwise, the boss announced it had to be stirred the other way.

"What difference does it make?" I asked. "I can stir more quickly with this hand in this direction."

"Don't argue with me, Greener Tuchas. You'll do it my way."

I even challenged him to a contest in which he stirred in his manner and I stirred in mine, and we would see which was more effective. Surprisingly, he accepted the challenge, and it turned out that my batch, stirred my way, was finished ten minutes ahead of his.

"Do you see," I asked. "My way is faster and it is easier for me."

"I don't care," was his reply. "You will do it my way or not at all."

And as I wretchedly obeyed his order, and stirred the mucilage, my mind began to work. His way or not at all? Maybe not at all would be better than this degrading taking of arbitrary orders in a meaningless activity for twenty-one dollars a week. As I stirred, some of the fire that had gone out of me returned. I grew angry, but remembered that in the woods, where survival was a daily question, anger was a luxury that could produce trouble. In the woods, when we were wronged, we didn't just get angry. We got even. I decided I would leave that job, but when I left, the boss would remember the Greener Tuchas. And I made my plans.

The Liberty Ink Company made its ink in a huge vat that filled the space of the warehouse. Perhaps ten feet high, it held thousands of gallons of water. The technology here was to fill the tank with water and mix the black powder that was the coloring of the ink with electrically powered paddles. When the ink was thoroughly mixed we attached one end of a rubber hose to a spigot at the bottom of the tank. The other end went to the devices I operated to fill the bottles. When the tank was emptied, we would wash it out with brushes and fill it and repeat the operation.

It was during one of these periodic changeovers, when the tank was empty and we were cleaning it, that I took a cork from one of the mucilage bottles and wedged it into the aperture inside the tank through which the ink would drain. With a wire, I wedged the cork into place in the hole and finished scrubbing the tank; we began to refill it. I could feel the depression lifting from my spirits. I was taking charge of my life again.

By the end of several hours, the tank was full and the ink mixed, and it came time to empty it into bottles. The hose was attached, and I worked the apparatus, but nothing came out. "There must be some dirt clogging the hole," the boss said, and he climbed up on a ladder and reached over edge of the brimming pool with a rod to try to poke clear the obstruction. Of course, the more he poked, the tighter he wedged the cork into place. He didn't know this, and so he worked a number of wires and rods in and out of the hole, but to no avail. If only he could get a different angle, one less awkward, he could probably clear the obstruction. And so, he piled some boxes on a table, and put a ladder on the boxes and climbed up and reached over with the rod. He reached and he poked and he reached some more from this precarious perch. And as he stretched further and further, the boxes became more and more unstable. As I stood next to the boxes and the ladder, I wondered how such a shaky structure could maintain itself. And in a few moments we learned that it couldn't. "Help, help. I'm drowning." The tyrant had somehow ended up swimming in the black ink, thrashing about to save himself, unable to clamber back out of the tank. Somehow the pile of boxes and the ladder had pitched him in.

Eventually, the boys pulled him out, black from the ink, sputtering with rage and fright. And as he stood there, dripping black ink all over the floor, he pointed his finger at me and shouted, "You did this Greener Tuchas. I know that somehow you did this, and you're fired." And I replied back to him with something resembling my old spirit, "Guess again, boss. You can't fire me because I quit last Friday."

I left that day, being owed for half a week's wages that I had already worked. I never collected that money, and I never cared. This was the best day I had experienced since I came to America. I had reestablished my control over my destiny, a condition I have tried never to relinquish in the fifty-five years that have passed since then. This was the beginning of my new life in America.

My Four Weddings

It sounds like a riddle. How can I have had four weddings and only one wife? Maybe we were married, divorced, and remarried? No. Even if we did that, we wouldn't do it three times. Give up? Let me tell you the story of our four weddings.

I met my wife in Cracow when we had both been masquerading as Polish Catholics. She had worked for a German construction firm, and I was in the Polish army. We had both grown weary of keeping our true identities secret from everyone but a few of our closest friends. We decided to be married under our true names by a rabbi in a Jewish ceremony under the *hoopa* (the canopy symbolizing the home that shelters the bride and groom in a Jewish wedding ceremony).

The rabbi in Cracow was Moshe Steinberg. He had come to me on many occasions seeking help with problems of Jews in trouble or with proposals to improve the welfare of Cracow's Jewish survivors in general. I had always been very receptive to him, and we had a strong, close relationship. He was delighted to be asked to perform this ceremony, but as we prepared to do it, he asked me who the *interfihrers* would be.

I hadn't thought about that. Jewish law required that we have two married Jewish couples, who have had no previous marriages, give us away in marriage. Usually it is done by the parents of the young couple, but both sets of our parents had been killed. We looked at one another. We had no people alive in Poland. Not only had we lost our entire families, we also had no friends who met the requirement. Most of our professional friends were Polish and didn't know we were Jewish. Those who did know had either lost a mate or had never been married. We had no one to serve as *interfihrers* for us, and so, despite our closeness, Rabbi Steinberg couldn't marry us and we had to abandon thought of a Jewish wedding.

Subsequently, I was reassigned to Wroclaw (Breslau), and we decided to be married there under our Polish names. I had a friend who was the vice mayor in Wroclaw, and he performed weddings. This involved his filling out a paper with our names on it and then our throwing a big party in celebration. I remember the party well, because I invited every high-ranking Polish and Russian official in the region. There were officers from the army, from the government, from the KGB, from the police. Poles and Russians are not famous for their abstemious drinking habits. Everyone got roaring drunk at our wedding party, and we were toasted so many times you might say we were toasted to a crisp. And so Tadeusz Zaleski and Felicia Milaszewska became man and wife.

Our stay in Breslau was to be short lived. It became urgent that I leave for personal security reasons, and we fled to Germany in anticipation of going to Palestine. For either purpose we would need documents proving we, Naftali Saleschutz and Amalie Petranker, were man and wife. Despite two previous attempts, we had none. We went to the local *Standesamt*, or justice of the peace, in Munich to have yet another ceremony. He was an elderly man, a little hesitant with the request. I brought him a salami and a kilo of butter, and he gave us a certificate certifying our marriage under our real names.

And so it was that in January 1947 we left Europe and came to America to start a new life. I have written about the hardships of gaining a foothold. With the exception of my Uncle Shulim, I found very little enthusiasm for my commercial value among the many uncles and cousins I had here. There was one relative of my wife's, however, who welcomed us with enthusiasm, a great aunt named Esther Engelstein. One day she asked us where we were married, and when I related to her what I have just related here, she felt it was awful that we had never had a Jewish ceremony.

"You must have a Jewish wedding," she insisted, and then proceeded to invite twenty relatives to attend yet another ceremony to be presided over by her cousin who was a rabbi. We had everything. I borrowed the rabbi's *kittle* because a Jewish man should be married in the white ceremonial garment, and we had a *hoopa* and *interfihrers;* we stepped on the glass and gained a *ketubah* that resides now, half a century later, with the several other wedding certificates in our collection.

My Aunt Raisel, who was my father's sister, is part of our family legend. It seems that when she was eighteen years of age and eligible to get married, the matchmaker came and proposed Chaim Zelig to my grandfather. Chaim Zelig, who was the nephew of my grandmother and some fifteen to twenty years older than Raisel, seemed ideal. He had a substantial textile business, a house, and was already a member of the family. My grandfather readily agreed to the match. Raisel was less enthusiastic. She didn't much care for her betrothed's personality or appearance. Besides, she had her own romantic ideas about the perfect mate. Regardless, her wishes in the matter counted for very little. The match was agreed to, the date set, the guests invited, and a grand ceremony and celebration took place in Kolbuszowa in 1880. After an appropriate interval, the couple stole off to spend the blissful wedding night together.

The next morning Chaim Zelig was discovered battered and bruised lying on the bedroom floor, and Raisel was missing. She had run off, apparently, after beating up her husband. It was really a small community, however, and she couldn't stay missing very long. She was soon found and she told a bitter story. "He was no gentleman. In fact he was horrid. He tried to rape me on my wedding night. I hate him."

Now in Jewish law it is written that a wedding must have one of three requirements occur in order to be final. These are (1) *B'kesef,* or money, and this is usually present in the form or a ring; (2) *B'shtar* or a contract usually represented by the *ketubah;* and (3) *B'biah,* or intercourse, usually occurring then, as now, on the wedding night. It turned out upon inspection that this marriage lacked all three. He hadn't given her a ring; the documents lacked the signatures of the necessary two witnesses; and,

This picture was taken at the Salsitz' 50th
wedding anniversary. On the same occasion
they celebrated Norman's 75th birthday as
well as the fiftieth anniversary of their
liberation from the German occupation.
Sitting left to right: Norman and Amalie.
Standing left to right: Michael, Dr. Bruce
Dezube, Dustin, Aaron, and daughter Esther.

of course, thanks to the fact that Raisel was bigger, stronger, younger, and
more motivated than her husband, the marriage had not been consum-
mated. The rabbis declared the wedding to be void.

Thus liberated, Raisel was free to eventually marry Beryl Rothbard,
and to bear him seven children—Abe and Gossi, who were twins, Yankel,
Ryfka, Moshe, Saul, and Schmuel, who became Sidney. Eventually, all of
the children but Moshe went to America where Saul and Sidney operated
a dental laboratory that became quite successful—successful enough for
them to bring their mother Raisel to America after the First World War.
There, she lived out her days. And there, her grandchildren, if asked, may
tell you the interesting story of their grandmother's two weddings.

Giant-Size Bloomers

No. 5X

Situation wanted. Can smuggle, bargain, trade, and fire a gun. Speaks Polish, German, Hebrew Yiddish, Russian . . . some English." That's how my want ad would have read when, in 1947 I emigrated to the United States after leaving the Polish army. I had held a high rank and was used to giving orders, not taking them. I was capable of making life-and-death decisions and had done so on innumerable occasions. People had depended on me, and I had not disappointed them. What sort of position did this qualify me for in my adopted country? Not much.

The early years in America were difficult and disappointing. I frankly didn't expect them to be so hard.

Eventually I got a start in my new country the way countless other Jewish immigrants have over the years: as a peddler of goods to other immigrants. In this case it was as a seller of plastic tablecloths, knives, and spoons. Each day, I would set out with my hundred-pound sample cases to my territory in Jersey City. First, I caught the elevated on Lorimer Street and Broadway in Brooklyn. From there I went to Canal and Fulton Streets, where I changed trains and took the Hudson tubes to Jersey City. The trip took two hours each way, and to compound my difficulties, the typical customer lived on the fourth or fifth floor of walk-up apartments. In this job, my lack of good English was no handicap. Some spoke Polish, some spoke Yiddish. Almost none of the customers spoke English any better than I.

After a few weeks of this I thought it was the road to financial salvation, but unless I found a line of merchandise that weighed less than the plastic goods I carried, I wouldn't live long to enjoy it. I discovered something that the railroads had realized long ago. You are better off carrying something with more value relative to its weight. Soon I was selling nylon stockings and men's and children's socks and underwear. In the course of my travels I observed that many of the Polish women were very heavy. My goods didn't fit them. These ladies needed extra large bloomers. I searched for a source of such exaggerated underwear all over the area and eventually found one in New York.

I clearly remember the day. I set out on my rounds with two large suitcases filled with even larger underwear. Off the elevated and into the subway I went. As usual, the rush hour crowds pushed and shoved, and as

I wrestled my two outsized suitcases onto the car, I suddenly felt them lighten considerably in my hands. I looked down and saw that my suitcases had sprung open, and my entire inventory of 4X and 5X bloomers were lying on the dirty subway floor.

All around me people began to laugh. These bloomers were huge, and the sight of them inspired delighted roars of laughter from my fellow passengers. For me of course, it was a different matter. If I didn't pick up all the bloomers at once, people would soon be stepping on them or stealing them. Suddenly the humor of the situation broke through to me. I picked up one of the huge bloomers and said loudly, "Who wants to buy seat covers with built in steam heat?" And I took a pair of size 5x bloomers and spread them over my head to show how big they were.

The people laughed and, seeing my concern beneath my joke, helped me pick up all the underwear and stuff it into my broken suitcases. Two men even took off their belts to wrap around the broken suitcases. Soon we arrived at Canal Street. My suitcases were fixed, and they helped me carry them to my next stop.

I was so grateful to those American people who helped a stranger in need that my happiness spilled over into my work. When I returned home that evening my suitcases were empty. My steam-heated seat covers had sold like hotcakes. That day I made a profit of one hundred dollars.

Maybe my relatives had turned their backs on me. No matter. I realized that I had found a new home among the good-natured subway riders who helped a stranger with spacious bloomers out of a tight spot.

Two Tales of Jewish Life

I enjoy listening to the stories Jews tell about one another. They often reveal a lot about the values and lives of our people. We are mandated to be charitable, to be supportive, to do good deeds, and we often find ourselves fulfilling these mandates in a hostile and antagonistic world. Yet, we do our best to cope. Let me tell you two of my favorites.

One involves two old Jews who shared a hospital room. Both suffered from some degree of paralysis, and they were largely confined to their beds. Neither received visitors, and their worlds were largely limited to the room they occupied and the experiences they shared with one another. The layout of the room placed one old Jew, Moshe, by the window with a view of the world, while the other Jew, Chaim, had a bed that was back in the darker interior of the room. Every morning, at least part of the day would be spent with Moshe reporting to Chaim on the events that passed before his view through the window. Even though he couldn't see the street outside the hospital for himself, Chaim knew every detail of the scene. It existed as a stage set in his mind's eye.

"*Nu*, Moshe. What kind of day is it today?"

"It's sunny today. It looks a little chilly because people are wearing coats."

"Can you see anybody doing anything?"

"Yes. There's a young mother in the park with her little boy. They are playing together. He has a dog, too, and the dog is running and bringing back a stick that the boy throws. Oh, yes. It looks like the mother has brought a picnic lunch basket. What a nice day for it. They can sit in the garden and eat. Wait. Here comes a little girl dressed up with bows in her hair. I think she must be part of the family. They are both hugging the mother. I guess the father must be at work."

With that, or similar reports of the events outside the window, Chaim would lay back on his pillow and reflect on his own family, now long gone, and on his own youth and how it had been for him and his wife so many years before.

The next day would bring news of the policeman's activities, or those of the shopkeeper around the corner, or of the tailor who had the shop next to his, or of the butcher. No detail of the little community outside the hospital window went unreported. No activity was too minor to note. Moshe's daily reports were Chaim's link to the outside world, and for two months the two old men passed the time with one reporting and the other visualizing the details of life on the outside.

The two old men were in the hospital for a reason, however, and with the passage of time, Moshe grew weaker and his condition deteriorated, until one morning, he lay quite still. The doctors came with their needles and medicines, but to no avail. Chaim's friend and companion Moshe had passed away.

As the authorities covered and removed the body and gathered up the few belongings Moshe had, Chaim realized that his link to the outside world would be lost unless he could be assigned Moshe's bed by the window.

"I imagine you are going to put someone else in the room with me," he said.

"Yes, we can't leave the bed empty."

"Would it be all right if I took the bed by the window then? The new person can have my bed."

"If you like, we can arrange to have you moved to this bed."

And so the attendants lifted Chaim from his bed and carried him over to where his departed friend had so recently lain. The curtains were drawn, and after he was settled in, Chaim waited patiently for the attendants to leave so he could open them and take in firsthand the activities of the world he already knew intimately from his friend's description.

But when the attendants had left, and when he opened the curtain to view the street, and the shops, and the flowers, and the dog, and the children, in all the yellows and reds and blues of a vibrant world, he saw instead, only the gray brick wall that had always faced the window of his hospital room.

I always liked the message of that story: how the love and imagination of one Jew could enrich the life of another. A different path to a similar destination emerges from the next tale.

This one takes place on Long Island, where Schmuel Goldstein's son Irving has moved. Irving lives in a big house in a nice, mixed community of Jews and Gentiles. Since his children have gone off to college, he has several empty bedrooms, and it seems only natural that he has his aging father move in with him and his wife. Schmuel is an Orthodox old Jew who spends his mornings reading the *Daily Forward* and sitting around his son's fancy kitchen, wondering how he can fill his days in this pleasant, if somewhat alien environment. Time hung heavily on him, so when the festival of Sukkoth came around, he readily undertook to build a *sukkah* (a temporary structure that Jews erect on Sukkoth) out in the back yard. He gathered the boards for the walls and branches for the roof and began to fashion the frail structure.

But all is not heavenly in suburbia. A Polish family lived next door, and they also had his father from the old country living with them. While as modern Americans living in a diverse society the children are willing to tolerate having a Jew next door, the sight of the old man with the skullcap dragging the boards into the yard and building the *sukkah* was driving the Polish father to distraction. Each day he watched as the old man joined the boards, built the walls, braced them, and topped the structure off with the makeshift roof. When the *sukkah* was just about finished, the old Jew was confronted by his Polish neighbor who demanded to know what he was doing.

"I'm building a *sukkah*. What does it look like I am doing?"

"It looks to me like you are building a house in your son's back yard," replied the Pole, "and you aren't allowed to do that."

The Pole, who had worked in construction in America, knew a little about local zoning laws, and he went on to explain to the Jew that there were building codes to protect neighbors from one another. Nothing could be closer than ten feet from the side lines of the property. He was too close.

"Where is your permit for building that structure?" he asked.

The Jew said he had no permit. He didn't know about zoning or permits or side lines. All he knew was that on Sukkoth you build a *sukkah* and that was what he had been doing, and that was what he was going to continue to do.

After a series of "No, you won't," "Yes I will" exchanges, hostilities escalated on both side.

"We'll see," said the Pole. "I am going to the police on this matter."

And so he went to the town hall and told the police chief that a father had moved in with his son next door to his own son's house, and the father was breaking the law by building without a permit. The chief took careful notes on the citizen complaint and promised to look into the matter immediately. He drove out to the Goldstein residence and sure enough, just as described, there was the old man building the *sukkah*.

"He's breaking the law," shouted the Pole. "Make him tear down that building."

The chief looked at the Pole, and at the old Jew, and at the *sukkah* and at his notes that he had taken, and at length said,

"You are right. He is not allowed to build a structure in the back yard. He is certainly not allowed to do it without a building permit. He is in violation of the zoning ordinance."

"So what are you going to do about it?" demanded the Pole.

"I am going to do what the zoning ordinance calls for. I am going to issue a fifteen-day notice that says he has fifteen days to tear this thing down."

The Pole glowered triumphantly. The building would be torn down.

The Jew smiled quietly to himself. Sukkoth only lasted eight days. After that he would have taken the *sukkah* down anyway.

And so with almost rabbinical wisdom, the police chief had satisfied both parties. After the Pole left to report his victory to his son, the Jew said to the police chief.

"You know, I would have torn it down in eight days anyway. Thank you. You must come into the house for a snack. My daughter-in-law makes wonderful gefilte fish. It will be a treat for you."

"No, thank you," said the chief. "I really have to go. Besides, my wife also makes pretty good gefilte fish every Friday."

Some Help and Some Hindrance along the Way

By the time I came to America, life had taught me that luck—both good and bad—can be more important in determining an outcome than all the plans in the world. Time and again, whether I was a survivor in the German labor camp, a fugitive in the Polish woods, or an officer in the Polish army, I had seen chance intervene with plans to produce a most unexpected outcome. Nothing changed along those lines when I came to America.

One such episode occurred when I bought my first car, a 1932 Chevrolet. With it came the opportunity to get out of the city into the surrounding suburban areas. Of course, with it also came the hazards of driving in the congested streets of Brooklyn and New York. One day, as I approached the Williamsburg Bridge from the right, a very expensive Cadillac was approaching it from the left. We each thought the other would yield and when neither did, we collided. Both cars had arrived at the same spot at the same time.

I was upset, but the other driver was furious. His beautiful Cadillac had a seriously damaged fender, and he hollered at me about my driving, my license, probably my parentage, and God knows what else. Since my command of English wasn't too far along, I was spared understanding half the things he called me. A crowd gathered and with it, a policeman arrived at the scene. He took notes and advised us to exchange licenses. I gave the driver of the Cadillac mine, and he gave me his, and as we went to record one another's personal information, he suddenly said,

"My God, your name is Salsitz. Do you have an uncle who is a dentist named Max?"

I said I did, and when he asked if I had a brother Al, and I once again responded in the affirmative, he clasped me by the hand and said,

"My name is Max Ratner. I know your whole family. We heard you had come from Europe, but didn't know where to find you."

The crowd began to lose interest as the hostilities turn into handshakes; Max turned to the policeman and said, "Don't write anything down. I will take care of it." And he turned to me and said, "Don't worry about the damages. I am insured. Here is my phone number. If you have any damage, take it to my garage and they will fix it. And please get in touch with me. I want to help you."

What a lucky accident that was. It turned out that Max Ratner was a distant cousin who lived in Brooklyn. He was also a sales representative—obviously a successful one—for a large manufacturer who made living room furniture. At the time, I was struggling to get established financially and was peddling small items such as socks and underwear. It wouldn't be long, however, before I would expand to installment sales of furniture. Max's company maintained a showroom in Brooklyn where buyers could come to see their furniture on display. Since I had no store, I had no place to show the furniture to my customers. Nor could I buy direct from the factories to resell to my customers. That privilege was reserved to stores. But Max could arrange for both, and what's more important, he did. Max Ratner, whom I met by crumpling the fender on his Cadillac, helped me along enormously by regularly arranging both for my customers to come to his showroom, which is usually reserved for the trade, and for the factory to sell to me direct.

I don't know what became of Max. What I do know is that fate brought us both to the Williamsburg Bridge at the same moment, and it turned out to be a lucky moment for me.

Of course, I needed a little luck. After all, we had a large family in America, and I was counting on them to help me get established. With the exception of my Uncle Shulim, they were of little help. In fact, they did more to discourage me than any other group I met in those early years. One of the people my Uncle Shulim brought me to for help was a first cousin of mine who had a large business employing several hundred people. We went to his beautiful house on Long Island one Sunday, and after my uncle introduced me, I told him in my broken English that I needed a job and he proceeded to question me, partly in English and partly in Yiddish.

"What can you do?" he asked.

"I can do everybody," I said. "If somebody works with a wheelbarrow, I can work with a wheelbarrow. If somebody figures with a pencil, I can figure with a pencil. I want a job and can do what everybody can do."

He asked me in Yiddish, *"Di host a kile?"* meaning, "do you have a hernia?" He checked my arms and asked if I had muscles. I resented both questions. We weren't getting along. I didn't like his questions, and he apparently didn't like my answers. Even though I was anxious for a job, and even though he was my father's brother's son with plenty of jobs to give, he wasn't about to give me one that day.

I didn't see him again for ten years, and by then I had becomes established and was doing well financially. When we met, I asked him if he remembered when I came for a job, and he said he did.

"Why didn't you give me a job? You knew I needed one," I asked.

He said, "I didn't give you a job because you were a wise guy. I didn't like your answers."

"What do you mean? What did I say that made you think I was a wise guy?" I asked.

He said, "When I asked you what you can do, you said, 'I can do anybody.' That meant 'I can outsmart anybody.' Well, you weren't about to start with me."

I guess that's how we learn idiomatic English. I had never heard of that expression. I was simply trying to say, "I can do what anybody else can do." I don't know whether he was being sincere or not. What I do know, is I got no help from him.

Nor did I get any help from another cousin, a clothing manufacturer, when I was in what I called the *"remnantses"* business. Again, my English faltered enough so I thought the plural of "remnant" was "remnantses." I had rented a room to use as a warehouse, and I was managing to eke out a small profit based on the price of two to four dollars per pound that I had to pay middlemen to get my remnants. While complaining about this to a relative one day, he told me I should visit our cousin who had a clothing business and who certainly had remnants for sale. I inquired, and sure enough, he had remnants; and he was selling them for forty-five cents per pound.

My English wasn't good, but my arithmetic was, and it told me I could improve my business considerably if I got my remnants from my cousin. He said he would be happy to sell remnants to me, but I would have to provide him with a financial statement and a bank statement showing a balance of at least twenty-five thousand dollars. That was a sum well beyond my means, but when I told this to my cousin, he simply shrugged and said that was the way he did business and he wouldn't be able to supply me. I was stuck with the middleman's rate of two dollars per pound.

Some time passed, and I had branched out into the furniture business, peddling door-to-door. This was after I had the fortunate accident with Max Ratner, and I was looking for space to use as a store. It happened that the same cousin I had tried to deal with for the remnants also had several shopping centers. Again, I approached him with a proposal. I thought that if I could have a spot in his center for selling furniture, I could make a good living. He said I could certainly rent from him. I would need to present him with a financial statement and a bank statement showing a net worth of at least $250,000. When he told me that, I began to laugh.

"What's so funny?" he asked.

I told him, "Last time I wanted to do business with you, you wanted me to have $25,000. I didn't have it then, but I have it now. Now you raised it to $250,000, which I don't have, but in a few years, I will. Then you will say I need a half-million dollars, which I will go and get. You are good for me, never giving what I need but always insisting I get more. And I do. If I keep this up, I can become a millionaire."

Later on, I was able to use Max Ratner's manufacturer's showroom, which suited me fine.

While my own family turned out to be of little help, my wife's family was wonderful. I think most fondly of her great-aunt Esther and uncle Azio Engelstein. Esther was the sister of her grandmother, who had gone to Palestine in 1934 after her husband died. Esther had married Azio, and they had a son, Harold. They were established in the United States when we arrived, and they all came to see us right away. "How can we help?" they immediately asked.

And they certainly did help. When my wife wanted to become a Hebrew teacher she needed papers. Harold was able to help her get a permanent license through the union. Another time, I was short of cash to finance my merchandise. It was before Christmas, and the customers bought more than usual on credit and wouldn't pay me until after the holiday. I mentioned my problem to Azio, and as we sat there, he took out a check, signed it, and told me to fill in whatever amount I needed. It was a wonderful and generous gesture. As it happened, even though I needed the money, I never used the check because, despite his generosity and trust in me, I was reluctant to write in an amount. Nevertheless, I am grateful to this day.

But the thing I remember them most for was the wedding they arranged for us. Yes, we were already married by the time we got to America. In fact, we had been married at three ceremonies: once in Poland, another time in Breslau, and another in Munich. However, we had never had a Jewish wedding, and we had never been married by a rabbi. Each time we were married, we were pretending to be someone else. When we told this to Esther, she knew just what to do: get us married a fourth time. And so she arranged for her cousin, who was a rabbi, to perform the ceremony. She invited twenty relative; we took our vows under the *hoopa*. And this time the contract was sound. This time, we got a *ketubah*.

I think that of all the family I had in this country, only a few people stand out in my memory: my Uncle Shulim, who was unusual for his kindness to us; my wife's Aunt Esther and Uncle Azio; my wife's aunt, Rosa Petranker, and her children; and my cousin Esther Rothbard, with her children, Regina, Frances, and Berl.

The Crossroad

We come to so many crossroads in life. We know where the path chosen took us. What we can never know for certain is where the other road might have led. In my own case, my choices led to survival against very long odds, a happy marriage, grandchildren whom I dote on, a successful business career, an active philanthropic life. My path led to many prosperous, happy years. And yet, alone at night with the distractions of the day removed, I have had serious regrets—regrets over the road not taken.

It was 1949. I stood with my friend Lolek Lehrer, a major in the Israeli army at the Jordanian border of the then divided Jerusalem. Lolek had worked for me when I was commandant of security for Breslau, or Wroclaw, as it was known by the Poles. That was before we both decided the proper road to take was the one leading out of the Polish army. He had gone to Palestine, arriving in time to fight in the war of independence. I had escaped from Poland to Germany and worked with the Bricha, an organization that smuggled Jews into Palestine. My intention was to help them until my turn came to be smuggled in as well.

Since the immigration of Jews into Palestine from Europe was essentially blocked by the British, we knew that choosing that path carried the possibility of capture and internment in a displaced persons' camp in Cyprus. Although she wanted to join her family in Palestine, my wife decided she didn't want to attempt to do it illegally. She didn't want to risk being placed in a camp. We elected to go to New York instead and on January 18, 1947, the liberty ship *Ernie Pyle* had completed its storm-tossed voyage and deposited us in the New World.

Lolek pointed to an area of the wall dividing the Israeli half from the Jordanian half of Jerusalem, where new cinder blocks had been installed.

"It has been repaired now," he said. "We tried to breach the wall there to capture the remainder of the city. We nearly succeeded, but were driven back. Many were killed that night. They rebuilt the wall. I guess it will be there forever."

Neither of us could imagine then that eighteen years later, another war would allow Israel to seize what was then walled off. We just stood and looked at the clean, new cinder block patched into the older, darker wall. The patch represented to me what might have been. A wave of regret overwhelmed me, and I began to sob.

Lolek had never know me to show any weakness in Poland. Quite to the contrary, I had sealed off the loss of my mother, father, sisters, cousins, friends. My energies had gone into being a crisp, efficient Polish army officer, and there is no place for weeping there.

"Why are you crying?" he asked.

"Because I wasn't here," I replied. "You couldn't take it because I wasn't here."

"Nonsense," he said. "What difference would you have made? The only difference is you might have been killed like the others, and now you are alive."

I told him, "I don't mean that I alone could have meant the difference. I mean that there were hundreds and thousands like me who could have been here—should have been here fighting for freedom, and weren't. We would have made the difference."

When we landed in New York in 1947 our plans were to go to Palestine as soon as it could be done legally. Meanwhile, I made contact with one of the Zionist groups that was raising money and buying arms for the Haganah. In those days we were like the Irish IRA support groups: a loose-knit confederation of secretive organizations. Our group collected guns that American veterans had brought back. We cleaned and oiled them and packed them in barrels. They would be smuggled into Palestine in preparation for the war.

The operation, of course, was outside of the American laws and contrary to its foreign policy, and one night the police raided the apartment we were working in. They confiscated the barrels of guns and arrested us. We were taken to the station and held overnight. American police really didn't frighten me. I had been exposed to much worse. In fact, as a Polish policeman, I had been much worse. What did worry me was the fear of deportation. Here I was, a newcomer to this country, and now I had been arrested. The next morning we were called out of our cells, questioned, and then told to go home. There was no prosecution, perhaps because the Zionist movement had penetrated the upper reaches of New York politics.

I was extremely depressed. My efforts to establish myself economically had led to a series of humiliating, low-level factory jobs. My living quarters were shabby. I had no money and no trade. Why, I wondered, had I survived so much in the war only to come to this dead end in America. Now that the group I was with had been broken up I felt more than ever that I should have gone to Palestine. Torn by regret, I felt like a traitor because of my choice to come to America, instead of going to fight for the homeland.

I took up with a more militant Zionist group at this point, a group that was forming what they called the George Washington Legion. A

Major Weiser, who I believe was a South African Jew in the British army, was recruiting a unit that would go over to Palestine, fully equipped, to join the Jewish forces. The group met in the McAlpin Hotel in New York City, and each week new volunteers would appear, to be inducted by Major Weiser into the George Washington Legion. There were mostly Jewish veterans from the American army, but they were also joined by soldiers of fortune of various stripes, eager to fight in any cause. The group had some blacks, some Irish who wanted to fight the English any place they could, some Holocaust survivors like me, and some idealists. Marilyn Petranker, one of my wife's cousins, volunteered her services as a nurse to the legion. She had been born in Berlin, and her family had left Germany in 1938, when the Nazi's policies were becoming more evident. There were some pilots among the veterans who were desperately needed to fly the ragtag air force the Zionists had managed to assemble in Palestine. When Major Weiser learned of my background in security, he assigned me to be head of the military police unit for the legion. We were a credible force, trained and ready to fight for the liberation of a Jewish homeland.

And then we learned that U.S. government policy would not permit a unit such as ours to organize and go to fight on foreign soil. The George Washington Legion, if it were to fight for the Jewish homeland, would have to get surreptitiously from America to Palestine. Its arms would be shipped ahead.

We met and decided that instead of going as a unit, we would go as individuals, booking passage in twos and threes on the voyage that went through Marseilles and then to Palestine. Some didn't want to go under those circumstances, but I agreed that I would, as did my wife's cousin Marilyn Petranker. I remember the pride I felt in myself at realizing at long last the goal I had deferred by coming to New York.

That night, I came home and told my wife that I would be going to Palestine in the morning. I was going, not as part of the George Washington Legion, but as an individual who would book passage to France and then to Palestine. I would offer my services to the Haganah to fight for the Jewish homeland. I was brimming with enthusiasm as I made this announcement to my wife, who at the time knew only that I was involved with the organization of some sort of military unit.

As a counterpoint to my agitated enthusiasm, she stood very still. My wife of two years, whom I loved very much, stood very still. My wife, who had lost her mother, father, sister, and two hundred relatives, and who was alone but for me, stood very still, waiting until my talk subsided, and then she said in a quiet voice.

"If that is what you want to do, I cannot stop you. There is just one thing you should know. If you go, I will not be here waiting for you to return. I have lost too many people in this world to risk waiting home while I lose another. I will simply put you out of my mind. I cannot bear the thought of waiting to hear that you have been killed or wounded."

These were indeed sobering words. I agonized over the decision, but I had only overnight to do so. In the morning Marilyn Petranker and another comrade left for Marseilles without me. I had come to another crossroad and elected a path to travel. Marilyn, I am happy to report, not only survived the war, but while there, met a British orthopedic surgeon who had volunteered to serve in Palestine. She married him, and today they live in Canada. I reluctantly turned to work in America.

By 1949 the homeland had been established. My wife and I, having met with some material success in America, planned to go to the new State of Israel to settle there. There was nothing to keep us in the United States, and this, after all had been our intention from the beginning. We went to Israel, with plans to stay. But times were bad in Israel in 1949. The country was struggling. We were told: "It is too late. Two years ago you could have contributed. Now, you are just two more mouths that we would have to feed. Go back to America. If you want to help Israel now, you can best do it by sending us money. We need your money more than we need you."

The sobbing had passed. I stood with my friend Lolek Lehrer and looked out at the Jerusalem wall and thought of what might have been.

I had taken one road that had led to another and then another. It was too late now to turn back.

And we never did.

On Becoming an American

Cholesterol. Who knew from cholesterol? Growing up in Poland, we longed to have a fat-filled diet, not a fat-free one. Fat was a delicacy. The trouble was, Jews couldn't afford the luxury of fatty beef, fatty lamb, fatty goose, or fatty pork, which of course they wouldn't eat even if they could afford it. The meat with fat hanging from it sold for a premium because it represented more time and more feed invested in the animal before it was brought to market. The rich Polish farmers kept the best, fattiest cuts of meat for themselves. When the Jews selected their poultry and meat cuts they usually had to choose from among the leanest, the stringiest, the most undernourished offerings—what today's cardiologists rave about, but yesterday's *bubba* (grandmother) accepted with resignation born of need.

One day, just a few months after I had come to America, I found myself entering Katz's delicatessen on the Bowery for lunch with my friend Leibowitz. In those years I was scraping along, peddling watches, trinkets, and jewelry items supplied by Leibowitz and a few other jobbers like him, and it happened that as noon arrived we had just agreed on terms for the goods I would sell. Leibowitz was feeling good about the transactions and said, "Come, have lunch with me. I'll buy."

Such offers were few and far between, and I quickly said, "If you'll buy, I'll eat."

We walked the two blocks through the cold, blustery winter air of lower Manhattan and entered the humid warmth of Katz's. I can still smell the aroma produced in the restaurant by the pastramis and turkeys and frankfurters hanging behind the counter and giving off an essence that hung in the air and clung to your clothes and fogged the window with droplets of moisture laced with what we now call low-density-lipid proteins. This was literally fat city, and to me it smelled like heaven.

I walked to the counter to check out the possibilities, and there was the counterman in a dirty apron trimming a huge corned beef. He expertly wielded the butcher knife, cutting the fat off and piling it up at the corner of his work bench. As I watched him I realized that he was taking this rich fatty layer to set aside as a premium cut. This was the part of the meat my father would usually eat in recognition of his leadership of the household. Scarce as fatty meat was to Jews, when it was available, it always went to sustain the energy of the family breadwinner.

The waiter came over with his order pad poised, and Leibowitz told him he would have a cream cheese sandwich on white toast. Duly noted, and when the waiter turned to me I told him I would have one of those delicious corned beef fat sandwiches. He raised his eyebrow, then smiled and told me I could have as much corned beef fat on the sandwich as I wanted. I looked at Leibowitz, who seemed unconcerned, and told the waiter I was very hungry and to pack the bread thick with filling.

What a treat. The fat was hot and tasty and the sandwich must have been piled six inches thick. Great slabs of corned beef fat were piled on to the Jewish rye bread. While Leibowitz daintily nibbled on his cream-cheese-on-toast sandwich, I wolfed down the juicy treat set before me.

In this picture, taken in 1947 in Brooklyn, N.Y., we see that Amalie and Norman are wearing the latest American styles and have clearly adapted to their new country.

The flavor saturated my taste buds. Juice ran from the corners of my mouth. I ate as though I hadn't had a meal in a week, and indeed, I had never had a sandwich so burdened with such a delicacy. As I noisily smacked my lips and licked my fingers, the other patrons of the restaurant watched me and nudged one another and whispered and smiled at me, and I knew they must envy me this rare treat, available not at all in Europe and surely very dearly here in America. What a country! Leibowitz paid the bill, and I thanked him for his extravagance on my behalf. He assured me I was entirely welcome, and we parted, he back to his store already half hungry from his meager cream cheese sandwich, and me brimming with energy from the corned beef fat.

It must have been three years later that I was back on the Bowery with Leibowitz. I had prospered relatively well and continued to sell an expanded assortment of jewelry items. My business had brought me as far as South Jersey and up into New York State, and I had become a young man of acquired culture and panache. Once again Leibowitz suggested lunch at Katz's, and once again the warm humidity embraced us as we entered. As if we had left yesterday, the counterman was at work trimming the corned beef.

"What will you have, gents?" asked the waiter. "What will it be?"

"Cream cheese on white toast." said Leibowitz.

"Very well, sir," said the waiter. And as he turned to me he asked, "And what will you have, sir?"

I looked at him. My mind flashed back to that day three years before when I had eaten with such gusto a sandwich made of a pound of the scrap fat that I later learned they threw away into the garbage. I thought of myself, mouth full, juice dripping, jaw working over that sweet-tasting waste. I thought of how delicious it had been and how everyone had

watched me, apparently not in envy,
but in amused horror at what I was
eating.

"The same," I said. "Cream
Cheese on white toast."

I had become an American.

A Few Blemishes on America the Beautiful

In this 1950 picture, Amalie and
Norman were matron of honor
and best man at the wedding of
one of Amalie's cousins.

When I left Poland for America, I
thought I left anti-Semitism behind.
After all, Poland was an old-fashioned
country in which generations of
church teaching had produced an un-
reasoning hatred of Jews. Pogroms and
systematic discrimination were taken
for granted. Jew and Gentile, by mu-
tual agreement, led separate lives. The
Jews, for the most part, eked out a living and were content with their existence that revolved around the *shul*, the family, and the comfort found
in study and observance. All around them smoldered resentment and
suppressed hostility that occasionally would be fanned by a rumor, a sermon, an event, into the flame of open violence. The peasants' self-esteem
lay in their certain knowledge of their superiority to the Jews.

America, by contrast, was well known for its credo that "All men are
created equal and endowed with certain inalienable rights." Here, there
was no official church, no police protection of anti-Semites. Here,
government officials were sworn to protect those without power. Here,
there would be no discrimination. Or so I thought. I would soon lose my
innocence.

By 1951 I had been in America for four years. They had been difficult
years, and in many ways disappointing. I had come with no profession
and no job, and in spite of my expectations, I had received no help from
my family. Through a great deal of hard work I had managed to make a little progress economically, and my wife and I decided we owed ourselves a
vacation. We planned to drive to Florida in my 1932 Chevrolet, the first
car I had ever owned, accompanied by my friend Yanek Susskind, who at

the time was looking for an American girl to marry so he could stay here. Rounding out our group was a single young lady named Leah who was a friend of my wife and who wanted to see Florida.

By then I had some idea that blacks weren't well treated in the South. We had seen on TV that the relationship of the blacks to the whites was not too different from the way the Jews were treated by the Poles. Just knowing of this flaw in the American character was a great disappointment to me. But as in so many things, knowing of it and experiencing it were two very different things.

It first hit home when we were in a store in Florida where my wife was shopping for a pair of shoes. While she was being fitted, I walked back to the bathroom. There it was: a sign on the door that the bathroom was for whites only. So, too, was the drinking fountain. It took a moment for the significance of these signs to register. And then it hit me. This was exactly like Poland, where the Jews couldn't travel and enjoy many of the freedoms the Gentiles took for granted. I became incensed and began to yell, "Don' t buy anything in this store. Don't spend your money in a place where they treat people like dogs." No one knew what I was talking about. Customers stared at me like I was crazy. No matter. I kept on yelling and my wife got up, put her shoes back on, and we left the shop without buying.

We stayed in Florida for two weeks. More and more, we saw instances of the discrimination against the blacks that we had read about or seen on TV, and more and more, it became evident that this was the way things were in the South. We didn't like it, but there seemed little we could do about it. It was in that frame of mind that we stopped off in a diner in South Carolina to get something to eat.

As we sat down, I joked that Leah, who was quite dark, might not be served here. She could be taken for black. Some joke! The waitress heard a part of the remark and in a moment the manager was standing next to our table telling us to leave the restaurant. "Why should we leave?" I asked. "We're hungry." He never told me. He just repeated the order to leave. I argued with him that we came in to eat and we wanted to order. Two minutes later, two policemen responded to the manager's call and said we should get up now and leave. Through the window I saw that there were two more policemen waiting on the sidewalk. I knew enough to stop arguing, and we got up and walked out of the restaurant with the two officers right behind us.

Once outside, the police asked if we had a car. When I told him we did, he said we should get into it and drive immediately out of town. Again, I started to argue, but when he threatened to arrest us we quickly got into the car and started it up. As we left town I could see that behind me there were two motorcycle policemen following to make sure we kept on going. And so we did, a good deal wiser and extremely disappointed in this reality that we found in our adopted homeland.

When we got home, I was still brooding about this incident. I called the editorial office of the *Forward* newspaper and told them about the story. They laughed. "That's not news. That's the way it is in the South." Even the Jewish newspaper, the paper of immigrants had come to accept the systematic mistreatment of a whole class of people in America. It was a rude awakening.

Many years and many encounters with discrimination later, I am a good deal less idealistic about America. In fact, experience as a landlord in Jersey City had built up a degree of understanding of the basis for some of the ill will. Nevertheless, active discrimination against people for simply being who and what they are still upsets me greatly. I just handle it better.

A few years ago I was in a courthouse in New Brunswick, New Jersey, the county seat of Middlesex County, waiting for a case I was involved in to be called. I was standing in the ornate marble rotunda of the building observing who was coming and going, when my eye fell on the name plate worn by one of the sheriff's officers staffing the building: Rutkowski. A good Polish name, I thought, and on an impulse I went up to him and began speaking in Polish. My efforts were greeted with a broad smile and an enthusiastic reply in a long unpracticed and broken version of the language.

Rutkowski was obviously pleased with whatever mastery of his mother tongue that he possessed and in due course, asked what I was doing there. "I have a case that has to be heard. I am waiting for the judge to call it," I answered him in Polish.

"Who are you against in your case," he asked. "Are they Jewish?" Before I could answer, he confided in his fellow Pole, "If they are Jews, you will lose. All the judges are Jews. I have worked here for years and I know the Jew judges always decide in favor of the Jews."

Once again, I was disappointed that an officer of the court, a member of the sheriff's office, would believe such a thing. I was disappointed, but not surprised that a Pole would confide such a thought to his fellow Pole. We were many miles and many years from the ghetto, but some things yield to neither time nor distance. Anti-Semitism was one of them.

Before I knew it, Rutkowski and I were exchanging stories like long-lost friends. The mother tongue was eliminating all inhibitions. At length he said that he thought I would understand a particular dilemma he had. What was that? His mother, he told me, had told him a story that he knew to be true. Yet whenever he told it to his neighbors they scoffed and told him it wasn't true. What did I think, he asked? Since I hadn't yet heard the story, I urged him to repeat it. I would give him my judgment then. This is the story he told me:

"Every year, in the town in Poland where my mother lived, around Easter, a group of Jews would kidnap a little boy. They would tie him up and put him in a barrel that had holes cut in it all around. The Jews would then surround the barrel, and stick needlelike tubes into the holes in the barrel and suck out the blood from the little boy. It happened every year in her town and in others as well, and no one did anything about it. Everyone knew about it, but no one did anything to stop it."

When I listened to this story all I could think of was Yitzhak Shamir's observation that children became anti-Semites in Poland when they drank their mother's milk. Here was an American-born officer of the law telling me a story that came straight from the dark, Jew-hating heart of Poland. Time and distance counted for nothing.

"Do you believe it?" he asked.

"Why shouldn't I believe it," I replied. "After all, your mother told you the story didn't she?"

As it turned out my case was postponed by the court until the following day. Since I was coming back anyway I told Rutkowski I thought this was an extremely important thing for people to be aware of and asked him if he would repeat the story the following day if I brought a tape recorder. He readily agreed, and the following day he repeated into the microphone this age-old tale that has been used to persecute Jews for centuries, just as naturally as if he were telling a story about going downtown to the movies.

Anti-Semitism is commonplace in Poland, but it obviously didn't stay there. Recalling the incident with Rutkowski brings to mind a similar moment that occurred while I was still working as a door-to-door peddler in Jersey City. I covered the Polish neighborhoods with my goods because I could speak their language and had an advantage comparable to the disadvantage I had when selling to native, American-born English speakers.

One day, I came to an apartment where the door was open, and the mother, with her back to the door, was hollering in Polish at her two-year-old little girl who was crying. She didn't know I was behind her as she told the child, "You better stop crying. If you don't, the Jew will come with the sack and take you away in it." When she turned around and saw me, I asked her why she told her child that story, and she said, "Oh it's just a story my mother used to tell me. It frightened me enough to make me stop crying, and it works with my daughter as well."

America is very good to its immigrants. They come here with their talents and their ambitions, asking for an opportunity to use them in freedom to find a better life. Unfortunately, they come here with their prejudices and hatreds as well. These, too, travel across countries and oceans intact. Leftovers from the old country, they persist in poisoning one new American against another for generations.

Two Paths to Salvation

When I came to America I sold housewares in Jersey City. You'd be surprised at how many interesting people you met selling door-to-door in the Polish-speaking part of New Jersey during the 1950s. One I remember clearly was a girl named Sofia S. As a peddler I practiced one of the older professions. Sofia had a profession even older than mine.

She was a call girl who two or three times a week would go across the river to New York from Jersey City to practice her trade. She spoke frankly with me about her profession, seeming to find no shame in it or apparent concern that it might conflict with the deeply religious sentiments she felt for the Catholic Church. Each Sunday she went to mass, and she regularly went to confession. It was this latter act, she explained to me, that made her career as a call girl okay. As long as she could confess to the priest, telling him in great detail of her professional activities, she could continue to be absolved of her sins. I thought this might be a little hard on the celibate priest, but it was good for Sofia. Sin all week and confess on the weekend. Her conscience was clear, and her position with the church secure.

How convenient for the conscience this arrangement was. No wonder Catholicism has such appeal to so many. I thought about it with a sense of superiority because it all seemed so superficial, so shallow. I thought about it, but then I began to reflect back on a situation from my days in Kolbuszowa that was not too different.

Fifty zlotys was a lot to pay in 1933. But then again Szymon Kapka was unloading a big burden. The pious Jew stroked his beard and studied the contract the rabbi had drawn up. At this time he was well into his late seventies, and his face bore the expression of a man with a deeply troubled conscience who was on the verge of setting his accounts right with

God. Across the table sat Szayle "Goi" D. He seemed young and light-hearted without a care. He wore the bemused look of one to whom good fortune had sent an unforeseen windfall. He, too, scanned the contract, but with considerably less intensity than Szymon Kapka.

What was in this document, written in Hebrew, that brought these three together? Nothing less than the transfer of sins from the older to the younger man. Despite his wealth, his farm, his animals, his large house, the knowledge that his children in Germany and America were well provided for—despite daily, almost constant prayer at the most religious house of worship in Kolbuszowa, Szymon Kapka knew he was estranged from God, and as long as he remained so, he would have no peace of mind. This fortunate bargain about to be entered into promised the peace of mind he sought. For fifty zlotys the younger man would assume the older man's sins.

Szymon Kapka had been a labor recruiter of sorts. The labor he recruited was young Polish girls whom he would arrange to send to Germany to work on the farms. Szymon Kapka had contacts in both Germany and Poland that made his position possible. The peasants of Poland came frequently from large Catholic families. The women were strong but dirt poor. Most jumped at the opportunity to improve their lot by going to Germany to work in the fields for what by local standards were attractive wages. In Poland, they were lucky to get enough to eat.

As the middleman in this arrangement, Szymon Kapka earned a handsome commission, and he grew wealthy from this trade. In addition to his fee, however, Szymon Kapka had added a fringe benefit for himself. Before sending each girl off to Germany, he assured her safe passage by sleeping with her the night before her departure. He was well aware that the girls were so eager to get the opportunity to leave home that they readily submitted to this exit tax. Szymon Kapka had been pursuing this activity for many years before World War I, praying in the *shul* by day and sleeping with the peasant girls at night. And the more he prayed and the more he played, the more he became concerned for his soul.

That had all gone on years before he moved to Kolbuszowa. By the time he came to our town, age had dulled his appetite but sharpened his sense of guilt. He had sinned and needed to be forgiven. It was with this need that he came upon the carefree Szayle "Goi" D, to whom this all seemed like so much nonsense. He readily agreed to accept his neighbor's sins. Fifty zlotys, after all, was a substantial sum, and if Szymon Kapka believed that by paying it he would be purified, that seemed okay to him.

I don't know what the moral of this story should be, if indeed there is a moral. There certainly don't seem to be any morals. Fifty zlotys for salvation for Szymon Kapka. Sofia got it for nothing. We think of Szymon Kapka as an old fool, while Sofia is recognized as being in harmony with the precepts of her faith. The only thing evident is that, as usual, things came harder to the Jew.

The Judge

I had been looking forward to this one for fifteen years. It was the late 1960s, and invitations to participate in public events came to me constantly during that period of my life. I was active in so many groups: United Jewish Appeal, Anti-Defamation League, Magen David Adom, Israel Bonds, Holocaust survivor groups—you name it, and I was either an officer, a board member, or a financial supporter. Each would have a program to honor someone, or to commemorate some event, or simply to raise money, and they would invite me as a speaker. I had acquired a reputation as an entertaining storyteller, and since I also brought the prestige of office or the virtue of generosity with me as well, I was in big demand. I tried to accept as many invitations as I could; but at times my calendar would simply be overwhelmed, and I would have to turn down a deserving organization. Or my wife would say, "Enough already. Sit home, for a change."

I probably would have turned this one down if I hadn't read it through completely. I was invited to speak in Jersey City on the work of the Magen David Adom, the Israeli Red Cross. As president of the suburban chapter in New Jersey, I had raised thousands of dollars in its behalf. I felt it was time to broaden the base of the organization's support. Other leaders in the group should gain experience in representing it in public forums. As I read the remainder of the invitation, however, I saw that there was more. In addition to my speaking about Magen David Adom, I was to introduce the honoree of the evening, a certain judge who was Jewish to whom a plaque was to be awarded. I could not refuse. The judge was a man to whom I owed a great deal, and this would be my opportunity to repay it.

There were several hundred people in the audience that night, including the judge's wife and family, friends, and colleagues. We had chatted before the program began, and I wasn't surprised that the judge didn't recognize me. Fifteen years had gone by, and the circumstances had been very different. Although I had been given the judge's formal biography, I thought I had enough personal anecdotal material to make the evening memorable for both of us.

Here is how I introduced the honoree that evening:

"When I came to this country twenty years ago, I was penniless. The only money I thought I had, two one-hundred-dollar bills sold to me before I left Germany, turned out to be counterfeit. I started at the bottom, schlepping goods from Brooklyn, where I lived, to Jersey City, where the immigrant Poles lived. I went door-to-door selling stockings, underwear, blouses, and similar things to this Polish-speaking population. Gradually, I added items to my merchandise such as jewelry and furniture, thereby changing my status from a simple peddler, to a customer peddler, to an installment dealer, to a decorator installment dealer. The titles changed and the money changed, but the work was the same: door-to-door.

"One day I called on a customer who told me that the camera I had sold her on payments the month before didn't work. It wasn't a very expensive camera, and since it was on warranty, I took it back and sent it to the factory. A short while later the factory advised me that the camera didn't have a manufacturing defect. It had been broken by the owner, either dropped or deliberately smashed. I went back to the apartment and this time a tall, husky gentleman answered the door. I explained that I could not take the camera back because it had been broken by the owners. What about the payments? Of course, they would have to pay for the camera.

"Well, they couldn't see paying for a camera they couldn't use, and I couldn't see refunding money on a camera that didn't work because they had abused it. The discussion ended when the gentleman hit me in the mouth with his fist, splitting my lip and producing a lot of blood and pain.

"I went to the police to press charges and papers were served on the customer. Eventually the matter came to trial in a court of law.

"At the trial I said that the defendant had hit me and inflicted bodily harm. The defendant replied that I had sold him a bad camera.

"I said I hadn't and besides, that had nothing to do with him hitting me.

"The judge then said to me, 'You came to this country and were given an opportunity to succeed in business. You have an obligation to be honest in your dealings with people. You cheated this man.'

"I interrupted the judge. 'Your honor. That is not true and it is not relevant. We are here because this man hit me. I am not here to receive a lecture on business ethics from you. We are here to decide the assault.'

"The judge interrupted me. He told me to be quiet or he would lock me up for contempt. Having no desire to suffer further injury, I shut my mouth.

"The judge glowered at me for a moment, and then banged his gavel and said, 'Case dismissed!'

"I was amazed, and I must confess, shocked at the justice system I saw in America. It was no different than the show trials in Germany. I lost a lot of respect for the law, and I lost complete respect for the judge who behaved that way. Two lawyers I knew were waiting in the courtroom on other matters, and they came over to me and expressed their shock at the judge's behavior. One said that perhaps it had something to do with the fact that the judge's father had been a peddler.

"And tonight, ladies and gentlemen, it is my pleasure to introduce that judge to you. He is none other than your guest of honor, the recipient of your plaque."

Everyone in the room was shocked. The judge turned white and then red and then white again. I am not sure if they were more shocked by the story I had told or by my telling it. I didn't care. I just hoped he felt a small portion of the humiliation I had endured in his courtroom fifteen years earlier.

One thing you learn when you are running and hiding in the woods, and being mindlessly abused by an enemy, is to strike back if the opportunity ever presents itself. It did for me, and I am pleased to report I took every advantage of the chance fate had offered that night in Jersey City.

A Miracle in Jersey City

My car was missing. Frantically, I ran up and down the block to see if my recollection of where it was parked was wrong. No, I knew where I had left it, and I was slowly accepting the painful reality that while I had been peddling my wares to earn a few more dollars, it had been stolen from the curb in Jersey City. I was sick. Losing the car was bad enough. What was worse was that locked in trunk were boxes of the merchandise I sold, including a consignment collection of small diamonds worth several thousand dollars, or about half of my net worth at the time. I had no insurance.

I had started as a peddler once it became clear to me, and to numerous former employers, that I wasn't cut out to work for someone else. I had had a lot of jobs since coming to America. They had each ended with my telling the boss how he should be doing it to make it better, or showing the boss what I thought of him when he rejected my advice. Having survived the Holocaust by using my wits and initiative, I found it difficult to adjust to an environment where blind obedience and repetition were required. I would not have lasted more than two days employing those tactics in the woods.

It all began when I lost one final job that had paid twenty-one dollars a week. "Why don't you go into business for yourself?" I was asked. "There is a whole Polish community in Jersey City. Get yourself some merchandise and see if you can sell it to them."

Could I do it? I was determined to find out. I started out with children's socks. I bought a hundred dozen pair on the Lower East Side in all sizes and colors. I paid $1.50 per dozen and decided I would try to sell them at the rate of $2.50 per dozen. We lived in Brooklyn at the time, and I packed the socks into two big suitcases and brought them by Hudson tubes to Jersey City. I started going door-to-door on Henderson Street, speaking in Polish to the women who were at home. I guess they appreciated what they thought was one of their own selling to them. I remember the first customer I called on. She was a lady named Zielinska who, upon learning I was selling children's socks said, "I have no children." "But" she added, "since you are a nice Polish boy trying to make a living, I will give you a dollar."

I appreciated the gesture but refused to take her dollar. I pushed on and began to meet with more success. Before the day was over, I had sold the entire hundred dozen and realized I had made one hundred dollars. While I am not a mathematical genius, I do know that one hundred dollars a day beats twenty-one dollars a week. This was for me. It was true that there was gold in the streets in America. You just had to know how to pick it up.

Gradually, I added other items such as underwear, dresses, coats. I bought a car. I added furniture, and in a few years started selling door-to-door watches, brooches, rings, and other jewelry that had been given to me on consignment. I was particularly successful selling engagement rings on time. When someone was getting married my policy was always to sell the diamonds for less than their appraisal value. I would invite the customer to have it appraised, and as a result I established a good reputation as a source for merchandise of all sorts. Business was booming until that fateful day when I was parked on Pavonia Avenue with a trunk full of merchandise, including an assortment of diamonds, and came out to find the car missing.

Naturally, I reported the theft to the police, and they said they would look. But I was in despair. The value of the merchandise I had lost represented a lot of doors knocked on. I went home and was depressed and inconsolable.

One day, about four weeks later, I had occasion to go to New York. It was a mark of my prosperity that I was driving my wife's car. Instead of taking the highway to the Holland Tunnel, as I usually did, I went through Jersey City to run an errand. A traffic light turned red, and as I halted I couldn't help reflect that the car in front of me looked a lot like the one that had been stolen. It was the same make, the same color. What was even more of a coincidence, it bore the same Springfield New Jersey PBA sticker in its rear window that mine did. My God, it was my car!!

I pulled around it when the light turned green and cut it off. As I got out, two young men opened their car doors and took off on foot. Let them go. With trembling fingers, I took the spare key to the trunk that I carried on my key ring and opened it. Unbelievably, the trunk looked undisturbed. Evidently, without a key, they hadn't forced it or looked in it. Holding my breath, I opened the case that had held the diamonds. There they were.

The rest was routine. The police took care of the fact that I now had two cars in Jersey City. My wife was overjoyed, not just to get the merchandise back, but to get me back from the depression that was weighing on me. I was elated with the notion that perhaps God had smiled on me after I had experienced so much grief in my life.

How else can you explain the miracle that occurred in Jersey City that day in 1954?

The "Shpitz" of a "Koiledge"

Modern science has been working for mankind for some five hundred years, and medicine, perhaps two hundred. God, however, has had his reciprocal arrangement with the Jewish people for six millennia. I must admit, despite my strict Orthodox background and my yeshiva education, my first approach, when in need of medical help, is to the doctor and not to the rabbi. I have to have pretty well exhausted all that medicine has to suggest before turning with any enthusiasm to seek divine help.

After ten years of marriage, my wife and I still had been unsuccessful in conceiving a child. We had been to a number of doctors who checked and rechecked, counted and recounted, and pronounced us 100 percent okay. "There is absolutely no biological reason that you shouldn't have as many children as you want— maybe more than you want," one told us with a wink. We know he meant the wink to be reassuring. However, we had heard this so often and had found it to be so untrue, that the wink became associated with insincerity, someone telling us something that wasn't really true. And so it had gone. Medical science not only told us we should be able to conceive children without helping us to do so, but in telling us this, it effectively blocked our opportunity to adopt. Since we should be able to have children, the agencies told us, we were ineligible for adopting one.

One evening we had an opportunity to put our concerns on hold. Moshe Rubin, now known as the Diniver Rebbe, an old childhood friend who was the son of the *dayan* from Kolbuszowa, lived in Monsey, New York, and had invited us to the bar mitzvah of one of his sons. Moshe was extremely religious, as well he had to be, for he had married the niece of the Satmar Rebbe. The Satmars were an ultra-Orthodox sect who were against secularism, Zionism, and the founding of the State of Israel. It was their belief that only when the Messiah had come could a Jewish homeland be restored.

When we arrived and had greeted those guests we knew, Moshe Rubin told me that the Satmar Rebbe, his uncle, was attending the bar mitzvah and he had asked to speak to me. The Satmar Rebbe wanted words with me, a Zionist and military man? What could we have to speak of? I quickly learned. Moshe Rubin, to whom I had confided my problems in getting my wife pregnant, had in turn mentioned it to the Rebbe. He requested that I see him, so I found a moment during the party.

"I understand you are having trouble having a child," he said. Somewhat surprised at this direction of the conversation, I indicated that such was the case. He said, "Take the *shpitz* of the *koiledge* (the end of the braided challah eaten on holidays) and have your wife eat it. I think you'll see a change." And with that he broke off and handed me the tip of the braided challah.

He took no offense at my raised eyebrows and my inability to suppress my skeptical expression. I thanked him and took the end piece and went to look for my wife to tell her of yet another crackpot suggestion. Since it was an Orthodox affair, she wasn't in the same room as we were. I had to seek her out among the other women. She laughed at the suggestion that eating a piece of challah would make her pregnant.

"Norman, this is the twentieth century. You are bringing me reme-dies from the Middle Ages," she said.

"I know," I said, "but let's humor the old man. At least it is not a drug, or harmful, and he did go out of his way to seek me out."

"Okay," she laughed, and with that, she chewed and swallowed the hard end of the *koiledge*. That night, we resumed our efforts at extending the lineage.

As I said, I am not too given to belief in miracles, or the expectation of immediate response to the prayers offered each Sabbath. Of course I be-lieve in God, but I know he has the problems of keeping the universe in order, not my difficulties at conception. What I do know is that nine months to the day that we received that *shpitz* of the *koiledge* and advice from the Satmar Rebbe, our daughter Esther was born.

What does my wife think? She believes we waited too long and tried unsuccessfully for too many years for this to be a coincidence. She thinks that the blessing of the Satmar Rebbe on the *koiledge* made the difference between our having no children and having a family that now extends to three grandchildren as well. She may be right. Who knows?

Certainly not my doctor.

Whatever one believes about the rabbi's miracle, the baby Esther, shown here with her mother, was born exactly nine months after following his directions.

The Adoption

Perhaps we had already had our share of miracles. To begin with, we had survived the Holocaust, a miracle denied to all but a tiny remnant of Polish Jews. We had then met one another while masquerading in unlikely guises as Polish Catholics. Amalie had been left behind by the retreating Germans with orders to blow up Cracow, and I had been a Polish army officer assigned to stop her. We had married and come to America, penniless, and had established ourselves as members of the middle class, verging on prosperity. We were now seeking one more miracle, the miracle of new life. The passage of ten years had allowed us to come to terms with an agonizing question that had bedeviled us: "Does it pay to bring a child into such a cruel world?" Our vote was in the affirmative. We wanted to have a child.

Miracles should not be taken for granted. While populations were exploding all over the world, and careless, as well as caring couples soon found themselves pushing baby carriages, we discovered that we were unable to conceive. We made the rounds of the medical profession, and doctor after doctor assured us that there were no physical reasons why we shouldn't be able to have children. Perhaps so, but as the months turned to years, hope turned to despair. We decided to adopt.

The Louise Wise Child Adoption Committee was the principal organization for Jewish adoption, and we went there to make our application. At the interview we established that we were financially capable of supporting a child. My business was growing, and Amalie worked as a Hebrew teacher. We did the paperwork and left financial statements. The lengthy process of personal investigation proceeded, and a case worker came to our house and discussed with us the obligations that would come with parenthood. We assured her of our readiness and showed her the separate room we had set aside for the child. We felt she was satisfied with everything she saw and heard during the five separate visits or interviews we had, and that was confirmed when we received a call from our case worker with the wonderful news.

"Congratulations. I can assure you that you will have a happy Thanksgiving. I am recommending that you be given a child."

We were overjoyed. While this approval didn't qualify as a miracle, it certainly was an omen of continued good fortune. We prepared the child's room and anxiously awaited the call to come to pick up the baby.

Four weeks went by before we received a phone call from the Louise

Wise agency. When we answered, the voice on the other end identified herself as the case worker on our adoption application, but it was immediately evident that this was not the case worker who had made the previous call. It seems that her workload had been redistributed, and this new case worker, a woman named Miss Rath, had received our folder and wanted to look into the matter a little further. She made an appointment to come to the house.

You don't survive the Holocaust without developing instincts about people and situations. When I hung up the telephone, Amalie immediately said, "That is a bad omen. We are not going to get the child."

A few days later Miss Rath came to inspect our situation. When she walked in, a chill seemed to come in with her. A plain woman, she offered a poor physical comparison to the glowing beauty of Amalie. Her conversation conveyed no spark of imagination or vitality. Somehow, I got the impression that there was resentment on her part against my wife. I thought there was jealousy there that did not bode well for us or our application.

A week went by after Miss Rath's visit. We had not heard from the agency, and I called to inquire. Rather than the optimistic report offered just a month before, I received a noncommittal, "We are still looking into it."

Two weeks later the Louise Wise Agency did call. They were very sorry, we were informed, but the decision was not to give us a baby. There was nothing personal. It was just that they had so many eligible applicants. No, their policy was not to give specific reasons for these decisions. They just couldn't give a baby to us.

Amalie and I were heartbroken over this news. Our expectations had been raised by the first case worker, only to have them mysteriously dashed when the new worker had assumed responsibility for our file. Arbitrary as it was, the decision was final.

I was determined to find out the truth behind our rejection, and ultimately I did gain access to information contained in the file.

Miss Rath, as we suspected, had recommended against us. Her reason stunned us. While it was true that we were financially stable and had the ability to support a child comfortably, she didn't believe that Holocaust survivors could be normal parents for a child. We were once again being punished for the accident of being born Polish Jews and for living through and surviving the war.

Our first effort was to try to get the decision reversed by getting some important people to vouch for us. If there was something suspect about our character, it would be helpful to get character references.

The first person I went to was Dr. Emil Rosenhauch, a prominent ophthalmologist who was well known in Europe and New York at the time. I had known him in Cracow under different circumstances. As the war was winding down, and the Germans were retreating to the west, he and his wife had come out of hiding, desperately poor and totally stripped of resources. At the time I was Tadeusz Zaleski, an officer in the Polish army, in a position of considerable influence. Among other favors I extended to the doctor, who at one time had been a colonel in the Polish army, was the granting of permission for him and his wife to eat their meals in our army officers' mess. Since there was little food available for anyone, and none for surviving Jewish doctors coming out of hiding, this favor had been critical to his survival and recovery. Dr. Rosenhauch was grateful for the opportunity to return my favor, and he wrote to the agency describing us in glowing terms.

I also went to Harry Schein, a successful businessman whom we had sponsored and brought to the United States after the war, and I told him of our problem. He, too, sent off a letter to the adoption agency. None of this helped, however. The woman in charge of adoptions informed us that their decisions were final, and we would not get a baby through them.

Our resolve to adopt a child was not diminished by this rejection. If we couldn't get a baby through conventional sources, we would investigate adoption through the black market. Our inquiries led us to an agency in Philadelphia where the screening process and review of character references were less meticulous than those at the Wise agency. In Philadelphia, it consisted mainly of our willingness to deliver eight thousand dollars in return for a baby. We agreed to pay this sum, indicating our preference for a newborn baby girl. It would be a matter of a few weeks, we were told, and we went home to await the call. When it came, we were to bring the eight thousand dollars with us in cash.

It appears that God had one miracle left for us after all, and it came to us a few days before we would receive the phone call from Philadelphia. During the interval, my wife announced to me that she missed her period, and the rabbit announced a few days later that, after our years of trying, and after our frustrated efforts at adoption, she was indeed gloriously pregnant. We were overjoyed, but tempting as it was, we decided not to be greedy. Raising two infants who were within a year of one another in age would be unfair to both.

When the long-distance call came from Philadelphia a few days later, I thanked them with what must have seemed a strange lilt in my voice, and told them that we wouldn't be adopting after all.

Rachel's Ring

It was our daughter Esther's third birthday. Our apartment rang with celebration—celebration of our being alive in America; celebration of the
miracle of our child, conceived and born after eleven years of marriage,
and just as we were about to give up hope of ever having our own children; celebration of signs of our succeeding, of making it in America. Esther, as she toddled around the room in her party dress, going from
adoring relative to relative symbolized all of that for us: the hardship of
the past, the joy of the present, and the promise of the future.

For this special day and this special child, I had a special gift. It was a
child's ring with a small diamond. I took her tiny hand and I slipped it on
her finger. It fit perfectly, as if it had been made especially for her. But it
hadn't been. It hadn't just come from the jewelry store, but in fact, had
been made many years before. I had carried it with me when my wife and
I left Europe. Nor had the ring been made for Esther. That fact was easily
confirmed, for inside a name was engraved in Hebrew letters—the name
Rachel.

I came into possession of the ring during the time I was chief of security in the city of Wroclaw (Breslau). We arrested what we took to be a
German civilian and in the process of investigating him learned that he
was actually a man named George Schlosser, a sergeant in the German
Shupo (*Schutzpolizei*, or civil police) who had been commandant of a police unit in the Polish town of Czestochowa.

Tall, blond, with blue eyes, he eventually told us under interrogation
about his past. We learned that he had been involved in the Jewish ghetto
at Czestochowa and responsible for some of the atrocities committed
there. When we searched his apartment we found a bag filled with dia-
mond-and-gold jewelry: watches, pins, and rings. He told us it was the
booty he had taken from transports that had come through from Belgium
during the war. The poor Jewish souls on the train, anticipating relocation, brought their valuables with them in hope of having something
with which to start over in their new homes in the East. But there were
no new homes—only the camps and death. Schlosser had engaged in the
normal German practice of stripping the victims of their valuables, but
rather than turning them in for shipment back to Germany, he had kept
some small portion for himself. We confiscated the bag for the Polish
authorities.

One by one I looked through the items, recording them on an inventory to be turned over to the state treasury in Warsaw: a diamond pin, a diamond brooch, obviously items of considerable value. Our standard practice was not to record these as diamonds because we lacked the expertise to certify that they were real. Instead, we would write entries such as "ring with white stones," not to be evasive, but simply to be as honest and as objective as possible. I didn't indeed know for sure what these stones were, and I must say I was scrupulously honest in recording and turning over everything that came into my hands.

Eventually I reached into the bag and took out the child's gold ring with the tiny diamond. It was so simple, so small, lost among the glittering gems at hand. I took it, turned it over, and saw the small Hebrew letters spelling "Rachel" inside. Schlosser merely shrugged when I asked him about it. He didn't remember who it came from—just part of a Belgium transport's valuables.

He didn't remember, but I understood immediately what this tiny child's ring with its diamond chip represented. I could picture the little girl that had owned it. I could picture her just as I could see my own nieces, pretty, innocent, proud. I could picture the ring being taken from her finger, and I knew this unknown Rachel, probably the child of wealthy Belgium Jews, had been robbed and promptly sent to her death. The ring was all that was left, and I knew that for once I would breach the honesty I had shown in handling appropriated jewelry. I wanted to keep this ring to preserve the legacy of the little girl Rachel and pass the ring along, if possible, to my own little girl, should I be fortunate enough to have one.

Schlosser was sent back to Czestochowa, where his wartime activities eventually led to his trial and execution. The ring remained in my pocket and ultimately came to America, where it reappeared in our apartment on the occasion of our daughter's third birthday.

How pleased she was. All day she wore it, holding her hand out in front of her, looking at it, showing it off, first to one and then to another of us. And at length, when it was time to go to bed, she kept it on her finger, took it under the covers with her, and fell asleep happily playing with it.

The next day it was gone. When my daughter Esther arose, the ring was not on her finger. Surely, it was in her bed, among the covers, in the mattress, on the floor. Surely the ring would turn up. No, it was gone. To this day, I cannot imagine how the ring disappeared or what happened to it. It came from Europe to America, was worn one afternoon, and during the night, it vanished.

It is forty-three years later as I write this. I have no more explanation today than I did then of the fate of the ring bearing the name of the child Rachel. I only know that the shadow of her existence came to me through the ring, and that it was passed on to my daughter, where it lingered for no longer than a day, and then, like a shadow does when the clouds gather, it faded out and was gone.

My Polish Neighbor in New Jersey

Daughter Esther slept with Rachel's ring one night, and when she awoke, it was gone. It was never found.

It was ironic. After five thousand miles and twenty years, I had worked my way up to a house in the suburbs in Springfield, New Jersey. I had come far away from Poland and the bitter memories it held for me, only to find myself living next door to an old Polish woman named Mary from the village Gwoznica, located near Strzyzow in Galicia. When I found out who my neighbor was, I thought it a bitter twist of fate. Here I was, once again living next door to a Polish peasant. I knew how troubled coexistence could be.

As it turned out, I was wrong about her. Instead of harboring the anti-Semitism I had come to expect from Poles, she had an open acceptance of Jews. When the weather was nice we would greet one another outside the house and gradually, from this, came invitations into the house, where we would talk Polish and exchange stories about our experiences. It was from one of these exchanges that I was reminded again, how different the experiences of Polish Jews and Gentiles were and how impossible it was for them to get along in the old country.

She had been one of a dozen children born into a poor Polish peasant family. Each had to work to eat, and more often than not, there wasn't enough food to go around. Because of that, she thought it had been a stroke of rare good fortune that led her to a job with a Jewish innkeeper, Mendel. She worked for him as a housemaid, cleaning the rooms and scrubbing the pots. In exchange she got a small amount of money, but more importantly, she got enough to eat. She could finish every day with

a full stomach, and on Friday night and Saturday, she got a piece of challah and a meal containing meat. We can't appreciate how rare meat was in
the diet of the Polish peasant. Most raised a few chickens, but they never
ate them. Instead, they would be taken to market and sold for whatever
they would bring. It was quite exceptional to be able to look forward to a
meal at the end of the week that would reliably include a piece of meat.
She was extremely happy working for Mendel and the envy of her friends.

Just as she ate meat every Saturday, she went to church on Sundays.
One Sunday, after she had been working for Mendel for about two years,
the priest stopped her as she was walking out.

"I understand you work for Mendel the Jew," he said. When she nodded, he told her she could not continue to do that.

"Why not?" she asked. "He treats me well, pays me fairly, and I get
more to eat than ever at home."

"No, you simply may not work for a Jew," he told her.

When she began to protest, he cut her off by saying, "If you persist, I
will not take your confession; and if I do not take your confession, you
can never be buried in a Catholic cemetery."

The injustice of this edict crushed her. She needed the church as she
needed air. At the same time, her job meant the difference between
hunger and comfort. That, she told me, was when she decided to come to
America. She could resolve this dilemma by running away from it.

The rest of the story is ordinary. She came here alone at the age of fifteen, met and eventually married a furrier named Drazek, raised a family,
and found prosperity in the New World, just as I had done. America offers
opportunity for all.

As it turned out, the priest's intolerance had been her salvation. Because of it, she had left Poland. When I heard the story, I thought she
hadn't been the only one to leave Poland because of the church's attitude
toward Jews. That type of intolerance had led countless Jews to flee also.
Things worked out well for most of those who fled the bigotry. But the
Catholic Church, through priests such as this one, had laid down the
seeds of hate that were to grow into bitter fruit for those who remained
behind.

Coming from as large a family as she did, Mary had a number of
nieces and nephews who would come to America to work. Some stayed
on, and others, after earning a little money, would go back to Poland.
Zoska was one who did just that. She lived with Mary for about six
months, worked as a maid and housekeeper for several families in the
area, but eventually decided that she preferred to be back among her
brothers and sisters in Poland. While she lived next door we came to

know Zoska and thought of her as a pleasant, if unsophisticated young women who usually said whatever came to her mind, appropriate or otherwise. This tendency on her part eventually caused me pain. Here is how it happened.

One day a stray cat showed up in the neighborhood. It had probably been abandoned, or gotten lost, and it just went from house to house looking for food. Zoska and Mary responded and put food out, and the cat quickly adopted this as its new home. Mary never really took the cat in. She just kept feeding it, and it kept coming back for more. I don't know what kind of communication network cats have. All I know is that pretty soon Mary's cat brought a friend, and then another. It wasn't long before the neighborhood was overrun with what must have been fifty stray cats, prowling around, looking for food, yowling at night, and making a general nuisance of themselves. It wasn't long after that when someone on the block called the SPCA and reported the condition.

The authorities responded. They dispatched their dogcatchers, turned catcatchers, to our Springfield neighborhood, and they began rounding up the stray animals. These were a wary and elusive group of cats, however. They were clearly accustomed to being on their own and very suspicious of human contact. While the SPCA people were able to catch most of the wild cats, a few continued to elude capture. Rather than beat the bushes indefinitely, the SPCA left baited traps that they knew sooner or later would tempt the hungry animals. And so they did. Within a day, the last of the neighborhood cats had yielded to temptation and was trapped, waiting to be taken off to likely extinction.

While all this was going on, our daughter Esther watched with quiet disapproval. She was a typical teenager, given to acceptance of most of God's creatures and, I suspect, complicit along with Mary and Zoska in the feeding of this feline assembly. None of them was terribly sympathetic with the SPCA's capture of the strays. Esther came home from school one day and discovered that the last of the cats was meowing loudly within one of the traps. It had been lured in and couldn't get out. Perhaps it was teenage rebellion. It may have been an act of sheer compassion. At any rate, my usually studious and law-abiding daughter opened the trap door and freed the last cat, which scampered off and, as far as I know, is still running.

As it turned out, Zoska was watching these events through her own window, and she saw Esther open the cage, liberating the cat. Zoska later told us about Esther's deed in these words.

"You know, Mr. Salsitz, what Esther did for the cat was just like what some Polish people did for the Jews. I remember when railroad cars were stopped. Polish people sometimes opened the doors and let the Jews run away to try to survive."

When I heard her say that I felt a terrible chill. Zoska's comparison of the beleaguered Jews of Poland to the cats seemed terribly insensitive. It was so upsetting to me, that I remained cool to Zoska from that day until she went back to Poland. It seemed like something that belonged with the same mentality that had driven Mary to leave Poland originally.

The tragic thing is that the image of a group being pursued by authorities who are bent on their extinction because some in the community feel them to be a nuisance was not so far off the mark. Perhaps that is why my revulsion at the time was so strong. The Jews of Europe had had no more power and no more chance than Zoska's cats. There hadn't been enough Esthers interested in saving them.

My Dealings with the NAACP

By 1957 I was in a position that today has become a cliché: I was a Jewish landlord with black tenants. I came here as a penniless immigrant. I had worked hard, shown initiative and enterprise, enjoyed a little good luck, and prospered in America. I invested some of my money in residential property and thus found myself a Jewish landlord with Polish tenants in Jersey City and Italian tenants in Hoboken. It wasn't long before these once stable communities began to change, and before I knew it, almost all my tenants were black. The color of my tenants' skin really didn't matter to me. I was more interested in the green of their money, but in the case of the tenant on the top floor of the eight-family building I owned on Monroe Street and Fourth in Hoboken, I hadn't seen any for a long time. That didn't stop things from going wrong, however. His wife had called one night to say the toilet wasn't working.

A couple of nights later, Wasyl Lenczuk and I showed up to take care of the complaint. Wasyl was a handyman I had come to use in matters such as this. Although Wasyl wasn't Jewish, his arm bore the tattooed numbers that attested to his history as a concentration camp survivor. He was a Ukrainian who had been sent to Auschwitz for reasons he never made clear to me but which the Germans had evidently understood perfectly. He was a reliable worker, and we got along well.

The neighborhood had once been solidly middle-class Italian. In fact, Frank Sinatra's old house was next door. The well-documented sequence of events that turns middle-class white neighborhoods into run-down black ones had long since run its course. Wasyl and I climbed the stairs, knocked, and entered the large, chilly apartment on the top floor. My tenant was home. He was a big-framed man with a loud voice who had told me at the very beginning of our relationship that he was the president of the local chapter of the NAACP—the National Association for the Advancement of Colored People. I well knew and respected the organization.

He showed us the problem he had with the toilet, and Wasyl was able to take it apart and fix it. Having done this, I took the opportunity to remind him that, by the way, his rent was overdue.

His reaction was not what I would have expected from the president of the local NAACP. With little preamble, he glowered at me and said, "That's the trouble with America. We have too many Jews here. We need a Hitler in America to kill all the Jews, but if Hitler won't do it, we blacks will."

The onslaught had me momentarily speechless. However, Wasyl, who rarely said anything to anyone, responded, "Why do you talk about Hitler? Hitler was bad. I'm not Jewish and he had me in a concentration camp. Why do you want him in America?"

My own wits returned, and I added, "You know, Hitler hated the blacks more than the Jews. Look how he treated Jesse Owens at the Olympic games. If Hitler was here, you would be in the gas chamber before me."

With this, he grabbed me, hit me, and threw me out of the apartment.

My experiences had certainly exposed me to greater bullies than this one. I knew that when you are pushed, you better push back harder. My first action was to call the New York office of the Anti-Defamation League. I had been very actives with the league, and described to Robert Kohler, its director, what had happened. He said he would get back to me, adding that "this man has no right to be the president of the NAACP."

A few weeks later, Mr. Kohler called me to report that a meeting had been arranged in the New York office of the NAACP to be held the next day. He wanted me to be there. I, in turn, called Wasyl and asked if he could attend the meeting. Since he was a working man, I offered to pay him for the day he would miss, and he agreed to join us.

The next day, we were ushered into the conference room in their spacious offices in midtown Manhattan. There were a number of people seated around the table, including the head of the national office of the organization, several secretaries, four or five lawyers—Jewish lawyers, I should add—my tenant, and three of what were represented as "witnesses." He was extremely cordial and joked with the national director, whom he obviously knew. The meeting got under way, and after introductions were made, the tenant and witnesses were asked to leave the room while I told my story to those present. The national director asked a few questions. Wasyl spoke and confirmed everything I had said.

At this point the tenant and his witnesses were called in, and he was asked what had happened. He smiled and confirmed that he had thrown me out of the apartment, but said he had good reason. I had called him a "fucking nigger" and had said, "If you don't pay me the money right now, I will get a dispossess order and throw your black ass out of the apartment tomorrow."

This produced a murmur among the group. He sat back, obviously wounded by the wrong I had dealt him and pleased with what seemed the board's sympathetic reaction.

I asked the national director if I could ask the tenant a few questions. He agreed and I asked,

"How many apartments are there in the building?"

"Eight," he said.

"Where is your apartment?"

"On the top floor."

"How many of the apartments are occupied by black tenants and how many by white?" I asked.

He said, "All black."

"What time of the day or night did this take place?"

He said, "It was eight or nine o'clock in the evening."

"Was it dark outside?"

"Yes."

"Did I say or do anything else besides call you a fucking nigger and threaten the dispossess if I didn't get my money?"

"No."

I thanked him, and turned to the lawyers and asked, "Gentlemen, do you think it is logical that I would go at night into that house occupied by eight black families, in a black neighborhood, go to the top floor from which I could not easily flee, call him the name he says I did, and speak to him in the manner he says I did, and expect to come out alive?"

Brows furrowed. Eyes wandered. At this point, when asked, the witnesses had nothing to say. They didn't believe it was logical either, and they admitted that they hadn't actually witnessed the event. They had come to attest to their friend's good and honorable character.

The lawyers and director conferred for just a few minutes and told my tenant, "You are not fit to represent this organization. From this moment on, you are no longer the president of the NAACP chapter. What is more, you are not fit to even belong to the organization. You no longer belong to the NAACP." They not only took his office away, they took his membership away.

A few weeks later I completed the outcome. I took his apartment away. I got a dispossess notice from the court, on the basis of his being a habitual late payer, and the sheriff came and enforced it. I was both pleased and surprised to learn that, instead of being upset, the other tenants were grateful. It seems his bullying behavior had been common in their dealings with him as well, and they were pleased to be rid of him.

I offer this story as an example of my experience with men of goodwill in America. I relied on the sense of justice that I was sure must exist in an organization such as the National Association for the Advancement of Colored People, and I am happy to report I was not disappointed.

An Unexpected Encounter

By 1965 I was a well-established suburbanite in Springfield, a middle-income community in central New Jersey. Its Jewish community included both a Reform and a Conservative congregation. My personal affiliation was with the Conservative synagogue, Temple Beth Ahm, but one of the people in the community whom I liked very much was Israel Dresner, rabbi of the Reform temple.

While I had slipped away from Orthodox observance many decades before, I did retain a knowledge of Judaism and Jewish matters gained from my Hasidic upbringing in Kolbuszowa. Many evenings over the years, Rabbi Dresner and I discussed matters of Jewish custom and observance.

One year, Rabbi Dresner had an inspired idea. He realized that his Reform congregation of Westernized Jews had not the remotest acquaintanceship with the fervor with which the ultra-Orthodox practice their shared religion. He organized a bus trip to Brooklyn on the holiday of Simchat Torah (the eighth and last day of Sukkoth, the Feast of Tabernacles) that year, bringing interested members of his congregation to observe how the Hasidim celebrate this holiday, the Festival of the Rejoicing of the Torah. To the Orthodox, this is one of the most joyous of holidays, celebrated by frenetic dancing with the Torah by those selected for that honor. To the Reform, it is yet another of those minor holidays—

if it isn't Rosh Hashanah or Yom Kippur, it is minor. Rabbi Dresner's trip was in the order of an anthropological outing for the Reform group. They would observe the Orthodox in celebration much as they would consider some Alaskan Indian tribe at a potlatch. The rabbi asked me if I would like to go along, and I readily assented. It had been many years since I had been with the Hasidim at Simchat Torah.

The bus arrived in the Eastern Parkway section of Brooklyn, and we found ourselves surrounded by thousands of Jews outside the Lubavitcher *shul* that Rabbi Dresner had selected to visit. Attired in their holiday finest, the men of the community were in high good humor as they crowded their way off the sidewalk and into the *shul.*

The Springfield Jews stood back to observe, but I suddenly found myself back in an element that was all too familiar to me. To get in, one had to push. To push, one had to use sharp elbows. Throwing myself into the crowd, I jostled with the best of them, pushing, shoving, and ultimately finding myself inside the *shul* where the men were standing on benches and tables, each with a small paper cup of vodka waiting to catch the rebbe's eye. When they did, they would exchange the traditional greeting, *L'chaim,* to life, and bolt down the small amount of vodka. In the excitement, I was handed a paper cup of vodka, and I climbed up on a table. As the Springfield Jews outside looked in through the window, I caught the rebbe's eye, we toasted each other and celebrated in the tradition of the Lubavitchers. I think the Springfield Jews were impressed with one of their own.

Next, Rabbi Dresner took his small flock to the *shul* of the Bobover Rebbe, Shlomo Halberstam, a smaller, ground-floor synagogue, once again surrounded by thousands of the faithful. Here, the European origins were more clearly discernible. The Bobover Hasidim wore heavy beards, were silk coated, and were capped by elegant, sable fur *streimels.* Once again, as the Springfield Jews stood back in reserve, I plunged into the crowd, elbows flying, and in a matter of moments they could see me through the window. Here, the celebration featured the Rebbe, his head covered by his *tallit,* dancing with the Torah for hours on end. For this purpose, he held a special miniature parchment scroll in his embrace and whirled and whirled. I stood again on a table, clapping my hands, singing and shouting alongside the Hasidim.

Part of this custom is the *hakafot,* or giving out of honors to deserving congregants who dance with the Torah and the rabbi. The first *hakafot* are usually given to the Kohanim (members of the priestly tribe), and then if there are more Torahs than Kohanim, the remainder are given out to the important congregants. Seven times during the evening, one has a chance to be so honored, and as the crowd cheered, a silk-coated Hasid, resplendent in fur hat and flowing red beard standing on a chair next to the ark called out the names of those to be so honored. With each name, an eager worshiper reached forward to take the Torah and join in the wild dance with the rabbi. Although I am in fact a Kohen, this fact was unknown, and I was content to remain on the sidelines.

But then the man with the red beard held a Torah out and called "Zaleski, I give this honor to Zaleski." When no one in the congregation responded, once again he called, "Zaleski" and as I turned from facing the crowd to look at him, I realized that the Torah was being thrust toward me.

Zaleski. I hadn't thought about using that name for twenty years. Zaleski, the name I had adopted while masquerading as a Polish Catholic in the army. Tadeusz Zaleski. This Hasid with the red beard was honoring Tadeusz Zaleski with the *hakafa*. In bewilderment, I stepped down from the table and accepted the Torah, and as the group from Springfield peered in through the window, I whirled around the *shul*, Torah in my embrace, dancing with the Bobover Rebbe.

At length, I yielded up the scroll and tugged at the arm of the man who had called my name. "Why did you give me the scroll?" I asked in Yiddish. "How do you know me as Zaleski?"

"I owe you a debt," he replied, "and I am glad to repay some small part of it by giving you this honor."

"But I don't know you, I protested."

"Yes, you do," he said. "Do you remember back in Cracow, when you rescued two boys who were being held in a coal bin in the police station?"

Two boys in a coal bin. My mind raced back to before America, before Germany, before escape from Poland, Two boys in a coal bin . . . Yes, I remembered.

It was winter, 1945. By that year, I had advanced within the Polish security forces to the position of head of the State Security for the County of Cracow and its neighboring communities. For a known Jew to hold such a position in the Polish government would have been impossible. However, only a handful of people within the government knew I was Jewish. To the rest, I was Tadeusz Zaleski. I spoke perfect, unaccented Polish, had a characteristic Polish face, and clean-shaven, there was no reason to believe I was anything other than the Roman Catholic officer I claimed to be.

After the liberation of Poland by the Russian forces the few Jewish survivors gradually began to drift back into the cities. Cracow was no exception, and as the number of Jews grew, they organized themselves into Jewish Committees to look after Jewish interests. Shortly after I arrived in Cracow I made it a point to visit the leadership of the Cracow Jewish Committee, a lawyer named Stulbach and a woman named Marianska, to take them into my confidence by revealing that I was a Jew, and to let them know that I was available to do whatever I could, unofficially, to ease their circumstances.

Although I could do little within the formal structure, there was a great deal I might do unofficially. The small Jewish community was extremely vulnerable to both governmental and personal abuse in Poland at that time, and my offer was gratefully accepted. At that time, Rabbi Moshe Steinberg, a rabbi who by some miracle had survived the war, served as spiritual leader of the threadbare Jewish community of Cracow. With my permission, Stulbach told Rabbi Steinberg about me, and the rabbi would, from time to time, arrange to have me contact him so I could learn of Jewish needs in the community.

It was through Rabbi Steinberg that I learned one day of two Jewish boys from a small town outside Cracow who had been arrested by the police for black market dealings, and had disappeared. The police had caught them transporting a truckload of sugar, confiscated the vehicle and its cargo, and taken the boys into custody. From that point on, they had vanished with no satisfactory answer ever given to the concerned inquiries of the Jewish Committee. The rumor was that the authorities had kept the sugar for their own profit and turned the boys over to the Cracow Militia to be held somewhere in a Cracow jail.

As head of the State Security I was indirectly superior to the local militia. While we didn't report through the same chain of command, our political sponsorship placed us in the dominant position. However, this political dominance could not prevent simple lying. It never has. The next morning, I inquired from the chiefs of each of the precincts whether or not they knew anything of the fate of these two brothers, arrested some two weeks before, but, not surprisingly, none did.

So I set out on a precinct-by-precinct inspection of the jail facilities of the twelve precincts in Cracow. To appearances the inspection had nothing to do with the missing Jewish brothers. It was simply an inventory of the jail cells in the city undertaken for bureaucratic reasons. One by one, I visited the dingy jails in the basements of the precinct headquarters. One by one, the cell doors were thrown open for my inspection. Some cells were occupied, others vacant. Most contained the occupants called for by the records—criminals and political offenders of various stripes.

At length, I came to one precinct in the building called Wolnica, and the inspection was proceeding just as the others had, except at the end of the dark basement corridor, there was one door still locked tight. When I inquired about it, the police chief assured me that it was just a bin used for the storage of coal.

Nevertheless, I persisted in being allowed to look inside. The keys were nowhere to be found. They are lost, I was told. I backed everyone away and shot the padlock off the door. As the door swung open, I was able to discern in the dim light of the bin two filthy figures—the missing Jewish boys I was seeking. As the chief dissembled about lost records and confused paperwork, I relented in my chastisement of him. "Just clean them up and get them to my headquarters. I will take care of this matter myself." Relieved that his obvious impropriety had not led to anything worse, the militia chief readily assented, and by the end of the day the prisoners were presented.

They told the story that the Jewish Committee anticipated. They had been arrested, beaten, and locked in the dirty bin two weeks before. Although they had been fed on a daily basis, they had never been charged. Frightened and hungry, they stood before me, the embodiment of the power of the state, expecting only the worst.

Relief flooded through them when I told them I had been sent to look for them by Rabbi Steinberg, that I was Jewish, and that I was going to let them go, providing they left the Cracow territory and I never saw them again. And so it was that the two brothers fled into the Polish countryside, spared and freed to continue life.

And so it also was that on this fateful Simchat Torah in Brooklyn, New York, twenty years later, fate presented me with an encounter with the red-bearded Hasid who handed me the honor of dancing with the Torah as repayment for the good deed I had done him in Poland two decades before.

"How in the world do you recognize me?" I asked the Hasid. "I don't know you at all."

"I could never forget your face, especially your eyebrows," he said. "I have constantly thought of how we were delivered from that coal bin in Cracow, and the minute you walked in, I knew it was you and I was overwhelmed."

He went on to point out that in Cracow, I had been an adult, clean-shaven then, and so I was now. He, by contrast, had been a youth who had now matured, grown a beard, and put on a black coat and was virtually a different person than the one I had set free. Joseph in Egypt, he pointed out, had similarly not been recognized by the brothers because Joseph had been a young boy and he had changed in much the same way I did.

"No, it is you, Zaleski," he said. And as the people from the Springfield suburbs in New Jersey stared through the window of the *shul* in

Brooklyn, their neighbor, who had toasted the Lubavitcher Rebbe and danced with the Bobover Rebbe, now fell into the embrace of a red-bearded Hasid, dressed in the black silk coat and fur *streimel*, his face wet with long-suppressed tears of joy.

The Button and the Cap

The need for American Jews to buy Israel Bonds was always clear to me. As a survivor who had lost his entire family in the Holocaust, I vividly recognized that a Jewish homeland could have saved millions of lives had it only existed when no one else would take us in. I did everything I could to promote the sale of these bonds, so when in 1968 the bond office asked me to chair the drive in Essex County, New Jersey, I readily accepted. While Jewish pride was at its height following the Six Day War, so, too, was the urgency to add to the capital assets of the struggling Eretz Israel (literally, Land of Israel; figuratively, Jewish homeland). I would invest all of my energies to achieve a record sale.

The major bond-selling event each year was a big dinner that would be attended by four or five hundred of the region's most prominent citizens. It was not unusual to have senators, congressmen, industrialists attend this black-tie affair at which a prominent representative from the State of Israel would be present to brief the audience on events in the Mideast and to urge the purchase of bonds. This year's representative was to be an Israeli army colonel named Peled, who came in his full-dress army uniform to address the audience. My job as chairman would be to make a speech as well, and to introduce the colonel. The bond office had prepared a speech for me and sent it for me to read.

Although I was very comfortable in the role of chairman, I have always felt extremely uneasy reading a speech that either I or someone else has prepared. Storytelling was my forte. Speech reading inevitably ended up disastrously because I would get mixed up as I read, looked away, and then back again to the paper. In Polish or Yiddish it would have been no problem. In English it was a formula for confusion.

I sat at the dais between my wife and the colonel, growing more uneasy by the moment. The bond office speech was in my pocket, and as the program moved forward to my part I was upset because I knew how important a big sale would be and how little I could do to promote it by stumbling through someone else's written words. I leaned over and whispered to my wife, "I am not going to read the speech they gave me." She looked at me with surprise and then worry as I added, "I am going to tell them a story instead." She immediately began to kick me under the table.

"Don't start with your stories."

"Don't worry," I assured her. "You will see that it will work out fine." But it was myself that needed assurance. I didn't have the faintest idea of what story I could tell.

At length, my time came. I got up, and as I walked past the colonel to the microphone, inspiration struck. I would tell them a story from the works of the great Sholom Aleichem, who at this time was particularly popular among Jews and non-Jews alike. *Fiddler on the Roof* was enjoying great success on Broadway.

"This evening and this occasion," I said, "remind me of a short story that Sholom Aleichem wrote many years ago called *'Dus Knepel in der Dashek,'* otherwise known as 'The Button and the Cap.' Since he lived around the turn of the century, Sholom Aleichem didn't know if it would ever come to be a reality, but in this story he asked God, 'When will we Jews have a shiny brass button and a leather brim on our cap?'

"Why was a button and a cap so important? Because in the time of Czarist Russia, everybody who was an important government official wore a jacket with silver or gold buttons. And he had a cap with a shiny leather brim. These were the trappings of power in those days, and they were forever denied the Jew. A Jew couldn't have them because a Jew could never be a governmental official. Even a dogcatcher wore a jacket with golden buttons and a cap with a brim. But a Jew couldn't even be dogcatcher. So Sholom Aleichem prayed and asked God, 'When will we Jews have a *kneppel* in a *dashek*?' meaning when will we Jews be able to participate, to be somebody important, to be part of the government?

"Sholom Aleichem didn't live long enough to see the Jews get the recognition he prayed for. True, there were Jews who attained buttons and a cap, but they were not Jewish buttons and caps. They belonged to someone else. I had worn the uniform of the Polish army. Other Jews who were in the U.S. Army had similarly worn a military uniform, but no matter how elaborate these uniforms had been, the fact remained that they were not Jewish uniforms. They had been borrowed from another power and were worn by Jews only through the indulgence of those powers."

As I talked, the audience wondered where I was going. They were soon to find out as I asked Colonel Peled, who was to follow my talk with his own, to please stand up.

The author stands at the far left of this group from the dais at the Israeli Bond dinner. The Israeli officer in uniform is Colonel Peled, the subject of Salsitz' remarks that evening.

The colonel stood, and I asked him if he would put on the cap to his uniform that he carried with him. He did so, and he stood before the audience, dressed in his well-pressed military uniform, its buttons gleaming, his ribbons attesting to a career of combat and danger.

"If only Sholom Aleichem were here today, he would see his dream answered," I said. "Look, here we have a man who has silver and gold buttons. They're ours. Look at his hat. He has a shiny brim. It is ours." As I spoke I became quite emotional and my eyes filled up with tears.

"Sholom Aleichem dreamed this, and we have lived to see it. Now, will we let these buttons tarnish? Will we let this cap lose its luster? They need money in Israel. They must build up the army. They need us to buy bonds to sustain Sholom Aleichem's dream."

The audience responded emotionally. Many showed tears in their eyes as they pledged many thousands of dollars of bond purchases to preserve the Jewish *knepel* and *dashek*. The colonel hardly had to say a word. His presence, in his Jewish uniform told it all.

As the evening wound up, I received the handshakes and congratulations of everyone at the dinner. My story had been a great success. One friend whom I had at the dinner, Dr. Elijah Bortniker, national chairman for Hebrew education in the United States and Canada, came over and said, "That was a marvelously appropriate story, Norman, but tell me: Where did you come upon that short story? I know Sholom Aleichem's works quite well, but I don't remember reading that one before."

I smiled and confessed to my friend: "Well, maybe Sholom Aleichem didn't exactly write that story. Actually, it is a Norman Salsitz original. But if I would say Norman Salsitz had this dream, it would have no importance. For Sholom Aleichem to have written of his dream seventy years ago—that's different. He would be happy, I am sure," I added, "to lend his name for the people of Israel."

That night the lending of his name was paid back in full. The Essex County drive set a new record in Israel Bond sales.

The Miniature Megillah

My house is filled with Judaica. Pictures with Jewish themes crowd the walls. A curio cabinet in the corner of the living room displays Kiddush cups, menorahs, *mezuzahs*. There is little doubt that a very proud Jew lives here. Each of these possessions was gathered with love. Many were saved from pre-Holocaust Poland, and when I look at them and hold them I recall the households in which they were cherished and the fates of those who owned them. Ask me about any of them, and I will tell you the story. What about that little megillah in the silver case studded with semiprecious stones? Ah, that one is my most prized possession of all.

In our town of Kolbuszowa lived a very wealthy Jew named Jacob Ekstein. Before World War I he was one of the very few Jews in Galicia who owned two entire villages. My grandfather, Naftali Saleschutz-Dubaser, was the manager in one of his villages: Dubas. Usually only Polish nobility held title to such estates, but Reb Yakov, as he was called out of respect, had been smart enough to earn a fortune as a businessman and had been even smarter in the charitable use of his wealth. He was generous to Jew and Gentile alike. From the brewery for vodka that he owned, he would distribute bottles of vodka to poor Poles on non-Jewish holidays. On Jewish holidays, he would likewise distribute vodka to the poor Jews.

One year when the Austrian army held maneuvers in Galicia, Reb Yakov took over and said he would supply hay, straw, and oats to the cavalry. Two gold medals were issued by Emperor Franz Josef of Austria-Hungary after the maneuvers. One went to the governor of Galicia. The other went to this Jew from Kolbuszowa, Jacob Ekstein. My father used to say that on national holidays this distinguished patriot with the aristocratic face and long gray beard came to the synagogue with a silver cane, wearing this gold medal on his black coat.

He was revered by Jews and admired by Gentiles until the day he died in 1935. He was buried on a cold winter day, attended by the entire Jewish town as well as by a delegation from the state government. Before the funeral the city government cleared the snow, which was two meters deep, for the three kilometers from his villa to the Jewish cemetery. Reb Yakov was so respected that the municipal government named a street after him: "Ulica Jakuba Eksteina."

Unfortunately, the gift of business acumen bestowed on Jacob Ekstein turned out to be only a temporary loan. After World War I, fortune began to smile on others and frown on his enterprises. Little by little he lost his property, his villages, his businesses, until by the time he died Jacob Ekstein left only a good name, good deeds, and the beautiful villa in which he lived, furnished with many beautiful and precious antiques.

Most of his children moved away from Kolbuszowa, and the three grandchildren who remained were likewise without the business sense their grandfather had. By the time the Germans came to Poland the grandchildren were reduced to selling off the antiques to hold body and soul together. And so it was that one day I bought from Reb Yakov's grandson the small megillah now housed in my living room, for fifteen loaves of bread. Some thought I overpaid. Who needs a kosher megillah in the ghetto? But as you can see, this megillah was something special. It was already over 150 years old, having been made by a gifted silversmith in Czechoslovakia. Inside, the story of Esther had been written on parchment in letters so small you needed a magnifying glass to read it. If Esther would save the Jews from one tyrant, we would save the telling of that story. My brother, Leibush, hid this megillah with all our other valuables in a double floor that we built in the attic.

Time passed. By 1941 my family lived with Leibush because his apartment was in the ghetto, and we had already been thrown out of our home. Gestapo Landskomissar Walter Twardon, who influenced our lives

This miniature megillah, salvaged by the author from the Kolbuszowa ghetto, occupies an honored place in his house today.

in the ghetto like no one else, kept us in a state of constant uncertainty with his unpredictable torment of the Jews.

One day in September of that year he and the Kreishauptmann, a Doctor Ehaus, came to the apartment to search for contraband. Only Chancia, Leibush's wife was at home. When they found a five-kilo bag of flour the Gestapo men undressed Chancia and beat her so badly with sticks that her body took on the look of a black piece of meat. Whether they had knowledge or not of what was hidden is uncertain. We do know that they then searched the remainder of the apartment, found the double floor with all the things my brother and my father had put away, and confiscated everything. The megillah was in the hands of Haman.

Misfortune followed misfortune. In June of 1942 the ghetto was to be completely liquidated. My father had been murdered, and my mother and sisters taken to the Belzec death camp where they were gassed. Leibush and I, however, were spared. Through a strange twist of fate our knowledge of the merchandise looted from our father's business became our passport to survival. Twardon needed laborers to dismantle the ghetto and remove all traces of its existence. He also needed a warehouseman to identify, pack, and ship items of value from my father's inventory back to Germany. We were selected to be part of the Kolbuszowa labor gang, and while the other members of the family were killed, we were sent back to work. Some days we worked dismantling the ghetto. Some days I was sent to the warehouse, where I made packages of coffee, tea, sugar, cocoa, and soap—things they didn't have in Germany—to ship back to Twardon's family. Each night, as I left the warehouse, the German policeman who let me out searched me to be sure I hadn't stolen back some piece of Twardon's loot.

One day while working in the warehouse I opened a wooden box that had been nailed shut and discovered all of the possessions that had been taken from the double floor of our apartment the day they came and beat Chancia. There was our flatware and our candlesticks and jewelry. They seemed so important then and so meaningless now that the family was dead. I wasn't interested in any of it until I found, thrown in with the rest, the antique megillah. It had come down through one and a half centuries to end up in a dusty box, part of the booty gathered by the pirates. I held it in my hand, admiring the intricacy of its carving and became obsessed with getting it back. But how? I put it back and closed the box.

"You're crazy," Leibush told me. "If they find it when they search you, they will kill you." I had told him of my discovery and my intent to steal back the megillah. Of course, I knew he was right, but I also knew I would find a way to smuggle the megillah out of the warehouse.

When I went to work each day I wore an old army cap along with my Jewish armband. Just as the armband marked me for eventual destruction, the cap signified that I should be spared for the time being. It was recognized as part of a uniform that meant I shouldn't be stopped or arrested. It was also the means by which I would steal the megillah.

In our camp we had a Jewish tailor and I asked him to make a double lining in the cap with a little opening. He fashioned it as I requested and the next evening, after working a whole day making packages for Twardon, I took the megillah and pushed it into the lining of my cap. With a needle and thread that I brought in with me I sewed the opening shut. At about 6:00 P.M., I put the cap on my head, and waited for the policeman to let me out.

The next minutes passed like hours. The policemen had me raise my arms and as usual, they searched my body. They patted me down and turned my pockets inside out. They looked everywhere but in the hat. Satisfied, they told me to pass and, elated over one small victory won over an enemy that had inflicted so many defeats, I returned to the labor camp and my brother Leibush. Oh, how we celebrated that night.

I still celebrate. Sadly, Leibush is no longer alive, but each Purim as I look at that tiny antique scroll, I marvel at the strange twists of its destiny. It traveled from Czechoslovakia to Poland, to the villa of Jacob Ekstein, to the Kolbuszowa ghetto, to Twardon's treasure house, to the Polish woods outside Kolbuszowa where I hid out for the rest of the war, then to Germany when I escaped from Poland, and finally to America, to a comfortable house in suburban New Jersey where it occupies a place of honor—a small but brilliant symbol of perseverance, of survival, and of redemption.

Another Voice

The following was written by Helen Schreiber (Honig)

We couldn't believe it was over. After two years of being hidden by various Polish families in bunkers, in barns, under the ground—after two years of fear and hunger and cold, we were able to come out and celebrate. The Russian army had liberated Chrzastow, which is a small village near Mielec in South Poland. We had survived: my parents and I, the Rosenzweig brother and sister, Mrs. Kanarek and her daughter Mira, the Spalter parents and their daughters Giza and Hela, and Marc and Frania Verstandig. We had survived the misery and the danger of hiding from the Germans, and we were entitled to celebrate.

But it quickly became apparent that our celebration was premature. We had survived the Germans, but the Polish underground home army known as the Armia Krajowa, or AK, was just as bent on our destruction as the Germans had ever been. As soon as the occupiers left and the Jews come out of hiding, the soldiers of the AK began going from house to house where they suspected Jews might be hiding and systematically wiping them out. "Not one Jew should remain alive," was their oft-quoted motto.

One night ten men with rifles came to the place where the Verstandigs were staying. They were members of the AK. They lined the family up and marched them toward the woods. It happened quickly. Four of the family were killed outright. Frania Verstandig was heavily wounded, while her husband Marc managed to jump into the canal and swim away. When he came back he found Frania had been hit by a dum-dum bullet that tore a large piece of flesh out of her back. She survived and today bears the large scar that resulted.

Realizing our vulnerability if we remained in such a small village, we set out on foot from Chrzastow. As we walked, a truck filled with Russian solders stopped, picked us up, and brought us to Kolbuszowa, a town that had been liberated on July 29. We are forever grateful for the kindness shown us by the Russians. Not only did they help with our transport; when we arrived, the local Russian *comendatura* (military headquarters) assigned a house to us that had recently been abandoned by some Polish collaborators who had fled with the Germans. We had found a sanctuary.

It should be clear how large a role chance played in determining who survived in those days and who didn't. Chance shaped every aspect of our lives. Once again, chance intervened when, on the very day we came to Kolbuszowa, a tired-looking, shabbily dressed young man came to our door. "Someone told me there were Jews in this town," he announced with a spirit that was clearly in contrast to his shabby appearance. "I want to see Jewish girls," he exclaimed. "I never expected to see Jewish girls again." When the four of us came to the door, the weariness left his face. "Ah, Jewish girls," he cried. "Which one of you wants to marry me?" Despite the troubling times, we were accustomed to longer courtships. We laughed, asked him his name, and invited him in.

"Naftali Saleschutz," he said. "I was born in Kolbuszowa and grew up here." And as we spoke that day, he told us his own story of the death of his family, his escape from the labor camp, and his survival hiding in the woods and living off of the land. He knew about the AK, having joined them while pretending to be a Catholic Pole. He alternately made us cry and laugh and cry again with stories of survival and betrayal experienced by his friends during those years. At length, he made one more light-hearted proposal of marriage. When we once again turned him down, he announced that he was going to pick up a suit of clothes being held for him at a friendly Pole's house and perhaps that would make us change our minds. He told us we should get out of Kolbuszowa. It wasn't safe for a group of Jews because the AK would learn of us and come in the night and kill us. That night, we left for the larger city of Rzeszow.

About a year later, we were settled in Cracow.

We were feeling relatively safe from the AK, but life was tightly controlled by the government and its bureaucracy. One of our friends, caught up in the delay that strict adherence to the rules created for anyone trying to register a car, offered a bribe to a Polish official. I don't think it was the bribe that offended the Pole, so much as the fact that a Jew already owned a car. He became furious and had our friend arrested.

Alarmed at this dangerous turn of events, we frantically inquired about what we could do to help. Who could we turn to? Several Jews advised us of an official in State Security who seemed friendly toward Jews. His name was Tadeusz Zaleski, we were told, and he had interceded on several occasions on behalf of Jews caught up in the system before. There was even a rumor that Zaleski himself was Jewish.

I went to his office, had my name announced to him through the security apparatus in the building, waited for several hours, and eventually was admitted to a spacious office. Seated behind the desk, well groomed, and elegantly dressed in his officer's uniform was none other than my one-time suitor for an afternoon, Naftali Saleschutz. I could scarcely believe my eyes. "That must have been some suit his friend was holding for him," I thought.

He couldn't have been more gracious. I explained to him what my friend's problem was and asked if he would be willing to help. After all, he had been willing to marry me just a year ago. "Of course I will help," he told me, and he proceeded to advise who I could contact in the government, what lawyer I should procure to handle the case, what should be said, and to tell him "Zaleski sent me." The lawyer and the official managed to resolve the issue quickly, and the unlucky car buyer was set loose.

Within the year, we left for the United States.

Thirty years passed. We had prospered in the security of our adopted country, and one evening, while watching a program on the TV on Polish anti-Semitism, I saw a man discussing what had gone on just after the war in his home town of Kolbuszowa. The voice had a familiar tone. There was something familiar about the gestures. Suddenly the realization of who it was became clear. He was older—we all deserve credit for living to get older—and his features had softened with the fleshing out of his face. But there was no mistaking those eyes, and particularly the bushy eyebrows that had been most striking. All night, I relived experiences I hadn't thought about for thirty years, and the next morning called a friend and asked her if she had been watching the program on TV. Not only had she been watching, but it turned out that the speaker, now known as Norman Salsitz, was a good friend of hers from the Wagro organization.

As I write this, it is twenty years later. Norman, who recalled immediately who I was, called, and I visited him and his lovely wife Amalie. They went on to write a narrative of their survival of the war in a book appropriately titled, *Against All Odds*. Norman and I have remained good friends, and we often get together to talk of the old times, good and bad, in Poland and Israel. We speak easily with one another. We have shared a lot. After all, if I had seen him in that suit, we might have been married.

A Stamp Collector's Tale

There are many dangerous hobbies. If you skydive, the chute may not open. If you climb mountains, you may fall off a cliff. One of my hobbies is stamp collecting, a pastime not normally ranked high on the list of hazardous activities. Yet I nearly got killed pursuing it. Here is how it happened.

While I collect stamps from all over the world, I particularly specialize in those from Poland, Russia, America, Germany, and Israel. In fact, I have every stamp ever issued by the State of Israel, gathered through a standing order I have left with the Israeli post office. I have them send the stamps with a variety of cancellations, including all the first-day covers. When a new stamp is issued to commemorate an important historical event, the post office pastes it onto to a specially designed envelope and uses a unique cancellation on the stamp to memorialize the date. The stamp and envelope are called a first-day cover.

One such occasion for issuance of a new stamp was Egyptian President Sadat's trip to Israel, where he spoke to the Knesset and signed a historic peace treaty. Israel honored the event by issuing the Shalom stamp. It shows a part of the Western Wall with a slip of paper offering a prayer to God stuck into a crack. When I received it in the mail I recognized that it memorialized a major event in Israel's history, and I decided it would be fitting if I could get it autographed by the three men who were instrumental in bringing about this peace: President Anwar Sadat of Egypt, Prime Minister Menachem Begin of Israel, and President Jimmy Carter of the United States.

I began with President Carter. I sent the first-day cover to him with a letter explaining my purpose and requesting that he autograph it. After a few weeks I received a reply containing an autographed portrait of the president. The first day cover was also returned, but, was unsigned.

Disappointed, but by no means discouraged, I next sent the cover off to President Sadat with a glowing cover letter describing the admiration that I and the rest of the world felt for him. Six months went by, and one day I received an envelope from Cairo that contained a letter from him, thanking me for my interest. He had signed the cover in Arabic and in English.

Now my life became a little more complicated. With Sadat's signature on the cover, I really didn't want to risk losing it by sending it through the mail to any of the others. I figured that the next time I was in Israel, I would attempt to get in to see Mr. Begin and have him sign as well. However, when I tried to get in to see him, I had no success. Since my time in Israel was coming to a close, I decided to give the task to my wife's niece, who happens to be a beautiful, six-foot-tall, blue-eyed, blonde, and very striking member of the Israeli army. A lack of chutzpah has never been one of her faults. She went to Begin's office in full uniform, stated her purpose, and was promptly denied entrance.

Raising her voice, she said, "Do you know who this is for? It is for my Uncle Naftali, who is a very important person in America. He is the president of Israel Bonds, president of Magen David Adom (the Israel Red Cross) in America." On and on she went, and as she was once again being refused, the prime minister heard her from his inner office, came out, and inquired what all of the fuss was about. She showed him the envelope with Sadat's signature, told him of my intention to get all three signatures on it, and asked that he put his on it as well. I guess the old warrior recognized a kindred spirit. Begin told my niece, "Your uncle should be very proud of you for standing up for him like that. Of course I will sign it," and he did.

Now I had Begin's signature along with Sadat's. At about this time

Sadat was shot and his autograph became a real collector's item. With just the two signatures I already had something very special. Still, I wanted President Carter's signature as well. However, my dilemma was that I certainly wasn't going to let the document out of my sight.

One day I read in the paper that President Carter was coming to New York to work with Habitat for Humanity remodeling some houses. I went to the site and found hundreds of people standing around watching him. His public relations woman was standing there, and when I spoke to her, she said, "give it to me and I will have him sign it and send it back." No, I didn't want to take the chance of losing it, so she suggested I try to catch him at lunch and get him to sign. No luck. The police wouldn't let me get within fifty feet of him.

A few weeks later, I read that he would be in a New York bookstore signing copies of his book. An idea jumped into my mind. As long as he was signing books, there was no reason for him not to sign the first-day cover as well. I would get his autograph by going to the signing.

When I got to the bookstore, I found hundreds of people there ahead of me, lined up with their books. For thirty-five dollars I purchased his book, which I confess I haven't read to this day, and took my place at the end of the long, long line. We inched forward at a snail's pace, down a corridor and up a few flights of steps. At the end of three hours I was on the threshold of the room where the president was seated at a desk. Everyone in the line was handed a sheet of paper with instructions on the procedure to follow and bearing the warning not to give him anything but the book to be signed.

When my turn came, I found myself at a barrier about six feet away from the seated president who was surrounded by two Secret Service men and two New York policemen. One of them would take the book from the person, give it to the president to sign, and then return it. As the policeman took my book, I pushed the barrier aside and followed him into the space, approaching Jimmy Carter. The Secret Service men thought I was going to shoot him, and they grabbed me and lifted me off the ground. As they did, I shouted, "Mr. President, Mr. President, I have a letter for you from Sadat."

They were about to hustle me off to God knows where when he said, "Wait a minute. See what he wants."

I said, "I have a first-day issue signed by Sadat and Begin and now I need only your signature to make it complete."

He said, "Let me see it," and when I showed it to him, he said, "Yeah, yeah, you are right. This is unusual." I noticed that while I was the one

The author has framed his collection of First
Day Covers of Israeli stamps issued in honor
of significant steps taken toward peace, along
with the authenticated autographs of the
participants. The top is signed by Clinton,
Rabin, Perez, and Arafat, the one in the
center by King Hussein, Clinton, Rabin, and
Perez, and the one at the bottom by Sadat,
Carter, and Begin.

who was excited and frightened, he spoke with a slight stutter. While the
Secret Service men held me, he autographed the first-day cover and returned it to me.

President Carter may have been satisfied, but the Secret Service men
weren't. They picked me up bodily between them and carried me from
the fifth floor to the street. All the way down they kept telling me that I
was lucky they didn't shoot me when I approached the president. They
told me to get out, to disappear, and I did, with my precious first-day
cover complete with its three important signatures. Getting the assassinated Sadat's signature had been easy. Getting the old Stern Gang warrior
Begin's a little harder. But getting my own President Carter, the gentle
home builder, to sign had nearly gotten me killed.

In addition to the first-day cover commemorating Sadat's trip to Israel, I have two others issued for other peace initiatives. One is in honor of King Hussein of Jordan's making peace with Israel. This one is signed by Hussein, Yitzhak Rabin, Shimon Perez, and President Clinton.

Happily, these signatures were gathered less eventfully than the Carter autograph. I sent the cover to Hussein with a letter similar to the one I had sent Sadat. He signed it. Then I used another of my wife's relatives in Israel, this time a great-nephew who works for the Mossad. He was able to get signatures from both Perez and Rabin, the latter signing just two days before he was assassinated. I am beginning to think giving me an autograph can be an occupational hazard. The final signature from President Clinton was easy to come by. I entrusted the first-day cover to my congressman, who was able to get the president to sign.

A stamp also came out commemorating Israel's handing over of Gaza and Jericho to the Palestinians. I sent the cover to Arafat, in Jericho, who signed as president of the PLO and returned it. Ironically, when he returned it, he mailed it with Israeli stamps since there is no Palestinian post office. My wife's great-nephew was able to get Rabin and Perez to sign it at the same time they signed the other, two days before Rabin was killed.

The great-nephew also sent me three photos that the Israeli government had had taken at each of the formal signings: one with Carter, Begin, and Sadat; one with Clinton, Hussein, and Rabin; and one with Clinton, Rabin, and Arafat. I have had the six items—the three first-day covers and the three photos—mounted and framed, and this memento of the peace process and of the two leaders killed in the effort to achieve it, hangs prominently in my house.

Chutzpah, Israeli Style

Many Yiddish terms have invaded the English language. It is not unusual to hear words like *kibbutz, schlepp, schnor,* and *schmate,* pepper the conversations of New Yorkers. Go a little west, and the incidence of Yiddishisms probably drops off sharply until you arrive at the other coast. One term that seems to have made its mark on the language across the country, however, is chutzpah. Perhaps it was Alan Dershowitz's selection of *Chutzpah* as title of his widely read book that established it once and for all as a quality innate to Jews, but acquirable, to varying degrees, by others. Some may find chutzpah hard to define precisely, but like the judge said about pornography, it is clearly recognizable when encountered. And nowhere is this quintessential Jewish trait more likely to be encountered than in the Jewish state of Israel. During the thirty-one trips I made to the Holy Land over the past fifty years, I think I have become an expert at experiencing chutzpah, Israeli style.

On one of my trips I had to go to a bank on Lilienblun Street in the financial district of Tel Aviv in order to straighten out a problem that came up in an account I maintained there. I also wanted to cash in some Israeli bonds I had. The government encourages Americans to do this since it pays them off in local currency and saves the dollar drain. I knew that it was established practice in Israel for the banks to close from 12 noon until 3:00 P.M., and then to reopen for the balance of the day. I arrived at 11:30 A.M. and asked a teller which window I needed to use to straighten out my account. He sent me to one, and from there I was sent to another and another and eventually, I ended up at the spot where I had originally inquired. I assumed he had made an innocent error, and we were able to clear up the account matter quickly.

I then informed the teller that I had the bonds to cash as well. By this time it was 11:45. He nodded and proceeded to pick up his briefcase from under his desk, open it, and take out a large napkin that he spread on top of his desk. Next, he removed a thermos, a cup, a package containing a sandwich, silverware, and a piece of fruit. He placed the sandwich on the napkin, poured a cup of coffee from the thermos, and seated himself at the desk. This all took a couple of minutes, and I stood watching him while he was quite evidently preparing a meal.

I asked, "Are you getting ready to eat?"

"Yes."

"When do you intend to eat this meal?"

"Right now. We eat lunch at twelve."

"But it isn't yet twelve. It is ten minutes to twelve," I replied quite reasonably.

He said, "Yes, but it will take longer than ten minutes to process your bonds. You will have to wait until we reopen at 3:00 P.M." And with that, he sat down at his desk.

It seemed to me that I had a choice. I could meekly yield to this rude display, or I could show him he had no monopoly on chutzpah.

"Listen," I said in a loud voice, "I was here on time to transact my business before twelve. You sent me running all over the bank when I wanted service. If you take one bite from that sandwich, I will take the rest of it, shove it down your throat, and pour the coffee down after it."

He looked at me for a moment as did the other bank clerks who were sitting at their desks. Apparently he recognized genuine anger when he saw it. He stood up, folded his napkin, poured back the coffee into the thermos, wrapped the sandwich and piece of fruit, adjusted his tie, cleared his throat and said, "What can I do for you."

I handed him the bonds, he took them, and within five minutes, our business was finished. As other customers looked on approvingly I said, "See. Now you are behaving like an American banker."

Something not too dissimilar happened to me in the post office. I had been standing patiently in a long line, inching my way toward the window, when a man came in and walked right to the front of the line, ahead of all of us, and began talking to the clerk.

"What are you doing?" I called, and came up to him out of the line.

"I am in a hurry. I have a store in the neighborhood and I can't wait in line," he replied.

For a moment I paused. My father had had a store in Kolbuszowa. I knew how inconvenient it was to be away for a long time. As I wavered, he added, "And besides. The postal clerk is a friend of mine."

That was the wrong thing to say, although it was probably a closer approximation of the truth of the situation. I became furious.

"We'll see about this," I said, raising my voice. "I want to talk to the postmaster." Now, all the people in the line with me began to shout at the intruder. "Get to the end of the line."

Quite a commotion began, and the postmaster came out of his office to see what was going on.

I told him what had happened, and the other customers enthusiastically offered their support for my story. Under the circumstances, the postmaster had little choice. The interloper returned to the back of the line muttering something about foreigners. The clerk sold me my stamps, his face red with a combination of anger and embarrassment. The crowd chattered approvingly. Once again, a policy of fighting chutzpah with chutzpah had proven correct.

On another occasion, my wife and I were staying at the Hotel Sharon in Herzelia. This resort community is about a half hour from Tel Aviv by taxi. One day while we were making this trip in a cab, a man waved, and the taxi driver pulled over. The man opened the door and got in and sat beside us. He didn't say a word to us, nor we to him. The incident didn't seem unusual, however, because *sheyroot,* or the practice of sharing rides, is not uncommon in Israel. As long as two parties are going in the same general direction they commonly ride together and split the fare. Our companion wasn't exactly going where we were headed. He directed the driver to take him to the center of Tel Aviv, and after threading our way through the heavy city traffic we pulled up in front of the city hall. Still without a word to us, our passenger opened the door, got out and began to walk into the building. "Hey, wait a minute," the driver called after him. "What about the taxi fare?"

The man turned and said, "Why should I pay? They will pay."

I said, "What do you mean, we will pay. You rode with us. You should pay your share."

He shifted his briefcase from one hand to the other and said to me, "Do you know who I am? I am a *pakid* (a clerk) in the city hall."

I told him, "*Pakid* is only part of what you are. You are also a son of a bitch."

It rolled right off of him. He smiled, turned, and walked into the city hall, leaving us to pay his share of the ride.

These examples of chutzpah, however, are child's play compared to what transpired one day when we took the bus to Tel Aviv from Afula, the town nearest Kfar Baruch, where my sister-in-law lived. It was the last bus on Friday, and as usual, it was crowded with riders. Since buses don't run in Israel on Saturday, all those with last-minute reasons to be in the capital jammed themselves onto the Friday buses. We found all the seats occupied, and passengers were standing in the aisle for the two-hour trip. One bench had two little girls, about five and eight years old respectively, seated on it. Their parents were seated behind them on the next seat. It looked as if there was more room on the little girls' bench, and I asked them if they would squeeze over so my wife could sit down. They did so, and my wife gratefully squeezed in. As soon as she sat down, however, their father told her to get up. "I paid for those seats," he said. "You can't sit there."

I said, "What's the problem? There's room. Why should my wife stand for two hours when there is room for her to sit?" The man answered me by grabbing my wife by the arm and pulling her off the bench.

One insult led to another, he pushed me, I hit him, and in the process he tore my shirt. Meanwhile, everyone on the bus began to take sides in the argument, some with him and some with me.

"You are going to pay me for that shirt," I yelled at the Israeli.

"I will not," he stubbornly replied.

Meanwhile, the bus had not moved. The driver wouldn't go while all this chaos was taking place on his bus. The passengers were getting nervous. They knew that the bus would have to stop at sunset, and they were afraid they wouldn't get to Tel Aviv if they didn't leave at once.

It happened that one of the passengers on the bus was a Druse border policeman. He said that he couldn't mix in, he would have the bus driver stop at Natanya, a few miles down the road, where there was a police station, and we could file a report with the police.

And that was what happened. The bus pulled up at the police station. My wife and I got out, as did the man, his wife, and the two children. The bus drove away, and there we were, still angry with one another and still a long way from Tel Aviv.

In the police station, an officer, who happened to be from Poland, took our statements. I told him I demanded to be paid for the torn shirt, and the other man adamantly refused. The policeman said it would be up to a judge to sort it out, and in two weeks we would be called for a hearing. I realized that in two weeks I would be back in America, but I wasn't going to tell him that. Okay, I agreed, and we both gave our statements, which he dutifully recorded. Afterward I asked him if he would call us a taxi, since there were no more buses, and we wanted to get to Tel Aviv. He did, and in about fifteen minutes the taxi pulled up to the station.

As my wife and I were getting into the cab, the man with whom I had had the argument on the bus demonstrated why Israelis personified chutzpah.

"As long as you are going to Tel Aviv," he said holding the hands of his children, "take us with you. You can save us the fare."

Now that was chutzpah!

Housing for the Jews

Fifty years separates the events in this story. I juxtapose them because they share two common elements: the bigotry Jews faced when they moved into a neighborhood, and my reaction to it.

Life right after the war was chaotic for Jews returning from their places of refuge. They found other people had moved into their houses and had taken over their businesses and property. The government was likely to be of little or no help. Armies had just passed through. Providing adequate food, water, and electricity was challenge enough. Ironing out disputes involving a few Jews was low on any official's set of priorities.

I was the exception to this official indifference. In my position as an intelligence and security officer in the army I made it my business to look out for the welfare of the Jews whenever I could. Usually, the cases that came to my attention were those steered to me by the local

Jewish leadership. Some knew I was Jewish. Others simply heard that I would give them a fair hearing and exert my influence to improve their circumstances.

One day, Serla Lische, the sister of my brother-in-law, Szaya David Lische, came to my office. She had survived the war by hiding in the Ukrainian woods. Her husband was Szya Rokeach, the grandson of one of the famous rabbis from the town of Przemyslany, and she and he came to see if I could help them get an apartment. They told me that before the war, his brother had owned a house on a street called Bozego Ciala, which had been in the center of Kazimierz, Cracow's Jewish quarter. I agreed that I would try to get them an apartment in that house. Then they told me that there were others who had returned to Cracow who also had no apartments to live in. I decided to get the house back for them so the other Jews could live there as well. Since the head of the housing authority in Cracow, Rutkowski, and his assistant, Zawadzki, were friends of mine, I felt I could accomplish this without too much trouble, and I did. The house on Bozego Ciala became a residence for a number of Jewish families.

It wasn't too many weeks later that a frantic man arrived at my office and told my secretary that he had an urgent need to get in to see me. When he was admitted, he was in a great state of agitation. "They are throwing us out of the house," he cried. "The police are at the house now and putting us into the street."

"Who, what? Calm down." I quickly learned that he had been sent by Szya Rokeach to tell me that the police were evicting the Jews from the house. Some townspeople were claiming that Jews had no right to the housing.

I promptly dropped whatever I was doing and drove in my car to the house on Bozego Ciala. There I found four members of the local militia were removing all of the furniture from the house and piling it in the street. I got out of the car and asked who was in charge. I was directed to one of the militiamen and was soon able to figure out what was going on here. It turned out that the parents of the officer in charge were the janitors for the building. They were using their son to evict the Jews from the building so they could rent the apartments themselves to tenants of their choice at higher rents. Since I had gained the right to the apartments through official channels, their efforts were not only contrary to my wishes, they were actually illegal. I told the militiaman that they were breaking the law and couldn't force the Jews out.

"Who are you?" he asked.

I identified myself as the commandant of the security police, although I was in civilian clothes at the time, and I showed him my credentials. He stared at the book of credentials for a long time, before declaring that I was a fraud.

"These don't say you are a security man. They say you are in the insurance business," he said. He barked a command and two other militiamen raised their rifles and pointed them at me.

I realized what had probably happened. In Polish, the words for insurance and for security are a little similar in their spelling. Insurance is *"ubezpieczalnia"* and security is *"bezpieczenstwo"* In all likelihood, his literacy wasn't too highly developed, and he had mistaken one term for the other. It was a silly mistake, but given the circumstances I realized that I found myself in some danger. The militiamen had their guns trained on me, and the excitement attracted a cluster of local people to see what was going on. The rumor began spreading among them that the police had arrested a Gestapo man.

"Take me to your militia commander," I said. "He will tell you who I am."

And so, under armed guard and people in the street urging the police to "kill the Gestapo man," I was marched off to the precinct house to be dealt with. It had suddenly become a dangerous situation.

When we arrived, the precinct commander, who knew me, couldn't believe his eyes. Here was the commandant of security police of Cracow marched in by four of his men who were pointing rifles at him. I told him what was going on. I explained they had been trying to evict legally placed tenants to illegally rent out the apartments. I told him I would file charges against these police, and they should be relieved of their duty and placed under custody.

The precinct commander apologized over and over again. He placed several officers at my disposal, and we went back to the house where the Jews were still standing next to their furniture in the street.

"All this goes back," I said to the police with me. "Help these people put their belongings back in place."

The residents were dazed by this rapid turn of events. Life had not been kind to Jewish survivors. They had grown accustomed to random and arbitrary abuse. My ability and willingness to reverse this latest misfortune shocked and bewildered them. They were more amazed when I had the janitors who had initiated the situation evicted from their ground-floor apartment, and made it available for another Jewish family that had just returned from Russia. At that point, the building was 100 percent occupied by Jews.

This story played back in my memory on the day in 1996 when I had a visit from three of my neighbors. I lived then, as now, in a pleasant split-level house in the suburban community of Springfield, New Jersey. For the most part, people in Springfield mind their own business, and while the community has a balance of different ethnicities represented among its population, people stay pretty much within their own community. The group at my door contained an Italian, a Jew, and a third man.

"Did you hear about the Jehovah's Witnesses church?" one of them asked after the normal pleasantries of neighbor meeting neighbor had been exchanged. The reference was to a sprawling, red-brick building located on a street around the corner from me. Although it had originally been a residence, it had been sold some ten years before to a Jehovah's Witnesses congregation and been used as a place of worship since.

"No, what about it?" I replied.

"The Witnesses are selling it and are moving to a bigger church."

"So, that's okay with me. They never gave me any trouble."

"It is not them that's the trouble. It is whom they are selling it to."

"Who is that?" I asked.

"They are selling it to strange people. They look different and dress in peculiar ways."

I asked them who these strange people were, and they explained that there was a school for rabbis (a yeshiva) located on Morris Avenue now, and that they were going to expand it and put it in the Jehovah's Witnesses church. "Those black-hat people with their long, black coats are going to be all over our neighborhood if they do that."

My visitors went on to elaborate on the peril that would follow such a turn of events. They don't wash, they don't sleep, they continuously go in and out twenty-four hours a day, and most significantly, our property values would drop.

There was to be a meeting in the town hall the following week at which the local zoning board would consider the application to move the yeshiva. This delegation, I learned, had come to my door to enlist my cooperation in opposing the intrusion of the strange people, the Hasidim, into our neighborhood.

I politely listened to them while they made their petition to me. Then I asked to be excused for a moment, and went to my room to retrieve a picture I had there.

"I have been your neighbor for forty years," I then said to one of the visitors. "Do we get along well?"

"Yes, of course we do."

"Is my lawn clean? My flowers pretty?"

"Yes, yes."

"Do we have trouble?"

"No."

"Well, it may surprise you," I said, "to know that until I was seventeen years old, I dressed just like those people. I am a product of these people. I was one of them. My father was one of them all of his life." I put before them a picture taken of me in my black coat and hat with my side curls.

"You are wrong about these people on every count. They must bathe three times a week by religious law. They are up all night studying. They are too tired for much else. There will be no mugging or stealing from them. And as for property values going down, it will be just the opposite. In Brooklyn they raised property values because people want to move in to be close to the yeshiva."

They seemed at a loss for words, at least long enough to allow me to ask, "When did you say the meeting of the zoning board is? I want to be sure to attend to give support to the application."

The delegation of three left. One of them doesn't speak to me to this day. As for the yeshiva, it was approved by the zoning board and has been operating for six years. Everything I said was true, except for one thing. The boys are not too tired from studying to do anything else. Every Friday afternoon, just before Shabbat, they come out and play basketball in the playground in the park.

Reflections on "Saving Private Ryan"

The motion picture *Saving Private Ryan* has received a great deal of comment due to the realism of its opening, twenty-minute-long battle scene. The ear shattering, gut-wrenching brutality of war is vividly portrayed. Arms are blown off, intestines are spilled, men and officers are shot dead in their tracks. The sea runs red with the blood of soldiers who never put a foot onto the beach before a bullet found and felled them.

As I watched the picture unfold in a darkened theater in New Jersey, I was moved, as were my fellow moviegoers. Certainly the realism of the scene caught me up in its intensity. But something else about the picture got to me as well; something that I am sure wasn't experienced as acutely by the other viewers: the theme of the picture, the effort of the U.S. government to find and to rescue a sole surviving son from the battlefield. There were other families and other sons and other armies I knew about, and the mission wasn't to hunt down the surviving brother to save him, but to hunt him down to kill him. Let me tell you about two such families.

Psachie Reich and his wife Toba raised seven sons and two daughters in our town of Kolbuszowa. Rarely has God been so generous as He was when endowing the Reich children. One was more handsome than the next; one more intelligent than the next. They were the cream of Jewish youth. The boys excelled as scholars, and after Psachie died, the oldest daughter, Chacia, a beautiful girl married to a young man from Cracow, proved her mettle by operating a store with Toba. Together they provided a comfortable livelihood for the family.

When the war started, many Polish Jews fled east to territory under control of the Soviet Union. Certainly, they knew that the Russians and Ukrainians were not likely to provide a very hospitable environment for them, but the fear of the Germans was enough to warrant uprooting the family and leaving homes and businesses. The Reichs joined the exodus, and they joined the other Jews resettling themselves in the eastern part of Poland that had been partitioned off and that was occupied and controlled by the Soviets. As the Jews moved into the area, the Russians decreed that they were welcome to stay, but on condition that they register as Russian citizens and denounce other allegiances. In the event they refused to register, they would have to return to the western sector that had fallen to the Germans.

This presented a dilemma for many Jews. True, they had left their houses and businesses, but they hadn't permanently abandoned them. Their friends were still in the western sector, as were their relatives and the graves of generations of their ancestors. Russia had seemed all right as a temporary haven, but they hesitated to commit permanently to it. Besides, the early months of German occupation had been relatively benign. Jews were accustomed to discrimination, and the reports of experiences under the Germans were that they were difficult, but bearable. As the deadline for registration approached, the majority of those who had fled decided to return home. The seven Reich boys, their mother, and their sisters were among those electing to go back.

The Russians announced that transportation would be provided, and the Jews gathered and were loaded into trucks for the return trip. By now, history has recorded Stalin's paranoia. The Jews didn't recognize it then. Instead of repatriating the Jews who didn't want to remain, the Russians declared them enemies of the state. The trucks brought them to the train and the train headed, not west, but east—all the way east to Siberia. A total of four hundred thousand Jews who signed up to go back to their homes were instead exiled to the gulag.

As this was occurring some had an opportunity, in the confusion, to slip away. The Reich family was among those doing so, hiding out, and eventually mingling in with those who did remain and settling in the town of Kozova.

Fate intervened in the course of events, in a manner far stranger than any film writer might create. The Jews sent to Siberia as punishment for their disloyalty suffered mightily from hunger and exposure in the cold and desolation of that land. A full 150,000 of the 400,000 sent away died. That seems a heavy toll until one realizes that the 250,000 who survived represent the largest block of Polish Jews surviving the Holocaust. Compare that figure with the 50,000 Polish Jews remaining under the control of the Germans who were alive at war's end. Punishment became salvation for these Jews as events unfolded, for had they gone back as they planned, they would certainly have perished in the gas chambers and ovens.

What of the Reich brothers and those who escaped the deportation to Siberia? The seven of them neither went back to the western sector nor were they sent to Siberia. Instead they remained just over the line, living in relative security in the Russian-controlled sector. And they might have remained there, had not Hitler violated his treaty with Stalin and mounted the fateful war against the Soviet Union.

Those of us who have read books such as *Hitler's Willing Executioners* know that right behind the advancing *Wehrmacht* came the *Einsatzgruppen,* a unit whose charge was to follow the wave of battle with a wave of slaughter of Jews. There were no roundups, no camps, no internment. There was just an instant killing of Jews in the towns captured. And that's how Yidel, Nusyn, Szyia, Shulim, Meilech, and the two other Reich brothers whose names I have forgotten, were all killed on the day of the invasion, for the German forces immediately overran the partitioned eastern sector of Poland. There was no sparing of the surviving son as in the case of Private Ryan. There was just annihilation. I am quite certain that these seven, intelligent and resourceful as they were, would have survived the gulag—had they not been intelligent and resourceful enough to avoid being sent to it.

Amazingly, the mother and two daughters survived the German invasion of Russia. They were overlooked by the *Einsatzgruppen,* and they lived to bear witness to the killing of the seven brothers, when they returned to Kolbuszowa afterwards.

I have already told you another story in a similar vein. I called it "A Mother's Grief."

The Germans were arresting members of the Judenrat. On the list of those to be arrested was a young man named Boaz Feuer. When the Germans couldn't find him, they arrested his three brothers and his brother-in-law as hostages until Boaz turned himself in.

Concerned about his brothers and brother-in-law, Boaz did come to the police station to give himself up. They promptly arrested him, but instead of releasing the other four who hadn't been wanted in the first place, they bundled them all off to Rzeszow prison, where they were held for a few weeks pending shipment to Auschwitz. Eventually all were killed: four sons and a son-in-law dead. They came for one and took them all.

There was to be no story of saving Private Ryan here.

Some Yom Kippur Daydreams

In the fall, we Jews will be observing the ten-day period of repentance and atonement that begins with Rosh Hashanah and runs through Yom Kippur. I will take my place in the choir stall of Temple Beth Ahm, as I have for each of the past forty years, to sing the melodies and chant the prayers that have become second nature to me by now. The service will unfold this year pretty much as it did the year before; and I know that at times my mind will wander and I will daydream a bit and my thoughts will bring me back to another time in another congregation, where I also sang before the congregation at Yom Kippur.

It is 1930. I am a precocious ten years old, a *cheder* student with side curls and a bent for mischief. As the youngest of the nine children of Isak and Esther Saleschutz, with five older sisters to spoil me, it is little wonder that I am always in trouble. My father is one of the pillars of the Jewish community of Kolbuszowa. He is the owner of a successful general store and earns more than enough to place the Saleschutz family at the upper end of the local income scale. As a pious Jew, he gives *tzedakah* to support the synagogue and the rabbi, as well as the many charities and service organizations that make up the social support system of Jewish life. He is a Kohen and occupies a high station in synagogue life by virtue of his lineage as well as of his charitable deeds.

I am afraid I am a disappointment to my father. I would rather play than study. Skepticism is a stronger element of my thinking than faith, and my hands often bear the mark of blows from the teacher's stick. The principal joy I derive from religious services is the opportunity to sing before the congregation with my brother-in-law, an outstanding scholar, who serves as one of the leaders of the service. Since I have always been gifted with the ability to learn and sing melodies easily, I get to participate in the service more actively that I would by virtue of my religious devotion.

I have another role to play during Yom Kippur that is an even more valuable service to the congregation. Armed with a bottle of ammonia (*schmekehts*), I am responsible for reviving worshipers who grow faint from the ordeal of the day. When I see people swoon, I abandon my song or my prayer and race over to them, placing the schmekehts under their noses so they may continue their devotions. I remember one woman worshiper who regularly fainted at the same point in the service each year, and I would anticipate this and position myself near her as we approached that point in the prayer book.

Yom Kippur for the pious Jews of Kolbuszowa began well before Kol Nidre. For us, it began with my mother's purchase of a chicken for each family member for the *capuroth:* roosters for the male members and hens for the females of the family. These were kept until the morning of Kol Nidre. Then each of us would take our chicken and recite the *"b'nai adam"* prayer, which states in part, "This chicken is going to be killed, and I shall be admitted and allowed a long, happy and peaceful life." At the same time we performed the ritual that transferred our sins to the sacrificial chicken, thereby allowing us to atone. The chicken's legs would be trussed up and we would each hold our chicken over our heads and twirl it around while we prayed. Mothers would perform the ritual for their very young children. A pregnant women would perform it for her unborn child. We would all be cleansed of our sins after which the chicken eventually found its way to the *shochet* to be slaughtered for a later, post-Yom Kippur meal.

In the afternoon, my father and the other pious men would gather in the synagogue to humble themselves by receiving and accepting punishment for the sins committed during the year. Hay was spread around one portion of the synagogue and each of the Jews knelt on it and received a series of five or six blows from a whip wielded by the sexton. Regardless of their station in life, the Jews willingly accepted the blows and humiliation as punishment for their sins and a partial price for redemption.

Atonement then took on the more tangible form of charitable giving. Plates were lined up on a long table in the synagogue. Each was for a special service organization or needy group in the community. These included plates for the rabbi, the assistant rabbi, the *shul*, the library, the schools, poor people, people who visited sick people, people in jail, synagogues and rabbis in different communities—in short, every element in the social fabric that held the Jews together. The only agencies omitted from this charitable giving were the Zionist organizations, which were construed to be secular rather than religious in nature. Into each plate, each Jew put a small amount that was appropriate for his station in life. My father would generally donate half of a zloty. Others usually gave less.

After this, each sought out those competitors or rivals whom he may have offended in the course of business during the year, and begged forgiveness. The new year would begin with a clean slate, and for my father, active as he was in business and community affairs, the number of apologies needed to clean the slate was large indeed.

We would then have our Yom Kippur dinner that would have to sustain us for the next twenty-four hours. My mother had a special Kol Nidre apron, which she wore only on this occasion. She would put it on after she had finished cooking the dinner, and she would visit her older brother and her older friends to wish them a good fast. Each year she repeated the same routine, and each year the same thing happened. She always cried on the eve of Yom Kippur and always came back with tears in her eyes.

After the dinner, my father went to the synagogue, where he would remain for the next twenty-four hours. He stood and prayed and meditated all through the night, occasionally napping on one of the benches.

Yom Kippur day saw my fasting father back on his feet, and he would stand in his socks for the entire day without once sitting down. Religious Jews wouldn't wear leather, and unlike today, there were no synthetics. So they stood in their socks, on a little hay that had been spread to soften the burden on their feet. He stood throughout the day because to pray while sitting would be offensive to God. The seat that he owned by virtue of inheriting it from his father would remain vacant.

All seats in the synagogue were privately owned by their regular occupants, and there was a healthy market in seats when another was needed for a new son-in-law or one became available by virtue of a family moving away. My father stood near the eastern wall and davened while my mother remained in her own seat, inherited from her own family many years in the past.

Each of the men had in front of him a three-foot candle that had been lighted the night before and that was expected to burn for the twenty-four hours of the holiday. And so the scene was one of several hundred men in black silk coats, each with a head-covering yarmulke, wearing a white *kittle*, (worn only on Yom Kippur, Passover during the seder, on one's wedding day, and after one's death), a *gartle* (a two-inch-wide silk sash worn around the waist to separate the head and heart from the lower parts of the body), and a heavy wool prayer shawl collared with silver ornamentation and pulled up over the head, each bowing and swaying and delivering his personal prayer to God. Next to each burns a thick candle—several hundred in all—giving off smoke and aroma.

Behind them in the balcony, the wives alternately pray and gossip. Outside, the unmarried women tend to their younger brothers and sisters. And in the midst of this scene of devotion and repentance a young boy, curls flying, alternately sings, prays, and runs with his ammonia bottle to revive some devotee who has momentarily swooned from the rigors and raptures of the day.

And as I smile at the recollection and sigh at its loss, a sharp elbow brings me out of my reverie. The organist has given the cue, and I fumble with the music to find my place and once again sing before the congregation. I clear my throat, and I hope no one notices a bit of choking in my voice, or the little tear that has managed to escape my eye and is trickling, ever so slowly, down my cheek.

Similarities and Differences

Most Americans were shocked by the brutality of the killing that took place in Jasper, Texas, in 1998. Three white men chained a black man to the back of a pickup truck and dragged him along a road to his death. The subsequent trial detailed the suffering involved as the victim sought to ease his contact with the rough surface of the road. Then his body hit a drainage pipe, breaking his shoulder and tearing his arm from his body. The guilty verdict and death sentence met general approval.

As I watched the network coverage of events in Jasper, I recalled a similar incident that took place during the war. At least the brutality was similar. There was no trial and punishment of these perpetrators. Such activities under the Germans were normal.

The Freifeld family was by no means unusual. There was Hirsch, the father; Ruchel, the mother; and their five sons and one daughter. They were all bright, good-looking, and talented; each played a musical instrument in the local orchestra. Hirsch Freifeld had taught his own trade of tailoring to each of his five sons, and the family had established a reputation as reliable, skilled craftsmen. Like most Jewish tradesmen in Kolbuszowa, they got along better spiritually than financially, eking out a modest living through long hours of painstaking work. Oddly enough, under the German occupation their skills were more in demand than before because there was little opportunity for people to buy new clothes. Rather, they had to extend the life of whatever they possessed by constantly having it mended and altered.

The Freifeld boys would travel outside of our town to the neighboring villages, setting up shop for a few days to fix clothes people brought them. In return, some of the peasants would pay them in local produce, and they brought back quantities of eggs and meat and vegetables to Kolbuszowa, thereby raising all of our standards of living. When, in due course, the Germans collected the Jews and forced them to move into a ghettoized area, they restricted our movement in or out. The Freifelds could no longer go out of town to fix clothing, and outsiders couldn't come in. They lost much of their livelihood, and we all missed this source of food.

So every now and then, the youngest of the sons, Mendel, who was some three years older than I was, would slip out of the ghetto and go to a neighboring village to offer his services. As before, he was well received, and he would stay for a day or two in a place, and then return as quietly as he had left, bearing fresh food for the ghetto. Of course, his being out of the ghetto was entirely against the rules, so he made these commercial journeys at some peril. But after a few successful trips, his wariness diminished.

One night Mendel was in the neighboring village of Dzikowiec, and a Polish peasant went to the police and informed them that there was a Jew in the village. I guess the peasant didn't need any special incentive to do it. It just came naturally. Two policemen responded to this news by going to the village and seizing the tailor. I know who the policemen were: one was Rusiniak, and the other, Bartelmus. Both were Volksdeutchen (ethnic Germans) from Bielsko, Poland, on the Czech border.

The policemen decided that their duty required them to return Mendel to the ghetto in Kolbuszowa. So they tied his hands in front of him, and then took a ten-foot length of rope and linked him to one of their horses. Then, as they rode the five kilometers back to our town Mendel Freifeld was forced to keep up with them. At first they walked along at a steady pace, and Mendel could trot along behind. Then, they increased the horse's gait, forcing Mendel to run in order to maintain his footing. Eventually, however, he couldn't keep up and he fell and was dragged along for a while. The policemen would slow, allowing Mendel to get back up, only to prod the horses into a gallop that once again pulled the tailor from his feet and dragged him along the road.

This game of stopping and starting, pulling and dragging went on for the five-kilometer distance to town, and by the time they arrived, the tailor was dirty, bloody, bruised and broken. When the horses finally stopped at the gate to the ghetto, the two policemen untied him, and as the dazed Mendel staggered to his feet, and while we all looked on, Rusiniak took out his gun and shot and killed him, right there in the street in front of all of us.

Cruelty isn't limited by time or place. These deaths, so similar in nature and separated by half a century and half a world, remind us of that. What seems different is people's reactions: official outrage in Jasper, official indifference in Kolbuszowa. I hope I am not being deceived, and that this appearance of difference is real.

Mendel Freifeld, 1936. The Germans tied him to a horse and dragged him 5 kilometers from the village where they captured him to the gate of the ghetto. There they shot him.

•

Trips to the Holy Land

In 1998, the nation of Israel celebrated its fiftieth anniversary. When my wife and I went there to celebrate that milestone with our people, it was our thirty-first trip to the Holy Land. At the end of the war, our plans had been to settle in Palestine. Circumstances led us to stay in the United States instead, and as an imperfect substitute, we have found ourselves shuttling back and forth for half a century, visiting relatives and friends, and reliving other times. When I reflect on the highlights of those thirty-one trips I realize they mirror the history of Israel. I guess they also provide a little insight into my own personality. Let me tell you about five of the trips, each memorable for a different reason.

Our first trip took place in 1949, shortly after the War of Independence. We made this trip, in part, to assess whether in fact we would move to Israel as we originally planned. El Al wasn't flying yet, and we booked tickets on Swiss Air. Jet airplanes weren't yet flying either. Those who think the flight today is a long one will be interested to learn that in those days the trip took thirty-six hours. The plane made stops, mostly to refuel, in Newfoundland, Shannon-Ireland, Switzerland, and Italy before arriving in Israel. When the plane set down at the threadbare airport in

Lod that then served international traffic for the country, the passengers cheered. People were laughing and crying simultaneously. Spontaneously, they began to sing the "Hatikva" and patriotic Hebrew songs. I myself, was not embarrassed to get down on my knees and kiss the ground we landed on. The feeling of pride we felt was overwhelming. After so many millennia in the Diaspora, the Jewish people were at last home.

The trip had originally been organized by the Jewish Board of Education in New York to bring a group of American Hebrew school teachers to Jerusalem to take courses. From the beginning, we stood out like a sore thumb from others in our group of travelers.

To begin with, we weren't yet American citizens. That presented the problem of documentation each time we encountered an official checkpoint. We had no visas, no passports, only official letters explaining our circumstances. The lines would breeze past immigration authorities until they came to us. Then they would stop as officials called for superiors to come and interpret our status. Our presence certainly accelerated the pace others set to get to the immigration officials. No one wanted to be caught behind us.

Our second distinction—or rather my wife's—was that only she, among the American Hebrew teachers, spoke perfect conversational Hebrew. The rest wanted their educational courses in Hebrew to be conducted in English. This struck her as defeating the purpose of the experience, and when she made this sentiment known—well, let's just say it separated her out from the others.

But those were details that were quickly forgotten when we were reunited with my brother David and his family, who waited for us at the airport. We also met those members of my wife's family who had settled there. They had lost two hundred family members in the Holocaust; but her grandmother, three uncles with their families, and a few others had managed to get out from Germany in 1934, and her sister had left in 1939. As the youngest child in a large family, I had never known a living grandmother, and I quickly adopted my wife's as my own. It seemed that this already established extended family would make a wonderful and welcoming nest into which we could comfortably settle when we moved there permanently. However, they quickly disabused us of that idea when we discussed the possibilities.

While Israel had won independence within the past year, it was a desperately poor nation. They could have used our help in the fight, we were told. However, now that it was over, the country didn't need two new displaced persons to assimilate at this point. Rather, we were encouraged to go back to America, where we had already established ourselves. We should make a lot of money there that we could send to support the new nation. At the time, I had not yet found much in America to support the idea that I would make a lot of money there, but we came to accept this logic that changed our destiny.

Details of our two-month stay remain vivid in my memory. During that time the body of Theodor Herzl was returned to Israel for reburial in Jerusalem. He lay in state for two days in Tel Aviv, which is unusual since Jewish law calls for burial within twenty-four hours. Thousands paid homage to this tireless worker for the cause of Zionism. The first Yom Ha'atzmaot, anniversary of independence, occurred during our stay. I have pictures that I took of the parade of Israeli military might that took place in Haifa that year. Israel was so small, it was like a family celebration. Crowds lined the street, with people cheering and waving at a son or nephew. I recall, amidst the euphoria, being dismayed by the poor condition of the relatively light armaments of the Israeli Defense Force. I had only recently seen the very heavy armor with which the Russians had rolled through Poland in beating back the Germans, and the Jewish equipment seemed almost frail by comparison. I feared for the ability of our infant homeland to grow into adulthood.

My 1967 trip followed a severe testing of Israel's viability. I arrived in Israel two days after the Six Day War had ended. If the 1949 trip was the most momentous in terms of history, this one was the most emotional. The Jews had recaptured Jerusalem. The wish voiced over and over again in the liturgy had been realized. The Jews held Jerusalem, and I wanted to get to Israel quickly before the Arabs counterattacked to take back our holy place.

Upon landing in Israel, I immediately went to the Western Wall. There we saw thousands of Jews, mostly in military uniform, praying, swaying, singing, chanting, expressing in every way imaginable their joy at being able, after so many millenia, to touch the wall and speak to God. Tears flowed freely, my own included. We were at the holiest place the Jews had known. I thought of my father, who had dreamed of such a moment. I thought of him praying in the synagogue, praising God and pleading with Him for the return to Jerusalem. And I thought of the Germans shooting him down in the ghetto. As I reached out to touch the wall with one hand, I imagined that the other was reaching back and taking his. I was a spiritual link between his aspiration to experience such a moment and our realization of having done so.

During the 1949 visit, I had met one of my old comrades from Poland who had fought in the War of Independence. They had fought for

Three days after Jerusalem was liberated in the six day war, the author journeyed to Israel. It was unclear at the time whether the Israeli's could hold the city and he wanted to visit the Western Wall at least once, in case it was lost. The author is in the center and praying with him at the right is Leon Warhaft, also a survivor from Kolbuszowa.

Jerusalem, but had failed to seize all of it. He showed me the site of the battle and explained how they had fallen short of their goal. As we looked across the valley at the still occupied portion of Jerusalem, I had wept. I felt great guilt that I had not been there. I believed that I, along with thousands like me, might have made the difference. With our participation we would have seized all of Jerusalem. At last, our omission had been undone. Jerusalem was in Jewish hands.

After Jerusalem we journeyed to Bethlehem, significant to the Christian religion as the birthplace of Jesus, but also to Jews as the site of Rachel's tomb. We went to the Tomb of Rachel and again found many soldiers in uniform. But here, along with the warriors, were the mothers. Hundreds of women, mostly Sephardic women, stood by the tomb, talking to it, telling it stories, pouring out the facts of their lives to the "Ima," the mother who lay there. They called her "Ima'le" and "Mama'le" and talked to the tomb as if it were a living person. They seemed to find great

One of the highlights of the author's visits to Israel was Rachel's
Tomb in Bethlehem. Rachel was regarded as a surrogate mother by
many who had lost their own mothers in the Holocaust.

comfort in the opportunity to share their wishes with one so understanding. Jerusalem may have been at the heart of Jewish longing, but Rachel's
tomb touched the very soul of the mothers who gathered there each day.

While the 1949 and 1967 trips marked significant events in Jewish
history, an event that occurred during another trip I made, in 1960, when
my daughter was three and a half, put a mark on me that still remains in
my thoughts.

My wife's sister lived on a farm in Kfar Baruch in Emek Yizreal, the
Valley of Jezreel. Our visits to Israel always included a time at this quiet,
rustic place away from the tumult of Tel Aviv. It was especially important, we felt, for our daughter to experience the particular Jewish pride
that seemed to radiate from those who worked with the soil in Eretz Israel. We put her into the local kindergarten where she could play with the
children of the community, and it didn't take long for her to meld with
them, learning the songs, and beginning to speak the language. We were
there that year during the celebration of the War of Independence, and I
watched proudly as she marched with the other children singing songs
and waving the blue-and-white Israeli flag. Simple as it was, this moment
reminded me of the difference the State of Israel meant for our people. In

Poland, Jewish children were not allowed to wave Polish flags. We had been made to realize that we were outsiders, a people without a country, although our families had lived on the same soil for centuries.

During that trip, one Friday, we had to travel from Kfar Baruch to Herzelia. We wanted to be there for the Sabbath, and since the buses had proved to be unreliable on another occasion, we decided to rent a taxi. The driver took a shortcut that would bring us to our destination before sundown, and we found ourselves traveling on the back roads of the kibbutzim, past farms and orchards and through an area of orange groves. The radio was playing. It was late in the afternoon, and the sun was dropping lower in the sky.

Suddenly, at a moment during that motor trip, I experienced something so magical that it remains with me to this day. It happened as the radio began to play a song written by the famed Hebrew poet Chaim Nachman Bialik called *Hachama Meyrosh Hailanot Nistalka.* It was a song we had sung at home in Poland, and its lyric went

> The sun has slipped behind the trees,
> Come, let us greet the Sabbath Queen.
> She is now descending, the holy one,
> Surrounded by gentle angels of peace.
> She comes the queen, she comes the bride.
> Greetings to you, O angels of Peace.
> O beauteous one, with rays of shining light
> A night and a day—and then you depart
> We receive you adorned in raiment so fine
> With prayer and song and feasting and wine
> O peace so sweet, O peace so complete,
> Give us your blessing O angel of peace.

Outside of the cruising taxi, I could see a sunset, with its brilliant red and yellow rays, slanting through the trees of the orange grove. It was the very scene that was conjured up in my mind by the song. The groves were lighted, with almost theatrical beauty as the dust in the air danced in the light and the tree trunks cast long purple shadows on the ground. It was a remarkable experience. Here we were in Israel, with the Sabbath approaching. The radio was playing a song from my childhood that described the arrival of Queen Sabbath. And the vision was of such beauty as to make one believe that only God in his heaven could have created it at that moment.

We actually saw the Queen Sabbath arrive that day in Israel. I might have forgotten that feeling of awe by now, except that it returns each Friday night during the service, when we sing *"L' cha Dodi."* We turn at that point to the entrance door of the sanctuary to welcome in the Sabbath bride. I turn to greet an old friend whom I had seen so vividly that day in the Israeli orange groves with our invitation, *"boi kala, boi kala."* "Come in, oh bride. Come in, oh bride."

During one of our trips in the early 1970s I had another experience that could only come in the Holy Land. I acquired, and have to this day in my home, two stones from the foundation the Jews built for the tabernacle in Shiloh. The tabernacle, a square, portable tent fashioned by the Israelites during their forty years in the desert, housed the Holy of Holies, the Ark of the Covenant with the stone tablets containing the Ten Commandments. It served as the first sanctuary where the Kohanim and Levites conducted services and offered sacrifices.

When the Israelites settled in Canaan, they established a permanent location for the tabernacle in Shiloh, and there it stayed until Kind David later moved it to Mount Zion in Jerusalem. King Solomon installed the Ark of the Covenant in the First Temple, where it served as the centerpiece of Jewish worship and devotion. Its subsequent disappearance is one of the great mysteries of all time, and as most moviegoers know, the search to locate it continues to this day.

I learned while I was in Israel that a group of archeologists were excavating in Shiloh to unearth the foundation on which the tabernacle had rested before it was moved. The archeologists intended to bring it to Jerusalem. I visited the site and found they had indeed exposed the foundation. I also found that in the process of its being moved, some stones had broken off. The archeologists said they had no interest in these pieces, and I was able to simply pick them up and carry them home with me. As a member of the Kohanim, or priestly caste, I am particularly interested in the tabernacle and its history. The two stones I have, part of the four-thousand-year history of our people, are among my rarest possessions.

Our last trip to Israel produced a situation that deserves the word "bizarre." I think it could have only occurred in the Holy Land. We were staying this time in a hotel in Tiberias, on Lake Kinneret, or the Sea of Galilee. One day, some American friends and I took a boat to visit the Yigal Alon Museum, which was at the Kibbutz Ginosar, located on the other side of the lake. The day at the museum went by quickly, and before we knew it, it was time for us to return. Only then did we learn that the boats leave every two hours for Tiberias, and the last one for the day had departed some fifteen minutes earlier. This was a real problem since my wife was waiting at the hotel and we were expected back. In a state of considerable agitation, we went to the seaside to see if there was some way we could get transport back across the lake.

There, standing at the dock was a group of about two hundred nuns, a few priests, and a group of lay people, standing around and talking to one another in Polish. I went up and began speaking to them in Polish and soon learned that they were a group of clergy and parishioners from Chicago who had made a pilgrimage to the Holy Land. They had a chartered boat waiting, and when I explained our situation they agreed that we could join them for the trip across the lake.

When the boat was halfway across, the bishop who was leading the flock had the captain stop it so he could conduct a service here, at the midpoint of Lake Kinneret, where Jesus had walked on the water. The bishop put on his ecclesiastical gown and conducted a mass. My friends and I stood back and observed, and at the close of the service, the bishop opened a box of songbooks that he had brought for the group to join in song.

It quickly became evident, however, that the priests and the nuns were not too familiar with the melodies and lyrics they were attempting. They were old Polish hymns that the nuns, being from Chicago, were not quite familiar with. The singing was as aimless as the floating boat out there in the middle of the lake. They needed someone who knew the songs to lead them.

When I glanced at the songbook, I realized immediately that what it contained were all songs that I had sung in school in Poland. I knew them by heart. Church and state are not separated there, as in the United States. If you went to public school, you learned to sing religious hymns. I approached the bishop and told him that I knew the songs they wanted to sing, and with his permission, I would be pleased to lead the singing. He was greatly relieved to have my offer, and while my American friends looked on with amusement, I, a Jew, singing from memory, led a group of two hundred nuns in a Catholic service out there in the middle of Lake Kinneret. It was an unlikely scenario, but one that endeared me to our hosts.

The bishop wanted to know where I had learned this music, and I told him that I had studied for the priesthood at one time in Poland. I had given it up when I fell in love with a woman who I eventually made my wife, and to whom I was still married. Since the conversation was taking place in Polish, my friends didn't quite know what was going on. What they did know was that the bishop embraced me and gave me, as gifts, mementos of the American and Polish Catholic Church. He thanked me for my help in the service and invited me to join them then next day in Tiberias for mass.

Thanking him for his gifts as well as for allowing us onto the boat with his group, I explained that I would not be able to join them the next day. And so we parted, but not before I had experienced one of the highlights of this, or any other trip: my leading a Catholic service in the middle of Lake Kinneret.

Each trip to Israel offers new insight, new experiences, new wonders.

My Three Homelands

Nationalism can be a powerful force. Pride in one's homeland has produced some glorious moments in history as well as some dreadful ones: armies fighting on the battlefield, crowds cheering at the Olympics, mobs rioting in soccer stadiums, Jews dying in pogroms and in concentration camps.

During my lifetime I have at one time or another called Poland, Russia, Germany, Israel, and the United States home. My residencies in Russia and Germany were matters of simple expediency. Each country provided a temporary refuge from a situation that had become untenable. Neither generated patriotic feelings in me; quite the contrary. Poland, the United States, and Israel, however, were different. I have very strong feelings for all three and, as a result, consider myself to have not one, but three homelands.

While Poland was an *"ojczyzna,"* a fatherland to me, it was an abusive father. I loved Poland, but it was an unrequited love. I studied and treasured its history and its literature. I sang its anthems and wanted to march in its parades of national celebration. I would have been proud to serve in its army. But for all my ardor, for all the love I offered my homeland, I was rejected because I was a Jew. Jewish children in my public school weren't allowed to wave the flags on national holidays. Jews didn't serve in the army as officers. They couldn't even join the scouts. I didn't fight for the country of my birth until I posed as a Catholic. I loved Poland, but it considered me an outsider as long as I lived there. And so were all Jews, with the possible exception of my father, who, through his prominence in the community and activity in the *"Partia Ludowa,"* Peasant's Party, found acceptance among some Poles despite maintaining his strict Jewish observance. In fact, my father didn't join his six brothers and sisters in emigrating from Poland to the United States because he felt that only in Poland could he maintain his strict religious activities; living in the United States, he feared, would tempt him and his children away from orthodoxy.

The relationship of the Jews and the Poles in Poland dates back a thousand years. In medieval times and throughout its 123-year occupation by Austria, Prussia, and Russia, there were Jews. My own family traces its Polish roots to 1773. You would think such a history would be esteemed. It would be for most peoples, but not for Jews. Their welcome depended in some measure on the historical ownership of the town in which they lived.

Some towns were land grants received by a nobleman from the king. Here, the Jews were most welcome, because chances are, they performed needed financial and administrative functions for the nobleman in running his fiefdom. Polish aristocrats were rarely interested in day-to-day details of governance, and they valued the skills Jews brought with them. In other towns owned by the gentry or townspeople, however, skills practiced by Jews placed them in direct competition with Polish tradesmen. Jews worked in such common trades as carpenter, butcher, tailor, shoemaker, blacksmith, and so forth, and, given their circumstances, they were often better at their craft and worked for less money than their Polish neighbors. Here, the direct economic impact of the Jew on the Poles bred resentment, and fired by the antagonism of the church, resentment evolved into hatred and opened the Jews to noneconomic reprisal. Pogroms were not unheard of. Loans were defaulted with impunity. Persecution was common. Still, Jews in these situations were better off than in the towns owned by the Catholic Church. There, the policy was clear. There were no Jews allowed to live in church-owned towns and villages.

As a boy I overlooked the anti-Semitism that was part and parcel of living in Poland. In spite of it, I remained a patriot. The war, however, turned common anti-Semitism into something much more deadly. Poles betrayed their Jewish neighbors. They would tell the Germans where they were hiding, or even worse, kill the Jews themselves. When I offered to join the Polish underground to fight the Germans, our common enemy, I was betrayed, and shot by the boyhood friend who was a leader in the local Resistance. I contrast this with Yugoslavia, where Jews fought alongside Serbs in the underground, and where, in fact, the second in command under Tito was a Jewish general named Moshe Piade. Today, I have few illusions about my Polish homeland. It is like an old romance, a love that might have been, a disappointment experienced and survived.

The United States, in contrast, has repaid our faith by granting us opportunity. It has rewarded hard work with freedom and with economic riches. When I came to the United States in January 1947, I had nothing: no money, no trade beyond a soldier's skills. Here, I found energy and imagination were all the qualifications one needed to succeed. I found Polish-speaking families to whom I could peddle merchandise. Little by little, I added to my product line and to my clientele, until, in this wonderful golden land, I have been able to flourish beyond my dreams. Sure, there are flaws in America. I discovered the depth of discrimination against black Americans the first time I drove through the South. So, too, did I experience anti-Semitism. But, unlike Poland's anti-Semitism, it is neither official nor sanctioned by the government. I have been slighted, but not persecuted. I have been insulted, but not beaten because I was a Jew.

In America, I truly believe I can achieve anything to which I aspire, short of becoming president. And that is not a matter of bias. The law requires that I be born here. The success I have experienced, and my awareness of the achievements of Jews who head major corporations, who are mayors and senators and presidential advisors, who are prominent in the educational, legal, and medical establishments of American life, have built a love in me for this miraculous land. In America, not only can we dream; we can become what we dream. I would willingly lay down my life for my second homeland, the United States of America.

And what of my third homeland, my *moladity*, Israel? That is where my heart truly lies. Three times a day Jews pray to return to the Holy Land, Zion. It is ingrained in our souls to want to be there. When, after two thousand years, a Jewish state was created in my lifetime, I had fully intended to be among those who went. I had escaped from Poland to Germany and worked with the Bricha, an organization that smuggled Jews into Palestine.

My intention was to help them until my turn came to be smuggled in as well. Since the immigration of Jews into Palestine from Europe was essentially blocked by the British, we knew that choosing that path carried the possibility of capture and internment in a displaced persons' camp in Cyprus. Although my wife wanted to join her family in Palestine, she did not want to attempt to do it illegally. She refused to risk being placed in a camp. As a professional soldier I could have contributed to its greatest need at the time, and one of my greatest regrets is that I wasn't there to fight for Israel's independence. Instead, I have made frequent visits— more than thirty trips, beginning with 1949, the first time after the war that tourists were allowed in.

During a visit in 1991 by supporters of Magen David Adom, the Israeli Red Cross, the author read from the Torah at the Western Wall. He is wearing a *tallit* designed by the Israeli artist Agam, and is standing under another Agam *tallit*. These were given to the group by the artist.

My wife and I have many relatives who settled in Israel. When we travel to the country, we visit them, but they are not the only ones we see. People ask, "What do you do there?" and I tell them "We visit old friends." I have many old friends that I, and all Jews like me, grew up with. The tomb of Maimonides, who was also known as Rambam, or Rabbi Moses Ben Maimon, is located in Tiberias. Rabbi Meyer bal Hanes, for whom my father used to collect money in the pushkas, is also buried in Tiberias. Rabbi Simeon ben Yohai, the originator of Kabbala, is buried in Meron near Safed. My forefathers, the patriarchs, rest in Hebron, and my adopted mother, Rachel, is buried in Bethlehem. So, too, in Israel lie my friends of more recent memory, Theodor Herzl, Chaim Nachman Bialik, and the soldier Trumpeldor. I visit places that I first read about when I studied the Bible as a child. The principal characters from our ancient and modern history are buried in Israel, and when I am there, I feel as one with them. In my heart and soul, Israel is my homeland.

Those, then, are my three homelands. Historically I am from Poland, the land that rejected the affection I offered. Legally, I am an American. I

In 1954, Amalie and Norman Salsitz visited the Capitol of their adopted homeland for the first time.

belong to the land that took me in and nurtured me and brought me to robust health. But emotionally, the country that calls to my spirit and my soul is Eretz Israel, the homeland for all Jews.

Daily Reminders of the Holocaust

It is sixty-three years since the Germans came to Poland: six decades, and still I remember the events of the occupation as if they were yesterday. I am conflicted over this ability to remember so clearly. On one hand, I want to remember. I want to tell the world what happened, and over the past six decades, I have done so in my books and through my lectures. For that purpose my memory is a blessing. On the other hand, I want to sleep at night. I want to be able to walk past everyday, ordinary objects without having flashbacks to the Holocaust. I want control over my thoughts. Time has helped, but still I have had—and continue to have—daily experiences that lead me to make associations with dreadful events so long ago.

This menorah, the symbol of the state of Israel, was designed by the Jewish artist, Benno Elkan, and donated by the British Parliament to the Jewish people in 1956. It stands before the Knesset in Jerusalem where it was visited by Amalie and Norman in 1991.

One time a few years ago we were driving to Florida. As we passed through the rural countryside, we stopped at a restaurant to eat. There was a tractor trailer parked in the lot. It was taking a load of animals—I think they were sheep—to market. I could hear them bleating, and when I walked past the truck I could see the eyes of the animals staring out at us between the slats. They were sad eyes. I had seen that expression before in the eyes of the Jews locked in the transports: hopeless and pleading, desperate, yet already resigned. It was the eyes that triggered a flashback to the scenes at the railroad sidings; desperate, hungry, thirsty Jews surrounded by indifference. Whenever I encounter a truckload of animals on their way to the slaughterhouse, I have the same vision, and it fills me with despair.

The New York subway during its rush hour is a trying experience for anyone. As the train makes its way uptown, more and more people pack themselves into the steaming cars. Passengers are crushed closer and closer to one another. All semblance of personal space is lost. Our bodies are merged into those of the total strangers standing next to us. We inhale what they exhale. Our breathing becomes synchronized. Our sweat becomes commingled. And at the next stop, the subway guards push still more in. I can't make that trip anymore. My associations of that crowding are with the experiences of the Jews packed into the boxcars. Others on the subway feel only their personal discomfort of the moment. I feel that suffocating agony of the millions of Jews who were made to take the trip to the death camp. Only instead of a ten-minute journey from 14th to 42nd Street, theirs was destined to last days and weeks until they arrived—or died on the way. I no longer take the subway. The associations are too painful.

I have trouble when I am driving and pass an old car belching exhaust fumes. Fortunately, one of the by-products of emissions testing is relief from the vision I had from such an encounter. My mind's eye sees an old Russian tank backed up against the gas chamber in Belzec. They didn't all use Zyklon-B gas. At Belzec the carbon monoxide from the idling Russian engines was piped into the sealed and inhumanly crowded cells, where it displaced the oxygen in the blood of the Jews, draining the life from their straining lungs. The sight of auto exhaust coming from passing cars conjures that vision for me.

In my hometown in New Jersey each fall, the road department comes by to collect leaves and pick up fallen branches. The workmen gather up the tree limbs and feed them into a machine that grinds the wood into chips. The honest men of the road department have no way of knowing that this simple activity of theirs triggers in my mind visions of one of the greatest horrors of the Holocaust. The crematorium consumed the flesh of the Jews. It left the bones to be ground up for fertilizer in a mulching machine very much like the one that sits in front of my house processing tree limbs. Each time I come upon this scene of a work crew nonchalantly going about its business, my heart beats a little more rapidly, my breathing becomes more shallow.

Crossing bridges is increasingly traumatic for me. Living in the New York area, it is not unusual for me to go over the Verrazano, George Washington, or Tappan Zee Bridges. I recall similar bridges that spanned the Danube in Budapest, Hungary. The ever-imaginative Hungarians—the "Nyilas" (the Arrow Cross, whose leader was Ferenc Szalasi) used these as killing grounds as well. They would tie together three or four Jews, binding them tightly to one another. Then they would shoot one in the head and throw the group into the river from the bridge. The living would kick and struggle to save themselves, but the dead weight of their companion's body inexorably pulled them under. Bridges retain this significance for me, and I am alarmed whenever I must cross one.

When it snows and I look out from the warm comfort of my suburban home, my mind takes me back to the time I spent living, unsheltered, in the woods in Poland. We had no roof, no clothes to change to when the ones we were wearing became wet, no dry boots. We had only the boughs of the trees to deflect the snowfall, and it was not unusual to awaken to find that a foot or more of newly fallen snow had buried us overnight. It was so cold. I am not alone in this association of snow with suffering.

A few years ago the newspaper carried a story of a woman Holocaust survivor who had walked across the Williamsburg Bridge between Brooklyn and Manhattan during a blizzard. She was prosperously dressed in her mink coat and wore sturdy boots; and instead of riding in the subway, or staying home during the storm, she carried, by hand, a thousand-dollar check from her home in Brooklyn and delivered it to the headquarters of the United Jewish Appeal in Manhattan. They asked her why she had walked through the storm, and she said it was because it reminded her of her flight with her little girl from her house into the woods the day the Germans came to take them away. She had hidden herself and her daughter and remained there while the others vanished from her life, and somehow she had survived. She wanted to thank God for her deliverance from the deportation by repeating her flight through the woods to give to charity.

My list of daily activities that I associate with the Holocaust goes on and on. Chimney smoke coming from the tall smokestacks found around power plants and factories has all too obvious an association. My mother and my five sisters, as well as their husbands and children all passed through the chimneys of the death camps.

Preparation for my daily shower never fails to cause me to stand shivering uncontrollably in the bathroom. Even though the shower runs with water that is so warm it produces clouds of steam and fogs the mirror, I shiver as if I were back in the woods. There I had no alternative for washing but the icy water of the river, or the melted snows. We had to maintain some degree of personal hygiene, and that often meant bathing under brutally cold conditions. We had no warm towel to wrap ourselves in afterwards. We had no fresh clothes to put on. All we had were leaves and branches and the rags we had been wearing day in and day out for months. I shivered then as my muscles involuntarily responded to the Polish winter's chill, and I shiver today as my mind involuntarily responds to the memory of those frozen showers taken more than sixty years ago.

I am troubled by the bug zappers found in our yards. They remind me of the electric fences that surrounded the camps. Other insect killing devices allow entry but no exit. How similar this principle is to penalty rooms in which the Germans kept the Jews with no opportunity to sit down or straighten up for days at a time until they died.

When my daughter took part in a scavenger hunt as part of an adolescent party, I had a terrible flashback. The Gestapo had come into the ghetto demanding that the Judenrat gather a collection of specific goods from the population and present them. The list contained such items as silk stockings, leather gloves, strawberry jam, a canary. All of these items were nearly impossible for people who were in the ghetto to find. Nevertheless, we tried.

People who had passes to go out from the ghetto ran to Polish neighbors and offered to pay excessive amounts for the items demanded in an effort to satisfy what was to be proved an insatiable enemy. I myself was sent to find jars of strawberry jam, and I managed to buy some from a man my father had done business with before the war. I paid ten times its value, and to this day, I cannot eat strawberry jam without a flashback to that terrible time.

Catered banquets tend to be outstanding for the degree of excess they present the guests. Tables laden with meats and cheeses and fruits and fish and vegetables and sauces are presented to please the palate and tantalize the imagination. And so they do for most. Alas, to me the banquet table containing so much food that is destined to be thrown away at the end of the evening is a source of profound sadness. I remember the bewilderment of my nieces and nephews when their hunger went unattended. "Don't you love us anymore?" they would ask. We would have given anything to relieve their hunger. But there was no banquet in store for these wonderful children. The time and place of their brief lives didn't allow it.

When I see today's children in a line being led someplace by their teacher, I see children of that earlier time being led to the gas chambers. A gutter filled with dust appears to me as a gutter filled with ashes. A policeman blowing a whistle in traffic reminds me of the whistles the SS blew when commanding Jews to undress. A dog barking sounds like the dogs the Germans used to terrorize the Jews and tear their flesh. A baby in a crib reminds me of the helplessness of the infants torn from their mothers' breast and dashed on the ground. Once, in Morocco, we visited a Jewish kindergarten as part of our tour. I broke down and cried. My nieces and nephews were right around the ages of the children in the class.

And so my life has been blessed with my survival, and my opportunity to tell the story of the Holocaust to audiences whenever I can. I do that. I believe it is the reason I was spared. My life is also burdened, however, with the associations I cannot escape. Daily events are constant reminders of the cruelty I survived.

It is sixty years, and I can't forget for a moment.